AGELESS AGEING

The Natural Way to Stay Young

Leslie Kenton

CENTURY ARROW

LONDON MELBOURNE AUCKLAND JOHANNESBURG

For Maurice
with admiration and affection

This is a book about ageless ageing – a way of living designed to prolong youth, vitality and good looks. It is not about illness and how to cure it. The material in this book is intended for informational purposes only. None of the suggestions or information is meant in any way to be prescriptive. Any attempt to treat illness should come under the direction of a competent physician who is familiar with nutritional therapy. I am only a reporter, although one who has for many years had a profound interest in how to look good and feel great as the years pass. I write in the hope that some of my research may be of use to others who, like myself, want to live long and well and would like to 'die young late in life'.

A Century Arrow Book
Published by Arrow Books Limited
62–65 Chandos Place, London WC2N 4NW

An imprint of Century Hutchinson Ltd

London Melbourne Sydney Auckland
Johannesburg and agencies throughout
the world

First published 1985
Century Arrow edition 1986
Reprinted 1986

Printed and bound in Great Britain by
Cox & Wyman Ltd, Reading

ISBN 0 09 946690 2

Contents

Acknowledgements

Many friends and colleagues have contributed to make this book possible. So have a number of brilliant and humanitarian age-researchers. It would be impossible to thank them all properly. There are a few to whom I am particularly indebted: Johan Bjorksten, Herman Le Compte, Linus Pauling, Ralph Bircher, Dagmar Leichte von Brasch, Franklin and Alice Bircher, Phillip Kilsby, Stephen Levine, Bob Erdmann, Gordon and Barbara Latto, I. I. Brekhman, Robert O. Becker, Julian Kenyon, Robert Erdmann, Alan Cott and Lilla Bek. I am especially grateful to Monica Fine who offered to help me in her own spare time research the book, to my daughter Susannah who set aside several days of her holiday to correct my *apauling* (appalling) spelling and to edit the text, and to my son Jesse 'the scientist' for meticulously vetting my own inadequate language of science.

Introduction

Pick up any book on ageing and you are likely to be dazzled by the scientific confusion into which you've been plunged: a score of complex and contradictory theories expounded in hundreds of polysyllabic words none of which have much meaning to the man or woman who simply wants to know what he or she can do right now to protect him or herself from premature ageing and degeneration, to maintain youthful good looks and to live a long and productive life. The talk is of free radicals, cellular clocks, hormones, enzymes, heredity and immunity. And the disagreements are rampant. On the one hand you have highly respected conservative scientists claiming there is no way we can lengthen life appreciably. On the other you find Nobel prize winners who insist not only that it can be done but that it can be done with relative ease now. Then there are the real eccentrics—I call them the 'immortalists'—who believe that death itself is little more than a mistake, an event which we have been programmed to expect and which therefore becomes a self-fulfilling prophecy. Alter your expectations, they say, and you can alter reality. There is no reason why you cannot live *forever* they insist—yes you—right now. So get on with it.

Amidst so much confusion where do you find sense? Is there strong evidence that we can alter the individual rate at which we age? Can we live longer? And not just longer but *better*—a healthier, happier, more productive and creative life? Can we look younger in five years than we do right now? Are the knowledge and the tools available now to give us control over the rate at which our body ages? And what about rejuvenation? Is it just another of those old-fashioned notions which went out with romantic forties films—a notion which hard science has banished to the scrap pile of fantasy? Or can you use natural means to transform an ageing body into a younger one? And, if so, where do you begin?

These are a few of the questions which were plaguing me ten years ago as I began to research the scientific literature into ageing and rejuvenation. What set them off? What led me to spend hours in dusty medical libraries plowing through esoteric papers on longevity, the immune system and anti-oxidant nutrients? Why did I set out to interview scientists all over the world who had spent their lives studying the process of ageing?

The notion of writing a book about ageing had never entered my head. Yet I found myself passionately committed to the research. I *needed* to know; and it was a need which sprang from no abstract sense of scientific curiosity: each spring as I looked into the mirror I would notice that a few more tiny lines had appeared. Sometimes when I went out for a run I'd sense a certain stiffness in my muscles which wasn't there last year. Or was it? In short, ageing for me, as it is for most people, was a highly personal experience. I knew that I was doing it, and I figured there was nothing I could do about that. But by heaven I was going to do it *slowly*! I was going to find a way to live which kept me looking good and supported the needs of my body and mind at a high level of vitality and awareness well into my forties . . . sixties . . . nineties.

Now, after almost a decade of digging and mulling over contradictory facts and figures, trying out endless techniques and rejecting many which seemed worthless before trying more, I believe my search has been well rewarded. Oh, don't get me wrong. I have found no fountain of youth—no magic pill which you can take one morning and make biological time stand still. But I have come upon a great many techniques which I believe really work to keep you young and even to make you look and feel younger. Much to my surprise, I have also discovered that, amidst all those contradictory theories about why and how the body ages, and what can be done to slow down the process, there are unifying principles which we can put into practical use right now. There is necessarily a good deal of complex information to be digested in Part One of *Ageless Ageing*. Bear with me though, for it is background knowledge which will give you real understanding of the practical applications discussed in the later chapters of the book.

One of the things that worried me most in the beginning was the fact that so many of the anti-ageing techniques—from the use of high doses of anti-oxidant nutrients to the ancient practice of fasting—seemed quite contradictory. How, I asked myself, could massive doses of ascorbic acid have a similar effect to a high-raw spring-clean diet when it came to revitalizing the body, softening lines on the face and restoring high levels of energy? What possible relationship was there between the diet and lifestyle of the much studied long-lived peoples of the world—the Hunzas, the Vilcabamba Indians in South America, the Georgians in Soviet Russia—and the pill-popping anti-ageing culture that has grown up in the United States in the last decade? These were some of the issues which troubled me. Wrestling with them gradually forced me to look at the ageing process in an entirely different way.

I realized that ageing is far more than simply biological degeneration. That to begin to understand it, even to begin to answer some of my questions about why degeneration takes place and what can be done to slow it down, I would have to explore the nature of a living organism as an energetic system: a system with the remarkable property, unique to life itself, of sustaining a very high degree of order within a universe which the second law of thermodynamics tells us very clearly is *entropic*—that is, a universe in which everything tends to degenerate towards chaos. There was magic in it all. Gradually the sense of this magic took hold of me and wouldn't let me go.

When I began my research I had no idea just where it would take me. I certainly never suspected that a desire as narcissistic as wanting to prevent wrinkles on my own face would lead me to a view of age-retardation which has so deepened my respect for the living body and so expanded my sense of awe at the splendour of life processes that my original goal has often been almost forgotten. Oh yes, I've found ways of slowing down the wrinkle-formation on the skin, of restoring firmness and youthful contours to the body, of increasing vitality and encouraging the body to function in a more youthful way on a cellular level. And, make no mistake, I intend to use them: but in the midst of it all I have come to be aware of something which to me seems infinitely more valuable. I have come to stand in awe of the order and the perfection that is life. I have come to believe that for too long we have been fascinated by the elegance of scientific laws which govern inert matter yet we have remained blind to the natural laws which govern our own bodies and our consciousness. They are more obscure laws to be sure, but they are every bit as inexorable as the laws of the sidereal world. And they are laws which many farsighted people—from the physicians of ancient China to those which belong to the long tradition of natural healing in Europe—have examined, delineated and made use of to heal and to rejuvenate their patients.

Slowing down the ageing process depends greatly on exploring and then making use of these laws. For when in ignorance or disregard we transgress them, accelerated biological degeneration and a tragic waste of human potential is our reward. Get to know them and use them well, couple them with the latest biochemical techniques for protecting the cells of the body from age-related damage, and I believe you create a force for ageless ageing which has not yet been known in the recorded history of man.

But that's the end of my story. Let's begin at the beginning.

PART I

Hieroglyphs of Ageing

ONE

Why Ageless Ageing?

How long you live rests largely in your own hands. So does how *well* you live, how much vitality you have and how good you will look in twenty years' time. They are not, as most people still believe, accidents of fate. Neither are they heavily dependent on the kind of medical care you get, nor on your genetic inheritance—although both certainly have a part to play. Instead they depend mostly on two things: first, your lifestyle; second, how much use you make of some of the recently discovered tools for protecting your body against degeneration. Together these two form an integrated approach to ageless ageing which has two branches. The first branch I call *natural law*. It is based on what appear to be the biological laws of life. It centres around becoming aware of the quite specific needs of your mind/body/ spirit for optimum health and vitality and then on supplying them. These include psychosocial, physical, nutritional, environmental and spiritual needs which, when fulfilled, keep you in a state of maximum wellness year after year. The second branch of an integrated approach to ageless ageing, which I call *high-tech*, depends on making intelligent and effective use of the tools for age-retardation which have recently come to light thanks to research done in scientific disciplines such as free-radical biochemistry, submolecular biology, and biophysics and electrobiology.

Making ageless ageing work for you is simply a matter of exploring these two aspects of age-retardation in all their depths and then putting them into practice both to extend your life and to enhance its quality.

In the process it should soften lines on your face and prevent many new ones from forming, firm your muscles and help restore youthful contours to a body which is losing them, increase your vitality, and in many ways quite literally rejuvenate you by restoring your immune system to better functioning, lowering blood pressure which has become elevated, strengthening your heart and lungs and improving your body's use of oxygen at a molecular level—a major measure of biological age.

The First Branch—Natural Law

This two-pronged approach to retarding ageing is something which so far very few people, either within the scientific community or outside of it, have yet put into practice. Yet good solid information about how each branch can retard ageing, prolong youthful good looks and extend life is now available to anyone who is willing to take the trouble to dig for it and daring enough to make a few changes in the way he or she eats, thinks and lives to put it to work. The *natural law* branch—that of supplying an organism with all of its needs and living with an awareness of the biological laws by which we appear to be controlled—forms the foundation of every major tradition of natural health and healing throughout history, from ancient Taoist medicine in China and the Ayurvedic tradition of India to nineteenth-century European nature-cure and the jazzy 'holistic' approach to health becoming popular in this last quarter of the twentieth. It largely determines how susceptible you are to 'premature' ageing—a widespread phenomenon which makes faces wrinkle and arteries harden and which can be halted by such things as correcting any subclinical nutritional deficiencies which you may have, by altering your diet and by changing your lifestyle.

What modern scientific exploration has done for the first branch is to validate what natural traditions of health and healing have always taught—for instance it has shown how and why eating a low-calorie diet of natural foods, getting enough of the right kind of exercise, and enhancing your psychosocial well-being can strengthen immunity, slow ageing and preserve mental clarity and emotional balance. Laboratory and clinical studies have also been able to define better than ever before what the specific factors are that make up a natural lifestyle for ageless ageing, to show why they are important, and to present us with statistics that indicate that abiding by the natural laws of health we can live longer. We know for instance that non-smokers are less likely to end up with lung cancer, that exercise improves cardiovascular strength and makes you less likely to fall prey to a heart attack, that a low-salt diet should help protect you from high blood pressure. At one time these things would have to have been taken on faith, now many of them have been scientifically proven. Although for every hard statistic we have about what helps prevent disease, degeneration and early death, there are still a hundred as yet 'unproven' techniques, tools and morsels of anti-ageing wisdom buried in the natural health and healing traditions which can be put to use.

Learn about them, put *natural-law* anti-ageing to work for you, and you should be able to live a longer, more creative, more energetic and more satisfying life starting right now. Only when you do will you be able to live up to your psychobiological potential—something that as yet very few of us ever reach. This is the first step towards ageless ageing. Unless you choose to take it, no amount of fancy biochemical manipulations are going to do the trick for you. For some people this step alone may be enough. It has enabled such well-studied long-lived cultures as the Hunzas in Kashmir, the Georgians in Soviet Russia and the Vilcabamba Indians in South America to live active lives while most of our grandparents lay ailing in hospital beds. For it has great power.

The High-Tech Second Branch

The second anti-ageing branch—the *high-tech* scientific approach—is different. It is entirely dependent on scientific discoveries which have taken place, mostly within the last fifty years. These discoveries include a growing understanding of the role that the immune system plays in the rate at which we age, a knowledge of how certain natural and artificial chemicals known as the anti-oxidants can be used to prevent age-related damage on a cellular level and to strengthen immune functions, and how specific nutrients such as the free amino acids can be used to alter the chemistry of the ageing brain or firm sagging muscles, as well as an awareness of how specific pathways between mind and body enable your feelings, attitudes and expectations to play a major role in determining the rate at which you age. The use of anti-oxidant nutrients in animal experiments (one branch of the high-tech approach) as dietary supplements has been shown to substantially retard the basic biological process of ageing and to improve general well-being throughout the animals' lives. Human beings too can make use of them. We can also put into practice some of the recent findings about how dietary restriction boosts immune functions, rejuvenates the immune system and retards degeneration. Discoveries such as these have led even the most conservative scientific researchers to estimate that by the year 2000 we should be able to prolong life far beyond the proverbial three score and ten. For, unlike *natural-law* anti-ageing, which can banish the 'premature' factors in the ageing process, the *high-tech* approach aims at longevity by attempting to extend 'maximum' lifespan as well. (More about the implications of this later.) In effect it is involved in exploring the processes of ageing and degeneration in very specific terms—from the wrinkling of skin to the disruption of a cell's genetic material which is implicated both in ageing and in the development of cancer. Even more important, science is discovering specific and effective remedies for counteracting these processes of ageing and degeneration.

So when it comes to combating ageing, we live in exciting times. But we also live in fragmented times. It is always tempting to believe that thanks to the latest discoveries in free-radical biochemistry we should be able to load up on anti-oxidants from the local health-food store while we continue to smoke sixty cigarettes a day, to sunbathe *ad nauseam*, to eat rich desserts, to burn the candle at both ends, and still live for ever. Alas, it just ain't so—no matter how much a few sensational books and articles on the subject would have us believe otherwise. To get maximum benefits from what is currently known about age-retardation we need to fuse *natural law* and *high tech* into a single power for de-ageing. Used together they can not only have you looking good and feeling good twenty-five years hence, they can go a long way towards alleviating human suffering. For there are bonuses to ageless ageing: the very same tools, techniques and lifestyle changes which will keep you young-looking and full of energy will also go a long way towards preventing the degenerative diseases of civilization which have reached epidemic proportions in Britain and in the United States. That in a nutshell is what ageless ageing is all about.

Banishing Myths about Ageing

Most of us hold a lot of false notions about ageing and life-expectancy—ghosts which need to be laid before we can make ageless ageing a workable part of our lives. Two are particularly common. The first is the idea that degeneration—including a loss of good looks and the onset of longterm illnesses such as arthritis, coronary heart disease and cancer—is a 'normal' experience of growing older. The second is the belief that the 'miracles' of modern medical science have already significantly lengthened our lifespan. Both commonly held views are untrue. They are supported neither by vital statistics nor by biological evidence.

Degenerative diseases and the untold suffering they bring are by no means an inevitable part of getting older. Wild animals do not experience the slow and painful degeneration which takes so many forms in our society. They have been called 'diseases of civilization'—illnesses which orthodox medicine is unable to prevent and which lie behind the current crisis that medicine is experiencing. Neither, according to epidemiological and anthropological studies, do primitive cultures living on a sparse diet of natural foods suffer from this kind of degeneration. Throughout history most medical traditions—from China and India to ancient Sumeria—have taught that degeneration is *not* a normal part of ageing: that, provided we recognize the biological laws by which we are constituted and live with respect for them, we can live to a great age free of arthritis, heart attacks, cancer, lung diseases and the rest. These traditions have also taught that great age can be matched by great vitality so that we should be able—as an editorial in the *Journal of the American Medical Association* suggested not long ago—'to die *young* late in life'.

There are people who already do this. Not only the well-studied long-lived cultures, but aware individuals living in the urban environments of the high-tech West. I know a number personally—men and women of seventy or eighty or ninety who not only have the vitality of people fifty years younger than they, but who look wonderful and whose energy and creativity are an inspiration to everyone they come in contact with. Given an understanding of the basic laws of nature and the needs of our body as well as the means to care for it, there is no reason why, barring some untoward accident, we should all not also be able to 'die young late in life'.

Life Expectancy is Not Improving

The second big 'fiction' about ageing—the belief that medicine has already been able significantly to extend life—is as unfounded as the notion that degenerative diseases are inevitable. It is true that the average life expectancy of a baby born in Britain today is around seventy-three whereas in 1900 it was only fifty. (In America the statistics are respectively seventy-three and forty-seven.) But that is almost entirely due to a decrease in infant mortality thanks to improved child-bearing methods and better sanitation. Every baby who dies at birth drastically reduces *average* lifespan. Because we have fewer babies and children dying now than we had at the turn of the century, statistics show that *average* life expectancy has increased. But this figure gives little idea of *real* life expectancy. For statistics also show that once beyond childhood we have little chance of living much longer than our grandfathers did.

It is important to understand the distinction between *average* lifespan, which is often used to indicate life expectancy, and *maximum* lifespan, which is a major goal of ageless ageing. *Average* lifespan measurements give you an indication of the age by which half of a population of people or animals have died. In ancient Rome this measurement was twenty-two years, by 1850 it had risen to forty. At the turn of the century it hovered around fifty. It was sixty-seven by 1946 and now, thanks mostly to this drop in infant mortality, it is around seventy-three. But neither mass immunization nor high-technology hospital procedures have had much impact on the *real* life expectancy of somebody who has already reached adulthood. For they have had little impact whatever on *maximum* lifespan, which is an important measure of ageing. Despite miracle drugs, kidney transplants, and the other dramatic medical techniques for saving life, medical science has found no way of holding back the basic biological process of ageing.

How Long Can We Live?

Rather like the proverbial fisherman's tale, stories about how long man is capable of living tend to get more and more exaggerated. Moses, we are told, lived to be 120, Noah to 950 and Methuselah to 969. But scientific investigation has been little able to confirm such figures. What then is the *maximum* lifespan of man?

This is not an easy question to answer. In laboratory animals it is relatively simple. You take, say, a hundred rats, feed them the best quality of diet you can find and provide them with optimal environments and then you wait for the last one to die. That last death gives you your figure. For non-laboratory animals, such as bulls and elephants, turtles and thoroughbred horses, the procedure is to collect verifiable records of the oldest of a species. In the case of man these records are hard to verify. For while history abounds with stories about people who have lived to 200 years or more, we have no proof that this is so. Systematic birth and death records have only been kept in the past century and in many societies in the world these personal statistics are still not recorded. Scientists—such as Harvard Medical School's Alexander Leaf—who have travelled the world have often come back with stories of isolated communities which are well stocked with centenarians. The Andean village of Vilcabamba in Ecuador was found to boast nine individuals over 100 and one of 123 in a community of only 819, while in the Republic of Georgia in the Caucasus mountains of the USSR, 8890 centenarians were reported, 150 of whom were said to be between 120 and 170. But recently some scientists have become very suspicious of these reported ages and insisted that they have been highly exaggerated by the peoples themselves for whom vigorous old age is a status symbol. Dissenters insist that *maximum* human lifespan as of right now is probably between 110 and 120.

Two truths emerge from research into *maximum* human lifespan. The first is that whether it turns out to be 200 or only 110, practically none of us come anywhere near to approaching it. The second is that these long-lived peoples whose diet and lifestyles have by now been so well studied, by any standard, are able to live remarkably long, healthy and vigorous lives. At age 90 or 100 men are still siring children, riding horseback and taking daily dips into icy water—things that few of us Westerners would dream of doing past middle age. We can learn a lot from them.

Striving towards Our Psychobiological Potentials

To most people in the West old age brings ghastly images of decrepitude—not pictures of vigorous and sexually active old men and women intensively involved in work and looking forward to what comes next. The potential for creativity and enjoyment which is wasted in age-degeneration in the developed countries of the world is shocking. So is the cost to the state in providing medical treatment, hospitalization, food and care for people for whom ageing has become a nightmare of physical pain and emotional isolation. Few of us even come close to fulfilling our psychobiological potentials. Instead we look forward to a steady and inexorable increase in morbidity and mortality from one disease to another. The exciting thing about the principles of ageless ageing is that if we begin now to apply them we will not only be able to extend our lives but to improve their quality beyond all recognition. For all of the major causes of death and disability appear to be secondary to the progressive degeneration of ageing. And the same principles which help keep your skin smooth, your muscles firm and your vitality high can also reduce the incidence of chronic disease and postpone degenerative illnesses so that if they occur at all, they come only very late in life.

To arrest the diseases of civilization with which medical science has been fruitlessly wrestling we are going to have to take preventative action—action which draws on the optimum health practices implicit in *natural-law* anti-ageing as well as on recently discovered *high-tech* scientific techniques for protecting the body from degeneration. One American medical expert, Ernest M. Gruenberg, put it rather well when he said:

Now we recognize that our life-saving technology of the past four decades has outstripped our health-preserving technology and that the net effect has been to worsen the people's health, we must begin the search for preventable causes of the chronic illnesses which we have been extending . . . We will not move forward in enhancing health until we make the prevention of nonfatal chronic illness our top research priority.

What has become increasingly apparent is that to do this one needs to confront the ageing process itself. As famous age-researcher, Johan Bjorksten says we must aim to 'give as many people as possible as many more healthy vigorous years of life as possible'. He continues, '. . . every one of the major diseases tabulated is age-dependent. To attack the problems of these diseases separately, as is now the preponderant course of action, is akin to trying to stop a haemorrhage by closing all of the capillary vessels separately rather than ligating the main artery.'

Life-Enhancing Life-Extension

The ways and means of ageless ageing are as diverse as are the disease conditions which it makes possible for us to avoid. Some belong within the realm of *natural law*. These include high-potency low-calorie ways of eating which are in fresh foods, exercise techniques, mental tools to alter expectations, as well as sun, air and water treatments. Others are pure *high-tech* science based on the latest free-radical biochemistry. Together they can quite literally work wonders for the way you look and feel. For the pursuit of ageless ageing—with all that it implies—goes far beyond a narcissistic desire of the overprivileged middle classes for eternal youth. It reaches deep into the well of human possibilities for health, joy, and lifelong creativity. It can lead us to a time when instead of our elderly being a burden to their families and to the state, like the long-lived Hunzas, Georgians, or Vilcabamban Indians they will be able to contribute their experience, energy and wisdom to society. These are treasures which we can't afford to waste.

TWO

Story without End

The historical search for ageless ageing as a means of prolonging active life is a tale full of haunting legends, elegant alchemical theories, exciting successes and grandiose failures. It begins when, wracked with grief over the death of his friend Enkidu and fearful of his own impending death, the Sumerian hero Gilgamesh set himself to search for the herb of eternal life. No sooner does he find it than this magical plant is devoured by a serpent as he swims in a beautiful lake and the secret is lost for ever. Another chapter was written in ancient Greece: on returning from the voyage in search of the Golden Fleece, Jason entreated his bride Medea to use her magic powers to rejuvenate his aged father Aeson. The process took her nine days. She purified the old man with sulphur, fire and water. Then she prepared her formula of 'pebbles from the farthest Orient, hoarfrost gathered under the moon, wings and flesh of the infamous horned owl, entrails of a werewolf, the skin of the Cynyphian water snake, the liver of a long lived stag, the head of a crow nine centuries old and a thousand other things'. So successful was Medea's brew that Aeson's beard changed from grey to black, his body lost its lean and withered look and he took on the state of a man forty years his junior. And so powerful was Medea's rejuvenation mixture that its very smell transformed her dragons, causing them to slough off their old skins and to become young again.

Man has continually pined for the fountain of youth and been fascinated by the idea of ageless ageing. Down through the Middle Ages and beyond we have numerous records of special practices and potions designed to rejuvenate the body or to

extend life. It was this longing which spurred the ageing con-
quistador Ponce de León to make his sixteenth-century voyage
to the New World. It was the exceptional longevity of the
famous seventeenth-century British peasant Thomas Parr
which has not only made him a paragon of healthy old age but
which turned him into an object of fascination for the British
court.

Parr's life and death are no legend. They have been well
documented historically. A man who had lived his whole life on
a spartan diet of cheese, fresh fruit and a little bread, Parr was
summoned at the amazing age of 152 to the court of King
Charles I where he was lavishly feasted in the hopes of learning
the secret of his longevity. But overindulgence proved too much
for the frugal peasant. He sickened and quickly died. No less a
scientist than William Harvey, discoverer of the circulatory
system, performed the autopsy on Parr's body and wrote up the
case. Harvey relates in his report that he was astonished at the
peasant's superbly youthful brain and organs.

Brains, Brawn and Sex Organs

Modern ageing research goes back to the end of the nineteenth
century by which time the discovery of the endocrine system
had led some scientists to ask themselves if illusive glandular
secretions were not substances which could be used to regenerate fading youth, to restore flagging vitality and to prolong
life. In the spring of 1889, an eccentric seventy-two-year-old
physiologist named Charles Edouard Brown-Séquard carried
out some revolutionary experiments in which he injected himself with extracts taken from the testicles of dogs. Delighted
with the results, Brown-Séquard reported that the tone of his
muscles had improved and that he felt thirty years younger.
Unfortunately his experiments were taken seriously neither by
his family nor by the scientific community who insisted his
'results' were based on nothing more than an overactive
imagination. They made him a laughing stock. He died a few
years later in scientific disgrace. Yet a number of colleagues
were intrigued by his work. Many experimenters began to look
into glandular extracts as a workable means of rejuvenating the

body and to experiment with other hormone-related techniques which might be useful against age.

One longstanding myth about ageing is the notion that much vitality is lost in men through ejaculation. Soon after Brown-Séquard's downfall, a Viennese endocrinologist named Eugen Steinach decided to restrict this 'vitality loss' by tying off the sperm ducts—in effect performing a vasectomy—on animals, following the theory that in doing so male sex hormones would be redirected back into the bloodstream and would rejuvenate the organism. An impeccable technician, Steinach carried out elaborate experiments with rats. All his tests appeared to confirm the theory although no scientist either then or now has yet been able to explain why. Unfortunately for humans, so far there have been few reports of increased vitality in men who have undergone vasectomies.

From Apes into Man

As interest in Steinach's work declined a new star appeared on the rejuvenation horizon. He was a Russian (or at least so he said) named Serge Voronoff. An effervescent gentleman with a fascination for youth, Voronoff believed that you should be able to rejuvenate the body by giving testicular transplants. Working with farm animals, particularly rams and bulls, he succeeded in bringing back their potency and restoring their ability to sire offspring in old age. Voronoff quickly became a favourite amongst the agricultural community. Then in the spring of 1928, using anthropoid apes as donors of testicular tissue, he carried out his first ape-to-man transplant. This was followed by another 162 such operations in the next two years. Voronoff rapidly became the talk of Paris—famed for his 'monkey-gland' rejuvenation. And although medical colleagues at the time ridiculed his techniques, by the late 'twenties even Europe's orthodox medical profession had moved to a position of acknowledging that the eccentric surgeon's technique did have some therapeutic effect. A conference of a thousand leading surgeons in Austria agreed that while 'rejuvenation' as such was a misnomer (it is still a word which makes most scientists squirm), 'the gland transplantation operation devised by Dr Serge Voronoff afforded transient regeneration.'

Modern Cell Therapy

The work of Steinach and that of Voronoff with his curious glandular transplants served as inspiration for another famous and highly controversial 'youth doctor'—Swiss surgeon Paul Niehans. Aware of the problems of foreign-tissue rejection, Niehans turned to foetal glands taken from unborn sheep and developed a technique of fresh-cell therapy. Selecting specific organs, glands and tissues which had been determined by examination of the patient and tailored to his specific needs, Niehans injected these fresh cells into people to heal and to rejuvenate them. The technique has attracted wide interest from the rich and famous who claim it makes them look and feel younger. It has even been used to treat mental retardation in the young, often with considerable success. But since so far no one has ever done controlled studies to show that it works, the British and American orthodox medical profession insist vehemently that it doesn't. Niehans died, after an active, and very lucrative, professional life, at the age of eighty-nine. His clinic, La Prairie in Vevey, Switzerland, continues, with some variations on the original theme, to offer cell therapy at very high fees to thousands of patients each year.

Errors in Cell Immortality

Meanwhile another line of investigation was being followed in the United States by the brilliant French physiologist and Nobel laureate Alexis Carrel. In 1912 at the Rockefeller Institute in New York, Carrel initiated a study using fibroblast cells—connective tissue cells widely distributed throughout the organism—from a chicken embryo. This experiment was instrumental in forming scientific opinion about the ageing process for almost fifty years. Carrel grew the cell structure in a glass vessel nourishing it with a crude embryo extract. To the amazement of the scientific community it far outlived even

Carrel himself. The cells went on multiplying for more than thirty years at which point technicians terminated the experiment. Thanks to Carrel's long-lived chicken cells, the scientific community came to believe that ordinary cells in a living organism were immortal. Many scientists assumed therefore that there must be some substance in embryonic tissues with an ability to maintain youth and life. This belief, which was sustained for almost half a century, triggered a vast number of research projects in search of this natural youth serum—the elixir of youth.

The belief persisted until another famous age-researcher, Leonard Hayflick, carried out experiments which showed that cultured human fibroblasts *in vitro* are only able to divide about fifty times before they die out. This process takes but a few months in the laboratory. Hayflick discovered that when fibroblasts get to the limit of their dividing they do not suddenly just stop but the time needed for them to reach maturity gets longer as they approach their limit of fifty doublings. This eventually leads to the development of a group of cells which never reach confluence no matter how long they are incubated or how often the nutrient medium in which these cells are grown is renewed. In the end the cells undergo a variety of degenerative changes and then die. Looking more closely at Carrel's accomplishment it became apparent that his results were the outcome of a basic error. The embryo extract on which his cell culture was nourished was 'impure'. Inadvertently it had become contaminated with live chicken cells. One of Carrel's laboratory technicians even admitted later to Hayflick that she knew of the contamination, but so strong was the scientific community's commitment to the notion of cell immortality and to its search for the elixir of life which the belief implied, that she dared not voice criticism.

A Maximum Lifespan?

It was while doing cancer research at the Wistar Institute in Philadelphia that Hayflick happened upon the chance discovery that fibroblast cells appear programmed to die. Since then this finite lifetime of cultured human cells has been confirmed by researchers looking at fibroblasts as well as at other normal cell types including liver, smooth muscle, skin and brain. But, in keeping with the paradoxical nature of age research throughout history, it is now being contradicted by other scientists who claim that adding specific nutrients to such a culture can prolong its life—perhaps indefinitely.

The Nasty Immortals

One of the interesting offshoots of this cell research has been the discovery that, unlike normal cells which divide only until their limit is reached, some cells are actually immortal—they seem able to divide forever. These are cancer cells. By now a number of malignant strains have been cultured, mostly from animals. But the most famous of all is a human cell line which was derived in 1952 from cultured tissue taken from the cervix of a woman called Henrietta Lacks. It is known as the HeLa culture. Parts of this famous cell proliferation are still being studied in laboratories all over the world. Meanwhile the limit of about fifty divisions possible for normal cells on which many age-researchers agree has come to be known as the 'Hayflick limit'. And this fifty-division figure is important because, provided of course that Hayflick's findings turn out to be valid for cells *in vivo*—living cells within the body—they could be used to calculate mathematically the potential average maximum lifespan of any species. Employing Hayflick's mathematics, the average human lifespan should be somewhere between 100 and 120 years. Although many age-researchers insist this figure is far too low. But low or not, few of us ever get anywhere near this. Why? With this question, elaborate contemporary research into the mechanics of ageing began. And in an attempt to answer it gerontologists have developed complex, often contradictory and sometimes confusing hypotheses.

The Language of Ageing

Theorists tend to fall into two camps. Some believe that the causes of ageing are fundamentally cellular: these scientists spend their time searching for just where within the cells is located the trigger for Hayflick's limit. In the cytoplasm—the cell's gel-like interior? In the mitochondria, the minute organelles—the cell's powerhouses for energy? In the lysosomes—the cell's rubbish dumps which, when they happen to split open, pollute the cytoplasmic ocean with their toxic wastes? Or perhaps in the cell's nucleus itself? The fault could well be in the DNA molecule—life's coded blueprint. After all, they point out (as Hayflick himself showed), when you separate the nuclei from the cytoplasm of young cells and then recombine them with older cytoplasm, it is always the age of the nuclei, not the cytoplasm, which determines when their limit of doubling has been reached.

Other age-researchers—equally esteemed—disagree with the 'cell-focusers'. They believe that the primary causes of ageing are general, not cellular. Some scientists insist that a mechanism in one of your body's centres of control—such as the endocrine glands, the brain, the nervous system—triggers the production of some as yet unknown substance which signals your cells to die. Others believe that ageing is the result of wear and tear to the organism as a whole. The former speak of 'death hormones' and genetic clocks while their colleagues talk instead of stress, loss of *adaptive* energy and overload.

Twenty years ago the 'cell-focusers' and the 'generalists' seemed poles apart. Now, thanks to the vast amount of intellectual cross-fertilization in the discipline of gerontology and to rapid developments in the field of free-radical biochemistry and immunology most age-researchers have come to believe that there is no single factor which can be pinpointed as *the* cause of ageing. What has become obvious is that ageing is a multi-dimensional process involving many repair and destructive mechanisms both at a cellular level and systemically—in the body as a whole. Even more important, there now appears to be a strong relationship between age-degeneration being studied at a cellular level and the ageing of the body as a whole so that in a sense both the cell-focusers and the generalists are right. They are only looking at the phenomenon of ageing through different sets of binoculars. And, just as the practices involved in *natural-law* anti-ageing and the newly discovered tools of *high-tech* anti-ageing appear to work best when they are applied together, the whole process of ageing with all that it implies makes better sense when you try to look at it from a number of different angles at once. On a cell-focusing level these include investigating recent discoveries in the areas of free-radical biochemistry, electrobiology and submolecular physics. On a whole-body level they take in an awareness of the role that stress plays in age-degeneration, how ageing is related to a decline in immune functions, and new advances in the realm of psychoneuro-immunology—the study of how the mind affects the body's immune system. Each of these areas of scientific study has something to offer to an understanding of why your body ages. They also have much to contribute in developing a personal lifestyle for ageless ageing. Some of them can even offer ways of reversing age-related changes you may have experienced already: Let's look at the cell and at free-radical biochemistry first.

THREE

Mysteries of the Cell

The smallest structural unit in your body is the cell. It is truly a remarkable entity for it is alive. It moves, grows, reacts, protects itself and even reproduces. And so far, despite the most elaborate and learned research attempting to understand the nature of that aliveness, it remains a mystery. No matter from what perspective you view ageing, you are ultimately looking at changes in life energy which take place over a period of time. A major goal of ageless ageing on a cellular level is making sure that everything functions properly to ensure good energy production and to keep the life machinery of cells ticking over as the years pass much as it does in a healthy person of say twenty-five. To understand just how complex a task this is and just what is involved in fulfilling it you need to understand something about the structure and function of these little miracles of nature—the cells from which your body is built.

The Cell as an Energy Factory

Each cell—and there are trillions of them in the human body—is like a factory complex. The famous American biochemist Roger Williams describes this very well when he says:

> Every cell has its own power plant from which it derives its energy. The burning process from which energy is derived is a highly ordered, many-step process in which many different catalysts are involved. Each catalyst (enzyme) is protein in nature and is made up of hundreds of amino acids (and often

Top: A typical human cell. The organelles (specialized structures within the cell) are not drawn to exact scale.

The membrane is a basic feature of every organelle in the cell. The situation in the outer membrane of a mitochondrion is shown schematically in the final stage of the sequence of blow-ups (bottom); the picture would be similar for any of the other organelle membranes or for the cell membrane itself. The double lipid layer is a common feature. The heads of the lipid molecules have a high attraction for water and face outward; the tails, which prefer an oily environment, face inwards and towards each other, so that an oily layer is created inside the membrane.

The tails are the target of lipid peroxidation (see page 29), especially if the lipids are polyunsaturated. Vitamin E normally works to prevent this peroxidation but, if it is not there to protect the lipids, free radicals and oxygen can cause a chain reaction which ties them together and disrupts the membrane. This impairs the function of the organelle and possibly damages the cell as a whole.

A Simplified Animal Cell

vitamins) put together in exactly the right way. The power plant makes it possible for every cell to be highly dynamic. Something is happening every microsecond. Complex chemical transformations—filtering, ultrafiltering, emulsifying, dispersion, aggregating, absorption—are continually in progress. Tearing down, building up, and repairing are constantly going on.

He continues:

Cells have their own ways of designing and making blueprints; 'printing' and duplicating are very much in evidence. Cells also have their own versions of assembly lines. They have transportation systems; sorting, pumping, and streaming; and molecules riding piggy-back on others are common processes. Intricate mechanisms, including feedbacks, are used by cells to regulate their numerous activities. Cells have communication systems—messages and messengers. They have the equivalent of both an intercom system and devices for sending and receiving messages to and from the outside. Cells are equipped with sewage and disposal systems. They even have in effect pollution-control mechanisms whereby toxic molecules are converted into others which are relatively harmless.

This marvellous creation of nature—the tiny cell—is superbly *ordered* in its functions and structure. On this order depends your body's youthfulness and longevity. But because it is so complex each part of the cellular mechanism is also highly subject to *disorder*. And when a cell becomes deranged, its entire function can be seriously impaired. Multiply one deranged cell times the thousand million million cells in your body and you experience what is known in modern medicine as degenerative disease and ageing.

Cellular Order—Foundation of Ageless Ageing

At its outer edge each cell is surrounded by a protective membrane built mostly from lipids or fats. Through this membrane all nutrients and oxygen must pass to keep the cell alive and all wastes must be eliminated. Inside the cell lies a gel-like ocean of cytoplasm which contains a variety of subcellular bodies—fat-protein complexes called organelles which take part in cell functions. The organelles include microsomes which make new proteins, lysosomes which are like automatic waste collectors whose job it is to keep the cytoplasmic ocean unpolluted, and mitochondria—minute energy factories. Each cell also has a nucleus in its centre. Here all the genetic details of its structure and functions are carefully locked away in molecules of DNA, so that when a cell gets ready to divide, another nucleic acid called RNA carries the DNA's coded instruction to get the correct amino acids for the synthesis of new proteins.

Just like the cell itself, every organelle it contains is encased within a protective membrane. These membranes are very important to the integrity of a living cell and to protecting the body as a whole from ageing and illness. If they are disrupted, chaos can ensue: wastes can leak into the cytoplasm and cause the cell to poison itself, enzymes contained in the mitochondria can cause serious biological disruption, and damage to the DNA within the nucleus in turn can lead to a missynthesis of protein and the production of a mutant or damaged daughter cell. In fact all of these detrimental changes appear to take place as your body ages. Preventing them and protecting the integrity of each individual cell within any biological system is the central issue in preventing age-degeneration. And one of life's great paradoxes is that amongst the worst threats to cellular order and integrity on many different levels is the one element without which we cannot live even for a few minutes: oxygen.

The Two Faces of Oxygen

Two billion years ago—give or take a few million years—a profound change took place on earth which dramatically affected evolution: plant life came into being. These first primitive plants started to release oxygen into the atmosphere by breaking down water in the presence of sunlight through a process called photosynthesis. In the beginning this 'new' element oxygen was lethal to almost every living organism. The few creatures who managed to survive could do so only by continually adapting to

The carbon cycle of life is based on the sun as the ultimate source of energy. Solar radiation drives photosynthesis, which builds energy-rich glucose and other organic compounds from energy-poor carbon dioxide and water, releasing oxygen in the process. The fuels synthesized in this way are then broken down to carbon dioxide and water by animal cells, which use the energy extracted in the process to do their work.

Adenosine triphosphate (ATP), the common carrier of energy in animal and plant cells, is formed in the mitochondria (animals) and chloroplasts (plants). It supplies energy for muscle contraction, protein synthesis, transfer of nerve impulses, etc. The 'discharged' adenosine diphosphate (ADP) thus formed is 'recharged' by solar or food energy.

its presence in their system. Slowly these early simple animals evolved ways of doing this. They created protective mechanisms against oxygen toxicity. And they found ways of using oxygen to create energy—so successfully in fact that by now oxygen has become the potent impetus behind most metabolic processes that fuel complex forms of animal life.

Yet oxygen's toxicity is still with us. Expose yourself to levels of oxygen beyond what you are used to—around one fifth of an atmosphere of pressure—and you can become ill. For instance breathe in pure oxygen at 1 atmosphere for a few hours and you will develop inflammation in the trachea. Stay in such an atmosphere for days on end and, ironically, soon you will die from a condition called *anoxia* which means lack of oxygen. Even the oxygen we take in through the air we normally breathe is still highly toxic to many essential life processes on a cellular level because oxygen tends to combine with other substances and to wreak havoc with delicate cell structures causing *disorder*. It is a disorder which is central to the whole process of ageing.

Atoms, Molecules and Energy Exchange

In biochemical terms all the stuff of life—from the genetic material in your cells to the air that you breathe—is built out of atoms and molecules arranged in infinite combinations. A molecule is only a combination of atoms. And atoms are made up of a number of particles, the most important of which are the protons (which carry a minute positive electrical charge) and neutrons, both of which are found in the centre of the atom, and the electrons (each of which carries a small negative charge) which spin around in orbitals on the outside. Oxygen is the most important molecule we ever deal with.

What makes energy-yielding metabolism possible in the human body is only the ability we have evolved through evolution to convert nutrients taken in through foods we eat into chemical energy to fuel life processes by burning it. This is a process known as aerobic metabolism. And it is a highly efficient means of energy production and release. Specifically it involves the transfer of electrons from one molecule to another. In scientific terms this occurrence is known as an *oxidation-*

reduction or a *redox* reaction. So important are redox reactions both to life processes in general and to helping to slow age-degeneration that it is important to take a closer look at them.

Whenever an electron is transferred from one atom or molecule to another this complementary oxidation and reduction takes place between the two interacting species of molecules. In fact the word *oxidation* is a description of the process in which a molecule or atom loses an electron and the term reduction refers to the process whereby an electron is gained. So when molecules interact in any redox reaction one substance is *oxidized* (the molecule loses an electron) while the other is *reduced* (it gains an electron). For some time physicists have tended to view electrons not only as subatomic particles but also as basic units of energy. And the energy-producing metabolism which our bodies carry out can be described in biochemical terms as the *oxidation* or removal of electrons from reduced carbon compounds and the *reduction* of or transfer of these electrons by suitable carriers to their ultimate acceptor oxygen. It is a process which creates water as its by-product.

So long as we live these redox reactions are ceaselessly taking place. They are the basis of the oxygen-based metabolism which keeps us alive. And we need vast amounts of energy to stay alive. This we get by oxidizing biological substances—burning food as fuel. It is a burning which takes place not in some haphazard way as it would in a furnace. Instead it is ordered with superb precision: enzymes act as catalysts and oxidations occur in a carefully modulated series of small steps which are able to liberate the maximum amount of energy present for effective use while causing the minimum amount of disturbance to the cell. Energy which is liberated by such a process needs to go through many intermediate compounds which serve as electron-carriers in order to provide the control necessary. For if electrons were to reduce oxygen directly and not go through these intermediate steps then we would be unable to harness the energy released for useful purposes.

The trouble is that a number of highly reactive, potentially toxic and destructive species of molecules can be generated in the process. They are known as *free radicals* and they put us as human beings in the curious position of being dependent upon oxygen for our life energy and yet also susceptible to its toxic effects—what in biochemistry is known as *oxidizing stress* or *oxy-stress*. It poses a continual challenge to the integrity of our cells and tissues and it appears to be a central cause of ageing.

Friendly and Unfriendly Free Radicals

Free radicals are species of atoms or molecules which are highly reactive simply because they are electrochemically unbalanced. In stable molecules and atoms you'll find the positively charged protons and the negatively charged electrons in perfect balance so that the electrical charge the atom or molecule carries can be said to be nil. The molecule is neutral. Free radicals are different. Instead of having the usual orbitals occupied by pairs of electrons which spin in opposite directions these renegades have an odd number. Therefore they carry a small electrical charge. Most retain a single unpaired electron in an outer orbital. This not only creates the electrical charge it also gives the molecule astounding instability and makes it react with other atoms and molecules with which it comes into contact. It is a relatively simple matter to turn a stable non-radical molecule or compound into a free-radical species simply by bringing it in contact with another free radical from which it gains or to which it loses an electron. The whole exchange takes place in microseconds. Once a free radical is present it tends to propagate by generating other free radicals from chain reactions with the stable non-radical species which happen to be present.

Free radicals, which are common in all biological systems, are essential for the maintenance of life. Indeed free radicals are formed naturally during a wide variety of biological processes from respiration to the carrying out of enzyme activities which are a normal part of cell metabolism. However free-radical reactions are also responsible for many of the things that go wrong with the body on a cellular level. For when these free-radical reactions get out of hand they can precipitate a relentless process of destruction and degeneration in the body as a whole.

Molecular Rapists

Gerontologist Alex Comfort once compared a free radical to 'a convention delegate away from his wife: it's a highly reactive chemical agent that will combine with anything that's around.' Other researchers believe free radicals can be better likened to rapists whose union with other molecules, willing or unwilling, is nothing less than a clear attack. Free radicals can cut other molecules down the middle, chop pieces off them, distort cellular information and generally wreak havoc with living systems. They can cause injury, inflammation and destruction to parts of cells, cell walls and to collagen fibres—the body's most important structural protein.

An important source of free-radical harm in relation to ageing occurs through a process called lipid peroxidation. Lipid is simply the scientific word for fats and oils. Lipids are found all over our bodies: in the blood, they are stored as potential energy in the cells; they are joined to certain proteins called lipoproteins and are a part of steroid hormones. Lipids are particularly important to individual cells because they largely make up the membrane which separates a cell from its surrounding medium. The lipids in our bodies come from the foods we eat—saturated and unsaturated fatty acids. In fact it is absolutely necessary that we take in an adequate supply of unsaturated fatty acids for life and health. The trouble is that unsaturated fatty acids have a strong tendency to react with oxygen in the body to form chemical compounds known as peroxides. Peroxidation also occurs in the presence of oxygen in the atmosphere. This is what makes cooking oils or peanut butter turn rancid. Like free radicals, once formed in the body peroxides then tend to join with yet more lipids and to propagate yet more peroxides and free radicals. These can cause serious damage to organelles in the cells and to cell membranes, allowing cellular pollution and reducing the electrical potentials—thus lowering body vitality in yet another way. Protect your body from oxy-stress—free-radical and peroxidation damage—and you will dramatically slow down the rate at which you age.

Free-Radical Revolution

Recent findings in the field of free-radical pathology—the study of free radicals 'gone wrong'—are nothing short of revolutionary. They make it possible for the first time in scientific terms to formulate a *unified* theory of disease. Thanks to free-radical biochemistry, doctors well versed in the subject are beginning to make sense of a lot of what until now appeared to be contradictory clinical and epidemiological observations and to create a scientific rationale both for the treatment and for the prevention of a number of the major causes of degeneration and death: atherosclerosis, cancer, arthritis, dementia and other age-related diseases. For free-radical damage now appears to underlie the pathology of all of these conditions despite the difference in their manifestations in the body.

This discovery is perhaps the most important medical finding in the past fifty years. The discovery that oxy-stress—free-radical damage and peroxidation—can bring about disease and degeneration in the body and the development of ways and means of counteracting it are providing scientists with coherent and workable methods both for preventing illness—from allergy to many serious mental disorders—as well as for restoring much of the degenerative damage which is associated with ageing. The free-radical concept can also explain how many of the natural-law therapies work—therapies which we will be exploring in later chapters as a means of slowing down ageing and reversing pathological changes in the body—from chelation therapy and anti-oxidant supplementation to diet and lifestyle changes which are traditionally used to restore health to a chronically ill person. And, although it will take another twenty years before free-radical biochemistry becomes integrated into the work of the average doctor, it is already being used successfully by the few who know about the new findings and have begun to apply them.

Elmer M. Cranton and James P. Frackelton—two physicians who are experts in the field of free-radical biochemistry and its clinical applications—wrote recently in the *Journal of Holistic Medicine*, 'The field of free-radical biochemistry is as revolutionary and profound in its implications for medicine as was the germ theory and science of microbiology which made possible development of effective treatments for infectious diseases.' Methods for detecting and measuring the presence of free radicals in living systems have only just been developed. What they show is that the reason why many of the natural treatments for ageing and illness work is the fact that, in the words of these two scientists, '. . . physical exercise, applied clinical nutrition and moderation of health-destroying habits, all have common therapeutic mechanisms which reduce free-radical damage.' Free-radical damage now appears to be the very foundation of ageing as well. And if we want to counteract it we need to know how and why.

FOUR

Shoe-leather and Cross-linking

Proteins are made up of amino acids—the most important of all known substances in the organic world. For amino acids are the basis of life. They are used to build cells and to repair tissue. Your immune system—from its white blood cells to interferon—depends upon amino acids. Your bones and teeth are made with chains of amino acids in which minerals have been laid down. In your body over 50,000 different proteins are made from amino acids. Every enzyme is a protein—so, largely, are the hormones which direct organic functions, the muscle tissue which gives your body form and strength, and the vascular tissue which carries nutrients to the cells. Your cells' genetic materials—the DNA and its messenger nucleic acid RNA—while not themselves proteins are deeply involved in the process of protein synthesis. On the integrity of all these proteins you are entirely dependent for life and health.

When free radicals react with molecules of protein in the cell or in the tissue, these long-chain proteins can become *cross-linked*, which means they become molecularly bound together and tangled. As a result tissues lose their suppleness, skin wrinkles, veins and arteries become hardened and more inclined to build up deposits of cholesterol, your chances of developing cancerous growths increase and the genetic material in your cells, which is necessary for cell division and tissue repair, becomes garbled. Cross-linking is a phenomenon which is fundamental to age-degeneration—both at a deep internal level where it can cause arteriosclerosis and brain degeneration and superficially since it appears to be the major reason why skin wrinkles and sags. Prevention of excessive cross-linkage in your body is essential to any effective programme of ageless ageing.

During the Second World War a Finnish chemist named Johan Bjorksten was working for an American photographic company. In the midst of carrying out a routine task, one day, he realized that the changes which take place in the gelatins of film and plates are akin to those which take place in our cells when we age. These changes are the result of chemical bonds being formed—cross-linking—between thin protein molecules which make up the gelatin. They are also, he remarked, similar to the changes deliberately brought about in order to turn animal hides into strong leather. This cross-linking is responsible for the enormous difference in the way a finished piece of leather feels as compared with the skin of the animal from which it was taken. It was Bjorksten who coined the word cross-linking. He then went on to explore it as a central cause of ageing and to develop what is perhaps the most comprehensive theoretical approach to age-retardation of any scientist in the world today.

Factory Slow-down

To understand how cross-linking interferes with cellular metabolism and leads to degeneration Bjorksten explains that protein molecules—the most important chemical parts of the living body—are like long spirals. In all of them, along the chain there are points which can tie in very easily with other molecules or atoms. In fact it is thanks to these many 'sensitive' parts on the protein molecules that proteins are able to carry out so many useful tasks in the body and why they are so necessary to life processes. But when 'cross-linkers' such as free radicals or highly reactive oxygen molecules come along, rather like small rods with hooks at each end they can hook into these sensitive points on the protein molecules. And when they do this—with each end on a protein molecule—they bind proteins together. When two or more protein molecules are joined together in this way they can no longer move as freely. When they become linked up to many protein molecules in many places they finally get so jumbled up that they can no longer do their job efficiently.

Going back to our analogy of the cell as an energy factory it is easy to see what happens. Bjorksten once explained it this way to his child:

Imagine you are in a big room, where thousands of people are working. Each day some evil person comes in and slips a pair of handcuffs on a pair of people so that it ties them together. That makes it difficult for them to work, doesn't it? . . . Now if this goes on so that at the end of every day a couple more handcuffs are put on so that one handcuff is put on one person and the other end of it on another person, then you can see that things get more and more messed up . . . finally everything becomes so confused that nothing can get done, and the whole work or whatever they are doing in that hall has to stop. Think of the handcuffs as cross-linkers, and the people as those important protein molecules. When a person is young and in his prime, he hasn't many protein molecules that are handcuffed together to slow down the work of his body. But as he gets older more and more of the cross-linker 'handcuffs' slide into place and the work of his body slows down and he gets old and weak.

Wrinkles, Radicals and Radiation

The damage that free radicals and cross-linking can do to the collagen, elastin and reticulin in connective tissue is particularly worrying from a cosmetic point of view. It makes your skin sag and your muscles lose their firmness. Collagen, which is often considered the mortar of the cells, makes up more than 40 per cent of your body's protein. When collagen and other connective proteins are young they have almost a gel-like quality to them. They lend structural support to all the living cells. For these cells to be nourished, oxygen, moisture and nutrients have to pass through the collagen network. Through this network too are eliminated the cells' waste products. Collagen which has become cross-linked as a result of free-radical attack impedes proper cell nutrition and waste elimination and therefore lowers cell vitality and eventually the vitality of the whole organism.

Apart from natural body agents which cause a small amount

of cross-linking to take place even in the collagen of a baby, to give structure to muscles, the vascular system and skin, a wide variety of external factors also cause it to occur. They include industrial pollutants, polyvalent metals such as lead, cadmium, mercury and so forth, sodium nitrite which is used to preserve luncheon meats, radiation including x-rays, cosmic radiation and nuclear radiation in our food and atmosphere. When you are young your body produces enzymes which break down excess cross-linkages when they take place. Then there is an excellent 'balance of power' which keeps our skin and muscles and veins and capillaries strong but flexible and supple. But as the years go by cross-linkage tends to occur faster than these enzymes can undo it—probably both because enzymes tend to be reduced with age and also because we tend to accumulate more and more cross-linking substances in our system as we get older.

Cross-linking appears to be largely responsible for the loss of elasticity in our body's tissues that comes with age, for the increased brittleness of rigid tissues which is also a characteristic of age and for the decline in the percentage of bound water in the tissues which, because of the important role water appears to play in energy transfer in the body, can decrease vitality in tissues and organs—also a characteristic of advancing age. Animals kept on very low-calorie diets show dramatically increased lifespans. This, according to Bjorksten and others, is probably because a low-calorie diet creates a minimum of metabolic by-products which can act as free radicals and cross-linkers. The more you can avoid cross-linkage the smoother will stay your skin. If we could find a way of dissolving cross-linkage after it occurs then we would have a rejuvenation treatment *par excellence*. This has been (and still is) a major goal of Bjorksten who is director of the non-profit research foundation in America which bears his name.

Damaged DNA

Free radicals and the by-products of lipid peroxidation can also react with DNA, the cell's genetic material, and RNA, which carries the genetic messages, to disrupt genetic information so

Collagen and the cross-linkage of collagen. In this model of one type of connective tissue, each of the tube structures represents a chain of amino acids: three such chains twisted together in a spiral (a triple helix) are considered as a unit of collagen. Many of these units are joined end to end to form long, continuous threads; in turn, these continuous threads are stacked side by side to form larger strands. A small section of one of those strands is shown here.

During youth, only a moderate amount of cross-linking ties the collagen threads to each other (top). As a result, the collagen threads slide past each other, and the connective tissue is quite elastic. With increasing age, however, progressively more cross-linkages are formed, so that the sliding of threads past each other is greatly restricted (above), with the result that the connective tissue is less elastic.

that abnormal proteins are synthesized. As yet no one has been able to clearly understand how this takes place. What is known is that when genetic material is altered in this way cells no longer reproduce themselves accurately. This appears to be a major factor in age-degeneration as well as in the development of cancer. Bjorksten believes also that cross-linkages are formed between parts of DNA's spiral helices although other researchers disagree with him. In any case there is strong evidence that disruptions in genetic information do take place as we age, resulting in missynthesized proteins. The level of RNA decreases in middle age and it appears that RNA's susceptibility to misprogramming also increases. This may be the result of a reduction in protein and enzyme manufacture.

Missynthesized proteins cause problems in many ways. When the right protein is not made then the purpose for which it is intended does not get fulfilled and either the function of a structure or an enzyme is changed or impaired. Missynthesized proteins also tend to be bigger than normal proteins and to crowd them out, competing with them for available nutrients. They can also create wastes which pollute cells and, since the body needs to produce new proteins to replace them, can greatly lower a cell's vitality and drain its resources. Nucleic acids in the cell nucleus have a quite remarkable ability to repair themselves. But in order for this to happen there must be an adequate supply of ascorbic acid, amino acids, the B vitamins—especially folic acid, B_2, B_6, B_5 and choline— as well as zinc, manganese and chromium. A number of studies show that the sulphur amino acids, selenium, ascorbic acid and vitamin E together promote DNA and RNA repair. This is one of the reasons why these nutrients are included in the list of natural substances taken as nutritional supplements for ageless ageing. But to preserve genetic information intact it is necessary to protect DNA and RNA from lipid peroxidation and free-radical attack.

Anti-oxidant Defences

It is a challenge for which our exquisitely organized life processes have a double barrelled answer, in the form of complex anti-oxidant defence systems. The body in its wisdom has devised a number of mechanisms to protect itself from oxy-stress. Our first line of defence comes in the form of special enzymes— free-radical scavengers—with names you will find commonly mentioned in any treatise on age-retardation. They include: superoxide dismutase (SOD), glutathione peroxidase and catalase. Each enzyme has a specific and very important task to perform; all of these are involved in the processes of protecting living material from damage. The second line of defence is made up of the anti-oxidant nutrients we take in through our foods and which serve as free-radical quenchers to mop up reactive molecular species including singlet oxygen* and to neutralize their ability to cause damage. They include ascorbic acid, beta-carotene, vitamin A, certain amino acids, vitamin E and selenium. One of the most profound findings in biomedical research in the last few decades is that anti-oxidants are also anti-cancer agents.

About anti-oxidant nutrients we will be talking a great deal — not only because they can be useful in protecting your body from accelerated ageing and degeneration but because, as clinical applications of free-radical biochemistry are beginning to show, they have an important role to play in the treatment of many serious illnesses including environmental and food allergies. Also the same anti-oxidant nutrients which protect from oxy-stress have an ability to improve immune functions— another important factor in slowing down the ageing process. They can even be used for their anti-inflammatory properties. So important can these substances be for improving health that many doctors who use them in high doses for healing serious illness in their patients have now begun to incorporate similar high doses in their own lives for preventative purposes.

External Threats

Were the body's own metabolic processes the only trigger for free-radical production and cross-linking we would probably

---

*An oxygen molecule containing only one atom instead of the usual two atoms.

have little worry about age-related degeneration nor about supplying extra anti-oxidants for prophylactic purposes. Our own protective mechanisms might be enough to protect our cells, proteins and lipids from damage. But a myriad of external factors are also able to initiate and to accelerate damaging free-radical reactions in our body. Our environment is quite literally full of external triggers of free radicals. These include radiation of all sorts—from the sun's ultraviolet rays to emanations from nuclear power stations and even the electro-magnetic fields set up by high-tension electrical installations. They also include air pollutants such as ozone, nitrogen dioxide, and sulphur dioxide; cigarette smoke, solvents, pesticides and drugs; heavy metals such as lead, cadmium and aluminium; as well as certain foods, particularly those which are lacking in freshness. The eating of too much food, and the toxic residues from illness or prolonged emotional stress, also tend to increase free-radical reactions and cross-linkage. Even oxygen in the air we breathe brings about free-radical damage, not only because the majority of free-radical reactions involve oxygen but because oxygen in certain forms actually behaves like a free radical itself. Two forms of activated oxygen*—singlet oxygen and hydrogen peroxide—although technically not free radicals themselves nonetheless share with them a similar capacity to damage biological tissue and therefore to age the body.

The Fire, the Heat and the Screen

One useful way to look at the nature of free-radical reactions and the cross-linking they cause and understand how the body is able to protect itself from free-radical damage is through an analogy devised by an American scientist whose major focus has been on oxy-stress as an underlying cause of environmental allergies. An expert on clinical ecology, Steve Levine likens it to sitting in front of a fireplace watching logs burn. The burning of the wood gives off the energy needed to heat the room—akin to redox reactions which burn fuel for cell energy. And, thanks to the fact that in front of the fireplace is placed a good protective screen, the sparks which are emitted as part of the wood-burning

*Oxygen in highly reactive form.

process do no damage to our carpets or clothes. Think of the screen as the body's anti-oxidant defence systems. Think of the sparks as free radicals and other activated species of molecules. They are of course a normal outcome of cellular metabolism just as sparks are a normal occurrence when burning. Both are the inevitable result of inefficiencies in the burning process. If the burning process were total—completely efficient—then there wouldn't be any sparks.

Free radicals are potentially destructive and ageing to an organism only if the 'protective screen'—our anti-oxidant defence system—is damaged or worn, or if quite literally the number of sparks formed by the fire overwhelms the screen and sends it crashing to the floor, which is what happens in serious chronic illness and degeneration. The numerous parts of your body's anti-oxidant defence system must absorb the potentially damaging sparks—the free radicals and other activated molecular species. But when we are overwhelmed by environmental chemical exposure, or emotional stress or the trauma of infection, then there is an increase in sparks. And our metabolic machinery, which is basically burning fuel and deriving energy, ultimately has to deal with the sparks of metabolism. An inability to do this can result in illness, fatigue, degeneration and ageing.

Cellular Age Control

Age control on a cellular level entails preventing peroxidation of the foods we eat and inhibiting lipid peroxidation in the body, avoiding as much as possible the triggers for oxy-stress in our environment, and preventing free-radical damage and cross-linking by strengthening the body's anti-oxidant defence system. Many researchers believe, as Bjorksten does, that we may also be able to use certain chemical or nutritional agents to *dissolve* cross-linked proteins and repair free-radical damage which has already occurred as well. Bjorksten has actually discovered a means of doing this—a special strain of *Bacillus cerus* which is proteolytic (protein digesting). It can reverse the cross-links formed for instance in the tanning process, so that hide returns to its original soft shape even after having been turned into leather. But the enormous amount of research time and money necessary to develop such a find into a safe form of treatment which can be brought on the market has so far made this impossible.

Meanwhile biochemists continue to probe the secrets of the body's anti-oxidant system. It now appears that it is an over-taxing of this system—an excess of oxy-stress—which leads to the widespread incidence of both food and environmental allergies. Meanwhile strong evidence is emerging that free-radical damage is the underlying cause of the so-called diseases of civilization which plague our society. It is an exciting area of research which holds out many promises for healthier lives and slowing down the rate at which we age. The two-branched approach to ageless ageing relies heavily on new discoveries in free-radical biochemistry, as you will see in later chapters which deal with making use of anti-oxidants, amino acids, diet and exercise to lower oxy-stress and slow the rate at which you age. But it is by no means the whole story. For, lost in his world of electron microscopes, there is always the danger that the free-radical biochemist may lose his ability to see the wood for the trees. Even when I am most entranced by the elegance of their theories and the exciting implications of what can be achieved using natural anti-oxidant nutrients to protect the body from age-degeneration (and as you will see in subsequent chapters it is a great deal) I am still brought back to an awareness of the fact that after all we are dealing not just with a collection of cells, atoms and molecules but with a complex self-adjusting organism with, as yet, largely undefined control systems. It is an organism which, when attempting to penetrate the mysteries of ageing and the magic of age-retardation, has also to be viewed as a whole. When you step back from a microscope two important closely related areas of focus loom large on the horizon—stress and the immune system.

FIVE

Immune Power

The immune system is your body's natural defence against invasion, poison and disease. How well it is working determines to a large degree how rapidly you age. The immune system is like an enormously complex and highly organized secret police in a totalitarian country which—together with its special branch of armed militia—ensures that absolutely everything foreign, everything which does not carry the marker of 'self', is kept out. It guards against foreign proteins, viruses, bacteria and aberrant cells. And, just as a cell membrane must remain intact to protect the integrity of the cell, so your immune system must maintain its high-protection surveillance to ensure the integrity of your body as a whole.

The trouble is that as you get older two very dangerous things tend to happen to it. First its functions decline so that it is no longer an effective military force against invasion and aberrant cells. Second, rather like a secret police without proper control from the top, it tends to go haywire and fails to distinguish between self and non-self so that it not only is no longer able to protect you, it actually begins to attack and destroy the body's own protein. This not only leaves you vulnerable to invasion by disease-provoking microbes, it can also make you prone to a number of specific diseases known as the auto-immune disorders. They include multiple sclerosis, rheumatoid arthritis, rheumatic heart disease, and systemic lupus.

Immunity—Free-Radical Damage and Age Decline

The complicated system by which 'self' and 'non-self' are recognized appears to be regulated by a collection of genes

The immune system consists of the lymphocyte cells and the antibody molecules which they secrete. The cells and antibodies pervade most of the body's tissues, being delivered there by the bloodstream, but they are concentrated in the tree of lymphatic vessels and the lymph nodes stationed along them, the bone marrow (which is in the long bones, only one of which is illustrated), the thymus and the spleen. The lymphatic vessels collect the cells and antibodies from the body's tissues and return them to the bloodstream at the subclavian veins in the neck. Lymphocytes are manufactured in the bone marrow and multiply by cell division in the thymus, the spleen and the lymph nodes. *Right:* A highly schematic representation of the relation of the blood vessels and the lymphatic vessels.

found very close to one another on a single chromosome. It is a collection called the major histocompatibility complex (MHC). Interestingly enough some of the enzymes such as SOD and probably catalase—which, you may remember, are the body's natural free-radical scavengers—are also found in the same chromosome. Even mechanisms such as the repair of damaged DNA appear to be influenced by the MHC. Two well-respected age-researchers, Roy Walford at the UCLA (University of California at Los Angeles) Medical School and Ed Yunnis at Harvard have shown that the MHC is an important regulator of the rate at which we age. How well it works is closely determined both by the actions of free radicals and by how much decline has taken place in the immune system as a whole. For the functions of the body's anti-oxidant defence systems and those of the MHC and immunity appear to be inextricably intertwined. Take action to improve one and you improve the other as well. If science can find a way of preventing immune functions from declining and of preventing the immune system from acting against the 'self' of which it is a part, it will also go a long way towards slowing down or even reversing the ageing process. Immune dysfunction is a major pacemaker of ageing.

At the National Institutes of Health in the United States, researchers have been able to measure just how dramatic a decline in immunologic efficiency occurs as an animal ages. They discovered that when mice were subjected to measured doses of disease organisms designed to stimulate the immune system, the old mice demonstrated a response that was only 10 per cent of that of young mice. In other words, their immune system had experienced a 90 per cent decline. Translated into human terms one could say that at age seventy you are ten times more susceptible to disease and age-degeneration than you were at twelve years old.

The Master, the Police and the Militia

Just above your heart in the chest cavity is the master gland of immunity—the thymus. It is a gland which until recently was largely ignored because scientists believed that the thymus was only involved in the growth process and after that was simply redundant to the body. This theory they justified by the fact that the thymus tends to shrink dramatically after about the age of fourteen.

We now know however that not only is the 'thymus redundancy theory' wrong, the thymus is probably the single most important part of the body in protecting you from both illness and ageing. This small pinkish-grey body under your breastbone oversees your state of health from birth to death. The levels of hormones which this gland produces—called thymosin—appear to be related both to the state of your endocrine system with all its hormones and to many brain chemicals, as well as to how rapidly you are ageing. It is from the thymus that instructions come to the lymph nodes and the spleen to fight off bacterial invasions and to reject foreign cells. These tasks it relegates to the two major protective forces of the immune system—the secret police and the militia.

The thymus and its T-cells are the secret police. They make up about half of the resources for defence in your body. Another group of white blood cells called B-cells, whose main purpose is to protect your body against most bacterial threats and a few viral infections, make up the other half. They are the armed militia. These two branches work together but differently to provide constant vigilance against external threats—from bacterial invasions to chemicals which cause free-radical damage, peroxidation and cross-linking. Where the T-cells produce their single lymphokines, B-cells make antibodies.

T-cells, B-cells and Integrity

The thymus sends instructions to the lymph nodes and the spleen to fight off bacterial invasions and to reject foreign cells. It issues these instructions via a group of hormones which act as messengers to your body's defence system. They mobilize T-cell lymphocytes—your body's 'warrior cells'—and set them to work battling the thousands of potentially lethal microorganisms, cancer-inducing ultraviolet radiations from the sun or toxic chemicals from our highly industrialized environment. These warrior cells then produce another group of hormone-like substances called lymphokines which are considered the immune system's natural drugs. One of these lymphokines is interferon—now famous because of its demonstrated ability to fight cancer—but there are a number of others with strange titles like SIRS and IL-2.

When B-lymphocytes or B-cells locate a foreign organism they start producing antibodies against it. When T-cells spot an invader they produce their lymphokines to kill the organism or destroy a cancer cell directly. These T-cells can call upon another kind of cells too, called macrophages. The word means 'big eaters', since they are able to engulf and destroy bacteria or malignancies, or they can help B-cells to produce more powerful antibodies. By acting as 'suppressors', they also protect your body against the possibility that your B-cells and other T-cells attack its own tissue which is what happens in the case of the auto-immune diseases such as arthritis. So important to health is the thymus-mediated T-cell system that it is considered the brain of the immune response. If there is any imbalance between the different types of T-cells or if there are too few, your immune system falters and you become susceptible to the auto-immune diseases, early ageing and sickness.

Lymph Magic

At any moment there are about a trillion lymphocytes in your body ready for action. They weigh a total of 2lb and they are constantly dying and being renewed at a rate of almost 10 million a minute. The B-lymphocytes, whose major task it is to produce antibodies—important weapons in the militia's armoury—are highly efficient. Every second they release about 20 trillion antibody molecules into the bloodstream. Lymphocytes can monitor your body's internal environment and maintain its stable functions thanks to their ability to flow around the body in the bloodstream and to pass through capillary walls into the interstitial fluid so they have close contact with the tissue cells, and their ability to pass along the lymph vessels which carry fluids throughout the body. Flowing within the lymph system they pass through lymph nodes—lymph vessels with filters which work together with the cells to wipe out many disease carriers. The lymph system and all of the hardworking lymphocytes it carries are vital to the health of the body and to resisting age-degeneration. It helps keep you clean and safe internally by detoxifying the body of all the chemicals, bacteria and other toxic products which can cause free-radical damage, peroxidation and cross-linking. That is why a major focus of *natural-law* age-retardation has always been to use diet, exercise and various natural treatments such as hydrotherapy to encourage lymphatic drainage and stimulate circulation.

Ageing and T-cell Decline

To prevent ageing the body must not only ensure good lymphatic and B-cell functions. It must also keep T-cells in top condition so they can protect against bacteria, fungi, viruses, foreign cells and allergens and so they can help the body resist cancer and the auto-immune diseases. But as we get older the thymus gland tends to produce less and less thymosin—the hormones required for T-cells to function normally—and a decline in T-cells takes place. Defective T-cell function also occurs in most of the degenerative diseases such as rheumatoid arthritis, cancer, multiple sclerosis, diabetes mellitus and ulcerative colitis. For any loss of T or B cells indicates a decline in our immunological defence system and makes us increasingly vulnerable to degeneration and less capable of coping with destructive changes that occur in the vascular system, and with cancer.

A standard medical laboratory test—the T&B Cell Test—is used when organs are transplanted because physicians must artificially decrease T&B cell count just enough to keep the patient's body from rejecting the transplant but not so much that it would result in his death. The same test has now begun to be used as a means of determining how rapidly a normal person is ageing and as a means of indicating what kind of nutritional or hormonal treatment may be needed to slow any decline which has taken place.

There are a number of possibilities which science has so far investigated as means of slowing ageing and prolonging life by improving immune functions. Some researchers have discovered that (at least with cold-blooded animals) if animals are kept at a lower temperature than normal their immune functions are protected from decline and they live significantly longer than normal. Others have begun to use injections of the thymosin hormones to boost immunity in cancer patients, to increase people's resistance to stress, to improve brain functions, and to slow ageing. Animal experiments also show that putting mammals on a diet which is low in calories and protein yet provides a high degree of nutritional support from vitamins, minerals and other nutrients, can actually rejuvenate a flagging immune system and prolong life. (More about that in Chapter 10.) But perhaps the most relevant approach to improving immune status and cutting down on auto-immune responses so far developed centres around the use of relatively high doses of specific immune-supporting nutrients. And it is no accident that most of these nutrients—vitamins and minerals—happen also to be anti-oxidants which offer protection against oxy-stress—free-radical damage, peroxidation and cross-linking. For a close relationship between immunity and cross-linkage reactions has now been well established.

Nutrients Can Protect Immunity

T-cells contain a high concentration of ascorbic acid—vitamin C. As we age this level drops progressively; so does our resistance to illness. And when illness strikes—say in the form of a virus or a bacterial infection—ascorbic-acid levels in T-cells quickly drop. The more severe the sickness the lower the drop. Smoking also causes T-cell ascorbic-acid levels to fall. But experiments with both animals and human beings indicate that large supplements of vitamin C will actually improve the ability of T-cells to protect the body both from the intensity and from the length of an illness. Even more important is what occurs when these supplements are given *before* illness strikes. Research shows that vitamin C helps protect the immune system from degeneration. Many of the B complex vitamins such as vitamin B_6, pantothenic acid, B_{12}, and folic acid are also particularly important in maintaining a sturdy immune system and preventing age-degeneration. In animals, a folic-acid deficiency decreases T-cell count by up to 80 per cent. In humans folic-acid deficiencies are commonplace—particularly among women.

Vitamin E also has been shown to enhance immune functions and improve resistance to disease and ageing. So has vitamin A. Meanwhile research has shown that zinc—another nutrient widely deficient in the average British or American diet—is not only essential for the maintenance of T-cells, it has a stimulating effect on all reproducing cells in the body including those of the immune system and the thymus itself.

The Role of Slow Viruses

In an effort to discover why as we age the immune system has increasing difficulty in distinguishing between self and non-self and tends to begin attacking the body's own protein, scientists have recently been investigating the possible role that a certain kind of virus—known as a slow virus—may play in ageing. Viruses are known to produce three kinds of clinical disease. Some, such as those involved in colds for instance, appear to leave no permanent damage behind them. Others, such as the virus involved in poliomyelitis, are different. Although they cause quick initial damage to the organism they also leave behind the damage when they are gone. A third group which appears to play an important role in degenerative diseases and ageing are the slow viruses. With incubation periods which can be measured in years, perhaps in decades, these virus infections appear to bring about slow destructive changes over a long period of time. They are able to enter the body at one time but may not cause damage until years later. Slow viruses may be able to alter the genes in an organism although they don't inhibit the synthesis of RNA—the genetic messenger. They can live within cells for many years without destroying the cell although they can do damage to the cell's outer membrane and its organelles. Such damage can make the cell appear to the immune system to be 'non-self' so that cells are attacked by the immune system. Some viruses also appear to depress the immune system's ability to produce antibodies that will destroy other viruses. Many researchers now believe that the auto-immune diseases associated with age-degeneration are really the effect of slow viruses. It is an area which is currently being closely investigated.

The Psychology of Immunity

Another area of investigation which appears to be particularly important in finding ways of preventing immune-system decline and ageing centres around the influence that brain and behaviour have on immunity. The ability of the immune system to respond to foreign material or to attack depends upon thymus functioning which in turn relies on impulses from a centre of the brain called the hypothalamus which triggers immune-system activity. The functioning of the hypothalamus is highly responsive to emotions and mental imagery and is highly stress-responsive. Grief, shock, fear, and anger can all strongly suppress immune functions and encourage rapid age-decline. Positive emotions have been shown to have the exact opposite effect by enhancing immunity and making the body highly resistant to degeneration. We will look at this phenomenon more closely in Chapter 28 and also at some of the ways it can be used for ageless ageing. Meanwhile, let's investigate the area of age research which appears to tie together both free-radical biochemistry and immunity. Let's look at ageing in relation to stress.

The principal participants in the functioning of the immune system (see pages 42–50). At lower right are shown the results of the body responding or failing to respond to damage. At lower left the immune response is shown in more detail.

SIX

The Stress of Ageing

Everybody knows about stress. It is a word which is bandied about in the media—something we are all familiar with from long experience. Stress, the journalists tell us, is the kind of harassed feeling you get when you have too much to do in too little time or when some taxi-driver is rude to you or when you are grieved about the death of a close friend or the fate of your career. Or is it?

In truth, few concepts are as misunderstood as stress. Before we can even begin to create a lifestyle which works for ageless ageing, we need to clear up a few of the misunderstandings which surround the popular use of the word and to investigate what 'stress' in scientific terms really is and how it relates to ageing. For a real understanding of 'stress' can not only draw together recent findings in free-radical pathology and immune functions in relation to age-degeneration and how to prevent it, it is also the unifying principle which explains why, when the longstanding *natural-law* approach to age-retardation and its *high-tech* counterpart are used together, you are able to create a lifestyle for ageless ageing which is as yet unequalled.

Einstein, Selye and Energy

In 1905, while exploring the characteristics of inanimate nature, Albert Einstein gave the world access to a vast reservoir of energy which until then had been unavailable for use. He developed the *theory of relativity*. In the beginning this theory was only of concern to physicists and mathematicians. Eventually it led to the use of atomic energy. But the practical significance of Einstein's scientific discovery was not realized until forty years later. Since then it has completely revolutionized the way we view reality. Einstein had a strong sense that without a belief in the inner harmony of the world there could be no science. He also knew that the energy to which his theories gave man access could either be used for ill or good. And he struggled long and fiercely for peaceful applications of atomic energy.

What Einstein did for inanimate nature, another scientist, of Austro-Hungarian origins, Hans Selye, has done for animate nature. In the late 1930s Selye developed his *theory of stress*. In it he revealed a central law of animate nature. He showed that living organisms have access to an enormous reservoir of *vital* energy—what he called *adaptive energy*. On learning to draw on it and using it wisely the biological future of each individual life depends. Like Einstein's theories, which at first were only of interest to the scientific community, Selye's stress concept was first only applied in highly technical ways by specific branches of science and medicine. In fact, only recently has it begun to be used in a practical way. Probably the most practical application of all is in the area of ageless ageing and longevity.

Another thing which Einstein and Selye had in common was an awareness of the unity implicit in both the animate and inanimate worlds and a belief that all energy must be used wisely and well if man is to live in a life-enhancing rather than a life-destroying way.

The two scientists never met. But when early articles about Selye's work began to appear in the scientific press, Einstein was one of the first to recognize their importance. He wrote a letter to Selye in which he suggested that a *unified theory of medicine* might be able to be created. That was Selye's dream too—a dream on which he worked eighteen hours a day for fifty years until his death in October of 1982. Now, thanks to scientists who are building upon Selye's original research, and a growing number of doctors who are searching for ways of putting it into practice, such a unified theory is becoming a reality. It is a theory in which new findings in free-radical biochemistry, electrobiology, immunology and psychobiology all come together—a theory which is of central importance to anyone interested in ageless ageing.

First Beginnings

Born in Vienna in 1907, Selye began his medical studies at the University of Prague in 1924. The following year he and his fellow students were shown a number of patients all in the early stages of various infectious diseases. His professor then pointed out the specific characteristics of each disease. But what intrigued Selye was not so much the differences which were obvious between the various diseases but rather their similarities. Regardless of the specific illness from which a patient suffered, they all felt and looked sick: they had diffuse joint pains, intestinal disturbances, coated tongues and they showed a loss of appetite and weight. In Selye's words:

> The patients had a common syndrome, but the professor attached very little significance to the signs that were common to all these diseases because they were 'nonspecific' and hence 'of no use' to the physician in making a correct diagnosis or prescribing the appropriate treatment.
>
> I began to wonder why patients suffering from the most diverse diseases have so many signs and symptoms in common. Whether a man suffers from severe loss of blood, an infectious disease or advanced cancer, he loses his appetite, his muscular strength and his ambition to accomplish anything; usually the patient also loses weight, and even his facial expression betrays that he is ill. What is the scientific basis of what I thought of at the time as the *syndrome of just being sick*? Could the mechanism of this syndrome be analysed by modern scientific techniques?

It was a question which plagued the young scientist for more than ten years. During that time he continued his medical education at the Universities of Paris and Rome, returned to Prague to take both a medical degree and a degree in chemistry there, and became a research fellow at Johns Hopkins University in the United States and then at McGill University in Montreal.

It was in his laboratory—in the biochemistry department—at McGill that all of his ideas began to come together.

Trying to isolate a new hormone from the ovaries of cattle, Selye was testing ovarian extracts by injecting them into rats and then looking for evidence that the rats' organs showed unexpected changes which could not be attributable to any hormone already known. Much to his delight, he found that three important changes were taking place: (1) The rats' adrenal cortex became enlarged; (2) their thymus glands, spleens, lymph nodes and other lymphatic structures all shrank; (3) bleeding ulcers developed in their guts. At first Selye assumed that these changes were the reaction to a new hormone in the extract. But soon, working with other substances as well, he discovered that every toxic substance—whether from living tissue or not—which was injected in the rats would bring about the same three changes. His mind shot back to medical school and his notion of a *syndrome of just being sick* and he realized that with these toxic drugs and extracts he had just created an experimental replica of the sickness syndrome. This he described in a classic paper which appeared in *Nature* in 1936. It was called, 'A Syndrome Produced by Various Nocuous Agents'. Later it was renamed the General Adaptation Syndrome (GAS)—or the universal biological stress syndrome. He began to investigate it in depth.

Three Stages of GAS

He found that an organism, including the human body, experiences the same nonspecific reactions whenever it is *stressed*— that is, whenever it is faced with a challenge to its integrity. The challenge—which Selye calls the *stressor*—can be a biological or chemical agent, such as bacteria or an environmental poison, excessive heat or cold, overwork or intense emotion, or physical injury or shock, to name just a few possibilities. Selye defined 'stress' as the *nonspecific response of the body to any demand made upon it*. For all of these stressors trigger the GAS, the purpose of which is to maintain the structure and function of an organism in a steady state of homeostasis,* and by doing so, to preserve its life.

Working at first with animals, Selye discovered that the GAS occurs in three well-defined stages: *alarm*; *resistance* or *adaptation*; and *exhaustion*. The first stage—alarm—is the body's calling of its defensive forces to arms. During this stage the body's immune system is challenged, overall resistance is lowered, the sympathetic nervous system fires, brainwaves change, muscles prepare for action, circulation to the muscles increases and the adrenals secrete hormones. All of this is a kind of biological preparation to 'fight or flee'. The second stage—that of adaptation or resistance—follows close behind it, unless of course the noxious agent or stressor is so virulent that it destroys life. During the stage of adaptation many of the body's systems are stimulated into increased activity in order to meet the challenge presented and to protect the body from harm. In effect resistance is raised and symptoms which first appeared in the alarm stage often disappear. This second stage of the GAS can last for a long or a short time depending on individual make-up and on the intensity of the reaction to the stressor. But it cannot go on for ever. If the stressor or noxious element remains, sooner or later the third stage is reached—exhaustion. By the time the third stage of the GAS is reached, the body's adaptive qualities have become exhausted and its weakest systems start to break down. Chronic fatigue and illness are the hallmarks of the exhaustion stage. If they continue then eventually the body dies.

'The three stages', wrote Selye, 'are reminiscent of childhood (with its characteristic low resistance and excessive responses to any kind of stimulus), adulthood (during which the body has adapted to most commonly encountered agents and resistance is increased) and old age (characterized by loss of adaptability and eventual exhaustion).'

Is Adaptation Energy Finite?

This triphasic nature of the GAS gave Selye the notion that the body's adaptability or *adaptation energy* is finite. Experiments

*The tendency of the body to maintain normal internal chemical and functional equilibrium.

showed that when animals are exposed to cold, or intense physical effort, or haemorrhage and other stressors, they can withstand them only so long. After the first alarm reaction the organism starts to resist. How long it can continue before exhaustion sets in depends upon its innate adaptability and on the intensity of the stressor.

Neither Selye nor any of his colleagues could define exactly what this adaptation energy is which is lost but they knew it was not merely caloric energy—for food intake is normal during the period of resistance. One would expect, so long as an organism is fed, that it would go on for ever. But it does not. Adaptation energy appears to be finite. As Selye says:

> Our reserves of adaptation energy could be compared to an inherited fortune from which we can make withdrawals; but there is no proof that we can also make additional deposits. We can squander our adaptability recklessly, 'burning the candle at both ends', or we can learn to make this valuable resource last longer, by using it wisely and sparingly, only for things that are worthwhile and cause least distress.

So far nobody has yet discovered a way of synthesizing a 'fuel' for adaptation processes, although there are strong indications that nutrients such as amino acids, minerals and vitamins can be employed to restore flagging resources. But then when Einstein developed his theory there was no fuel for atomic stations either. The fuel was discovered only when a real demand appeared for making practical use of the great physicist's discoveries. There are already ways known of lending support to the body's adaptation energy. We will look at some of them which Russian scientists have been researching in recent years in Chapter 27. There are certainly many ways of slowing down its expenditure—from eating a high-potency-low-calorie diet, learning to let go of unnecessary worries and tensions and strengthening the body through regular vigorous exercise, to using anti-oxidant nutrients and free amino acids which can even alter your physical and mental response to many stressors. For—and this is one of the most important truths to come out of Selye's half century of work with stress—it is not the stressors which are dangerous to life it is the way in which you respond to them. More about this later.

Selye believes stores of adaptation energy cannot be replaced:

. . . we have no objective proof that additional deposits of adaptation energy can be made beyond that inherited from our parents. Yet, everyone knows from personal experience that, after complete exhaustion by excessively stressful work during the day, a good night's sleep—and, after even more severe exhaustion a few weeks of restful holidays—can restore our resistance and adaptability very close to what it was before. I said 'very close to', because complete restoration is probably impossible, since every biological activity leaves some irreversible 'chemical scars', . . . I look upon the irreversible process of ageing as something very similar. The stage of exhaustion, after a temporary demand upon the body, is reversible, but the complete exhaustion of all the stores of deep adaptation energy is not; as these reserves are depleted senility, and finally, death ensue.

Work, Stress and Ageing

Selye recognized that a close relationship between work, stress and ageing exists. Ageing, he said, is *the result of the sum of all the stresses to which a person has been exposed during a lifetime*. It corresponds to the *stage of exhaustion* of the GAS which is an accelerated version of normal ageing. Again in Selye's words, 'Each period of stress, especially if it results from frustrating, unsuccessful struggles, leaves some irreversible chemical scars which accumulate to constitute the signs of tissue ageing.' The biological wear and tear on the body is the result of stress and the *accumulation of the irreparable part of this attrition is ageing*.

This wear and tear manifests itself in biochemical terms as the accumulation of undesirable by-products of metabolism such as cross-linked proteins, the kind of ageing pigments which create brown spots on the surface of the skin and which clog the brain, heavy mineral deposits around arteries, joints, and in the crystalline lens of the eye. It shows itself in declining elasticity of connective tissue as a result of oxy-stress and free-radical damage and in a loss of cells throughout the body. To prevent the wear and tear of ageing and to preserve precious adaptive energy therefore becomes the goal. It is a goal which in part is achieved by how well we adapt to the stressors to which we are subjected and in part by eliminating or rendering impotent as many unnecessary stressors as possible. Let's look at the first challenge first.

The Adaptive Response

Stress, Selye believed, is neither good nor bad. It is simply a fact of life. And, although stress has been linked not only to rapid ageing but also to many diseases such as ulcers, kidney disease, heart disease and arthritis, it is not stress which is the cause but our reaction to it, especially when the reaction is negative—that is, one of *dis*-stress. Selye always insisted that '. . . stress is the spice of life. Being associated with all types of activity we could avoid it only by never doing anything. Who would enjoy a life of "no runs, no hits, no errors"? it is still not completely understood that *stress depends not upon what happens to an individual but upon the way he reacts.'* Illnesses such as emotional disturbances, stomach upsets, allergic reactions, rheumatoid arthritis, sinus problems and sleeplessness as well as circulatory disorders, and heart and kidney diseases, can all be triggered by what Selye calls 'faulty adaptation reactions'. The so-called stress-related illnesses are in fact not the direct result of any particular stressor but rather of these faulty reactions. And the reason why a particular stressor—say the death of a close relative—can cause quite different illnesses to develop in different people is due to each individual's inherited systemic weaknesses.

The Choice: Active or Passive?

The stereotype stress reaction of the organism to whatever demand is made on it can occur either in an active or a passive way. When you respond actively to a stressor, *catatoxic* hormones such as adrenaline are secreted into your blood. They trigger immune reactions and raise blood pressure. They cause blood sugar and fatty acid concentrations to rise all of which mobilize your organism to fight or to flee. When on the other hand you respond passively, *syntoxic* hormones are secreted which are exactly the opposite in their biological effects. They tell your organism 'no struggle, no mortal enemy is facing you' and they reduce immune reactions.

The choice of responding to a specific stressor is made by one's consciousness. Selye says:

> Suppose you meet a helpless drunk who showers you with abuse but is quite unable to do you harm, nothing will happen if you ignore him, in other words if you choose the syntoxic reaction. But if you don't estimate the situation correctly, then your organism will make a catatoxic reaction and throw itself into a state of preparedness. Stress hormones will go to work at full capacity. The result may be a fatal brain haemorrhage or heart attack, even if the drunk didn't touch you. This would be nothing less than *biological suicide*. Death is caused by choosing the *wrong* reaction. On the other hand if the man who attacks you is a homicidal maniac with a gun in his hand and you respond passively you are likely to end up with a hole through your head. It is clear that, contrary to common opinion, *Nature does not always know what is best, both on a cellular and an interpersonal level, we do not always recognize what is and what is not worth fighting.*

One of Selye's favourite personal maxims used to be 'Fight for your highest attainable aim but never put up resistance in vain.'

When I first met Selye, at an international conference in Monte Carlo, I was astounded by his vitality and his enthusiasm. I knew that six years before he had contracted a type of cancer called reticulosarcoma which is fatal in 99.5 per cent of the cases. Yet he'd survived it. I was told also that only a few months before he had been given two artificial hips as well. Yet I have never seen a human being more alive. His eyes sparkled. When he spoke his voice was rich with emotional depth. His intellect was as sharp as any I have ever encountered and when he walked with his two canes he moved more rapidly than most people do on two good legs. In medical school Selye developed the habit of rising at 4am and working all day until 6 virtually without a break. It was a habit which continued throughout his life. He travelled the world lecturing, wrote, researched, and indefatigably pursued his interests. Yet he showed no signs of 'being under stress'. When I asked him why his reply was simple. 'I love it. It isn't how much stress you are subjected to but how you respond to it. This determines whether it causes you to break down or brings you joy.'

The Individual Stress Response

Each person differs in his reaction to stressors. And what is a stressor to one may not be to another; although certain stressors such as burning or physical trauma affect everyone. We also differ in how much stress we can take before reaching the exhaustion stage. This depends both on how we have been conditioned to respond to difficulties and on the amount of adaptation energy we have been born with. One person will have a great deal—he may be on the move continually and is able to withstand a great deal of stress—while another, when faced with the same stressors, quickly reaches the GAS exhaustion stage. Selye himself had high tolerance to stress and adaptation reserves which were quite phenomenal—in no small part due to his passion for life and work. He used to say, 'If you are a racehorse you have to be a racehorse but if you are a turtle and you try to behave like a racehorse you are asking for trouble.' The point is that once adaptive energy is used up as a result of the wear and tear of stress it appears to be very difficult to restore it. This is exactly what happens as the body ages. To make use of Selye's findings for ageless ageing, each of us needs to become aware of our own stress patterns and optimum stress levels, remembering that it is as bad for a racehorse to be made to function as a turtle as it is for a turtle to be pushed into behaving like a racehorse. We also need to examine carefully how our adaptation energy is being used and if it is being used up unnecessarily, either by the way we are responding to emotional situations or by exposure to powerful stressors in our environment or our lifestyle which result in high levels of oxy-stress and the damage it does to the body on a molecular level.

Free Radicals and the General Adaptation Syndrome

Recently, biochemists have begun to relate Selye's GAS

specifically to oxy-stress. Research is beginning to show that this is probably the mechanism behind the development of both ecological illnesses such as food and chemical sensitivities as well as overall degeneration. So on a molecular level as well it appears that the 'rain barrel' concept of stress applies: each organism can only cope with so much free-radical and peroxidation damage and cross-linking (from whatever cause or causes they may come) before its limit of adaptive energy is reached. At that point the rain barrel of stress spills over, causing biological destruction and rapid ageing.

In a very real sense on the use of adaptation energy depends the ecology of the human body in the same way that on the use of natural resources and the protection of life depends the ecology of the earth. And the decision about how it is going to be used rests with each of us. As the highly respected Russian age-researcher I. S. Khorol has said:

> . . . according to stress-conception 'adaptation energy' is the main source of creation. The only holder of this source is a man . . . no machine will be able to surpass man if he doesn't himself exhaust or destroy this source by careless treatment of his own nature. Einstein dreamed of creation of a unified theory of *inanimate* nature structure. Selye's investigations are aimed at the general laws of *animate* nature. But modern science has proved that there is no insuperable barrier between the two. We believe that some day these theories will be created. We believe that they will come together in a unified metatheory of the Universe, that will allow people to build our future quite reasonably and harmoniously.

SEVEN

Information Lost

Despite the power of free-radical theory and the new immunology, despite the fact that they are beginning to provide a scientific basis for the treatment and prevention of the many causes of disability and death, they still have a couple of major drawbacks. First they tend to be self-limiting. The understanding of the ageing process which they provide and the practical applications which they make possible are strictly contained within biochemical parameters. Yet, no matter how much some longevists would have us believe otherwise, all life processes can by no means be explained according to current biochemistry. Second, despite the new unified theory of ageing, many scientists working with a biochemical approach to ageing and to age-retardation still have a strong tendency to be mechanistic and reductionist. They take an analytical and fragmented point of view—what I call the 'robot approach' to man. It treats the body as an obedient machine which adheres to all the laws of chemistry and physics, and they often neglect to consider the living system as a whole which is far greater than the sum of its parts.

Ignoring this reality can limit practical applications for ageless ageing to lists of anti-oxidant nutrients—both natural and artificial—which you swallow to cut down free-radical and oxidative damage and special sunscreens which you smooth on your face to protect from ultraviolet rays, to the exclusion of wider issues. For when age researchers break living things down into their constituent parts, somewhere along the line life itself slips through their fingers—that which they are most concerned about preserving and enhancing. Too many approaches to ageing still don't show enough awareness of the fundamental role which lifestyle—how you eat, think, exercise, breathe and are oriented spiritually—plays in either slowing down or speeding up the processes of degeneration. And often because the *high-tech* approach to age-retardation has as yet found no explanation for many clinically tried and tested tools for increasing vitality it tends to ignore them altogether. These include such practices as periodic fasting, the use of adaptogens—substances which increase the body's ability as a whole to withstand stress and ward off exhaustion—and the vitality-enhancing properties of a low-calorie-high-potency diet based largely on fresh foods.

To get full benefit from what is now known about life processes and age-retardation we must make good use of the biochemical model of ageing but we also need to go beyond it. How? First by asking a few provocative (and largely unanswerable) questions such as 'What is the nature of life energy anyway?' And, 'How can we preserve it?' Second we need to take a look at theoretical models now at the leading edge of science which can be applied to the ageing process. They include models built on information theory as applied to biology and on the new physics. These new scientific paradigms can be useful, not only in gaining a broader understanding of the ageing process, but also in devising a more comprehensive and effective approach to ageless ageing.

Laws to Be Broken

The biochemical view of ageing which we have been looking at is based on the assumption that life can be explained through an understanding of the laws of chemistry and physics. It looks at the way in which inorganic chemicals are used in a biological system to perpetuate the living state. Indeed this is the whole point and purpose of biochemistry and molecular biology—the major scientific models involved in most theories of ageing. The only problem is that the living body breaks all the rules.

In physics, the laws of thermodynamics focus on energy changes. These laws are really an attempt to understand events in the universe by studying the kind of energy changes which accompany them. The second law of thermodynamics is particularly important for our purposes. It is called the law of *entropy* and states very simply that, left to their own devices, things become disordered: iron rusts, buildings crumble, dead flowers decay and so forth. This is stated scientifically by saying that everything tends toward *maximum entropy*—a state of maximum disorder in which all useful energy is decreased. But what is so remarkable about living organisms (and what has been a great puzzle to some of the world's finest scientific minds) is the fact that, despite the second law of thermodynamics, living organisms are able to remain highly ordered. Our bodies are maintained in a state of fantastic improbability despite the innumerable destructive processes continually going on in and around us. Indeed there is every indication that in many ways we are continually involved in creating even more order. This we do both individually in the repair functions of our cells and enzymic systems and from an evolutionary point of view since living creatures differentiate into ever more complex and highly structured organisms.

Order to the Highest Degree

In a way which no one has ever been able to explain fully, unlike things in the inorganic world, living organisms are superbly ordered to maintain their systems. This is something which makes virtually no sense within the paradigms of physics and chemistry. Where by rights there should be little difference in the chemical and physical processes taking place in a living body and those of a corpse—since both follow the same scientific laws—in reality there is every difference in the world. In life, events are able to maintain the system in quite exceptional harmony (in scientific terms a high degree of negative entropy) despite the fact that events leading to maximum entropy in the universe as a whole are running wild to destroy it. In the words of Nobel laureate Albert Szent-Györgyi who has spent most of his life trying to penetrate this mystery of life energy:

> Life is a paradox . . . the most basic rule of inanimate nature is that it tends toward equilibrium which is at the maximum of entropy and the minimum of free energy. The main characteristic of life is that it tends to decrease its entropy. It

also tends to increase its free energy. Maximum entropy means complete randomness, disorder. Life is made possible by order, structure, a pattern which is the opposite of entropy. This pattern is our chief possession, it was developed over billions of years. The main aim of our existence is its conservation and transmission. Life is a revolt against the statistical rules of physics. Death means that the revolt subsided and statistical laws resumed their sway.

Age = Maximum Entropy

Since ageing appears to be the process which transports our body from a highly ordered internal state towards maximum entropy—ie death—to protect our body from ageing we need quite simply (or perhaps not so simply) to give it all the help we can to maintain that order. This can't be done only by manipulating chemicals in the system for that won't go far enough. To be effective and complete, any anti-ageing programme needs also to be holistic. It needs to take into account as many of the factors acting on an organism for good and ill as possible and to treat the living organism not as a machine but as a highly evolved and elaborate self-maintaining organic unity.

One of the first scientists to do this was physicist and Nobel laureate Erwin Schrödinger. He took a close look at the scientific contradictions implicit in the living state and concluded that so long as the human body is alive it avoids decaying into an inert state of equilibrium, death, through metabolism—by eating, drinking and assimilating information from the environment. As far back as 1944 Schrödinger wrote:

Every process, event, happening—call it what you will; in a word, everything that is going on in Nature means an increase of the entropy of the part of the world where it is going on. Thus a living organism continually increases its entropy—or as you may say, produces positive entropy—and thus tends to approach the dangerous state of maximum entropy, which is death. It can only keep aloof from it, ie alive, by continually drawing from its environment negative entropy . . . What an organism feeds upon is negative entropy . . . which is in itself a measure of order. Thus the device by which an organism maintains itself stationary at a fairly high level of orderliness really consists in continually sucking orderliness from its environment.

The body is often described as an *open living system*. As such we are constantly processing *information* which comes to us not only through the kinds and combinations of foods we eat and the way we prepare and process them but also from the air we breathe, the ideas on which we allow our minds to play, the electromagnetic environment in which we live and so forth. In other words, we need a constant supply of the right quantity as well as the right kind of information from the outside world to keep our bodies functioning optimally. Schrödinger believed, as a long tradition of natural medicine both in Europe and the Orient has taught, that to maintain a high degree of vitality and to protect the body from degeneration, we need to 'suck order' from our environment.

Although a number of scientists have noted the importance of Schrödinger's concept of living organisms feeding on negative entropy and it is mentioned in standard textbooks on biophysics and biochemistry such as Bray and White's *Kinetics and Thermodynamics in Biochemistry* and *Metabolic Pathways* by Pardee and Ingraham, it is still largely ignored by most nutritionists, biochemists and other researchers concerned with slowing down the rate at which we age. A few eminent scientists such as Ludwig von Bertalanffy, author of *Robots, Men and Minds*, British scientist and philosopher Michael Polanyi, and the Soviet biochemist I. I. Brekhman at the Far East Scientific Centre of the Academy of Sciences of the USSR, Vladivostok, have, however, taken it very seriously indeed.

Information Loss and Degeneration

Brekhman refers to information in relation to his main interests, food and the adaptogens—natural medicines with a long history of use which scientific research has shown have non-specific abilities to strengthen an organism's vitality and even to prolong life. Until recently man's interaction with nature has been seen only in terms of the constant change of *materials* and *energy*—the one a measurement of chemistry and the other a measurement of physics. Now, thanks in part to the development of cybernetic concepts, some farsighted scientists such as von Bertalanffy and Brekhman are beginning to add *information* to these categories. 'But this is not', as Brekhman points out, 'the kind of information about the external world which is received by the sensory organs and the nervous system and termed relative, free, or semantic information. It is information reflecting the degree of diversity and complexity of internal structure inherent in physical bodies. It is called absolute, connected or more frequently, structural information. From this we can see that there is a constant exchange of substance, energy and information between man and the natural environment.' To retard the process of ageing and degeneration, then, both the quantity and quality of this information must be as close to the ideal needs of our organism as possible.

Such paradigms have a number of important implications when it comes to the nutritional control of ageing. They make it clear that slowing down the ageing process demands more than simply supplying megadoses of those vitamins, minerals and other natural substances which lend support to your body's anti-oxidant and immune systems. They imply that it is necessary to approach the whole question of food not only from the point of view of energy (calories) and materials (specific proteins, vitamins, minerals, fatty acids, etc) alone. (If that were the case we would have nothing to worry about except the number of calories, how much carbohydrate, fat, etc we were consuming. But such an approach can never support a high level of well-being.) And they are stimulating some researchers to explore how nutrition for age-retardation is also dependent on the complexity of the way all of this energy and material is woven together by nature. For, as the eminent American biochemist Roger Williams has said, the body also extracts 'trophic factors' from the molecular balances of the entire food. Now, not only do specific nutrients which can be measured chemically—vitamins, minerals, protein, etc—appear important for age-retardation, so does the complexity of the way they and other (as yet unidentified) factors are combined in a particular food. This contributes to the 'quality' of energy in terms of the information which the food carries. Brekhman and others have shown that the heating and processing of foods which we carry out can decrease the quality of structural information which they bring to an organism and thus their health-supporting and age-retarding properties. Fresh foods appear to contain a higher degree of the structural information which the body can beneficially use than do cooked or processed foods. So do a number of natural medicines such as ginseng and eleutherococcus which can be enormously helpful in any serious programme for ageless ageing (see Chapter 27).

In experiments Brekhman has shown that foods high in structural information enable animals to carry out physical tasks for significantly longer periods than processed foods low in structural information even when the foods compared are equal in calories and therefore, by orthodox biochemical standards, supplying an organism with the same amount of energy. Brekhman and other Soviet scientists are particularly interested in those natural pharmacological substances which appear to supply a high degree of structural information to an organism and therefore to help support a high level of health and energy. They are now attempting to quantify the action of a plant substance or food on the body in terms of what he has called significant units of action (SUA) which is a way of measuring how long an animal can continue to carry out a piece of work when fed a particular food. One of the implications of his work in human terms is that how well your nutritional habits support your system for ageless ageing depends not only on how many of the anti-oxidant nutrients and immune-enhancing nutrients you take in but also on the ability which nature has to provide the right kind of structural information for high-level wellness in foods which are grown on healthy soils and have been little processed. This can never be gained artificially by measuring chemicals and swallowing pills alone.

Information Sources for Order

Of course food is not by any means the only kind of information which we take in and which is necessary to support the needs of the body for ageless ageing. We also need stimulation to the nervous system from changing environmental conditions, information taken in through the water we drink and the air we breathe, and even from the effects of body movement. All of these things act as stimuli to an organism. In terms of ageing their effects can be either good or bad. We need to make use of everything possible to ensure they are good. This is something which advocates of *natural-law* anti-ageing have been doing for generations in two main ways. First by applying stimuli to enhance bodily responses and increase vitality. It is on this principle that most of the natural methods of healing from Kneipp water therapy to aerobic exercise are based. Second by examining the quality of information which is coming to a person in terms of the environment in which he lives. If it is the right kind of information, if the air you breathe is rich in the elements such as negative ion particles known to produce a sense of harmonious well-being in most people, then it is something which belongs in any holistic programme for ageless ageing. If it is not—if, instead, it is full of industrial pollutants, and depleted in negative ions—then the opposite is true and you need to take action either to change it or to protect yourself from the negative effects of the kind of information your body is being forced to process. As a medium for information-transfer to living systems, nothing at the moment is more interesting as a possibility (nor less explored by most age-researchers) than electromagnetism.

EIGHT

The Body Electric

Life, we have been taught, is simply a collection of biochemical processes. The human body is nothing more than a machine which runs on fuel from the foods you eat and the air you breathe. It is as simple as that. But is it? New developments in information theory and high-level physics as applied to biology are leading many scientists to question this assumption. Some quite fascinating research into the electric and electromagnetic properties of living tissue are beginning to create new paradigms for life processes—paradigms which, like the unified theory of ageing now developing from Selye's work, are so revolutionary they threaten to shake classic biochemistry at its foundations. The new scientific models indicate that life and health are not just a matter of chemistry. The chemical changes in a living system which have been so carefully charted, from the way in which your body burns glucose to make energy to how it repairs damaged tissue when you are cut or burnt, now appear to be not *primary* but *secondary* events—events which may be controlled by an electronic dimension of reality that until now science has almost completely ignored.

Where classical chemistry and high-technology medicine have tended to be mechanistic in their approach to health and healing and to ignore the enigmas of life, the new electronic view of reality (a view which is now well supported by burgeoning experimental evidence) embraces them. Not only will it have profound implications for healing, growth, ageing, and consciousness in the next twenty years; it also brings in its wake a new vision of the nature of life itself and a new awareness of the potential dangers of twentieth-century electromagnetic technology to health and life.

The Body as Chemistry

Your body is a living organism which needs a vast amount of energy to carry out the chemical and physical work necessary to keep you alive. It gets this energy by oxidizing biological substances—burning food as fuel. This burning occurs not in some haphazard way as it would in a furnace. Instead it is ordered with superb precision: enzymes act as catalysts and oxidations take place in a superbly modulated series of small steps which are able to liberate the maximum amount of energy present for effective use while causing the minimum amount of disturbance to the biological order of cells and tissues. In scientific terms oxidation is defined as the loss of electrons from the outer orbits of an atom or molecule. This electron loss can either occur singly—that is one electron at a time—or in pairs, and paired electron loss can either take place in one step where both electrons are transferred at the same time or two steps—where one electron is transferred at a time and a free-radical species (see page 27) is momentarily formed as a transient intermediate.

One of the major problems for science has always been to unravel the precise mechanisms by which living tissues control this release of energy and orchestrate the myriad complex adjustments necessary to keep an organism functioning with only very small changes in temperature and minimal disruption to the life processes which are going on in an organism at the time. It is really quite a feat when you consider that in all the cells of your body there is a continuous process of repair and maintenance in which the chemical components are disassembled and resynthesized day in day out throughout your whole life. And thanks to the remarkable organization implicit in the living state, the entire architecture of your body's cells can be replaced without disturbing the normal activity, an example of superb order—negative entropy carried to the nth degree. How? These are questions for which the biochemist has no answer. They can describe the living machinery itself in terms of proteins, nucleic acids and nucleoproteins. And they can describe at length how electrons and nuclei form atoms, atoms molecules, amino acids peptides, peptides proteins and so on, but ask them to describe the nature of life's organization—

the basic principle by which two things are put together to produce something new, a thing quite different from the qualities of its constituent parts—and they are at a loss for words. They can chart the enzyme functions and alterations which control the energetic transformations on a cellular level but there still remains a very important, and until now almost completely unanswerable, question: what controls the controllers? This too is a question biochemists have been unable to answer.

Life processes which cannot be explained within a particular scientific discipline have a long history either of being ignored or misinterpreted. Yet these unanswered questions are central to an understanding of the ageing process. For when control processes go awry, disorder invades the organism and degeneration ensues. They are also biology's most intriguing problems. And therefore problems which make many biochemists very uncomfortable indeed simply because they are unanswerable in biochemical terms. Where can one find the answers? Or at the very least where should we be looking?

Electricity, Semi-conduction and Living Cells

One eminent scientist, Albert Szent-Györgyi, who won a Nobel prize for his work on oxidation and for isolating vitamin C, asked himself this question more than fifty years ago. He has spent almost every working moment of his life since in an attempt to answer it. He is often quoted as having posed the question at a dinner party: 'What is the difference between a living rat and a dead one?' By rights, according to the laws of classical chemistry and physics there should be no fundamental difference. Szent-Györgyi's own reply is simple yet revolutionary—'Some kind of electricity.'

Szent-Györgyi observed more than a quarter of a century ago that the molecular structure of many parts of a living cell, rather like crystals, might be able to support semi-conduction of electricity. It is a notion which, outside Russia where it has been vigorously researched ever since, has been largely ignored by orthodox scientists.

Semi-conduction takes place only in materials which have a highly ordered molecular structure such as in crystals where atoms are arranged in neat geometrical lattices enabling electrons to move with ease from the orbit of one atom or molecule to another. Szent-Györgyi postulated that molecules of protein in cells and tissues can boast this kind of molecular order, each offering a temporary 'hole' for mobile electrons, and that they may be linked together in long chains in the body in order that electrons can flow in a semi-conducting current over great distances without any loss of energy taking place. This kind of protein semi-conduction would enable energy to be passed along as *information* rather than being absorbed and stored in foods as chemical bonds—which is what takes place in the process of photosynthesis by which plants translate the sun's energy into the foods which we then eat and get energy from. In effect Szent-Györgyi is looking at a living organism not from a biochemical point of view but from an electrical one (which is the point of view most age-researchers have exclusively taken).

In the past thirty years, thanks to the miracles of electron microscopes, researchers looking at living cells and tissues have discovered that structures of crystal-like organization and complexity do indeed exist in living organisms. Meanwhile the exponential leap in knowledge which has taken place within the realm of solid-state physics has brought about advances in electronics, such as the development of transistors used in computers (something that was believed before to be totally impossible), which make the notion of electronic processes based on solid-state properties of highly organized structures in living organisms very feasible indeed.

The Élan Vital

Of course Szent-Györgyi was not the first one to consider that living things might have electrical or electromagnetic properties. Mystics and healers have long insisted that the transmission of thought, and laying-on-of-hands healing, are possible thanks to some kind of ill-defined electronic or electromagnetic phenomenon. And in the eighteenth and nineteenth centuries electricity looked to many scientists like the miracle find which would revolutionize philosophy and healing.

Luigi Galvani, the famous Italian anatomy professor after

whom the word 'galvanism' was coined, discovered as far back as 1794 that there is a 'current of injury'—an electrical charge generated at the site of damage in living organisms which is proportional to the severity of the wound. He tried to link electricity with the mysterious *élan vital* as the healing force— that enigmatic vital impulse of life which Bergson believed was the creative principle immanent in all organisms and responsible for evolution. Thirty years later in Pisa another Italian scientist, Carlo Matteucci, proved conclusively that this current of injury was real. He was able to measure it using the newly invented 'galvanometer'. But their findings and the findings of others experimenting with the relationship between electricity and living processes became enmeshed in a passionate philosophical debate between *mechanists* and *vitalists* and were largely ignored.

The Mechanists vs. the Vitalists

It was a debate the outcome of which formed the basis of classical chemistry and physics as well as the drug-based approach to medicine which has become the hallmark of treatment in the twentieth century. It went something like this. The vitalists (many of whose notions stemmed from Plato's idea of supernatural 'forms') believed that what made all living things different from inanimate objects was the presence of a spirit which they named the 'anima' or 'élan vital'. They divided reality into two parts: this vital force which they insisted was directional and purposeful, and the mechanical physical world. This abstract universal principle was for the vitalists more real than sensory phenomena. They believed that the passive, inert and unmoving universe was driven to change only through the actions of this élan vital (which Galvani himself believed to be electricity). The mechanists (who sided more with Aristotle's rationalism) didn't agree. They viewed matter as passively driven by a mechanical force in a totally determined manner. They denied the existence of any élan vital, treating it as so much spiritual hokum, and insisted instead that truth was objective—something which resides in the world outside us and which can be analysed and understood empirically simply by carrying out scientific experiments that alter the world with mechanical forces and measure the results. Truth, they said, is a phenomenon which can only be understood when fully analysed in terms of mechanical laws based on Newtonian physics—the fundamental concepts of mass, energy, space and time. That, claimed the mechanists, is the purpose of science.

Well supported by the philosophical tenets of Descartes from the century before, by 1850 the mechanists had largely won the battle. Galvani's notion of electricity as an élan vital was banished to the scrap heap of curious but untenable scientific curiosities and the foundations of our modern biology, firmly based on chemical principles alone, were well set. They have ruled supreme ever since. Anyone who has dared to suggest that electromagnetic principles underlie life processes such as growth, healing, metabolism and regeneration—a notion which suggests a subtle yet pervasive connection between mind and matter—has tended either to be ignored or ostracized from the scientific community.

Electronic Controls of Life?

Nevertheless, even in the twentieth century—that last bastion of mechanistic thinking—there have been a number of researchers who have tried. In the 1920s a Russian-born engineer living in Paris, named Georges Lakhovsky, suggested that the basis of life may lie in 'immaterial vibrations'. He believed that the cells of plants and animals were oscillating circuits—electromagnetic radiators—able, as a wireless set is, to absorb and to emit waves. In 1925 he reported a series of remarkable experiments which supported his notion that health is a matter of equilibrium in cellular oscillation. About the same time an American professor at Texas State University showed in experiments carried out over a period of ten years that plant cells produce electrical emanations. E. J. Lund developed a way of measuring minute electrical potentials in plants and demonstrated that they emit electrical waves and currents. These emanations not only change as does the health of the plant, they appear to direct and regulate plant growth and health. For instance, he found that in the growth of a plant bud (which chemists said was merely directed by plant hormones or auxins), electromagnetic radiations from the plant altered *before* any changes in hormone levels could be detected. In 1936 an American scientist named George Crile, a surgeon who founded the Cleveland Clinic in Ohio, wrote a fascinating book called *The Phenomenon of Life*, in which he suggested that, since electrical changes taking place in the cells seem to occur *prior* to chemical and physical ones, by measuring them in a living organism it should be possible for radiodiagnosticians to diagnose the presence of illness long before symptoms appear.

Life Fields

From the theories of Galvani, Crile and Lakhovsky and others about electronic and electromagnetic properties of living things, in the late 'sixties two Yale professors, a philosopher named F. S. C. Northrop and a doctor specializing in anatomy, Harold Saxton Burr, suggested that, since living things have electronic properties, they must also be surrounded by electromagnetic fields. And these fields might be the source of organization for life systems. To explore their theories Burr began measuring what he called life fields or L-fields around seeds. He discovered, as he expected, that significant changes in voltage patterns occur even when a single gene in the parent stock is altered. He also found that by measuring the intensity of an L-field of a seed he could predict how healthy the plant grown from it would be and that these fields could easily be diminished by subjecting the seed or plant to chemicals or heat. But with the dominant scientific view that chemical processes were controllers of life—a view which blurs the distinction between living and non-living things greatly—most of Northrop and Burr's research has also been ignored. Contemporary scientific knowledge of how living things are put together and how electricity is generated and transmitted contained no mechanism that would allow electrical currents to flow in any organized manner through living things.

Currents of Healing

When Szent-Györgyi's now classic book, *Introduction to a Submolecular Biology*, came along with his idea of proteins as semi-conductors and his notion of 'solid-state mechanisms' (see page 80) as a way of accounting for specific electronic properties found in living systems, among the farsighted scientists whom it inspired was an outstanding American orthopaedic surgeon named Robert O. Becker. In the past twenty-five years Becker has done more than any other living scientist to explore it and pave the way for its acceptance. Like other scientists working in the field, Becker (who in 1978 was nominated for a Nobel prize) asked himself a couple of important questions. First, might electronic conduction mechanisms form the basis of control systems in living organisms? In other words could they be the means by which life processes such as growth and the regeneration of healing take place? And second, if such systems do exist can they be influenced in a clinically useful way by applying appropriate electrical or electromagnetic energy from outside the body?

Electrical Bone Healing

Becker's personal interest and his field of expertise lay in using minute electrical currents to heal damaged tissue—particularly broken bones—in the body. By implanting tiny wires into broken bones and sending minuscule currents through them he has not only been able to speed healing but to restore normal functioning to patients whose broken bones simply would not join despite their having been treated with conventional methods such as bone grafts—patients who therefore faced the prospect of losing a limb. Becker has become famous worldwide for his high success rate in treating such cases. Indeed, had his work been confined only to the clinical application of electricity for healing, many of his colleagues believe, the Nobel prize for medicine would have been his. It wasn't.

A Second Nervous System

Guided by Szent-Györgyi's vision, Becker postulated a primitive analogue-coded electronic information system in the body which was related to the body's nervous system but which was not necessarily located in the nerves themselves. He reasoned that this system, as Szent-Györgyi had suggested, might use semi-conducting direct currents and that, either by itself or linked to nerve impulses, it might be responsible for regulating growth, healing and other biochemical processes. He repeated some of Burr's experiments on salamanders measuring voltages at nose, tip of tail and other points along the body. But to his amazement he did not find, as Burr had, that there was a *simple* relationship of positive voltage at the tail and negative at the head. Instead he discovered the existence of an elaborate field which followed the order of the nervous system and gave him quite a complex series of readings. He then went on to study electrical potentials in other vertebrates and discovered that such a system does appear to exist—an organized crystal-like structure with self-organizing and self-repairing properties based on semi-conductivity. In Becker's words, 'We found that the potentials are organized into an electrical field, represented by lines of force, which roughly parallels the pattern of the nervous system . . . Electrical potentials in a conducting medium such as the nerve cell implies there is also a direct current (DC) flow.'

Put simply, what Becker and his colleagues had uncovered was a 'second nervous system', a primitive data or information system, previously unknown to science—in the form of an organized pattern of electrical potentials which roughly parallels the gross anatomical arrangement of the central nervous system and which alters in a predictable fashion when an organism is damaged or repairing itself.

The healing process appears to be a kind of closed-loop negative-feedback cybernetic system in which DC currents linked to the body's nervous system via certain cells direct the healing process. When injury occurs to the body it causes cell damage. This changes local electrical charge which stimulates DC system input which on organization creates DC system output which in turn stimulates cell growth and repair. As healing proceeds, cellular activity diminishes until finally healing ceases and local electrical patterns return to normal. This control system also appears to regulate growth and healing. It can be used to control pain (which is probably why acupuncture is a useful method of pain relief and anaesthesia). It may even explain how hypnosis, psychic phenomena and the directed migration of birds work. It is also rapidly eroding the widespread notion that all life processes must have a chemical basis, and it is introducing into biology notions of cybernetics—the science of communication processes and automatic control processes—and of solid-state physics which deals with electronic processes that occur in organized crystalline-like solids, just as Szent-Györgyi postulated they might in living tissue.

Electrical Mind/Body Links

Becker's findings have wide implications for health and healing. In the area of age research alone a number of Soviet scientists have reported being able to lengthen animal lifespans and to slow down physical degeneration by placing the animals within electrical fields of specific intensity. As yet, no one has begun to apply their work to human age-retardation. But it is sure to come. Meanwhile the discoveries of Becker and a few other scientists working in the same area have led to an increased interest in the potentials of electrical currents for healing, explained how electro-acupuncture gets many of its good results and opened up an awareness of the body as an open system of negative entropy which is not only gaining its organization from chemicals it takes in in foods but appears also to be nourished by electronic or electromagnetic 'information'—particular kinds of which appear to be necessary for high-level health and slowing down physical degeneration.

What is in many ways even more fascinating is the way that Becker and his colleagues have shown that this primitive electronic communications system which he has uncovered appears to be a central means of regulating states of consciousness as well. Sleep, anaesthesia and hypnosis all show common changes in electrical potentials in the brain. And you can bring about similar alterations of consciousness by applying appropriate electrical currents across the brain. This is the basis of electro-anaesthesia. Even more exciting, Becker has discovered that under hypnosis and in certain altered states of consciousness we have the ability to change DC potentials in the system ourselves. And since the same electrical system which regulates pain and healing can be brought under the control of the mind it could be a powerful tool both for healing and age-retardation as well as for maintaining the body at high levels of health. This may also explain the phenomenon of 'miraculous cures' of illness by 'divine intervention' and much of psychic phenomena. But these new discoveries in electrobiology also have their dark side. And an awareness of these electromagnetic phenomena may be particularly important in protecting yourself from age degeneration.

The Earth's Electromagnetism

Something that is of real concern to Becker is the relationship between the body's solid-state data-transmission system and the kind of ever-changing fluctuations brought about not by the earth's electromagnetic field—a phenomenon to which we have been subjected throughout human evolution—but by the unnatural electromagnetic environment in which we in the industrialized world now live. Scientists looking at the circadian rhythms of the body and biological cycles of hormone secretions in living things have found that many are the result of rhythmic fluctuations in the earth's electromagnetic field. This field guides the migration of many animals. Alterations to its normal ebb and flow occur naturally as a result of storms on the sun that trigger magnetic storms on the earth. Indeed these things have been related to the occurrence of mental disturbances in many people. But, as Becker says, 'These kinds of natural changes in our electromagnetic environment are small compared with the kind of intense and chaotic electromagnetic phenomena we have created artificially from our twentieth-century lifestyle based on electric power and all that accompanies it. We are now

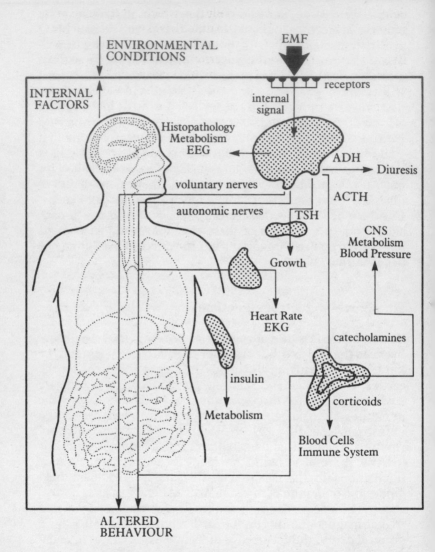

ENVIRONMENTAL
CONDITIONS

EMF

INTERNAL
FACTORS

receptors

internal
signal

Histopathology
Metabolism
EEG

ADH

Diuresis

voluntary nerves

ACTH

autonomic nerves

TSH

CNS
Metabolism
Blood Pressure

Growth

Heart Rate
EKG

catecholamines

insulin

corticoids

Metabolism

Blood Cells
Immune System

ALTERED
BEHAVIOUR

The effects of electromagnetic radiation on the body and brain as yet go
largely unrecognized by orthodox science except in Soviet Russia
where, as a health-protection measure, there are stringent controls on
electromagnetic pollution.

being subjected to electronic pollution which, unless it is taken seriously and controlled could do untold damage to human life.'

So far Soviet scientists are the only ones taking it seriously. In Russia there are legal limits governing environmental exposure to electrical power such as that which is emitted by high-voltage cables. Here and in the United States the notion that the electrical atmosphere in which we live affects life and health is not even given lip-service (except in defence departments where it has been investigated as a means of destructive warfare).

Becker in no way wants to eliminate electricity from modern life. But he insists that its environmental effects demand closer study. There have been far too many reports from farmers about inexplicable illness amongst animals and also from people who appear to be suffering the effects of living under high-tension electric pylons. There are even indications that sleeping under an electric blanket may contribute to the development of birth defects in unborn children.

Here, in Becker's own words are a few guidelines which we need to follow to protect ourselves from illness and degeneration:

- Don't use electric blankets on your bed.
- Don't use microwave ovens. The regulations governing their safety are not stringent enough to protect from leakage.
- Large-screen colour TVs produce strong fields not just in front but at the sides and behind. The bigger the set the stronger the field. These fields can go through walls into adjacent rooms. Always put the set against an *external* wall.
- Video display units on computers and word processors can cause reproductive disorders in women. As a result the state of Ontario in Canada has now adopted regulations for their use which include frequent breaks. No pregnant woman should ever work on one.

New Views of Healing

An awareness of Becker's findings is not sending us back to looking at reality through the eyes of nineteenth-century vitalism which is as dualistic a view as the mechanism with which science has been living for the past hundred or more years. But, the awareness is leading age-researchers and doctors to reject the view of living organisms as either mechanical systems animated by some mysterious élan vital or as machines which follow the biochemical laws based on Newtonian science. It is forcing us to revise our long-standing notions of cause and effect in health and disease in favour of an awareness of the body as a harmonious whole whose parts can only be understood through their interactions. Eventually, I believe, it is also going to force even eccentric longevists, committed to the notion that so long as you get your biochemistry right by swallowing massive doses of anti-oxidant nutrients you can dissipate your energies as much as you like and still expect to live for ever, to change their tune. The long-standing methods of life-enhancement and rejuvenation which have come out of the European tradition of natural healing now more than ever have an important role to play in making ageless ageing a living reality. Coupled with new discoveries in free-radical biochemistry, stress concepts and immunity, they should create a bastion against age-related degeneration which nothing else can even come near.

PART II

Elixirs of Life

NINE

The Two Faces of Ageing

Johan Bjorksten, who developed the cross-linking theory of ageing, is probably the most famous age-researcher in the West. What is remarkable about Bjorksten's work—apart from his profound understanding of the ageing process on a cellular level and his ability to construct lucid mathematical proofs of both his own and other scientists' various theories—is the fact that Bjorksten has an integrated understanding of the ageing process—on a molecular level as well as in the body as a whole. It is an understanding which may well be unequalled by anyone else in the world and an understanding which takes into account the important role that mind and spirit play as well. Bjorksten is also a pragmatist. Instead of getting lost in a mass of bio-chemical data as some researchers are prone to do, Bjorksten enters his laboratory, as he has done for the last half-century, with one major intention: to find out what works and then to put it into practice. Bjorksten points out that there are really two faces to ageing and each face needs to be approached in a slightly different way.

The Two Faces of Ageing

Bjorksten believes that our *maximum* lifespan is 157 years. He bases this figure on what he has found to be the highest reliably documented age for a man. This then, he says, is the first target for anyone interested in ageless ageing—to reach that age in tolerably good health. If we are not reaching this age it is because we are ageing *prematurely*. Premature ageing is the first face of ageing. Ways and means for counteracting it are available right now to anyone who wants to take the trouble to use them.

The next target is to deal with the second face of ageing: to develop and make use of techniques which will extend lifespan far beyond what now appears to be the human maximum limit—to, say, 200 years or even more. The strategies for wrestling with each face of ageing are quite different. Dealing with ageing's second face means developing ways of removing insoluble accumulations which have come as a result of chemical reactions in the body—for instance dissolving cross-linked proteins. It also means enhancing the speed of repair mechanisms for DNA as well, so that single-strand damage can be restored before mutated cells reproduce. The development of enzymes which are safe to use in the living body and which are capable of removing the broad spectrum of age-related accumulations has been a major goal for Bjorksten—a goal which has been often frustrated by a scarcity of funds for research. He has experimented with chelating agents and low-molecular-weight enzymes made by certain strains of bacteria such as *Bacillus cerus*—a bacterium present in soil. He has even used free hydroxyl radicals as a means of breaking up very dense aggregates which enzymes cannot penetrate. As yet it is too early for us to be able to safely make use of most of these techniques. This second face of ageing still hides too many of its secrets beneath its surface. But with a little effort we can go a long way towards smoothing out the wrinkles from ageing's first face right now.

Magnificent Redundancy

As Bjorksten points out, if an engineer wants to design a factory for trouble-free operation he builds into the system duplicates of all the essential equipment so that a spare will be at hand the moment anything malfunctions. This is known as *redundancy*. As human beings we have been designed the same way—two hands and feet and eyes and kidneys. Our brain is a superb example of redundancy with its 12 billion cells and innumerable pathways which enable us to recall a memory. Brain surgeons are continually amazed by the brain's powers of substitution when part of it has been damaged. Our metabolism too is built upon the principle of redundancy. Every biochemical process necessary for life has several possible paths all of which work, but often in very different ways. For instance there are at least five pathways for breaking down carbohydrates for energy and your body can make lecithin in at least three ways.

In order to protect your body from premature ageing and to promote long life, the reactions involved in its metabolic pathways need to be *efficient* and *clean*—they need to take place precisely, with as few by-products and as few hold-ups along the way as possible. When biochemical processes become sluggish, then toxic intermediate products which are formed in excess can build up to a point where they cause damage. Formaldehyde is a perfect example of such an intermediate. It is formed in at least eight normal metabolic reactions. There are two means of avoiding this dangerous build-up. The first comes under the auspices of *natural-law* anti-ageing. It consists quite simply of not eating more than your body's chemical processing plant can deal with cleanly and quickly and not taking into your body foods or chemicals which, in effect, can throw monkey-wrenches into the system. (More about what this means in specific terms in the next few chapters.) This in itself will take you a long way towards experiencing a youthful old age and looking good as the years go by. But, insists Bjorksten, '. . . it is not enough. The bottlenecks in the metabolic pathways must be widened to the largest extent possible to prevent hold-ups and secure smooth passage, even for occasional excess loads and to maximize safety margins and redundancy.' That is the task of *high-tech* anti-ageing. By bottlenecks, Bjorksten is referring to the enzymes which make biochemical conversions possible.

Precious Catalysts

Enzymes are the essential triggers for the metabolic machinery of every living thing—from daffodil to buffalo. They are complex organic substances which set off chemical transformations of materials—catalysts which bring about chemical changes but are not themselves changed in the process. Without the thousands of enzymes in each living thing there would be no life at all. Enzymes are extraordinarily powerful. For instance, at body temperature, a small amount of pepsin (one of the gastric enzymes we use to digest protein) will break down the white of an egg into small-chain peptides within just a few minutes. The same process can be accomplished in a laboratory only by boiling the egg white for twenty-four hours in a strong acid or alkali solution. The human body has a complex collection of enzymes, each of which has a specific task to perform; and in a healthy body these enzymes are constantly being renewed. In the liver alone there are some 50,000 different enzymes at work, on which your body's life and functions depend. They break down fats, proteins and carbohydrates into their constituent parts, which can then be assimilated into the bloodstream and carried throughout to the cells. So essential is the existence of the thousands of enzymes in our body that when there is a slowing down in the production of them in the digestive system or poor replication of them in the cells, health suffers and the body ages rapidly.

James Batcheller Sumner, who shared a Nobel prize in 1946 for crystallizing the first enzyme, insisted that the 'fortyish' look with its sagging skin, fat around the middle and lack of vitality was attributable to an enzyme shortage that occurs when the body is not efficiently replacing enzymes in its cells. Many highly respected age-researchers now agree with him. They say that an organism grows old when enough metabolic errors accumulate to injure the synthesis of certain enzymes. For instance, the enzymes directly involved in digestion such as those of the pancreas seem to play a vital role in preventing age-degeneration and disease. A sufficient supply of pancreatic enzymes appears to be a crucial factor in maintaining immunity to many degenerative diseases including cancer.

The Fallacy of the Recommended Dose

Enzymes depend for their actions on vitamins and minerals which are essential as activators for them. In order for enzymes to be able to carry out reactions with the precision and cleanliness necessary to protect against premature ageing, the supply of vitamins and minerals in your body must be *optimal*. It is not enough to simply see that you get the minimum required to avoid overt symptoms of vitamin deficiency.

All vitamins and minerals have multiple actions in the body. This is one of the major reasons they differ dramatically from drugs which are aimed at dealing with specific symptoms. For instance, nicotinic acid—vitamin B_3—is a component of at least fifty-four enzymes, and pyridoxine—vitamin B_6—of almost as many, including those most important for protein metabolism and for making brain chemicals. Nobel laureate Albert Szent-Györgyi, who was honoured for his isolation of Vitamin C, says this about the problem of the mechanism of action of vitamins in the body:

> I could illuminate this relation by comparing vitamins with lubricants, while comparing your own body with your car. *It is wrong to look upon a vitamin as a substance which just combats specific symptoms. Like a lubricant, the vitamin makes the normal working of your body possible* [my italics]. If there is not enough vitamin the working will be disturbed, leading to all sorts of damages which may accumulate and declare themselves in an early senescence and ill health. In your car, insufficient lubricant will declare itself in the wearing out of pistons and cylinders, with the result that after 40,000 miles your car will run as if it had done 80,000, and you will look at forty as if you were over sixty.

Pick up most books on diet or nutrition and they will give you the official line about 'recommended dosages' of vitamins and minerals necessary, they say, for health. In the case of most nutrients the amounts suggested by such tables are grossly inadequate if your body is to be protected against age-degeneration. These figures have usually been arrived at by slowly decreasing the supply of a specific nutrient in an animal's diet until he shows signs of severe symptoms of some kind. Then, the amount of a vitamin or mineral needed to banish these symptoms is taken to be the 'recommended dose'. What such a practice ignores is the fact that any organism leeches its reserves of a specific nutrient from as much as can be spared in all the enzymic pathways in which this vitamin takes part, causing vital metabolic processes to be reduced. As Bjorksten says:

Thus all these other processes suffer a drastic reduction of their respective reserves and safety margins. These are reduced to the point where the ability of the body to stand up to overloads in these is sacrificed. Therefore, for maximum longevity in good health, one of the prime requisites is a constantly maintained *optimal* supply of all vitamins . . . Other requirements are: adequate supply of the needed trace elements, but even more important the exclusion of the deleterious elements.

Premature Factors in Ageing

One scientist who has long concerned himself with discovering the ranges of optimal doses of nutrients for protecting the body from degeneration is Carl Pfeiffer, Director of Princeton's Brain Bio Center in the United States. Pfeiffer has also looked closely at many of the deleterious elements to which Bjorksten refers, such as the presence of heavy metals like lead and aluminium in the body. Pfeiffer speaks about both when he lists what he considers to be the *premature factors in old age*. And, while Pfeiffer's 'premature' factors are by no means exclusive, they give a good idea of what Bjorksten is talking about and are excellent guidelines for what to avoid if you are not to age prematurely.

1. Heavy-Metal Intoxication
This is one of the worst factors in premature ageing in industrialized societies where we are continually exposed to lead, mercury, aluminium, cadmium, asbestos, sulphates and phosphates. Even copper—one of the micronutrients necessary in minute quantities for health—acts as a heavy metal when it is present in too great a concentration in the body. Industrial pollutants released into the atmosphere produce acid rains which put aluminium into our drinking water by dissolving it out of clay in the earth. Lead enters our body from industrial emanations, from petrol fumes and when we drink water in houses which have been plumbed with lead pipes. Phosphate, which is a constituent of fizzy soft drinks, couples with white

flour, which is very low in usable minerals, to leach calcium from our bones. Silver enters the body from using silver cutlery for eating. Copper in excess can enter the body by drinking water—especially soft water—which comes in copper pipes. It can also build up in the brain if you are deficient in zinc or from taking 'multiple vitamins and minerals' which include copper but exclude zinc. Both copper in excess and lead can cause hyperactivity in children. Excess copper can make normal people into insomniacs or encourage the development of arthritis as well as of high blood pressure.

Heavy metals are potent cross-linkers. They can also inactivate enzymic functions. And they are poisonous to the body. Bjorksten has looked particularly closely at aluminium, one of the most powerful cross-linkers for proteins, and probably for DNA and RNA—the cell's genetic materials—as well, since these nucleic acids contain several sites to which it can bind. Aluminium appears able to inactivate the sensitive end organs of neurons, disturb intracellular transport of nutrients and to block genetic molecules. It has been found in high concentration in the brains of stroke victims. Yet it is still commonly believed that cooking with aluminium pots and pans, in which acidic foods—such as tomatoes—are capable of dissolving this metal into the foods we eat, is not dangerous. Most so-called authorities still believe that aluminium is not absorbed through the intestines. The avoidance of heavy-metal intoxication and the detoxification of any that may be present is an absolute necessity for ageless ageing.

2. Lack of Essential Trace Elements and Vitamins
Vitamins A, E, D and C are amongst those Pfeiffer lists as good candidates for preventing premature ageing and enhancing longevity. Trace elements which Pfeiffer lists amongst those which may provide longevity include sulphur, selenium, magnesium, calcium, potassium, zinc, manganese, molybdenum and iodine. He adds that we need riboflavin (B_2) to prevent cataracts, pyridoxine (B_6) to prevent atherosclerosis, chromium for the glucose-tolerance factor to prevent diabetes, and B_{12} to prevent anaemia and confusion. And we will be looking later at the anti-oxidant nutrients which protect the body from free-radical damage and cross-linking. Used as nutritional sup-

plements these nutrients can be enormously helpful in retarding age-degeneration. But never on their own. Thanks to the way the human organism has evolved through hundreds of generations, the *rule of synergy* always applies.

No single nutrient can do anything for age-retardation. As biochemist Michael Colgan says, 'It is the multiple interaction of nutrients, *not* their single actions, which are the basis of their biological functions. This principle has been only recently emphasized in nutritional science, although top scientists have known it for years.' In the same way that Bjorksten insists we need optimal quantities of nutrients for the smooth running of metabolic pathways, this rule of synergy demands that your body be supplied with *all* of the more than fifty substances necessary for health and life. Because of the complexity of interlinking metabolic pathways if even *one* nutrient is missing you are undermining your chances for vitality, longevity and health. This means we need to eat a wide variety of top-quality little-processed foods, a large portion of them fresh. For most of us in industrialized countries, where fresh foods organically grown on healthy soils are not readily available, it probably also means relying on nutritional supplements.

3. Loss of Calcium from Bones

The loss of calcium from bones, known as osteoporosis, is a common occurrence after the age of thirty; so are low levels of calcium in the body. They used to be considered a 'normal' occurrence in ageing by some scientists. In fact they are the result of such factors as inadequate nutrition, the build-up of aluminium and lead in the bones and brain which replace the calcium that should be there, a diet too high in protein, or just plain inactivity.

Calcium is the most abundant mineral in your body. About 99 per cent of it is deposited in your bones and teeth and the rest is in the soft tissues, circulation and extracellular fluid. Even a moderate calcium deficiency can lead to cramps, joint pains, palpitation, tooth decay, insomnia, impaired tissue repair and excessive irritability of nerves and muscles. It can also slow your blood-clotting and lead to the formation of brittle and porous bones which break easily. Calcium loss is something which must be prevented. You need adequate calcium for ageless ageing. How do you get it? First of all, like the long-lived Hunzas, Vilcabamba Indians and Soviet Georgians you get plenty of exercise. Regular physical exercise mineralizes bones and makes you able to make proper use of minerals and trace elements you take in in your foods. You also need to ensure you get adequate zinc, magnesium, calcium and manganese in your diet which together with optimal amounts of vitamin C can not only keep calcium and other minerals in good supply, but can also offer protection against aluminium and lead. And you need to avoid eating excess protein. As Pfeiffer says, 'Diets high in protein lead to increased urinary calcium excretion. Average calcium loss with such diets can amount to 30 per cent of the calcium intake. The affluent American is apt to eat a high-protein diet and many obese individuals use a protein diet to lose weight *and calcium and bone.*'

4. Loss of Vital Hormones

A number of important hormones decline with age. They include the sex hormones testosterone and oestrogen, thyroid, insulin and thymosin, which is related to immune functioning. Taking steps to stop this decline when it is occurring can effectively slow down the rate at which you are ageing. It can even help rejuvenate your body. Pfeiffer relates how in 1980 when the use of thyroid substance was introduced, '. . . this proved to be a miracle anti-ageing drug. The patients' heavy facial wrinkles disappeared, dimwittedness turned to laughter, hearts speeded up and body-swelling gave way to firm muscle and energy.' Of course this kind of improvement only occurs in people who are iodine- or thyroid-deficient. And Pfeiffer points out that for some people, '. . . even the iodine of kelp or seafood is enough to restart the synthesis of the thyroid hormone.' So important are the minute quantities of trace elements we need for protection from age-degeneration.

Most hormones are made from amino acids—the building blocks of protein—in the presence of certain vitamins and minerals. As people get older often the ability of their digestive systems to break down the proteins from the foods they eat into their constituent amino acids, from which hormones and enzymes and collagen and other body proteins can be built, declines. Sometimes this decline is the result of inadequate hydrochloric acid in the stomach or pancreatic enzymes in the gut. It can also often be corrected by nutritional supplements. Inadequate production of vital hormones may also be due to lack of specific trace minerals—for instance iodine in the case of thyroid hormone, and chromium which is necessary for insulin. Many of the most famous of the natural anti-ageing treatments, such as cell therapy, owe a great deal of their effectiveness to the way in which they appear to reactivate hormone production.

These are the major areas of premature ageing according to Pfeiffer—premature degeneration can be the result of lack of vitamins or essential minerals, lack of exercise and of mental stimulation, lack of hormones or contamination by heavy metals. Together they share a couple of important things in common. First, all of them are preventable provided we become aware of what is happening and take steps to stop it from happening. Second, either directly or indirectly all of them cause the problems of metabolic bottlenecks of which Bjorksten speaks and highlight the necessity of preventing them. Your body must be provided with optimal quantities of vitamins and minerals to do this.

The Orthomolecular Approach

Twice Nobel laureate Linus Pauling, and many other eminent scientists, have been saying the same thing for years—often to the distress of less informed nutritionists and doctors who still believe vitamins and minerals are only substances necessary in minute quantities to protect the body from gross nutritional diseases such as scurvy and beriberi. Pauling coined the word orthomolecular to describe the treatment and the prevention of disease by providing an individual organism with optimal quantities of specific vitamins, minerals and other nutrients in order that its metabolic processes take place smoothly and cleanly in the way Bjorksten insists that they must if we are to prevent premature ageing. 'Orthomolecular' means molecularly straight or correct. The orthomolecular approach to ageless ageing is aimed at providing the optimum molecular environment—especially the optimum concentrations of substances normally present in the human body. So far removed from this goal are the typical lists of 'recommended doses' of nutrients and the kind of common medical advice that you should eat a 'well-balanced diet' (which usually means the 'meat-two-veg' routine), that they can be considered virtually useless in any programme for ageless ageing. When it comes to devising a serious programme for preventing premature degeneration, only an orthomolecular approach will do.

Le Compte's Amazing Law

One physician for whom this approach forms the basis of all his work is the Belgian ageing expert Herman Le Compte. Le Compte is editor of *Rejuvenation*, a journal on ageing and age-retardation which publishes some of the most advanced work done in this area from the West and Soviet Russia. Now in his fifties but looking much younger, he is a man of extraordinary dynamism and a real renegade in his field. He is also the Robin Hood of age-retardation. For years in his clinic in Belgium he has been treating the wealthy and mighty and teaching them the skills of age-retardation as well as the poor and needy and charging for his treatment in direct proportion to a client's ability to pay. As a result of some thirty years as a clinician, during which time he was studying the ageing process and working to slow it down in himself and his patients, Le Compte came to formulate a law which is undoubtedly the most important guideline currently used to understand premature ageing and how to prevent it. It is called simply *The First Law of Le Compte* and it goes like this: *Ageing proceeds more rapidly where the deficiencies are greater and more numerous*. We'll take a closer look at the implications of Le Compte's Law in a moment. But the story of Le Compte's discovery of it is too good to pass up.

The African Connection

When Le Compte finished his medical studies, the prospect of starting up a practice in Belgium—what everyone expected of him—somehow didn't appeal to his adventurous spirit. So he and his young wife decided instead to go to West Africa where, after a short period as an assistant to a large hospital and after a few months of running a leper centre, he was sent to take charge of a brand-new hospital which served 50,000 patients and had 300 ward beds. Within a month of its opening he was treating up to 300 outpatients a day as well as paying house calls on others in remote villages. Working eighteen hours a day, seven days a week, Le Compte had no help except three European nurses and a dozen Congolese who were hard workers but who could neither read nor write. His operating room had neither electric lights nor running water and he had to carry out even major surgery under local anaesthetics for medical supplies were scarce. In three years he performed more than 3,000 operations, supervised some 2,500 births and dealt with sicknesses ranging from malaria to blackwater fever. And, despite the fact that he had no x-ray machinery, no cardiac monitors, no resuscitation equipment, and no laboratory, in all that time he only lost two of his surgery cases.

Drugs were as scarce as the proverbial hen's teeth and limited to local anaesthetics and penicillin. But the one thing Le Compte was never short of was vitamins. Because doctors in Europe used very little of the vitamins which were provided for them and because their surplus medical supplies were collected every few months by Boy Scouts who sent off unwanted medication to the 'poor Africans', Le Compte's storerooms were piled high with them—hundreds and thousands of bottles and jars and boxes of every kind of vitamin imaginable. 'Vitamins were considered useless,' says Le Compte, 'so they were all given away. Since I had nothing else I started to administer massive doses of all types of vitamins to my patients. I would keep a patient in hospital for a few weeks before a major operation to give him a chance to rest and gather his strength. During this time he would receive mega-multi-vitamin injections. Then, as now, my methods were empirical. I had little to guide me but my diagnostic instincts.'

His results were amazing. The recovery rate of patients treated before surgery in this way showed Le Compte that something quite extraordinary happened to the human body when you provided it with very large quantities of these natural substances—substances which he had been taught in medical school were only useful for preventing a few diseases of malnutrition. Not only that, on megadoses patients' resistance to illness and to degeneration after surgery was very high indeed. One rule Le Compte went by as director of the hospital was that he never refused an aged patient. In fact more than half of his surgery was performed on old people who, because of their poverty, had been refused help at hospitals in other regions and countries—the Portuguese Congo and the French Congo mostly.

Le Compte noticed from his contact with these people that not all Africans aged equally quickly. By means of sociological investigations he discovered that the difference in the rate of ageing had little to do with hygiene, housing, clothing or infections. It rested instead on how people were fed. The poor Africans were always badly nourished. They aged most rapidly. Those who were better fed aged more slowly.

Slow and Fast Agers

After three years of backbreaking work, leaving home before dawn each day and returning home late at night too exhausted to do anything but collapse into bed, Le Compte himself suffered a major heart attack at the age of twenty-eight. For three months he lay in bed unable to move. Then he was sent back to Europe where he faced a long period of recuperation. Fascinated by his discoveries in the Congo and by the process of ageing itself, he used his convalescent time to research intensively everything that he could get his hands on related to ageing and degeneration. It was then that he developed the simple but profound maxim which bears his name: *Ageing proceeds most rapidly where the deficiencies are greatest and most numerous.*

As with many fundamental scientific laws, it may appear so simple as to be self-evident and yet it is an essential foundation for any ageless-ageing programme. As a result of this basic statement, many important research projects have been started all over the world. Bjorksten himself has even published a detailed mathematical proof of Le Compte's first law. A close corollary to this law—one particularly important for ageless ageing—is this: *Ageing is maximally retarded where a maximum of potentially limiting strictures in the metabolic processes are widened.*

Oiling the Valves

Probably the most accurate way of analysing human metabolism is by viewing it as a network of interconnected pipelines where the maintenance of the necessary minimum flow in many critical areas depends on multiple interconnected valves and structures. In biochemical terms these valves or structures are enzyme-catalysed processes where the amount of processing depends largely on the availability of enzymes at appropriate multiple points. And this in turn depends mostly on how available are the materials for synthesizing the enzymes—vitamins, minerals and essential acids. Again in Bjorksten's words, 'Such a high level of the metabolic enzymes is maintained by a correspondingly high level of all the relevant vitamins, essential trace elements, and anything else that could become a limiting factor of any vital step in the normal metabolism.' In practical terms what this means is that, as Pauling and other scientists who advocate an orthomolecular approach to health and age-retardation insist, if you want to prevent the premature ageing (which is so common in our society as to have become the 'norm') then you need to begin now to provide your body with *optimal* amounts of all the nutrients it needs for carrying out its myriad metabolic processes smoothly, cleanly and without bottlenecks. That is quite a challenge. For most of us meeting it involves not only improving our diet, but also eating less, taking nutritional supplements and even ensuring that we get enough exercise to see that we prevent loss of essential nutrients. Let's begin by looking at the kind of changes in eating habits which can lead you closer to this orthomolecular state which forms the foundation of ageless ageing.

TEN

Eat Less and Live More

'Man lives on one quarter of what he eats. On the other three-quarters his doctor lives.' This observation carved permanently into an Egyptian pyramid more than 5,000 years ago should be chiselled into the brain of anybody serious about ageless ageing. Eat less and you will live longer is the simplest yet the most potent piece of advice you can follow. In 1973 E. D. Schlenker heading a research team at Michigan State University published the results of an interesting investigation of a group of ninety-seven women—middle-aged and older—whose histories he had followed since 1948. Originally, each woman had provided the research team with a list of foods and quantities eaten during one day as well as a health and nutritional history. At that time all these women were rated in good, fair or poor health following the qualitative index of ageing set out by the *American Journal of Public Health*. In 1972, those still living were again examined. Researchers found that women who looked younger than their years ate fewer calories. Also fewer of their calories came from fats and they managed to consume substantially more vitamins B_1, A and C than their older-looking counterparts.

Not only is avoiding obesity a major means of preparing for a good-looking and healthy old age, the avoidance of excessive food intake is important because, as you may remember from Chapter 4, eating more than your body actually needs is a major cause of oxy-stress to your system—free-radical damage and cross-linking. When animals are underfed yet provided with optimum quantities of all the essential nutrients in their diet they not only live longer, they tend to remain free of chronic infections and degenerative diseases including cancer, atherosclerosis and arthritis. Cut your calories but increase the quality of the foods you eat and you will dramatically *decelerate* the rate at which you are ageing.

Calorie Restriction for Life Extension

Back in the 'thirties a researcher called Clive McCay at Cornell University carried out a series of experiments in which he severely restricted calories in rats but supplied them with vitamin and mineral supplements from the time of weaning. He discovered that these animals lived as much as two times as long as a control group which were allowed to eat as much as they wanted. Not only that, their longer lives were far healthier.

McCay fed his experimental rats every day, starting from weaning, 60 per cent of the calorie intake of his control group. He then supplemented their diet with enough vitamins and minerals to make up for the 40 per cent deficit of these nutrients. By day 1000 of the experiment all of the normally fed rats were dead yet most of the underfed animals were not only alive and well, they were sexually active and showed little sign of ageing or degeneration. McCay's work was later validated by other investigators in a number of laboratories. Morris Ross at the Institute for Cancer Research in Philadelphia, for instance, was able to extend the maximum lifespan of rats by 50-60 per cent using similar methods. In human terms this would correspond to our being able to live around 170 years. Meanwhile other researchers found they could also extend an animal's lifespan by 'intermittent fasting'—fasting them every second day, every third day or every fourth day. This method brought about a 20-30 per cent extension to an animal's life. And, as with McCay's calorie-restricted animals, not only was their lifespan increased, the rate at which they aged was slowed. This was determined by what are known as *biomarkers of ageing*.

The All-Important Biomarkers

Biomarkers are measurements designed to determine how old

an animal or a human being is, not chronologically, but functionally and biochemically. You can have a chronological age of seventy-five yet your skin may be as smooth as someone twenty years younger, your heart and lungs may have the fitness of someone much younger and your immune system may work as well as a sixty-year-old's. In this case your *biomarkers* would indicate that you are much younger physiologically than your chronological age implies. Biomarkers include the degree of skin dryness, the greying of hair, level of blood cholesterol, patterns of liver enzymes, the incidence and the time of onset of cataracts and so forth. When researchers have tested calorie-restricted animals they have found that by all known biomarkers they are significantly younger than their chronological age indicates they should be. These animals are also highly resistant to degenerative diseases including cancer, heart disease and kidney disease. For instance in one study where 50 per cent of the well-fed group of mice developed cancer a mere 13 per cent of the calorie-controlled group did, while in another carried out on rats in Australia these figures were 64 per cent and 15 per cent respectively. Similar results were shown with other diseases as well.

Such findings caused great stir amongst those concerned with age-retardation. Yet for quite a while they seemed to have little relevance in retarding human ageing. For calorie-restriction from weaning is hardly something we can carry out acceptably on our children. First of all, a small percentage of these calorie-restricted animals die very early and no one could take such a risk with a human baby. Second there is always the chance that calorie-restriction might cause some kind of brain damage in a developing child. So McCay's findings and those of other researchers working in the same way were relegated to that place on the bookshelves of science which holds the curiosities of laboratory research. Then a dynamic American age-researcher at the UCLA (University of California at Los Angeles) Medical School began to play about with calorie-restricted diets and to design his own laboratory experiments which were variations on the McCay theme. His name is Roy Walford. He is a hard-headed sceptical research scientist of the highest order with an all-encompassing fascination with finding means not only of halting premature ageing but of increasing *maximum* lifespan.

A Workable Alternative

Walford reasoned that if you could start to restrict calories not from weaning but from middle age—all the while replacing any nutrients lost with supplements—then perhaps you could avoid the undesirable 'side-effects' of trying to do it from birth but still extend life. Trouble is, nobody had yet been able to do this by adult-initiated caloric restriction. The reason why, Walford reasoned, might be that they had made the changeover from normal diet to restricted one too rapidly. Together with his colleague Richard Weindruch he decided to try it more gradually. It worked. Walford and Weindruch were not only able to retard the ageing rate of these animals and to lengthen their *maximum* lifespan, they were even able to bring about some degree of immunological rejuvenation. This particularly intrigued Walford because, as you may remember from Chapter 5, immune response is a major biomarker of ageing. He says:

> One good biomarker test measures the response of critical agents of the immune system—white blood cells or lymphocytes—to a substance called phyto-hemagglutinin (PHA for short). PHA causes a lymphocyte to produce fresh DNA (the hereditary gene material in each cell) and divide into two new cells. The ability to respond to PHA declines with age. Dr Weindruch and I found that the lymphocytes of 16 month-old mice, who had been restricted since 12 months of age, responded to PHA at the same level as 6-8 month-old mice. (Natural lifespan in mice is 2½ to 3 years, so 12 months is well into young adulthood.) Evidentially, the rejuvenation does not involve *all* bodily systems, since the maximum lifespan of mice restricted as above is extended only about 20 per cent. But the results—displaying actual rejuvenation of at least one parameter of ageing—are encouraging.

In fact, Walford is being very modest about his findings which are almost revolutionary in a world where orthodox science has for fifty years insisted that rejuvenation of any kind is little more than a pipe-dream.

In common with animals whose diet had been restricted from weaning, Walford and Weindruch's mice also showed significant resistance to illness and degeneration. About 50 per cent of his fully fed mice developed cancer while only 13 per cent of the restricted mice did. The incidence of kidney disease, vascular disease and heart disease at 800 days old amongst the fully fed group was 100 per cent, 63 per cent and 96 per cent respectively while in their leaner counterparts the figures were a mere 25, 10 and 26 per cent. Also the restricted animals did not develop increased blood cholesterol as they got older. Their fat cells remained significantly more responsive to hormones (a decrease in responsiveness to hormones also tends to occur with age) and the auto-antibodies which are believed to be an underlying cause of senile dementia were greatly reduced. The findings of these two scientists have by now been well substantiated by other researchers such as those working at the Gerontology Research Center in Baltimore.

It is now generally accepted that their findings can be translated into human applications and that there is a high degree of probability that, started in adulthood, such dietary restrictions will bring the same benefits to people. For, as we have seen, ageing, like growth and development, is a *general* process—one of the most general of all biological phenomena. And biologists usually agree that such general processes are fundamentally the same within all mammals. They know that such a general anti-ageing tool as caloric restriction which works on mice and rats is likely to work for humans too. The prospects offered by such findings are very exciting indeed to anyone concerned about initiating an ageless-ageing lifestyle. For what Weindruch and Walford uncovered was a method of age-retardation, life-extension and prevention of degeneration which was not only effective but safe, simple and available to any with enough initiative and motivation to put it into practice.

Undernutrition without Malnutrition

Walford is quick to point out that his methods have nothing to do with going on slimming diets. Far from it. Neither are they some kind of crankiness as they might seem to uninformed scientist and layman alike. They are based on well-established and accepted scientific facts. Also, *under*nutrition is not *mal*nutrition. It is a way of nourishing your body on fewer calories yet ensuring you get a full supply of essential vitamins, minerals, fatty acids and so forth. What this means in practical terms is that as human beings we need *gradually* to restrict our calorie intake to about 60 per cent of what we would eat if, like his mice, we let ourselves eat as much as we wanted—about 1800 calories a day for the average man and 1300 for the average woman. And this caloric restriction should be achieved *gradually* over a period of five to seven years. Walford believes that you can also get the same results using intermittent fasting—in other words fasting on water for two days of the week—which would increase your daily restricted intake of calories on the other days to 2520 for men and 1820 for women. Slowly, such a restriction will lead to a 20-25 per cent reduction in your body weight. And there's good news for the person who has all his life fought the battle of the bulge because of a lowered metabolic rate which prevents him from eating as much as his thin cousin can without gaining weight. According to Walford this kind of person practising undernutrition without malnutrition may be able to live even longer still for his decreased metabolic rate and the lower body temperature characteristic of his body type are two factors which can increase lifespan.

Supremely Nourishing Foods

It is only possible to achieve 'undernutrition without malnutrition' by choosing your foods very carefully (more about that in the next chapter) and by eliminating all of the over-processed, nutritionally 'empty' foods which make up the greater part of most people's menus—from white sugar and white flour to margarines containing hydrogenated oils, soft drinks and potato crisps. Walford suggests a way of eating in which people in midlife—between thirty and fifty—get only 10-15 per cent of their calories in fats (the average Briton or American now takes in some 40 per cent or more of his calories in fats), 20 to 25 per cent of their calories in the form of protein and the remainder in *complex* carbohydrates such as grains, pulses, fruits and vegetables. Such a low-calorie-high-potency regime will need to be rich in fresh vegetables, preferably eaten raw to preserve as many of their nutrients as possible, and it is easier to achieve by combining grains, pulses, vegetables and fruits for your proteins rather than eating meat. Most meat contains too much fat and all meat is low in fibre. High fibre is another important characteristic of any ageless-ageing way of eating. It not only helps safeguard you against excess cholesterol formation, diverticulitis and cancer of the bowel, it also helps your body detoxify itself of many toxic substances which you take in from your environment and which are powerful free-radical formers and cross-linkers.

The final essential ingredient in this new approach to age-retardation is a good supply of extra nutrients from supplements of vitamins and minerals, essential fatty acids and possibly amino acids. The anti-oxidant nutrients are particularly important—vitamins C and E, the mineral selenium and the sulphur amino acids cysteine and methionine (see Chapter 16 for guidelines) because they act as free-radical scavengers. (Walford refers to free radicals as 'great white sharks in the biochemical sea' because of their ability to do untold damage on a cellular level.) But the other vitamins and minerals are important also. For, as we saw in the last chapter, all essential nutrients are *synergistic*—they work together and, because of the complexity of the web of metabolic pathways in our bodies, a nutrient without all its related nutrients is of no use against age-degeneration. Computer analyses of attempts to establish wholefood diets without taking nutritional supplements point up common deficiencies in descending order. They are: zinc, vitamin E, copper, magnesium, iron, niacin, vitamin B_{12}, pantothenic acid, calcium, riboflavin, folic acid, vitamin A, vitamin B_6, thiamine and vitamin C. Many studies show that four of these nutrients are commonly deficient in the average Western diet—vitamin C, vitamin A, calcium and iron—while zinc, chromium, manganese and potassium follow close behind.

Putting it into Practice

Walford advises anyone interested in pursuing this new dietary approach to age-retardation to begin by going through a health check-up with their doctor and having as many tests of bio-marker functions taken as are available. They can include measurement of blood pressure, blood cholesterol and tri-glycerides, treadmill tests for heart function, a glucose-tolerance test to detect blood-sugar disorders, and tests for lung and kidney functions. One of the simplest of all medical tests—a lung assay known as the forced pulmonary expiratory volume—is one of the best human biomarkers of all for indicating physiological as opposed to chronological age. It measures the amount of air you are able to expel in a specific length of time (usually a second) and gives a good indication of both the elastic recoil of your lungs and the integrity of your breathing passages. Having these checks done at the beginning of such a change in nutritional habits will do two things. First it will ensure that you are in good health and let your doctor know what you are planning. Second it will give you some hard data against which you will be able to measure your progress. People who have already begun to follow this kind of nutritional lifestyle (Walford among them) report these biomarkers usually begin altering for the better very rapidly.

What's It Like?

To most people the idea of restricting the number of calories they consume and leaving the sticky buns and chocolate out of their lives seems like some kind of terrible deprivation—an action which can only be carried out by a gargantuan effort of the will. In fact this is only the view of someone who has not yet experienced the enormous rewards that come with dietary temperance. My greatest health-fault has always been a tendency to eat far too much because I am such a hedonist by nature and because I learned early on from my grandmother (who raised me as a very young child) that if anything went wrong or you felt tired or tense or confused FOOD was the answer. Happily, since for many years the foods I have overindulged in have been top quality, I have suffered no serious health consequences yet. But since I have begun my own form of high-potency-low-calorie eating I can honestly say that the rewards far outweigh what at the beginning I thought would be the sacrifices. I not only look better, feel better and have more energy than ever, I actually enjoy food more than I ever have before. The dishes I prepare have become beautifully light symphonies of colour, and texture and taste. Like periodic fasting (see Chapter 14), such a way of eating keeps your mind clear and your senses heightened. It has enabled me to get greater enjoyment out of almost everything I do.

There are other bonuses in store from such a lifestyle too. Animal studies show that it should markedly increase your resistance to infection as well, for instance. Arthritic changes in the spine, the greying of hair and many of the other age signs should also be significantly delayed. Animals on such a regime are more active and more energetic. They also retain sexual interest and energy long after their fully fed brothers have fallen by the wayside. Let the last word on the subject be left to Walford himself: 'Appropriate dietary restriction will give you better vision, hearing, mental function, an improved sense of physical well-being, retained sexuality, and increased disease resistance in relation to your chronological or birthday age.' Here he quotes the Greek poet Hesiod who, some 2700 years ago, wrote:

> Fools not to know that half exceeds the whole,
> How blest the sparing meal and temperate bowl.

ELEVEN

The Seedbed of Ageing

Not only is the quantity of food you eat a central factor in how rapidly you age, so is its quality—and I am not only talking about how many vitamins it contains. Even ten years ago such a statement might have been considered crankish. Food was simply fuel for the body and so long as you got what was considered the right quantity of calories, protein, and fats, plus a few vitamins, that was all you needed to worry about. Food was believed to have little to do with health unless, like the starving Africans, you didn't get enough of it.

Now we know differently. Amost daily reports appear in the scientific literature and the popular press linking processed fats with arteriosclerosis or stressing the importance of fresh vegetables and fruits and fibre in the avoidance of stroke and cancer. The medical profession and the general public are keenly aware that there are many things wrong with the average British or American diet. We know now that most of us should eat less fat and meat and sugar, less white flour and coffee. We are also told that we would be healthier if we got more fibre and ate more pulses and whole grains—even if we don't always understand why. But what few people are yet aware of (probably because much of the research has been done in Europe and published in foreign languages) is that the *state* and *quality* of the foods you eat is one of the most important issues in determining how well you remain and rapidly you age. The state of our foods is determined by such considerations as freshness, the condition and health of the soil on which they have been grown and both whether and how they have been cooked or processed.

Nurturing the Cells

Your foods do not just supply you with vitamins, minerals, building blocks and energy. The state and quality of what you eat also determine the health of your capillaries and the condition of the *mesenchyme*—connective tissue, blood and blood system and the smooth muscles through which nutrients and oxygen must pass to nurture cells, glands and organs. This microscopic tissue element—the mesenchyme—carries the 'nutritional stream' to all parts of your body. The Swiss expert in the use of nutrition for healing and for retarding degeneration, Max Bircher-Benner, always referred to it as 'vegetatives Betriebsstuck'—*the seedbed*. Giving it this name is an excellent way of understanding its importance. For the mesenchyme is very much like a seedbed—a medium in which your organs and glands, like flowers, have to live. And any gardener will tell you how important it is to the health and beauty of flowers that the seedbed is not allowed to deteriorate. When it does they fade, wither and sicken. If the seedbed of the body is right—if it facilitates an easy passage of oxygen and nutrients and the rapid elimination of cellular wastes—then your cells' metabolic processes are carried out as they should be: *efficiently* and *cleanly*. Then you also get a high degree of protection from oxy-stress, free-radical damage and cross-linking. If not then the foods you eat—no matter how delicious or how much vitamin this or that they may contain—can slowly and persistently increase the rate at which you age.

What's Missing in Modern Nutrition?

Like much of modern science, most nutrition tends to be highly reductionist. Reductionism, you may remember from Chapter 7, is the world view which asserts that an effective understanding of any complex system can be gained by investigating the properties of its isolated parts. That is exactly the mistake made not only by nutritionists and food scientists themselves but also by most of the food industry as well. It is a mistake by which our health suffers greatly. The science of nutrition is based on the notion that the function of a vitamin or mineral or protein is encapsulated in its chemical structure. It assumes that man needs certain quantities of these nutrients as well as some protein, fat, carbohydrate and so forth in order to avoid gross nutritional deficiencies such as beriberi, pellagra and scurvy and it doesn't concern itself greatly with how he gets them. But it gives little thought to the importance of the complexity of how they are combined in natural fresh foods.

In truth the function of a vitamin or protein or any other nutrient can only be expressed by the interaction of this nutrient with its biochemical and physiological milieu. And unless you are reasonably knowledgeable about this milieu, its function cannot be understood. The body's biochemical milieu, like fresh foods grown on healthy soils, is highly complex. It includes vitamins, minerals and other accessory factors and there is much evidence that a shortage or an excess of one vitamin interferes with utilization of another. Once you begin to split off a nutrient from the milieu in which it occurs, even if later you combine it again with all of the known factors with which it was originally linked, you greatly emasculate its health-promoting potential. (This is a mistake many pill-popping longevists make when they assume they can eat anything they like so long as they take massive quantities of anti-oxidant nutrients.)

Structural Information for Ageless Ageing

As Russian biochemist I. I. Brekhman would say, we significantly alter the structural information which comes to us from the natural foods to which our bodies have become accustomed through our evolution. Brekhman and his colleague M. G. Kublanov have studied this issue at length examining scores of natural and artificial chemicals and foods from the point of view of the structural information for high-level health which they contain. He says:

Foods and drugs can be regarded as factors of chemical regulation of homeostasis. Since any regulation in the organism is an informative process the molecules of biologically active substances are chemical transmitters of information. Besides specific informative substances such as DNA, pheromones, endorphins, neurohormones, any compounds of complex composition and molecular structure can be 'informatively active'.

Brekhman has shown that drugs or highly processed foods which are relatively simple both in their chemical structure and in the low level of structural information they impart to the organism using them have little to offer either in terms of strengthening the organism's adaptive energy or in contributing to homeostasis. But vegetables, fruits—particularly when they are eaten fresh and raw—whole grains, pulses and so forth are complex natural compounds which carry a high degree of biological information necessary for wellness to the living organism. And, as you may remember from Chapter 7, this kind of biological information appears to be very important if we are to maintain the high degree of order or negative entropy necessary to resist ageing and degeneration.

Yet this is something of which most nutritionists and food technologists are still ignorant. Over 70 per cent of the foods we eat in Europe and North America continue to be factory processed. Modern food technology still disassembles the molecules of wheat or oats or corn and oil-bearing seeds and then modifies them in inventive ways to make our ready-in-a-minute meals and packaged and frozen products. Manufacturers also routinely add almost 200 chemicals to bolster the texture, taste, and appearance of foods engineered from modified starches, proteins, carbohydrates and fats, and there are several thousand more chemicals close at hand which can be thrown in for special purposes.

The American biochemist Roger Williams expresses our need for structural information in the maintenance of a high degree of negative entropy slightly differently when he says that the body extracts *trophic factors* from the molecular balances of the entire food for high-level health. We have great need of the trophic factors in natural fresh foods—the quality of structural information they contain. For only *it* can provide the right kind of seedbed for our cells and organs to make ageless ageing a reality. Even many of the positive effects of *high-tech* anti-ageing tools such as supplements of the anti-oxidant nutrients or free amino acids, which we will be looking at in Chapter 18, can be wasted if this internal milieu, through which they must pass to do their work, at a molecular level does not facilitate this happening.

The European Experience

To my knowledge most of the study of what kind of diet can do this comes out of Austria, Germany, Switzerland and Scandinavia. This is probably why the topic is so little understood in English-speaking countries like Britain and the United States. In continental Europe there is a long tradition of healing and age-retardation using natural foods—a high degree of them uncooked. European scientists have also carried out elaborate clinical and laboratory studies to determine how, on a cellular level, fresh foods are able to quite literally work wonders for the health of human beings. Their clinical experience and their laboratory findings can contribute greatly to *natural-law* anti-ageing. And as we will see, many of their findings—things about how raw foods increase the microelectrical potentials of cells and so forth—are directly relevant to the growing awareness of the body as a negentropic open system and probably also of the role that electromagnetic phenomena appear to play in growth, health and regeneration.

The tradition of using natural foods for healing is a long and interesting one involving the use of simple, often organically grown foods. For healthy soil is needed to impart the right kind of biological information for health to the plants grown on it. Many of these foods are used in their uncooked state for the treatment of serious chronic illness from cancer and arthritis to high blood pressure, arteriosclerosis, migraine and diabetes. In the finest European clinics for natural healing, a diet of such foods is combined with exercise, good stress management and simple treatments with air, water and sunlight. They are used to treat emotional disturbances, resistant obesity and addictions as well as chronic illnesses. The story of how the tradition developed, its phenomenal successes and how it is now being used is a fascinating one but far too long to tell here. My daughter Susannah and I have explored it in some depth in another book—*Raw Energy*. (The book also contains a number of recipes and nutritional guidelines.) But there are a couple of aspects of it which are particularly important to ageless ageing.

Rah Rah Raw

The foods which European physicians at those clinics commonly use, to perform what to the uninformed can seem like miracle transformations in their patients, are nothing special. They are the common-or-garden foods we see in our greengrocers and wholefood emporiums: fresh vegetables and fruits of all sorts, whole grains such as wheat and brown rice, and barley and oats, pulses and beans such as lentils, split peas, beans, and so forth. Those that are cooked are cooked simply but deliciously. The proportion of cooked to uncooked foods in a person's diet which these physicians employ while treating a patient are proportional to the seriousness of the illness being treated. The more serious it is the greater proportion of the foods will be raw. An all-raw diet is used to treat cancer, to induce safe and easy rapid weight loss, to treat diabetes and so forth. Then as the patient improves the physician gradually reduces the quantity of uncooked foods—fruits and vegetables, seeds and nuts and flaked grains plus yoghurt perhaps or cheese—to somewhere between 50 and 75 per cent. Once a high level of well-being is restored to the patient then he is encouraged to maintain himself permanently on a diet in which at least 50 per cent of the foods eaten are raw. Such a way of eating is the most powerful tool for *natural-law* anti-ageing you will find anywhere. It helps create a seedbed of the highest order as well as improving the efficiency with which your cells use oxygen. It also strengthens cell walls and improves cell metabolism. And it protects your body from a build-up of the toxic wastes we have been looking at which can cause the molecular damage of ageing.

Why a High-Raw Diet for Ageless Ageing?

The first, most obvious, reason is that fresh uncooked foods are higher in almost all of the anti-oxidant nutrients important in protecting your body from oxy-stress as well as in the other accessory nutrients which make it possible for them to do their work. It is well-established scientific fact that storing, heating and processing destroy vitamins and cause mineral loss. And as Walford insists, if we are to make use of calorie-reduced eating as a tool for ageless ageing, we need as much nutritional value from our foods as possible. But this only scratches the surface of the high-raw phenomenon.

What has recently come to light is the fact that cooking not only destroys nutrients. Four kinds of damage to amino acids can occur as a result of heating and processing protein foods:

● Under high heat food proteins can become resistant to digestion so that the availability of all amino acids is reduced.
● Lysine is lost when you heat proteins especially in the presence of reducing sugars—for instance as in the pasturization of milk.
● When protein is exposed to treatment with alkali as it is in many food-manufacturing processes then lysine and cysteine (one of the natural anti-oxidant nutrients) residues can be eliminated and toxic products such as lysinolalanine are formed.
● When oxidizing chemicals such as sodium dioxide are used in food processing considerable methionine from the protein is lost. Methionine is one of the natural anti-oxidant aminos which it is important to get plenty of as a protection against cross-linkage and peroxidation in the cells.

Another fact about cooking which has only recently come to light and which is probably relevant to why raw foods are so important for ageless ageing, is that cooking creates chemicals which are mutagenic and *carcinogenic*. Carcinogenic means cancer-producing, while mutagenicity is the ability to produce changes in gene patterns which can be transferred to future generations. Researchers such as T. Sugimura and others have discovered that the burnt and browned matter which results from heating protein during cooking is highly mutagenic. And a number of chemicals isolated from heated protein have been shown to be cancer-causing when they are fed to animals. Also the browning reaction products that come from caramelizing sugars and from the interactions of amino acids and sugars during the cooking of foods (such as the brown crusts on bread and toast) contain a wide variety of DNA-damaging substances.

The amount of this burnt browned material which is taken in the normal Western diet can be several grammes a day. Even coffee, which contains a considerable amount of burnt material, is a source of several mutagens. One cup of coffee contains about 250mg of the natural mutagen chlorogenic acid. Caffeine itself inhibits the cells' DNA-repair system and can increase the production of cancer tumours in animals. And there is now preliminary epidemiologic evidence that heavy coffee-drinking is associated with ovarian cancer as well as cancer of the colon, bladder and pancreas. Fats—particularly unsaturated oils such as those we cook with—have also been shown to change during heating and processing. Not only is much of their nutritional value lost, they too can produce mutagenic and carcinogenic compounds.

More than the Sum of Its Parts

A number of European scientists who have investigated the high-raw healing phenomenon believe that there are other important substances—such as the essential oils in plants, the chlorophyll and the saponins—with health-enhancing properties which are changed or destroyed by heat. Although ignored by orthodox nutrition, these substances are probably also part of the structural information biologically necessary to support high-level health and to slow degeneration. Also, unlike the average Western diet, a high-raw way of eating does not tax the body with excessive acidity and it is low in salt—particularly important when our high salt intake has been indicted as a possible cause of high blood pressure and vascular disease. Some experts on the relationship between a high-raw diet and health believe that the reason why orthodox nutrition has not yet twigged to the value of fresh natural foods is precisely because of the reductionist nature of the science. Ralph Bircher—biochemist son of Bircher-Benner—has spent the past fifty years compiling laboratory and clinical research in this area, has edited a scientific journal in Europe for more than a generation and has written almost a dozen technical books on the subject. He says:

> It is not the vitamins, nor the mineral salts in raw vegetable foods which do it, nor chlorophyll, nor the quality of the proteins nor the saponins, nor essential oils, nor excess of alkalines, nor fibre, nor the fact that this diet is low in sodium. The problem is complex and much more interesting than that. Heating and even wilting destroys many qualities the significance of which is not yet known and mankind will possibly never know it completely. But new analytic work of recent years has given interesting insight.

High-Raw Protects Immunity

Some of the work to which Bircher is referring was done by scientists such as Paul Kouchakoff at the Institute of Clinical Chemistry in Lausanne, who discovered that there are significant differences in the way the body responds to cooked foods and to raw foods. Kouchakoff found that a phenomenon which he called *digestive leucocytosis*, which was believed to take place whenever we eat food, doesn't actually occur if the food eaten is raw. In digestive leucocytosis, some kind of message triggers the release of leucocytes—white blood cells. These cells swarm out to the intestine walls—especially to the colon—as if to defend a front-line attack on the body. This was assumed to be a normal physiological phenomenon until Kouchakoff's discovery. He also found that it does not occur if you only *begin* your meal with something raw. Raw foods appear not to challenge the immune reactions in the way cooked foods do—leaving immune functions free to deal with day-to-day biochemical housekeeping. Kouchakoff's findings have been confirmed by other researchers as well.

Raw foods also contain natural enzymes which are destroyed when food is cooked. Orthodox nutrition pays no attention to these enzymes in the belief that they are rapidly destroyed by digestive processes as soon as we eat them and therefore can have no beneficial effects on the body. But researchers such as Kaspar Tropp in Würzburg and Nobel laureate A. I. Virtanen in Finland have shown that this is simply not true. Virtanen (who incidentally was Johan Bjorksten's teacher) found that many of these enzymes are broken down in the mouth as a result of chewing and their substrates react chemically with substances in saliva to produce new chemical compounds which appear to be beneficial to the health of animals and man. Tropp discovered that the human body knows how to protect many of these enzymes and escort them through the digestive tract so they reach the colon intact. There they attract and bind whatever oxygen may be present, thus removing the aerobic condition which can result in putrefaction, fermentations, intestinal toxaemia and dysbacteria or dysbiosis—a condition to which almost no attention has been paid so far in Britain and North America but which appears to have far-reaching consequences for human health.

Dysbiosis—An Insidious Menace

Dysbacteria or dysbiosis strictly means 'colonic dysfunction as a result of altered colonic flora'. The large intestine contains a colony or flora consisting of many forms of bacteria including various strains of *E. coli*, lactobacilli and so forth. In the colon are also smaller quantities of yeasts such as *Candida albicans* and some bacteria which can cause harm. The enzymes in raw foods appear to stimulate the production of the helpful bacterial flora such as the lactobacilli and *E. coli* which synthesize vitamins—particularly the B complex. When the bacteria present in the large bowel are abnormal then the body can suffer from insufficiency of some of these nutrients. This is a common occurrence in people who suffer from food allergies. When the flora is abnormal—as it is in dysbiosis—then the gastrointestinal mucous membrane becomes abnormally permeable, allowing the absorption of toxins from the bowel. These wastes can enter the circulation and be carried throughout the body to disrupt cell metabolism and cause toxic effects. Recently in America there has been great concern over the widespread incidence of high colon concentrations of *Candida albicans* yeast. It has been associated with a number of common illnesses from arthritis to chronic depression and fatigue.

Cell Power for Ageless Ageing

Even more interesting are the effects which raw foods have been shown to have on the body's circulatory system, the mesenchyme or seedbed and the cells themselves. A central issue in protecting the body from degeneration is ensuring that there is a constant interchange of energy, substance and information between the capillaries—the very ends of the circulatory system—and the tissue cells. This goes on simultaneously at something like a billion points in every part of your body. Its efficiency depends to a large degree on the electrobiological events such as those we were looking at in Chapter 8 which make exchange possible. Scientists such as Hans Eppinger at the University of Vienna have found that a diet high in raw foods significantly improves intra-extra cellular exchange, micro-circulation and waste elimination from the cells. Ralph Bircher describes this process rather well:

> The nutritive substances of the blood and the waste substances of the cells have to pass through two fine membranes and a narrow dividing interstice. In a dead body such an interchange would be ruled by nature's law of levelling contrasts, the principle called 'diffusion', but during life the cells overcome diffusion. They tend to create the exact opposite of levelling, ie antagonistic contrasts and tensions of a chemical, physical and electrical nature, by attracting from the blood what they need and rejecting other material.
>
> The stronger these antagonisms are the better, for in them life finds the power of defence against disorder and the power of healing illness. On the other side, ill-health is expressed by a partial loss of this 'selective' capacity of the cells, by undue and diffused exchange of minerals—salts penetrating the cell walls for instance—also by a lowering of the tensions, by distortion and spasms of the capillaries, by a sticky coating of the blood platelets and by a sort of 'marsh' resulting in the dividing interstices between the membranes by waste products being scattered around the cells. Cell life slows down. This is an insidious aspect of ill-health, a condition which may exist long before clinical symptoms appear.

What Bircher is describing in slightly different terms is what

Bjorksten is concerned with when he says that, unless metabolic pathways are kept open, biochemical processes become sluggish and toxic intermediate products are formed in excess to build up to a point where they cause damage. A high-raw diet protects from this happening which is one of the main reasons it can be so useful in ageless ageing. It restores the selective capacity of cells and ensures that nutrients carried through the bloodstream via the capillaries are available for clean and efficient cell use. In fact a substantial intake of raw foods was the only thing that Eppinger and his co-workers found which could do this in people already undergoing the effects of degeneration. Again in Bircher's words, 'Under the influence of a raw vegetable diet the life-giving antagonistic tensions grew and capillaries were slowly restored to their vigorous efficient state. You see how raw vegetable food works. It is an unspecific, general treatment, tending to restore the organizing centre in every cell in the organism.'

Light Quanta and Cell Order?

The discovery of Eppinger that raw foods have regenerative power and an ability to restore order as well as to encourage clean and efficient metabolic processes in organisms which have lost them still can't fully explain precisely how and why this happens. Bircher-Benner said that fresh foods are the *sine qua non* of natural health and healing because they carry to the organism eating them 'complex sunlight energies which have been stored in the vegetable kingdom during its construction of living matter, in the form of light quanta. This means that our blood, our organs, our tissues and our central nervous system are not being nourished by calories alone as was hitherto assumed, but by light quanta—very small but highly charged energy waves which show their rich diversity in the colours of the rainbow.' Because in the 'thirties what Bircher-Benner referred to as 'light quanta' (which he claimed we acquired through the electronic construction of living material) couldn't be measured the way we can measure calories obtained from combustion, his conclusion was not understood by nutritional science which was intent on devising tables of vitamins and on dismissing whatever was not explainable in chemical terms alone. So the famous Swiss physician was accused of 'mysticism' despite the quite exceptional results that application of his theories brought to patients. In fact they still do, at the same Zurich clinic, which bears his name but is now owned by the Swiss government. Yet still much about raw food's healing, organizing and rejuvenating properties remains shrouded in mystery.

Electron Clouds and Changing Shapes

Now, however, thanks to developments in submolecular biology and quantum physics, what once appeared 'mysticism' is beginning to be explainable in terms of scientific theory. The handful of scientists who from one point of view or another have tried to penetrate the mystery of life energy and how it is maintained within a living system—many of them Nobel laureates such as Erwin Schrödinger and Albert Szent-Györgyi—have come up with explanations very close to Bircher-Benner's own. Szent-Györgyi has said, 'An electron going around is a little current. What drives life is . . . a little electric current kept up by sunshine. All the complexities of intermediary metabolism are but lacework around this basic fact.'

What he means is, we know now that while a classic chemical reaction in a living system—called bivalent oxido-reduction (which is what chemistry concerns itself with)—involves a rearrangement of molecular structure, there also exist *monovalent* electron transfers. These are electrons going it alone—which do not necessarily involve such rearrangements. They belong to the world which Becker and scientists working in the field of electrobiology are now beginning to unravel. Bircher-Benner's 'sunlight quanta' which he believed to be the healing force behind the high-raw phenomenon—a force destroyed when foods were heated or processed or when they wilted—also appear to have a place within this world. For currents such as these—single electrons cascading down and giving up their energy piecemeal—as Szent-Györgyi says 'can do anything but cannot be expressed in classical chemical terms. A wandering electron belongs to the changing shapes . . . of those electron clouds which belong to the submolecular, dominated by quantum mechanics.' It is a world about which orthodox nutrition and biochemistry know nothing as yet. And it may be several years before it is charted. But you needn't wait until then to make use of the remarkable age-retarding benefits of high-raw eating. That can begin right now.

TWELVE

Eat for Your Life

If we make Walford's *under*nutrition without *mal*nutrition our goal then how do we go about achieving this orthomolecular state? What kind of foods do we need to eat and what attributes of these foods will be particularly important in forming the foundation on which we can build with anti-oxidant nutrients and other substances that can be useful for ageless ageing? Canadian expert on the orthomolecular approach Abram Hoffer has been treating people with anti-oxidant nutrients for more than a generation. But before he ever gives a patient nutritional supplements he insists that they get themselves into a new way of eating—a way of eating based on four principles:

1. Foods eaten should be whole foods, not fractions of foods which are the result of refining and processing.
2. Foods need to be as fresh as possible and as close to a living state as possible. They should be allowed as little time as possible for deterioration which comes as a result of oxidation. When they are cooked it should be as lightly as possible since cooking increases the carcinogenic properties of foods.
3. All foods should be non-toxic. They should not contain synthetic flavours, colours, preservatives or other additives used to cosmetically 'enhance' the food.
4. The diet should be varied for down through evolution the human body has adapted to a wide range of foods which offer a broad spectrum of nutrients.

Add to Hoffer's list of requirements for a healthy diet one more:

5. The diet must be low in calories. (How low depends on whether you are male or female and how high a level of

strenuous physical activity you have in your life. A top athlete for instance will need more calories than an office worker but for most people the calorie count will hover between 1200 and 1800 calories a day.)

and you have guidelines for an anti-ageing nutritional lifestyle which can't be beat.

Eating for Ageless Ageing

Following these guidelines will automatically provide you with anti-ageing nutrition of the highest order—a way of eating which is low in fat, low in calories, eliminates all chemically processed foods, and it is of necessity low in meat (meat tends to be far too high in fat) and rich in a full complement of essential nutrients. It is a diet rich in the structural information necessary to maintain a high degree of order or negative entropy in your body and therefore to protect it from degeneration. Provided your foods are fresh enough, and from 50 to 75 per cent of them are eaten raw, this way of eating should also carry with it whatever as yet undefined electromagnetic properties—what Bircher-Benner called 'sunlight quanta'—appear to give fresh foods their ability to retard degeneration and promote a high level of health in living systems. Such a nutritional lifestyle has three other attributes which are particularly important for ageless ageing as well: it is low in protein, high in fibre and an excellent source of *usable* essential fatty acids. Let's look more closely at all three and why they are important.

The Longest-Living People

Almost all of the world's cultures studied by scientists such as Sir Robert McCarrison and Weston Price which have had a very low incidence of degenerative illnesses, as well as all of the long-lived cultures—the Hunzas, the Georgians, the Vilcabamba Indians studied by Alexander Leaf—lived on a low-calorie diet. And it was a diet rich in fresh uncooked foods. Considering the effect that such a diet has on promoting healing in an organism and on increasing vitality, it is not far-fetched to assume that it is also likely to be the optimal diet for *us* to use in promoting human longevity. But there is another important characteristic which the diets of long-lived cultures have in common as well: unlike the normal Western way of eating, all of their diets are also *low* in protein. There are strong indications that any diet designed to retard age-degeneration and to prevent degenerative illness should follow a similar pattern. Cultures which have the lowest life expectancy in the world—the Laplanders, Greenlanders and Eskimos (it is only thirty to forty years)—live on diets high in animal protein.

The Dangers of Too Much Protein

So insidious and destructive are the effects of the high-protein diet, and so extensive is the research which demonstrates that excess protein hastens early ageing, that it is difficult to believe the 'lots-of-protein-is-good-for-you' myth still survives. A diet which supplies more protein than your body needs can cause severe deficiencies of many essential vitamins, including vitamin B_6 and niacin. Excess protein also actually leaches important minerals such as calcium, iron, zinc, phosphorus and magnesium from the body. And when your body metabolizes protein, complex by-products are formed, some of which, such as ammonia, can be highly toxic to the system, encouraging free-radical damage and cross-linking, and stressing your body's adaptive energy. Eating more protein than you need creates deposits of these toxic residues in the tissues leading to over-acidity, autotoxaemia, an accumulation of purines, and dysbacteria or dysbiosis of the colon, all of which can contribute to degenerative illnesses—from gum disease to arthritis and atherosclerosis, heart disease, cancer and even schizophrenia. Many animal studies have now shown conclusively that while a high-protein diet brings about early rapid growth, it also results in early and rapid ageing and disease.

Beware of Amyloid

Ralph Bircher and Henning Karstrom—a Swedish scientist well known for his work with nutritional methods of health promotion and healing—both stress the danger of a build-up of amyloid deposits, which occur on a high-protein diet. Amyloid is a fatty-waxy compound which is the result of serious and extensive cross-linkage. Associated with age-degeneration, amyloid builds up in the tissues of people on a very-high-protein diet—particularly one which contains a lot of meat. Professor of physiological pathology at Frankfurt University, Dr P. Schwartz, one of the world experts on amyloid deposits and their implications, refers to it as 'the most important and perhaps decisive cause of decline with age'. Amyloid in the tissues interferes with the transport of nutrients and oxygen between bloodstream and cells and with the elimination of wastes, as well as lowering immune functions. It creates a physiochemical environment which not only stifles proper cell metabolism but can damage genetic material and cell membranes. Its build-up in the body causes tissue and cell degeneration and leads to premature ageing. If you care about preserving the youthful integrity of your body it is certainly something you need to avoid.

How Much Protein Is Enough?

This is a question that can provoke heated argument, even in scientific circles. At the beginning of the century the idea that 'the more protein you eat, the better' developed. Recommendations for health made by Voit and Rubner were for 120–160g a day. Chittenden however showed that high-level health and peak athletic performances could be achieved on less than half that amount. And other studies such as those of Hipsley and Oomen indicate that good health is possible on as little as 15–20g a day. Ralph Bircher, who has studied the question thoroughly for fifty years, places the figure around 50–60g, which he says is probably on the high side and 'allows a good margin for error'. In Britain and the United States, recommendations usually hover somewhere between 60 and 100g a day, but an increasing number of scientists now insist that this is still excessively high. Expert on the relationship between diet and ageing, Dr Myron Winick of the Institute of Human Nutrition at Columbia University School of Medicine says that for maximum protection against ageing and degenerative diseases the 'recommended daily intake for healthy adult men and women of almost any age is 56g and 46g respectively'. And even that recommendation offers a 'high margin of safety'. People on a low-calorie diet—rich in a variety of vegetable foods—however, are likely to need even less protein. For it is not just quantity that matters, but quality. And the quality of protein in a mixed vegetable diet which supplies all eight essential amino acids in easily assimilable form is very high indeed.

The Meat Question

The long-standing notion that you have to eat meat or eggs to get enough protein is simply untrue. As Carl Pfeiffer, co-author of *Total Nutrition*, says, 'There is a general belief that only meat gives us protein and that vegetables could never be the equal. This is quite erroneous. It is a matter of calorie density: a helping of broccoli has a very high protein value in proportion to the calories consumed. There is also the advantage that the calories are in a high-fibre form.' Meat is also very high in fat yet low in fibre and essential nutrients apart from protein. It is virtually impossible to follow an ageless-ageing way of eating and eat much meat. The long-lived peoples of the world have all eaten meat but only occasionally—say once a week—and only in very small quantities. Most people find that as they increase the quantity of fresh raw vegetables and fruits in their diet and eliminate coffee and other stimulants, they no longer have much desire for meat. If you like it, by all means eat it—but not too often and not in large quantities. The best meats are the game meats such as partridge, pheasant, wild duck, venison and so forth. Fish is a good source of essential fatty acids and a good flesh food for health. But it too is a very concentrated source of protein. Enjoy it in smaller quantities. Both meat and fish are low in fibre and high fibre is an important constituent of eating for ageless ageing.

Fibre Power against Degeneration

The importance of the high-raw diet in promoting health and protecting the body from degeneration is right now in the same position that fibre was a decade ago. And, just as it has taken ten or twelve years for the value of fibre for health to be recognized—so is it likely to be with fresh foods. Ten years ago no one but old-maid schoolteachers and a few eccentric scientists concerned themselves with fibre. The rest of the scientific world aggressively dismissed any hint that fibre—bulk or roughage in the diet—could be important in reducing excess weight or protecting the body from illness. Wholegrain bread, they insisted, was no better for you than white bread. Theirs was a sentiment which received strong support from vocal food manufacturers, organizations intent on defending the virtues of white bread and sticky buns. Fibre after all was something unnecessary. It was the part of your food which, unlike the nutrients, was not assimilated into the body. Ten years back if you mentioned 'roughage' in your diet to your GP he dismissed you as yet another annoying 'crank'. In a decade however all of this has changed dramatically thanks to some pioneering scientific research into the relationship between a low-fibre diet and the development of degenerative diseases, as well as lots of popular publicity. Now 'How much fibre do you get in your diet?' is one of the first questions the average GP asks his patient. Meanwhile millions of people are sprinkling extra bran on their breakfast cereals or their baked beans, and most people think they know all about fibre. But do they?

In truth the fibre story is just beginning to reveal its mysteries. Did you know for instance that wheat bran is *not* the perfect form of fibre as some journalists and manufacturers of cereal products would have us believe? That for some people it can be an intestinal irritant and as such is actually constipating rather than laxative? Are you aware that supplementing your diet with high levels of bran can result in anaemia and the loss of several important minerals from your tissues? Did you know that lesser-known kinds of fibre appear to be far more useful for slimmers than bran and also as a help in preventing degenerative illnesses such as cardiovascular disease and diabetes? Or that some recently investigated forms of fibre can lower blood cholesterol and low-density lipoprotein (LDL) levels in the blood? (High LDL levels are associated with coronary heart disease.) At this point the fibre story is far from ended but the latest research into fibre, its importance in health and its usefulness in preventing and treating many abnormal conditions—from diabetes, gall-stones and obesity to intestinal stasis and heart disease—is so exciting it needs to be told.

What Is Fibre?

Dietary fibre is a biological unit not a chemical entity such as a vitamin or mineral. We get it in our diet by eating plant foods—whole grains, beans, seeds and pulses, fresh raw vegetables and fruits. From simple sugars plants make a number of carbohydrate polymers. Some, the starches which serve as energy stores for the plant, are almost completely digested and absorbed in the small intestine when we eat these plant foods. Others, the fibrous or viscous polysaccharides and lignin which lend plants their structure and form, we cannot digest. Instead they pass through to the colon intact where they are fermented to some degree before being eliminated from the body as waste. These indigestible polysaccharides which in the plant make up its cell walls, are known collectively as dietary fibre or fibres. Individually plant fibres have a number of different characteristics and qualities, and the chemical and physical properties of dietary fibre differ greatly from plant to plant. They are also influenced by the age of the plant and the conditions in which it was grown. So far there are at least six known kinds of fibre, which shows up in everything from porridge oats to strawberries. And as yet far too little research has been done to determine the inherent characteristics of each type although what is known is quite fascinating, for the differences in physiological actions of these six classes of fibre can be as varied as those between spring water and gin. Here they are:

Cellulose
This is the most common fibre in bran and is what most people think of when the word is mentioned. It is one of the structural fibres. Its main physiological action when you eat it is to bind

water which is why it increases faecal bulk and is helpful to some people in treating constipation. You'll find cellulose not only in bran but also in fruits and vegetables, wholemeal bread and beans. It even occurs in nuts and seeds. Not only does cellulose prevent colonic stasis, many fibre experts believe that it may also dilute and flush out cancer-causing and degeneration-encouraging toxins from the intestinal tract. It may also help level out glucose in the blood and curb weight gain. On the ageless-ageing regime you will have no need to supplement your diet with extra bran or any other kind of fibre because this way of eating naturally restores the high degree of natural fibre necessary for health which has been lost by the way we have been nourishing ourselves for the past hundred years in industrialized societies.

Hemicellulose
Its name sounds like it should mean 'half-cellulose'. In fact hemicellulose has its own character entirely but it usually occurs together with cellulose in natural foods and it shares some of its characteristics. It also helps relieve constipation, aid weight reduction and chase carcinogens from the bowel.

Pectin
So different in texture and character is pectin from other forms of fibre that it is hard to believe it is classified in the same group of substances. Unlike cellulose and hemicellulose it does not bind water. Instead, it is water-soluble. It has no influence on stools and can do little to deter constipation. However pectin appears to be an excellent substance for lowering cholesterol and may also help eliminate bile acids from the intestines thus shortcircuiting the development of colon cancer and gall-stones. Common sources of pectin are fruits such as apples, oranges and grapefruit, grapes and berries. Even bran contains a bit of pectin. Because of pectin's ability to bind cations and organic materials such as bile acids it is also used as a natural chelating (binding) agent to take up unwanted heavy metals such as aluminium in the system and to eliminate them from the body. This is a very important role in terms of protecting the body from age-degeneration. You may remember that heavy metals are potent cross-linkers and very dangerous to the functioning

of brain and body. That is why if anyone has heavy-metal poisoning pectin is usually given along with vitamin C and other natural substances as a nutritional chelating agent to remove the heavy metals.

Gums and Mucilages

These are the sticky fibres which food manufacturers make good use of as thickening agents in ketchups and making biscuits. They are not components of cell walls in plants as are many forms of fibre. Instead they perform the important task of repairing injured tissue in plants. They are widely used in cosmetics and are currently being investigated as nutritional supplements in an attempt to improve the quality of collagen in the skin and circulatory system. The gums such as locust-bean, karaya gum, guar gum, oat gum and others can lower cholesterol significantly. Guar gum, which is found in good quantity in the cluster bean, has proved itself particularly helpful in the treatment and prevention of diabetes because of its ability to stabilize blood sugar—something of increasing concern as you age.

Lignin

This is the woody fibre which you find in cereals, raspberries, strawberries, Brussels sprouts, cabbage, spinach, kale, parsley and tomatoes. It too is able to eliminate cholesterol and bile acids from the intestines and there is some indication that it may prevent the formation of gall-stones.

Because the ageless-ageing way of eating is high in all types of fibre, and because much of the fibre is uncooked and in its natural state, it offers help against biological degeneration on several different levels at once. It keeps the intestines clean and it helps detoxify the body of heavy metals and poisonous wastes (some of the fibres present in seaweeds and kelps are even able to clear radiation from the system). And eating in this high-raw wholefood way you need never again give a thought to sprinkling flaky bran on to your baked beans.

The Essential Fatty Acids

As important as the fibre which ageless-ageing nutrition offers is the perfect complement of unprocessed and unadulterated essential fatty acids (EFAs) it supplies. For many years lipids or fats were all but ignored by nutrition, for until relatively recently science understood very little about these fascinating chemical substances which, as we get older, our body tends to lose its ability to make proper use of. Fatty acids are the chemical building blocks from which oils and fats are made. They consist of chains of molecules strung together with carbon atoms. Some, such as those present in butter, contain hydrogen on their open links as well as carbon atoms, and are known as saturated fats. Others are called unsaturated. Instead of being connected to hydrogen atoms their chains link back to each other in double bonds. Some of these unsaturated fatty acids, specifically certain polyunsaturates, are absolutely necessary for life and health. They are known as essential fatty acids or EFAs. Science has discovered that there are two distinct families of EFAs which we need since, like most of the vitamins, your body can neither manufacture these EFAs nor can it convert from one to the other. The first family, called the omega n-6 group of acids, includes linoleic acid and its biologically active derivative, gamma linolenic acid—GLA. The second family, called omega n-3, includes the parent alpha linolenic acid and its biologically active derivatives eicosapentaenoic acid—EPA— and docosahexaenoic acid—DHA. These EFAs need to be supplied in small quantity through the foods we eat—primarily via the oils in vegetables and seeds, and from animal foods which contain them, such as fish and game.

EFAs have a number of important functions for ageless ageing and lasting good looks. For instance they are the building blocks of cell membranes and of the intercellular cement. When properly supplied they encourage proper cellular exchange of nutrients and oxygen. From a more cosmetic point of view, they help to ensure that the skin's moisture retention is optimal, thus protecting it both from dehydration and from some of the premature signs of ageing. They also help protect blood from clotting too rapidly and therefore appear helpful in improving one's resistance to heart disease. And EPAs are essential for the production of prostaglandins in the body. These are hormone-like substances (scientists have now delineated the functions of about thirty different prostaglandins) which perform such functions as ensuring the proper function of T-cells in the immune system—important in preventing premature ageing—and keeping skin soft and smooth and hair and nails strong, and helping to prevent susceptibility to heart disease, inflammatory disorders and even depression. Some prostaglandins affect the release of compounds from nerve cells which transmit nerve impulses, still others keep blood platelets from clotting together.

Conversion for Youthful Well-being

In order to make use of both EFA families (which we should take in through the foods we eat) two things are important. First, like the ageless-ageing eating plan, your diet needs to be one which is not rich in *saturated* fats from meats and dairy products nor in fats which have been highly processed—such as most margarines and vegetable oils you can buy on supermarket shelves, not to mention the many processed bakery goods which are full of these hidden highly processed fats. For processed fats can actually block the proper assimilation of EFAs, even when they are present in adequate quantities in the foods you eat. Second, your body needs to be able to convert the EFAs in your diet into their biologically active forms—GLA, EPA and DHA—a conversion which can only take place if there is adequate vitamin C, B_6, B_3, zinc and magnesium in your system. For it is only after these biochemical conversions have been made that your body can make use of the many positive attributes EFAs offer for health, good looks and age-retardation.

EFA Deficiencies Are Widespread

There is considerable evidence that in many people these conversions are not efficiently made or that they are blocked by poor dietary habits so that insufficient quantities of GLA, EPA and DHA are available in the body to prevent degeneration. In other words it appears that many apparently healthy people are deficient in EFAs. The consequences of such a deficiency, as shown by animal experiments, include a number of symptoms, from hair loss, dry scaly skin and poor tissue structure which can make a face lose its firm contours rapidly, to irritability, lethargy, a susceptibility to infections, painful swollen joints and premenstrual tension. In recent years a number of interesting clinical research projects have shown that supplementing the diet of such people with very small quantities of one or both EFA groups can have remarkable results in improving a great variety of conditions from eczema and simple dry skin to menstrual difficulties—simply by giving four to six capsules of 500mg per day of an EFAs preparation which includes the biologically active forms, DLA, GLA and EPA. And many longevists add these supplements to their formulas. Such supplementation is also proving a helpful means of lowering blood cholesterol levels and restoring the right balance of blood lipids in men prone to heart disease and in strengthening the immune system because of the action of the prostaglandins derived from them. GLA—usually given in the form of evening-primrose oil which is probably its richest natural source—has also shown itself to be effective in controlling rheumatoid arthritis in a substantial number of sufferers.

Getting the Most from EFAs

The ageless-ageing way of eating makes sure that you get the most out of what EFAs have to offer for age-retardation. It does this, somewhat paradoxically perhaps, by cutting down your overall level of fat intake from all sources, for you need only the smallest amounts of these important essential fatty acids—it is just that they have to be in a form in which your body can make use of them and free of the conversion problems caused by the presence of trans-fatty acids (the unusable form which occurs in heated and processed oils) in your system which block them. And the ageless-ageing approach eliminates hydrogenated oils in margarines, commercial mayonnaises and highly processed foods such as cakes, breads and biscuits which contain them. This helps prevent conversion problems. It also provides you with a good source of unadulterated EFA from seeds and nuts, grains, and fish (mackerel and other oily fish are particularly high in the biologically active forms of EFA) and also with the co-factors needed for their conversion into prostaglandins and other active metabolites in the body. However, many people who have been living on an average diet for years and have developed conversion problems as a result can gain help, at least at the beginning, from nutritional supplements of these nutrients. But one of the best things about ageless-ageing eating is that for most people the basic changes in food intake itself and the improvement in food quality are enough to restore normal metabolism relatively quickly.

THIRTEEN

Sensuous Austerity

If all this talk about fibre and fat and protein has led you to think
that following an ageless-ageing way of eating means gritting
your teeth and doing what is good for you but expecting to hate
every moment of it, there is good news to come. For the
hedonistic splendour of good ageless-ageing cuisine couldn't be
further away from the heavy stodge you get in some so-called
health-food restaurants. The variety of colours, textures, tastes
and culinary experiences which delicious natural foods offer to
anyone with an interest in food preparation and a love of fine
cuisine at the very least equals the best traditional cooking.
Many of the most beautiful 'nouvelle cuisine' dishes will be
found on the ageless-ageing table. And there is another advantage to the low-calorie-high-raw way of eating as well: thanks to
the effect of eating these fresh foods rich in 'life force' and to the
fact that you are living on far fewer calories than you were used
to before, your taste-buds, sense of smell and aesthetic awareness of food become dramatically heightened so that the
appreciation of all that you eat can be greater than ever before.

This has certainly been my experience and the experience of
many others I know who have tried it. From being someone
who used to love fresh cream and rich sauces I've become
infinitely more appreciative of the fine flavours implicit in
ageless-ageing cuisine. And I love it. Not only because I look
younger, feel better all round and have infinitely more energy
than before, but because the experience of eating itself has
become so much more delightful. Most of us eat far too much
and we dull our senses and our appreciation of food in the
process. Even the most subtle of Beethoven's late quartets begins

to dull the senses when you have too much of it. So can too much food even if it is the very best. Ageless-ageing cuisine revives them.

One Main Meal

Not only do most of us eat too much we also eat too often. And while growing children thrive on three hearty meals a day, most adults do far better on one—preferably eaten at midday but taken in the evening instead if you can't manage it then. Two light meals or wholesome snacks a day to go with your main meal create a way of eating which doesn't tax your body's enzymic systems and keeps you feeling light and clear headed while nourishing you well. There are several good books with recipes which fit nicely into the low-calorie-high-raw way of eating. My favourite is a real treasure-house from the Bircher-Benner clinic itself written by his daughter Ruth Bircher. It is called *Eating Your Way to Health*. It contains hundreds of recipes for main dishes, salads, sweets, breakfasts and suppers which are delightful and simple to prepare. *Raw Energy*, which my daughter Susannah and I wrote, also has a large selection of recipes, and *Raw Energy Recipes* will not only give you some recipes, it is also full of beautiful colour photographs to give you some idea of how splendid these dishes can be. Miriam Polunin's *The New Cookbook* can also be particularly helpful since not only does it boast some delicious and easy-to-prepare recipes, all of them are carefully marked with calorie counts. This can be especially useful in the beginning. After a few months of ageless-ageing eating you will find you no longer have to count calories. You will know from internal signals how much is enough and when you have stepped over the bounds.

Your main meal, like all your meals, should begin with something raw in order to avoid digestive leucocytosis and the immune challenge which it brings. This can be a piece of fruit or a raw salad or some crudités. Follow it with whatever you have chosen for a main dish—perhaps a casserole of pulses or vegetables with a little low-fat cheese atop it or a small piece of fish or game, or even a festive and large salad made from a myriad of vegetables and sprouted grains and seeds topped with chopped hard-boiled eggs. This can be accompanied by a baked potato or some brown rice or couscous or bulgar wheat. There are also some wonderful homemade peasant soups based on fresh vegetables, grains and legumes, which are a meal in themselves and are great taken with a beautiful salad. I make them using Marigold Swiss Vegetable Bouillon Powder as a stock (it is a delicious vegetable product which contains no additives and can be used for seasoning salad dressings, sauces, casseroles and soups). If your main dish has been cooked then have a side salad with it. If not then you might have some mixed vegetables lightly steamed or wok-fried in a small amount of butter or olive oil. There are also some wonderful low-calorie sweets. One of our favourites is 'Raspberry Freeze Fruit Pie' (in *Raw Energy Recipes*) which is made entirely from raw ingredients. Or you can serve some fresh fruit. The varieties of what you can prepare for a main meal are just about endless. Here are a few suggestions for main-meal menus for a week:

Day 1
RAW DISHES: melon; cauliflower and tomatoes mixed with red peppers and lettuce salad topped with yoghurt-herb dressing.
COOKED DISHES: Chinese steamed fish; wok-fried beans and peas; brown rice.

Day 2
RAW DISHES: lamb's lettuce, celeriac and wild-herb salad topped with chopped egg dressing; fresh pears and plumped raisins.
COOKED DISHES: cream of oatmeal soup with cashews; steamed baby carrots and basil; young peas with mint.

Day 3
RAW DISHES: mushrooms, watercress and chicory salad topped with Italian herb dressing; 'Raspberry Freeze Pie'.
COOKED DISHES: 'Luscious' lentil soup; wholegrain bread.

Day 4
RAW DISHES: 'Sunburst' platter of avocado, beetroot, cos lettuce, mushrooms, tomatoes, celery and peppers served with raw houmous dressing.

COOKED DISHES: carrot and coriander soup; Scottish oatcakes; strawberry whip dessert.

Day 5

RAW DISHES: 'Jungle Slaw' salad made from cabbage, tender green beans, carrots, spring onions, red or yellow pepper and raw unsalted peanuts served with citrus dressing.
COOKED DISHES: baked beans; black bread.

Day 6

RAW DISHES: gazpacho; pineapple salad stuffed with orange, mango, papaya and strawberries and topped with coconut.
COOKED DISHES: vegetable tart.

Day 7

RAW DISHES: 'Sandstone Loaf' made from carrots, lemon juice, almonds, pumpkin seeds, tahini and herbs; apple and ginger salad; homemade blackberry sorbet.
COOKED DISHES: bran muffins and almond cheese.

Small Meals

The two small meals of the day can consist of fresh fruit, some natural yoghurt, a slice or two of wholegrain bread spread with some low-calorie herb cheese or—best of all—fruit muesli. If you have never tasted real muesli (and it bears no resemblance to the flaky sweet stuff you can buy on the shelves of supermarkets) you have a real treat ahead of you. Fruit muesli was the invention of Swiss physician Max Bircher-Benner who devised it as the perfect light meal. It is a delicious and easy-to-digest completely uncooked dish which can contain all of the essential vitamins and minerals, and which is an excellent source of high-quality complete proteins and essential fatty acids. It can provide you with sustaining energy but will never lie heavily in your stomach. And it can be made low in calories.

Real muesli (often called Birchermuesli after its inventor) is not a grain-based but a fruit-based dish with only a very small quantity of top-quality fresh wholegrain flakes in it. It is usually made with apples and oats but there are so many varieties which you can make, calling on whatever fresh or dried fruits and whatever kinds of grains, nuts and seeds you have available, that you could quite literally eat it twice a day all the year round and never get tired of it. Children absolutely adore Bircher- muesli both as a complete breakfast and as a sweet after a main meal. A small bowl of muesli in the morning will keep you going all the way to lunch with none of the 'elevenses slump' that has many people reaching for a cup of coffee, and a pastry or a chocolate bar. It is also an excellent food to eat in the evening since it is so easy to digest that it never interferes with sleep. I do a lot of travelling and for many years I dreaded having to stay in hotels because the food available in so many hotel dining-rooms is so poor. I have got into the habit of carrying with me a small 'muesli bag' with a hand grater in it plus some grain flakes and minced nuts and a small bowl so I can make my own breakfast or supper whenever I want and not be forced to eat what I don't want just because there is nothing else. Here is the basic recipe:

Birchermuesli
For each person you'll need:

1 level tablespoon rolled oats soaked in 4 tablespoons water
1 heaped tablespoon raisins or sultanas
1 tablespoon lemon juice
3 tablespoons natural unsweetened yoghurt
1 large apple
½ banana
1 teaspoon raw honey (if desired)
1 tablespoon minced hazelnuts and almonds or other mixed seeds and nuts
1 pinch cinnamon (if desired)

The preparation can be done in the same bowl from which you will eat if you are only making enough for yourself or in a large bowl for the whole family.

Soak the rolled oats and raisins in water, preferably over- night. This begins to break down the starch present in the grains and turn it into natural sugar so it is easily assimilated. If you have no time to soak the grains then simply mix with the water (you will need slightly less water in this case) and carry on immediately.

Wash the apple(s) and remove core and stem but don't peel. Then, using a stainless-steel hand grater or a food processor, grate the apple into the mixture and, stirring, add lemon juice to protect it from discolouring.

Cut the banana into small cubes, add to the mixture with the honey (if desired) and mix with yoghurt. Sprinkle the top with the minced nuts and a little cinnamon if you like.

Instead of rolled oats you can use other cereal flakes such as wheat, rice, barley, millet or buckwheat. These are available from wholefood shops. I find I don't usually add honey to my muesli because it is so beautifully sweet already, thanks to the soaked grains and fruit. You can substitute a good unsulphured black molasses for the honey (it is rich in minerals). The best in Britain is made by Potters, and unlike most which taste medicinal it is delicious. You can also make muesli with soft fruit such as strawberries or raspberries, loganberries, red and black currants, blackberries or blueberries as well as with apricots, cherries, peaches, plums or greengages. Or you can mix your fruits together. Also you can make the muesli from dried fruit which has been soaked for twelve hours or overnight in spring water. But make sure you get sun-dried not sulphur-dried fruits to which no glucose has been added (it is commonly added to figs for instance) or you can end up with a gastro-intestinal upset.

Seasoning and Spices

Salt is unnecessary when you begin to prepare foods with all of the wonderful culinary herbs that are available. And the list of seductive possibilities seems almost endless: caraway, fennel, dill, chervil, parsley, lovage—the Umbelliferae; summer savory, marjoram, the mints, rosemary, and thyme—the labiates, which have a strong aroma and are particularly useful for seasoning; the Liliaceae such as garlic, onions, chives and leeks; and three of my favourites—basil and tarragon and horseradish. Herbs have a special role to play in any ageless-ageing regime. They contain pharmacologically active substances such as volatile oils, tannins, bitter factors, secretins, balsams, resins, mucilages, glycosides and organic vegetable acids each of which can contribute to overall health in a different way. The tannins, for instance, which occur in many common kitchen herbs, are astringent and have an anti-inflammatory action on the digestive system. They help inhibit fermentation and decomposition. The secretins stimulate the secretion of pancreatic enzymes—particularly important for the complete breakdown of proteins in foods to make them available for bodily use. Organic acids have an antibiotic action and are helpful in the digestion of fats and the bitter factors which are found in good quantity in rosemary, marjoram and fennel. They also act as a tonic to the smooth muscles of the gut and boost secretion of digestive enzymes. Use herbs lavishly in your meals and you will find you can create the most remarkable combinations of subtle flavours and aromas.

Drink Yourself Younger

Coffee, although not completely forbidden on any serious programme of ageless ageing, is not something to drink daily. The occasional cup after dinner is not likely to do much harm. More than that and you are really undermining your potential for age-retardation not only because it contains mutagenic and carcinogenic compounds which cause oxy-stress and free-radical damage but also because regular coffee tends to make cadmium (one of the heavy metals) build up in your system and can interfere with proper pancreatic functioning. Tea is OK in moderation—no more than a cup a day—but there are other drinks which are not only good for you, they can be highly enjoyable as well.

Alcohol is another substance you want to go easy on. Not only is it very high in calories yet practically worthless in terms of the nutrients it supplies, it also causes your liver to produce one of the most potent cross-linkers known—acetaldehyde. A glass or two of wine can be easily accommodated within the low-calorie limits. More than that as a daily intake is likely to seriously undermine your effort. And make sure it is good wine. The run of the mill *vin de table* is full of toxic substances which your cells can do without.

You'll find some delicious mixtures of herbs in ready-made tea bags if you comb through a few delicatessens and health-food stores. Some of my favourites have names like Cinnamon

Rose, Almond Sunset and Red Zinger. They are great to drink for pleasure and refreshment—the way most people drink coffee and ordinary tea. But there are others which are quite wonderful simply because they affect the body in specific ways. Lemon verbena, for instance, is a refreshing sedative, chamomile soothes the digestive tract, and both horsetail and solidago (goldenrod) are excellent natural diuretics. The teas I like best just before bed are orange blossom, which you make by boiling a few blossoms for 2–3 minutes in two cups of water, red bergamot and lemon peel, all of which are natural sedatives. This last tea comes from an Italian tradition. You make it by peeling the outer yellow skin off a lemon (which has been washed well) with a potato peeler. Pour boiling water over this and let steep for 5 minutes. Then strain and drink.

Make Way for a New Lifestyle

Eating for ageless ageing leads most people to a totally new way of living. You become more alert and more active. You will probably sleep less yet far better than before. This is because your whole system will be far clearer of toxicity than before and you will need less time for tissue repair and restoration than you do on a normal diet. You will also probably find that you are better able to deal with stress than ever. The low-calorie-high-raw way of eating provides you with high levels of potassium and rapidly restores the sodium-potassium balance in most people. This leads to increased resistance to fatigue and a greater feeling of calm stability day in day out. It may also set you slightly apart from your gravy-eating, hard-drinking friends and may even have them feeling slightly suspicious of you in the beginning. But it has been my experience that as soon as they find you are not trying to sell them anything—that you have a live and let live attitude to whatever they do—they show a similar respect for your new lifestyle. In fact, the people who have been the most resistant to what you are doing and the most opinionated are very often the ones who are first to become intrigued about what an ageless-ageing lifestyle might offer them. And they are usually the ones with the energy and interest to carry it out.

FOURTEEN

The Fast Way to Rejuvenescence

Few things seem as strange to the average person as the notion of going without food for several days. Just mention the idea in a group of people and wait for the reactions: 'But my dear, it's so dangerous! Don't be ridiculous, no one can fast for more than a few hours: I remember the day I skipped lunch and I felt terrible'; or 'I could never find the will-power.' In fact, almost all of the popular notions about fasting are untrue. Having personally followed more than three dozen fasts of varying lengths from one day to as long as three weeks, and having read everything I could lay my hands on about the subject over the past twenty years, I know first-hand that fasting can be one of the most rewarding experiences most people can have. There is also a mass of evidence from animal studies that regular short fasts—fasts of a day or two at a time—can slow ageing and prolong life. Periodic and controlled fasting is a superb way of detoxifying your body of cross-linkers and of reducing oxy-stress. And from an aesthetic point of view, such fasts can make you look great. They smooth out fine lines on your skin, make your eyes crystal clear and leave your face glowing with colour. Used wisely, fasting can be a highly successful technique for ageless ageing.

What is Fasting?

The word is used to describe total or partial abstinence from food for any one of a variety of reasons. There are religious fasts: Jesus went into the desert where he fasted for forty days to purify his body and prepare it to receive the Holy Spirit. In nature you find physiological fasts such as the hibernation or seasonal abstinence of specific animals or people when they feel they just can't eat. Some people fast to lose weight of course (by no means the best use of fasting, however) and then there are therapeutic fasts for the purpose of restoring and maintaining optimal health. None of these reasons for fasting are new. All of them have been practised since the beginnings of history. Pythagoras fasted for forty days before sitting his exams and then insisted that his students fast also before they could be taught by him. Ancient Egyptians used fasting as a tool for treating syphilis, and Hippocrates prescribed fasting for his patients during critical periods of illness. In the sixteenth century the famous Swiss physician Paracelsus insisted that 'Of all the remedies available, fasting is the greatest one.'

In the past century many thousands of therapeutic fasts have been conducted and recorded at such centres as Otto Buchinger's Bad Pyrmont in Germany. As a result a vast quantity of information has been collected about fasting, in Europe and America after the turn of the century, and more recently in Russia where Soviet scientists have found it to be a useful method for healing mental symptoms. Yet the orthodox medical profession remains largely ignorant of the value of fasting both for health and age-retardation. Meanwhile the average man in the street continues to regard with awe somebody who goes without food for even a day. So there are a lot of unanswered questions: Just what can fasting do? Why should anyone consider it as part of a lifestyle for ageless ageing? How safe is it? What are the pitfalls and how do you avoid them? Let's investigate the remarkable benefits of fasting as an anti-ageing tool. First let's look at the regenerative effects fasts have been shown to have on animals and humans. Then we'll explore what happens on a long fast—a fast of more than two or three days—which is something that on no account should be done except under medical supervision, preferably in a clinic atmosphere. Finally we'll examine short fasts of a few days and how for healthy people they can form an exciting and enjoyable (yes, *enjoyable*—most people who look on fasting with distaste have never experienced its physical benefits and the heightened state of mental and emotional clarity it can bring) vacation from the kind of habitual eating most of us find ourselves doing.

Rejuvenescence Starts Here

Rejuvenescence is an old-fashioned word which means 'the acquiring of fresh vitality and the renewal of youthful characteristics in the cells and tissues of the body'. It is a word which was used frequently early on in the twentieth century by clinicians and researchers investigating and making use of fasting as a natural technique for healing and for enhancing health. Like fasting itself, in the face of allopathic medicine, the word has rather fallen from use. But it is an excellent word to describe the remarkably revitalizing effect of going without food for periods of a few days (which most people can safely carry out at home on their own provided of course that their doctor approves) and several weeks—something that should under no circumstances be done unless you are in a controlled environment under medical supervision. If you want to look in depth at the physiological effects of fasting you have to look back to the time in which it was seriously studied.

The Invincible Worm

In the first decade or two of the twentieth century C. M. Child at the University of Chicago carried out lengthy studies of the effect of fasting on animal life. He took a group of flatworms which had become old and infirm and fasted them for months until they were reduced greatly in size. When he began to feed them again and they re-grew to normal size he found they were functioning as young animals again. Similar studies were carried out on earthworms by a British researcher about the same time. He fed these creatures their usual foods but one of the worms he isolated from the rest and fasted at periodic intervals. In every other way the life and diet of all the worms were the same. This isolated worm lived on while nineteen generations of worms in the colony lived and died. In 1915 Child published a book called *Senescence and Rejuvenescence* in which he describes the effect of fasting on lower forms of life. He says, 'Partial starvation inhibits senescence. The starveling is brought back from an advanced age to the beginning of post-embryonic life; it is almost reborn.'

Interesting though these results are, they were performed on very low forms of life—forms of life which, unlike human beings and other mammals, have an ability for regeneration lacking in more complex organisms. However a number of studies have also been done on mammals which also highlight the relationship between fasting and age-retardation. For instance, scientists at the Gerontology Research Center in Baltimore, Maryland, discovered that when rats are fed every other day they live sixty-three weeks longer than those allowed to eat all they want. They also remain more active later in life than their well-fed cage mates. Rejuvenescence effects have been often reported by people who have fasted and by fasting researchers. When researcher A. J. Carlson at the University of Chicago fasted a forty-year-old man for fourteen days he reported that at the end of the fast his tissues were physiologically in a similar condition to those of a seventeen-year-old. When Gandhi, an enthusiastic periodic faster, was examined in May of 1933 on the tenth day of a fast his physicians reported that 'despite his sixty-four years, from a physiological point of view the Indian leader was as healthy as a man of forty'. Otto Buchinger, who is generally considered *the* European expert on fasting, has conducted thousands of fasts in the treatment of many age-related diseases and has demonstrated that fasting can be an effective technique for healing—from high blood pressure and arthritis to rheumatism, early diabetes, angina, early arteriosclerosis, vascular ailments, menopausal symptoms, allergies and nerve disorders, to mention only a few.

Nature's Wrinkle-Banisher

The aesthetic benefits of fasting as an improver of good looks and a rejuvenator of skin are well known. That is why, often in modified form such as a juice fast, fasting is the cornerstone of treatment at most of the famous spas in Europe where people spend a fortnight and return home afterwards quite literally looking ten years younger. Lines and wrinkles on the face become softened even after a fast of a few days, and blotches, pimples and discolorations disappear. Skin texture and colour also improve and eyes become bright and clear. The elimination of wastes and toxic substances from the body which a fast brings about clears the skin and the eyes and can give the flesh a new softness which our polluted atmosphere and poor eating habits take out. It also helps restore elasticity to the muscles. People who hadn't seen me during my first fast were amazed at how it had changed me physically. Not knowing that I had been fasting, they came up with some rather amusing hypotheses to explain the improvement. The most common was that I must have fallen in love. (That, alas, is one of the things which fasting *cannot* do for you.)

Changes from the Word Go

Drastic changes take place in your body right from the first missed meal. Almost immediately wastes stored in your tissues are thrown off—sometimes at an incredible rate. This can lead (and usually does) to a coating of the tongue and teeth with an unpleasant tasting stuff and in some people even to a headache or a feeling of being unwell which lasts for from a few hours to a day. For this reason fasting experts generally insist that their patients follow a special diet composed of raw fruits, juices and vegetables for a day or two before beginning a medically supervised long fast, to start clearing the system somewhat and avoid too drastic an elimination of waste products all at once. Twelve hours after you begin your fast your body starts to use whatever glucose it has stored in the liver. This supply lasts less than a day. Then body chemistry begins to change. Abstinence from food forces the body to produce and circulate ketone bodies—normal products of fat metabolism which can be oxidized to produce energy. Elevated levels of ketones occur since fat in the body is being rapidly metabolized. There are two points during an extended fast during which acetone excreted through the urine and the skin reaches a peak—usually on the fourth and fifth day and then again on the ninth or tenth. This gives some fasters a scent of acetone on the surface of the skin and can make your system very acidic, which is why many experts in fasting insist that it is better to fast on fresh vegetable and fresh (non-citrus) fruit juices whose alkalinity can balance any excess acidity.

American researchers have found that your body adjusts itself to the fasting state by utilizing these ketones as fuel for brain and nerve cells. A mild state of ketosis on a fast is fine. If it becomes too severe it can be damaging, particularly if the patient already suffers from kidney or heart trouble or is pregnant. But in these conditions fasting is not advisable anyway. Fasting also tends to lower blood pressure, which is useful in the treatment of hypertensive patients. From the beginning of a fast there is also often a slight increase in temperature which lasts only a few days and which most fasting experts attribute to the rapid burning of stored toxins. Sometimes on about the thirteenth day the level of ketones in the blood serum rises drastically to as much as ten times above the previous level, while alkali reserves fall, and temporary disturbances can take place in the fat, cholesterol, sugar and diastase levels in the blood. Often on these days the faster feels slightly unwell. Doctors working with fasting have termed these periods the 'crisis of acidity'. They stress that it is a natural occurrence in the fast, nothing more than symptoms of the body's readjustment. These symptoms disappear quickly and don't occur again throughout the rest of the fast, but they can be a cause of great concern to the uninformed and only serve to underline the necessity for careful medical supervision on a long fast.

Cleansing the Depths

The healing, rejuvenating and regenerating effects of a fast come from its ability to eliminate toxic waste products from the body—sometimes wastes which have been stored in the cells and tissues for almost a lifetime. For a long time critics of fasting insisted that these wastes were the invention of overactive minds and that they didn't really exist. Now laboratory tests are even able to measure the fact that things such as xanthoprotein and indican are eliminated rapidly during a fast. Wastes which accumulate as a result of the build-up of metabolic by-products and from exposure to environmental pollution from foods and water, as well as from excess stress, are prime movers both in lowering vitality and in the development of degenerative diseases and ageing because they cause auto-intoxication of the system. Most of the metabolic toxins which play a decisive role in the origin of disease and premature ageing come from protein metabolism although carbohydrate metabolism also produces some, such as pyruvic acid and a form of lactic acid, as does fat metabolism.

An organism can only stay healthy and youthful so long as it is able efficiently to detoxify itself of its metabolic intermediary products, waste products or 'autotoxins' as they are sometimes called. On an extended fast the material which is burnt first from the body for energy comes from superfluous fat and un-wanted matter. Some experts in fasting believe that one of the reasons it is so useful in retarding the rate at which the body ages is that it may be able to break down and use as fuel cross-linked proteins which make it possible then for your body to build new collagen and new cells. Fasting may well be nature's own tool for breaking down and clearing out morbid cross-linked pro-teins—something which gerontologists such as Bjorksten and others have been searching for years to find a chemical way of doing.

The Fast High

The experience of fasting is a highly subjective one. Many fasters claim that their concentration is improved and that they are better able to carry out creative tasks like painting or writing. (I will often do a fast of a week or two before beginning to work on a book.) Naturally fasters lose weight. How much varies tremendously. Weight loss is greater in people who are most overweight. It usually varies between 4½lb to as much as 10lb a week. The average is about 7lb. You lose weight more rapidly at the beginning of a fast.

Most fasters sleep less than usual and feel better for it. Although this is usually not true of patients who previously suffered from insomnia. They often sleep more—sometimes as much as eighteen hours a day in the beginning. A few people, particularly those who have been chronically ill, experience a feeling of weakness and tiredness and seem to need a lot of time simply to lie around and do nothing. However there are also many cases recorded where just the opposite is true. Once-famous heavyweight fighter Harry Wills always used fasts during his training period before a big fight because he claimed they gave him strength, and both American and Swedish athletes have been known to carry out long walks—of two weeks or more—while fasting. Experts on fasting say that usually patients who are weaker at the beginning of the fast will tend to gain strength rapidly from the beginning of the period of abstinence. Sexual desire is usually reduced during a fast although in some instances people have reported an increase in sexual activity. In any case it returns almost immediately after the fast is broken—often with renewed vigour.

Keep Moving

Fasting for more than a day or two tends to lower your metabolic rate so that you can begin to feel rather sluggish and lazy. It is important that you don't let this happen, by making sure you get plenty of exercise such as long walks in the open air. I often use a bouncer—one of those mini-trampolines which you can tuck behind the sofa in the sitting-room when you are not using it—when I am fasting. Bouncing, or rebounding as it is sometimes called, is a pleasurable way of exercising either gently or hard. (I like watching films on a video or listening to music while I am exercising.) This kind of exercise encourages good lymphatic drainage and as such helps to get rid of the sludge that your body is burning up in its tissues and then to eliminate it. Long fasts also tend to lower body temperature. You will need to wear warmer clothing than you ordinarily would while on a fast.

Many uninformed people worry a lot about vitamin and mineral losses on a fast. While it is true that vitamins and mineral stores do get drawn on during a fast almost all physicians with much experience in fasting are quick to reassure you that it is nothing to worry about in a healthy person, for any loss is quickly replenished when you start eating again. In fact the fasting organism is exceptionally efficient. You use less of everything when you abstain from foods.

Fasting and Mental Health

American physician and fasting expert Alan Cott believes, as do most doctors with a long experience of fasting their patients, that a long fast can be a powerful force for restoring mental health. He has fasted about 300 chronically ill schizophrenics—the kind of people who tend to end up in the back wards of mental hospitals—and found that after twenty-five and thirty-two days without food about 65 per cent of them improved enough to leave hospital and return to life with some degree of being able to function in society. Of these people the ones who after their fast stayed on a well-balanced vegetarian diet were least likely to experience any relapse. At the University of Athens, scientists have recently discovered that fasting blocks the brain's uptake of the neurotransmitter dopamine. This may be one of the reasons why it can be useful in the treatment of mental illness, for many medications given to control schizophrenia do the same thing.

British and Russian scientists have found that fasting raises the level of serotonin—another neurotransmitter which is important in bringing relaxation to the body and mind and in harmonizing mood. Russian scientists such as Yuri Nikolayev have also had considerable success in rehabilitating mental patients. Cott quotes Nikolayev, who believes that fasting 'purifies every cell in the body. I am sure that 99 per cent of sick people suffer because of improper nourishment. People simply do not understand that they litter their bodies with many unnatural foods and . . . because of this . . . poisonous substances are collected in the body. If you are interested in being in good mental and physical health and in increasing your vitality, start to work today *with* nature, not against her.' Nikolayev believes, as does Cott, that fasting helps the body mobilize itself against many ills. And also that when you temporarily stop putting food into the body it gives it a chance to catch up with elimination, forcing it to draw off stored toxins from the tissues and then to excrete them. Finally, he believes that the practice biochemically rebalances the whole system. Both the elimination of toxic wastes and this rebalancing act are probably responsible for the way fasting brings a sense of being uplifted emotionally and very clear mentally.

Crystal Consciousness

The first time I fasted (about fifteen years ago), I did a three-week fast under the guidance of a doctor friend. I was going through a particularly difficult period of my life where there were serious decisions to be made and I felt somehow I didn't have the clarity to make them. My friend suggested that if I fasted for several days it might clear my mind so that I would be able to know better how I really felt. When I began the fast I had no idea how long it would last. The first three days passed quickly with the occasional pang of hunger, which I ignored. In fact, they were not hunger pangs at all, I learned later, but appetite demands, for when you are used to eating all the time (I have a real passion for food and have always tended to use it for comfort as much as for nourishment) and suddenly there is no food to be had, you feel hungry. But after the first three days this 'hunger' passed and never returned again during the whole length of the fast—much to my amazement. I felt well physically and I had lots of strength. However I found I needed to exercise every day or I tended to become sluggish, so I took long walks in the country. As the fast continued I found I felt more clear mentally and more emotionally centred—in fact more balanced than I had ever before in my whole life. I would awaken in the morning feeling full of joy. The world looked beautiful to me in a calm and quiet way. All the creatures I saw, from the spider on my bedroom window to the neighbour's dog, seemed marvellous, the way a coloured picture book looks to you when you are still six years old.

During the three weeks I was fasting I was working (something most fasting experts advise you not to do) but I tried to spend as much time as I could alone. My friend, the doctor, advised me not to allow myself to be with any people with whom I didn't feel at ease. 'If anyone tries to lay his problems on you,' he said, 'politely excuse yourself by saying you are fasting and can't be disturbed, and get away from him.' I did. A few acquaintances were offended at my insistence that I remain calm and not get involved in their troubles, but my real friends understood and encouraged me. They noticed that each day my skin became smoother and my complexion brighter, and my eyes clearer, and were almost as pleased about the changes as I was. Two of them even began fasts themselves after seeing what mine had done for me.

But no matter how pleasing the physical effects of my first fast, what were most important of all to me were its phychological ones. My head became clearer and clearer. After the first few days my vision was so sharpened it was as if I was looking at the world through a crystal glass. It is difficult to describe the changes that took place in my thinking and my emotions during the fast. I can only say that the world looked different. I realized that there was so much beauty around me which I ordinarily miss in my hurry from one task to another. Fasting made me stop and think, stop and feel. I found delight in the simplest of things—just sitting under a tree, or washing vegetables, or combing my hair. Everything seemed important. I felt I wanted to do everything with awareness. I also gained a sense of distance from my own problems which enabled me to make the decisions facing me calmly and quietly. As a result, since then, whenever I feel myself hung up over something or whenever I feel I am not seeing things clearly I will often quietly fast for a day or a few days until I feel clear again. To some people this may seem an eccentricity, but not, I suspect, to anyone who has actually tried fasting.

It Is the End that Matters

Something that almost nobody understands—except doctors proficient in fasting their patients, and people who themselves have undergone long fasts—is that the way a fast is broken is as important as the fast itself in bringing about lasting benefits. When you go without food for a week or even a few weeks, your digestive system has a complete rest. One of the results of this is that digestive secretions slow down and eventually stop altogether. Also your body becomes highly sensitive to whatever you put in it. With what and with how much food you break your fast matters a lot. Break it sensibly on small quantities of raw food and you will find that a week or two later you will continue to feel as well and as clear as you did during your period of abstinence but even stronger. Break it carelessly by eating too much or the wrong kind of thing and you can throw your organism into complete chaos—a chaos which can result in mental and emotional confusion, fatigue, and even serious illness.

Most experts believe that the best way to break a long fast—on which you have had nothing but water—is by eating a couple of apples throughout the morning and then taking a glass of fresh vegetable juice or wholesome homemade vegetable soup which contains no flour. Then the next day you can begin the 'build-up' programme which takes you back to normal eating *gradually* over a period of about a week: prunes or figs soaked overnight in water for breakfast, a fresh raw salad with a little yoghurt dressing for lunch and some fresh fruit with, perhaps, a piece of crispbread or a sugarless oatcake spread with about a third of an ounce of butter. On about the fourth or fifth day after breaking a fast you can have Birchermuesli for breakfast, and soup and salad for lunch and dinner, and by the end of the week you can eat your first fish or meat if you want them. This slow transition back to normal eating is absolutely essential in fasting. In fact, control over the breaking of a fast is one of two essential reasons why fasting for more than a few days at a time must be done under medical supervision. The other reason is that fasting, although a perfectly healthy and beneficial practice when carried out by the rules, is also quite an extraordinary state. It is *not* a game. And, until you are absolutely sure of how it works and have yourself experienced a number of fasts of different lengths, you need the support of a doctor or a trained professional who can guide you and reassure you. This is particularly important in the face of the kind of well-meaning but really very destructive 'advice' you tend to get from people who have never fasted and generally know nothing about it. Comments like, 'You mustn't fast—it weakens the heart and you could have a heart attack' or even, 'Oh you poor darling, you must be *starving*, do have just a little something with us' can be very detrimental to the inexperienced faster. The friendly medical practitioner who monitors your progress and reassures you that all is well helps counteract all this beautifully.

It is also important that while fasting your state of mind is a positive one and that you are at peace. A genuine willingness to fast and an optimistic attitude towards it are essential for therapeutic fasting. As Otto Buchinger, a European physician who is considered a world expert on fasting, says:

> The mental attitude of the patient is of fundamental importance in the direction of the metabolic processes of the whole body. (This is the reason why it is necessary to explain to the patient the nature of the cure before it is undertaken and to guide him psychically during the cure.) Hunger brings about an inward position of coercion and protest. This in turn leads, via the central nervous system, to a dysfunction of the capillary circulation as well as to disturbances of the organs.

Do-It-Yourself Fasting

For many people a long fast—a fast of between one and three weeks—carried out once a year (preferably in spring when the earth's regenerative powers are rising strongly) can be an excellent way of periodically eliminating any stored wastes, regenerating new tissue, clearing your mind, balancing emotions and making you look five or ten years younger very quickly. But it must be done either at a spa or clinic where fasting is well understood and regularly carried out, or under the wise care of a physician oriented towards natural methods of healing and age-retardation. Although fasters claim that complications are rare, if they do occur, they need to be dealt with professionally. Fasts of from one to three days are different. The general medical consensus (which includes the opinions of a great volume of doctors for whom the very idea of fasting is anathema) is that, so long as you are in good health, this kind of short-term self-chosen abstinence can only do you good (particularly in our overly indulgent world) provided you go about it in the right way and provided your doctor approves.

If you can, prepare for your fast by eating only raw fruits and vegetables the day before you begin. Then spend from one to three days on fresh spring (not tap) water. Drink herbal teas if you like but adamantly no tea or coffee. Be sure to get plenty of rest. Fasting is an ideal time to spend most of the day in bed with a good book every once in a while but make sure you also get whatever exercise is normal for you during your abstinence. If you get any symptoms such as a headache from going without food for a day or two this is a sign that your body is rapidly detoxifying itself. Rest if you can until it passes—for it usually does within a few hours. Your tongue can also be coated with white or yellow fur. This too is a sign of rapid elimination. After a few weeks of eating in a high-potency-low-calorie way you will find soon that you no longer get any symptoms at all except a kind of 'lightening' of mind and body and perhaps increased energy during the days of your fast.

Return to your everyday eating habits slowly. Your body needs time to readjust. Some longevists fast for a day or two a week all year round to decrease the number of calories they take in, to give their system a rest from food and having to deal with it, to eliminate wastes built up and to clear their minds. It is something which I have tried for periods and I must admit I thrive on it. While everybody else is making noises about how much will-power you must have to do this every week, you keep trying to tell them the truth and they never believe you: there isn't much will-power needed. The sense of reward which comes with regular fasts such as this and the uplift they bring far exceed any qualm about giving up a meal or two. Fasting like this can also make you so much more aware of the delicious textures, tastes and colours of food when you resume eating. For me, however, a short fast will never replace the quite exceptional pleasure of a longer fasting 'cure'. It is something that, having discovered its benefits more than fifteen years ago, I think I will never want to be without doing once a year. But whether you choose a short fast on your own or a long fast under supervision, one thing is sure: any technique as powerful as fasting needs to be treated with the utmost respect and never entered into lightly.

FIFTEEN

Spring-Cleaning for Youth

No matter how sparse and how good your diet or how many anti-oxidants you take, no matter how conscientiously you deal with stress and how enthusiastically you exercise—all of which are central to ageless ageing—it can be helpful periodically to spring-clean your body from within. Controlled fasts are not the only way of doing this. The *natural-law* approach to age-retardation and the long tradition on which it is based also offer a number of other simple methods. Some—such as a spring-clean semi-fast or the sauna—are helpful when used every few weeks, while others, such as techniques for improving lymphatic drainage, can be used to advantage every few days or even more often. The whole purpose of spring-cleaning is to stimulate your body's eliminative capabilities so that any sluggishness in the blood and lymph circulation and any stasis in the tissues is cleared away. Then whatever toxicity may be present—heavy metals and cross-linkers for instance—can be broken down and eliminated via the skin and lungs, bladder and colon before it can cause degenerative damage and premature ageing to your body.

Toxicity and Ageing

As we've seen, apart from inadequate nutrition, the primary cause of premature ageing—and all the fatigue, cell damage and disease which accompany it—is a build-up of waste products which are toxic to the system. They result in poor circulation to and from the cells and in a stagnation of cellular fluids. A continuous interchange takes place between your body's trillions of cells and their surrounding interstitial fluids. This is where nutrients and oxygen are exchanged for waste products from the cells. Wastes are then picked up by minute lymphatic tubules or ducts and sent through the lymph vessels to be detoxified. It is an exchange regulated by subtle electrochemical processes. Living cells will only thrive when both nutrients and oxygen are well supplied and toxic wastes are concurrently removed and eliminated from the body. The methods for encouraging this are extraordinarily simple yet their effects can be remarkably profound. Many are also immediately experienced in terms of improved good looks and vitality and a new-found sense of calm well-being. Let's look at the Long Weekend Spring-Clean Diet to start with.

Long Weekend Spring-Clean

This is a method I like to use when for one reason or another (such as after Christmas celebrations or living in hotels) I have not been able to eat the same kind of foods I do at home, or when I am feeling tired and need a lift. It takes three days to carry out. Ideally you should eat all raw foods the day before you begin but this is not always possible. It is an ideal way to regenerate yourself over a long quiet weekend.

On rising, or at 9am, each day you begin with a cup of herb tea—not too hot. You can sweeten it with a little honey if you like.

Day 1
9am   Herb tea
11am   8oz fresh fruit (not citrus) or vegetable juice
1pm   1 cup potassium broth
4pm   Herb tea
7pm   8oz fresh fruit (not citrus) or vegetable juice
9pm   1 cup potassium broth

Day 2
9am   Herb tea plus half an apple—be sure to chew it thoroughly
11am   Fresh fruit or vegetable juice

1pm   Cup of potassium broth
4pm   Herb tea
7pm   Cup of potassium broth
9pm   Fresh fruit or vegetable juice

Day 3
9am   A dish of prunes which have been soaked overnight in
      water
11am Fresh fruit or vegetable juice
1pm   Salad of fresh raw vegetables with a little yoghurt dressing
4pm   An apple
7pm   Fresh fruit or vegetable juice
9pm   Cup of potassium broth

During the Weekend Spring-Clean you can drink as much spring water as you like. It is important that you take a brisk walk in the open air for at least half an hour each day. You can continue to work if you like but it is especially pleasant to carry out over a long weekend when you have time to yourself. You must not smoke, or drink alcohol, tea or coffee. Herb teas are available from health-food stores. So is potassium broth which is made from fresh vegetables and herbs and contains no additives. It comes in little cubes over which you pour boiling water or in a powder form which I prefer. The best I have found is called Marigold Swiss Vegetable Bouillon. You can make your own fresh vegetable or fruit and vegetable juices (half an apple and half a carrot is a particularly delicious and effective combination to use) provided you have a centrifuge juice extractor. Otherwise look for those processed by low heat to preserve their natural enzymes and nutrients. They too are available in health-food stores. Aspall Apple Juice is excellent, as are the Biotta juices from Germany. Daily baths are a must during the Long Weekend regime and you will probably find you need to brush your teeth more often than usual since your body will be rapidly eliminating wastes and both teeth and tongue can become coated when this occurs. Skin brushing is excellent for hastening the eliminative processes. Do exercise regularly. Do not take a sauna during the Long Weekend Spring-Clean however. On the fourth day simply return to your normal high-potency-low-calorie way of eating with particular emphasis on raw foods for a day or two.

Skin-Brushing Works Wonders

Skin-brushing is an old and well-proven European technique for getting rid of toxic wastes from the body, both because it stimulates lymphatic drainage and because it increases the quantity of waste which is eliminated directly through the surface of the skin (a staggering one third of our wastes can be eliminated this way). I first learned the technique more than fifteen years ago. It was taught to me by a West Country physician named Phillip Kilsby who used it in conjunction with a high-raw diet as part of a programme for healing many kinds of illness—from migraine and arthritis to high blood pressure and depression. When he first told me how effective it was in eliminating wastes and toxins from the body I did not believe him. He suggested a little experiment by which I could prove to myself just how effective it was at eliminating rubbish through the surface of the skin. He said, 'Take a washcloth or flannel and wet it then wring it out well. Now brush your skin dry using the directions below. When you have finished rub the flannel over the surface you have brushed—all over just once. Then hang the flannel up and don't use it again until tomorrow when you perform exactly the same routine. After three or four days smell the flannel.' That was all the proof I needed!

You can either use skin-brushing on its own or together with the Weekend Spring-Clean. I use it regularly, year round, several times a week. Many of the natural techniques for detoxifying the body are more effective if your body is not allowed to become accustomed to them by doing them every day. Skin brushing, for instance, can be done steadily for three weeks with a week's break before resuming it again. After even a week of skin-brushing you will also notice an improvement in the look and feel of your skin. After a few weeks it even seems to improve muscle tone although I have never been able to figure out why this should happen.

Here's How
You will need a natural vegetable-bristle brush (the long-

handled kind is best) but a hemp glove will also do. Such brushes and gloves can be found in most health-food shops or good chemists.

The brush should be kept dry. It is best to brush first thing in the morning before you shower. Brush the entire skin surface, except for your face. Begin with your feet, including the soles, then move up your legs, front and back, with firm sweeping strokes. Brush from your hands up your arms and across your shoulders, then brush your back and buttocks. On your front, brush a little more gently—your neck, chest and abdomen. In the abdominal area use a clockwise circular motion. To begin with brush fairly gently, increasing the firmness of the strokes as your body becomes more accustomed to it.

After brushing take a shower. If you are brave you can alternate with warm and cold water (always beginning with warm and ending with cold)—this is an excellent way of getting the circulation going and speeding up elimination.

Stimulating Lymphatic Drainage

Skin-brushing is not only effective as a *natural-law* tool for detoxification because it stimulates the release of wastes through your skin's surface. It also encourages better lymphatic drainage—something which is vitally important to (as Bjorksten says) making sure metabolic processes run *cleanly* and *efficiently*. Your body's lymph system is, amongst other things, a kind of metabolic rubbish dump. It helps the body rid itself of dead cells, toxins, metabolic wastes, pathogenic bacteria, foreign substances and other assorted junk the cells cast off. Unlike the circulatory system, in which the circulation of blood is controlled by the pumping of the heart, the lymphatic system has no such pump. The plasma which has seeped through capillary walls gathers in the tissues and then slowly enters the lymphatic channels. These are tiny vessels with one-way valves in them for carrying lymph, along with whatever small bits of foreign matter, wastes and bacteria it has gathered, through the lymph nodes and eventually back into the bloodstream.

The normal contractions and relaxation of your muscles and the force of gravity on the body keep the lymph flowing. They act to pump the lymph back through its channels and eliminate these wastes. Regular vigorous exercise encourages this elimination. It brings about a general flushing of the wastes from interstitial fluid and then helps them be carried away through the lymphatic tree of vessels until eventually they empty into the subclavian veins and are eliminated from the body through the actions of all the excretory organs—the skin, lungs, kidneys and colon. In Europe some of the finest natural treatments for healing involve a kind of massage dubbed 'lymphatic drainage' which helps the body do this. It is not only used to treat serious chronic illness and fatigue but even as a beauty treatment for women on the face. Skin-brushing stimulates the tissues beneath the skin, encouraging efficient lymphatic drainage. It is an extraordinarily efficient technique for cleansing the lymphatic system and for clearing away waste materials from the cells all over the body as well as those which—as in the case of cellulite in women—have become trapped in interstitial spaces where they are held by hardened connective tissue and where they build up to create pockets of water, toxins and fat that make the skin look like *peau d'orange*. Skin-brushing is something any woman with cellulite should do twice a day.

The Breath of Youth

Chinese medicine (which I spent three years studying and working with) has a long tradition of *natural-law* ageless ageing. And a great deal of it centres around the use of the breath. This is something to which we give little attention in the West and it is strange to think that specific breathing techniques are so ignored when, as we have seen in Chapter 3, the body's use of oxygen is *the* central determinant of the rate at which we age. Every one of our cells needs a continual supply of oxygen. It is this oxygen that feeds our brain, sparks metabolism and calms nerves. One of the reasons why regular aerobic exercise is so beneficial in slowing down the rate at which you age and warding off degenerative diseases is because it improves your use of oxygen. So can learning to breathe fully. It can also improve your mood, increase your resistance to colds and illness, and improve sleep as well. Full breathing is also an important tool for encouraging waste elimination. It is a kind of spring-cleaning process that can go on all year round every day of your life.

Few people breathe fully. Most of us, particularly if we have sedentary jobs, *breathe high*—that is we breathe quickly and shallowly concentrating the inhalations in the upper chest area which is the part of the lungs which holds the smallest quantity of air. Not only does this kind of breathing inhibit oxygen intake, it can also encourage the lungs to atrophy and to lose much of their natural elasticity—something which is a common occurrence as people get older. Other people, who allow the air to flow deeper into their lungs are *mid-breathers*—an improvement over breathing high because it encourages the ribcage to move and brings more oxygen into the lungs for body use. But to make the best use of oxygen for ageless ageing it's important to develop the habit of taking *total breaths* so they become your normal way of breathing.

The Total Breath

This is not something which you can learn overnight for there is nothing more unconscious and habitual than the way we breathe and that takes time and a little persistent effort to change. In breathing totally all of your breathing apparatus comes into play—the chest and ribs are lifted but not by themselves. The intercostal muscles also expand the ribs outward to create a large space in which your lungs can inflate to their maximum. Finally the diaphragm moves down, pulling the lower ribs outward which lets even the very bottom of your lungs fill up completely with air. With total breathing a much higher proportion of your lung power is used, as are most of your chest, rib and stomach muscles. Practise it lying down for five minutes a couple of times a day—perhaps just on awakening or just before going to sleep—and gradually it will become an automatic way of breathing which will not only help in ageless ageing but will also improve your resistance to fatigue, improve the glow of your skin and help protect you from minor illness.

Here's How
1. Lying flat on your back with a small pillow beneath your

neck, place one hand on your abdomen and rest the other on one side of your ribcage. Now inhale slowly through your nose while imagining that you are sending your breath to a place about 2 inches below your navel. Your tummy will start to well outward rather like a balloon. This has the effect of filling the lower part of your lungs with fresh air.

2. As the in-breath continues, let it fill the rest of your stomach and then expand your ribcage outwards to the side as well as the mid-section of your chest. You can feel this side expansion by keeping your hand against one side of your ribcage and making sure it moves outward.

3. Now let the fresh breath fill the upper part of your chest area as well, watching it as it expands outward and to the side. (The whole process of inhalation should take about 5 seconds altogether.)

4. Hold your breath for another 5 seconds. (In time you will find you can hold it much longer which gives your lungs a good opportunity to absorb all the oxygen available to them.)

5. Now exhale following the same process you did in inhaling: first contract your lower abdomen gently to move the air upwards then as the lower lungs deflate you should feel the ribcage contracting again followed by the upper chest. This process too should take about 5 seconds.

6. Rest for a second or two before beginning the whole cycle again.

Whereas detoxification by improved breathing can be used every day of your life to advantage, the final technique for spring-cleaning—self-induced fever—is best used only periodically. But then it can work wonders.

Feverpower

Like many old wives' tales the adage 'sweat it out' is beginning to look like good advice. For generations medicine has tried to suppress fever, believing it to be a state detrimental to the body. Latest findings show that fever can not only significantly strengthen your body's defence system, it appears to be a critical component in immune functions. As such, so the new findings indicate, when it occurs naturally, for instance as a response to infection, it should not be completely eliminated by drugs the way we have been wont to do. Fever weakens the force of invading enemies and is a potent positive force for fighting infections. Some scientists now believe that, because of its many immune-supporting characteristics, even when fever is artificially induced in a healthy body by saunas, turkish baths or vigorous aerobic exercise it can act as a powerful prophylactic to ageing, it can increase vitality and it can help provide you with a high level of well-being.

This new approach to fever is anything but new. Ancient Greek physicians considered fever a beneficial sign of vitality in an organism. They believed that disease was the result of an imbalance between the four humours—blood, phlegm, yellow bile and black bile—and they considered fever a means of burning off the bad humours and clearing the body of them. To this end they employed sudorific (sweat-producing) herbs, steam and hot baths to induce fevers in their patients. Such practices went on well into the seventeenth century when the famous British physician Thomas Sydenham commented that 'Fever is Nature's engine which she brings into the field to remove her enemy.' Then in the middle of the last century, with the discovery of antipyretic (temperature-lowering) drugs such as aspirin doctors began to insist on reducing fevers when they occurred. Drugs such as aspirin not only lower bodily temperature, they also eliminate many aches and pains associated with fever, thanks to their analgesic properties. This makes patients feel temporarily better. So gradually both doctor and patient began to lean heavily on the use of these drugs to suppress fever, and fever came to be considered a negative thing—something to be eliminated as rapidly and effectively as possible.

Recently researchers such as Matthew J. Kluger, a professor of physiology at the University of Michigan Medical School, have begun to examine the phenomenon of fever afresh and to ask questions such as: Just what happens when the body is plunged into a feverous state? Why did evolution develop the phenomenon of temperature-raising fever in its creatures? What is the purpose of this remarkable response? What Kluger and others have discovered is that fever's occurrence is not a sign that something is wrong with your body's temperature control system. Instead, a superbly modulated deliberately chosen temperature has been created at which several important physiological and biochemical events occur to heal the body.

Fever's Bounty

Among their known benefits (and there are probably many as yet unknown), even slight elevations in temperature not only increase white-cell concentrations, they make the body's defence army of white blood cells more mobile so they can reach any site of infection quicker. There is also considerable evidence that fever makes them more effective in engulfing and destroying invading micro-organisms. Indeed it appears to make many other immune functions more effective too. For instance interferon, one of the body's natural anti-viral, anti-cancer (and therefore probably anti-ageing as well) chemicals, about which we have heard so much in the news lately, has been shown to be more effective at elevated temperatures. Of course illness is not the only way that many of the beneficial effects of fever can be brought about. EP stands for endogenous pyrogen which is a low-weight protein produced by leucocytes to help destroy infection in the body. After a good workout of aerobic exercise, substances appear in the blood which have identical characteristics to EP.

Naturopaths have long insisted that fever is an important force for healing the body. They claim that controlled overheating of the body also increases the rate of metabolic processes as a whole and stimulates the functioning of the endocrine system. Since Hippocrates—some 2400 years ago—doctors have been using artificial methods of inducing fever, for instance giving the herb Echinacea or putting people into sweat baths or steam baths and applying hot compresses—to improve their vitality or stimulate the body's natural healing processes. The new fever research has begun to explain why many of their time-tested methods work. It is also beginning to lend credence to the beliefs of the Turks and Russians that periodic steam baths are strengthening to health and vitality, and to those of the Scandinavians, who have used saunas as a means of both stimulating immune response and spring-cleaning the body from within—two useful tools for ageless ageing.

Words of Warning

Despite new findings that fever is of benefit to the body, there is every indication that it needs to be treated with respect and that your physician is the best guide to dealing with any illness. For extreme fever can have a damaging effect on a body. And there are some people in whom the benefits of fever may well be outweighed by the risks involved. For instance, in a pregnant woman a high fever could potentially damage her unborn child and young children with very high fever can be subject to convulsions. Also, fevers in very old people have to be carefully watched because of possible damage they could do to the heart. But for most of us the new findings indicate that it could be potentially harmful not to allow a fever to work its natural course. When Kluger and other researchers have given aspirin to infected animals the animals have shown a significant increase in deaths.

Fever as a Prophylactic

Provided you are fit, aerobic exercise such as cycling, running, walking very briskly, swimming, rowing or dancing is probably the best way of all to benefit from small elevations in temperature. Saunas too can be helpful provided you are in good health, don't overdo them and provided you follow the basic guidelines. A sauna helps make your joints more supple while it soothes your muscles and refreshes the mind. It is also an excellent adjunct to any serious anti-cellulite programme for a woman. And early spring, when one's body is suffering from too much heavy winter food and clothing, too little fresh air and exercise, is an excellent time to make use of it. Here are the guidelines:

- Give yourself lots of time. It will do most for you if you take it leisurely so you have time for several sessions in the heat, with short rests in-between and a rest of at least thirty minutes—preferably an hour—after you are through.

● Never take a sauna until at least two hours after a meal and never take a sauna during a juice fast. (It is an excellent idea to use the sauna the day before a juice fast or special eliminating diet begins, however.)

● Never take a sauna if you have the symptoms of an illness.

● Wear little or nothing in the sauna—a towel wrapped around you is more than enough. The more you wear, the less effective will the heat treatment be.

● Take off any jewellery and your watch. They become very hot.

● Stay in the sauna room for only 5–10 minutes at a stretch. Then plunge into cold water or take a cold shower and rest before going back in.

● Don't water the stones during your first session and be sparing with the moisture you put on afterwards.

● Lie down in the sauna room if you can or sit quietly. Once you are used to the heat you can move to a higher bench.

● Take at least a half-hour rest at the end to let your body readjust to the normal temperature of the room. This is just as important as the sauna itself to make sure you reap all the benefits.

● Don't towel-dry yourself afterwards. Instead let the air dry your skin naturally. Then you can have a shower.

Not only can heat applied to the surface of the body be useful as a spring-cleaning tool, it also has a role to play in skin-care. Steaming your face over a pan of hot water into which you've tossed a handful of herbs such as chamomile or peppermint can do for skin what the sauna does for the whole body. It will leave it deep-cleaned, fresh and glowing. Let's look now at what can be done using high-tech biochemistry to slow the ageing process.

SIXTEEN

Anti-oxidants — Keys to Ageless Ageing

Since the 1950s gerontologists have reported success in retarding ageing and promoting longevity using chemical substances, both natural and artificial, which protect living systems from oxidation and free-radical damage—anti-oxidant chemicals and free-radical scavengers. They are usually grouped together under the label 'anti-oxidants'. Using anti-oxidants, researchers have been able to significantly extend the life of laboratory animals as well as to prevent, or at least to postpone, much of the degeneration of illnesses such as cancer and lung diseases which are usually associated with ageing. Anti-oxidant chemicals slow down destructive peroxidation of lipids in your body by allowing themselves to be oxidized, thereby trapping unstable oxygen molecules in the process before they can destructively react with lipids. They then turn into relatively stable and harmless compounds which can be easily eliminated or metabolized. Free-radical scavengers work in much the same way. By reacting harmlessly with highly active free-radical molecular species, they deactivate these free radicals before they can do harm to cell membranes and DNA and RNA, and before they can cause dangerous cross-linking to the body's many other proteins. In practice, most substances which protect from peroxidation are also able to deactivate free radicals. Together with the high-potency-low-calorie way of eating, these anti-oxidants can create a massive bastion of defence against ageing and degeneration in your body. That is why they are a vital part of any serious programme for ageless ageing.

Home-Grown and Lab-Made Anti-Agers

Anti-oxidants come in two varieties: natural and artificial. The natural anti-oxidants are simple nutritional elements which occur naturally in the foods we eat. These include ascorbic acid, vitamins A, E, and many of the B complex, zinc, selenium, glutathione and the sulphur-based amino acids. The artificial anti-oxidants are man-made chemicals such as the food preservatives BHT and BHA. In some ways these man-made chemicals appear to be even more effective than natural free-radical deactivators and anti-oxidants. That is why many longevists swallow them each day in large quantities. Certainly excellent results have been gained in animal experiments using combinations of natural and synthetic anti-oxidants. But many people—I among them—feel more comfortable in relying entirely on those substances with which nature has provided us in our foods and to which, therefore, our bodies have been accustomed throughout evolution as anti-ageing supplements.

The Power of Synergy

Recently anti-oxidant nutrients have begun to receive a lot of attention. You will find long lists of them in books and articles on age-retardation and on the backs of bottles in health-food stores and pharmacies. The trouble is that much of the interest in them as age-retarders has come from a fragmented kind of thinking based on the assumption that if you take one or two— say vitamin C and vitamin E for instance—then you should be able to take advantage of their anti-ageing properties. In fact, anti-oxidants work together and no single anti-oxidant can do much for ageless ageing unless it is well supported not only by the other anti-oxidants but also by all the other forty or fifty nutrients essential for maintaining life. For it is not the single actions of these nutrients but their multiple interactions which make them biologically efficient in detoxifying your body and protecting it from degeneration.

Experts in free-radical metabolism Elmer M. Cranton and James P. Frackelton give some idea of just how complex and interrelated the body's natural anti-oxidant defence system is in relation to the anti-oxidant nutrients, 'Vitamin E (tocopherol), vitamin C (ascorbate), selenium in glutathione peroxidase, the amino acid cysteine in reduced glutathione, riboflavin and niacin are all interrelated in a recycling process which provides on-going neutralization of free radicals. If each one of these nutrients is present in adequate amounts, they can all be restored to their active anti-oxidant forms after reacting with free radicals.' This principle is too often ignored in anti-ageing programmes. It mustn't be. For as Le Compte's first law states quite clearly, *ageing proceeds more rapidly where the deficiencies are greater and more numerous.*

Clinical Applications of Anti-oxidant Nutrients

So potent are the anti-oxidant nutrients in protecting the body against illness that high doses of them are now beginning to be used in both the prevention and treatment of many serious illnesses from cancer to ischaemic heart disease. In addition to their ability to protect from oxidation destruction, they appear to have many other health-promoting properties as well, such as an ability to improve immune functions. They are also anti-inflammatory agents. In the words of another expert in the field, E. Crary:

> High but well tolerated doses of the nutritional anti-oxidants selenium and vitamins E and C (400–1000mcg, 400–1200mcg, 1g respectively) have significant immunostimulant, anti-inflammatory and anti-carcinogenic effects which are well documented in the existing biometrical literature. In addition, these anti-oxidants help to protect the structural integrity of ischaemic or hypoxic (oxygen-starved) tissues and may have useful anti-thrombotic actions as well. Supplementation with high-dose nutritional anti-oxidants may eventually gain a broad role in the prevention, treatment or palliation of cancer, cardiovascular disease, infection, inflammatory disorders and certain diabetic conditions.

He then adds:

> While there is little evidence at present that high doses of manganese, copper or beta-carotene will produce special

benefit, it is wise to assure adequate intakes of these nutrients, which play anti-oxidant roles. The apparent ability of beta-carotene to reduce lung-cancer risk in smokers merits special mention in this regard.

With all of this in mind let's take a closer look at some of these natural anti-oxidant protectors and the kind of wonders they can work to keep you looking good and to protect your body from degeneration. The first is ascorbic acid—so important it really deserves a chapter to itself.

Vitamin C—the Non-Vitamin?

Ascorbic acid or vitamin C was first isolated in 1928 by Nobel prizewinner Albert Szent-Györgyi. He extracted it from orange juice, cabbage juice and adrenal glands of animals and he called it hexuronic acid because of its chemical structure. A lack of it in the diet was found to be responsible for the development of scurvy and it was later dubbed vitamin C. Since then it has been the subject of much enthusiasm and even more controversy despite the fact that it has quite conclusively been shown that ascorbic acid helps prevent arthritis, that it helps cure the common cold, that it can slow down the growth of cancer cells, and that it can even help protect the body from airborne and waterborne pollution. High levels of ascorbic acid are essential in protecting from the kind of free-radical oxidation damage which is central to age-degeneration.

Many researchers, amongst them Szent-Györgyi himself, now believe that vitamin C has been badly misunderstood. They claim that it is not a vitamin at all but a unique substance which encourages energy transfer in the cells. Szent-Györgyi believes that on a molecular level vitamin C is capable of creating heightened electron exchanges and thereby raising the level of vitality in the cells and tissues. If this is true—and, thanks to current findings in electrobiology (see Chapter 8) it seems very likely—then its actions on the body in many ways parallel those of a high-raw diet—raising electrical potentials in the cells, increasing cellular exchange and stimulating cell metabolism. Certainly ascorbic acid is a powerful anti-oxidant with particular protective properties for proteins of all sorts—from essential hormones to enzymes, collagen and even nucleic acids. It even offers significant protection against radiation. And, among vitamin C's most important anti-ageing properties is its ability to detoxify the body of both organic and inorganic poisons (including the heavy metals such as mercury, lead and cadmium), arsenic and benzene. It can even clear away toxicity caused by such agents as spider and snake poisons, bacterial toxins and many industrial pollutants and contaminants.

Szent-Györgyi has insisted that once we come to understand how vitamin C really functions in the body we will probably learn many other biological secrets as well, such as why cancer cells reproduce and how to stop them. Many ascorbic-acid researchers have reported that this substance, vitamin or not, helps maintain physiological homeostasis throughout the system. Irwin Stone, one of the world experts on the vitamin and author of *The Healing Factor*, says, 'On a molecular basis, the whole living process is nothing more than an orderly flow and transfer of electrons. Therefore, having an abundance of a substance like ascorbic acid present in living matter makes this orderly flow and transfer of electrons proceed with greater ease and facility. It acts substantially like an oil for the machinery of life.'

Protecting Homeostasis

Vitamin C has been found to perform many important functions in the body: because it is a reducing agent, it acts as an anti-oxidant, disarming highly reactive oxygen molecules and free radicals before they can do damage to membranes, tissues and cells. It also promotes the formation of red blood cells, helps prevent internal bleeding which leads to bruising and broken veins, and is of central importance to the proper functioning of the controlling centres of the body, such as the pituitary gland, brain, adrenal cortex and even the eyes. It has also been found to speed the healing of wounds and burns since it facilitates the formation of connective tissue in the scar. Vitamin C (along with zinc and the bioflavinoids) is also an essential substance for the synthesis of collagen in your body. A truly adequate amount of it (more about adequacy later) strengthens intercellular cement, helps keep muscles firm and helps protect skin from sagging and wrinkling.

Ascorbic acid has well-demonstrated antibacterial and anti-viral actions. In part this is because as an anti-oxidant it offers cells and body tissues protection against colds and other viral infections. In part it is due to more direct actions which it has on the immune system. For instance vitamin C is essential in good quantity if leucocytes are to function at optimum capacity in their efforts to engulf and destroy invading bacteria. But studies have shown that this is not possible even on a daily intake of 250mg of the vitamin—already more than most official tables recommend as necessary for 'health'. To achieve this level of optimal activity, somewhere between 1 and 69 appear to be necessary for most people. Vitamin C also protects your body from the cross-linking damage that is perpetrated by acet-aldehyde—a toxic substance found in raised amounts in people who drink large quantities of alcohol or smoke many cigarettes. This is one of the reasons why it is a well-tried and proven remedy for detoxifying the body from alcohol and why it banishes many of the symptoms of hangover, particularly when taken with a little fruit sugar.

The Missing Enzyme

Irwin Stone spent most of his professional life studying the biological functions and activity of ascorbic acid and putting them to therapeutic use. He believed also that it had been misclassified when it was dubbed a vitamin. It is instead, he says, an important metabolite, and an ancient genetic mutation has led to our being one of the few animals (in company with apes, guinea-pigs, Indian fruit bats, rainbow trout and the coho salmon) who do not produce the substance naturally within their own bodies. In all the other mammals there is a chain of enzymes involved in the production of vitamin C from glucose in the liver. The amount of ascorbic acid an animal produces at any particular time is directly related to the animal's environ-mental condition. For instance, when subjected to conditions of stress, cold, illness or a polluted environment, more ascorbic acid is naturally produced than in normal low-stress conditions when the animal is well fed, peaceful and not faced with high-risk situations.

Man and the few animals who do not produce this substance naturally are not so fortunate. Not only are we entirely dependent on our diet for an adequate supply, the concentration of ascorbic acid in our blood falls dramatically just when we need it most—when we are under any kind of stress—making us more susceptible to infection, age-degeneration and fatigue. The reason we are unable to manufacture this metabolite in the body is that in this chain of enzyme-controlled reactions in the liver which produces it, we are missing the last enzyme of the series—a little gem called L-gulonolactone oxidase. This, Stone and others believe, is a result of a genetic mutation which occurred several million years ago and which eliminated this important enzyme from our biochemical make-up.

Beyond Deficiencies

Scurvy is the deficiency disease associated with insufficient vitamin C. The symptoms of severe ascorbic deficiency were first recognized in the eighteenth century when James Lind carried out controlled therapeutic trials on sailors suffering from scurvy and discovered that a simple daily prophylactic dose of 1oz of lemon or lime juice per seaman would prevent the dreaded disease which was costing the Royal Navy hundreds of thousands of men. It was an important discovery, for scurvy is a very nasty illness: first the complexion changes and the skin becomes sallow or muddy. Then vitality is lost so you tire easily and suffer from breathlessness, with a desire to sleep most of the time. There can also be pains in the joints and limbs, particularly the legs. The gums become sore and bleed easily and reddish spots appear on the skin. Sometimes the eyelids become purple or swollen, nose-bleeds occur, and blood is passed in the urine. As the gums become increasingly spongy the teeth start to fall out, the jawbone begins to rot and the bones become so brittle that they easily break. Finally death comes either through a secondary infection such as pneumonia or from collapse at even the mildest of exertions.

Optimum Levels of C

The usual way of determining adequate amounts of vitamin C has been to ask the question, 'How much of the vitamin will prevent scurvy?' The official answer has come back, between 45 and 60mg a day, because in most adults such an amount will prevent the *overt* manifestations of scurvy. Since science has been largely blinkered by the notion that ascorbic acid is a vitamin and therefore performs only one function—that of preventing gross symptoms of scurvy—it has tended to ignore another question which for most people is even more important, 'How much vitamin C do we need to live at *optimum* health and vitality and to retard the degenerative processes associated with ageing?'

This is a question which Linus Pauling, twice a Nobel laureate, has long investigated. He has come to the conclusion that while a few milligrams of ascorbic acid each day will prevent the symptoms of acute scurvy we need much larger amounts if we want to live in the best possible health, to prevent age-degeneration in the body and to promote longevity. Just exactly how much depends, as always, on biochemical individuality. But most people, he believes, probably need between 1 and 5 grams a day to remain optimally healthy. Some may actually be able to get along with as little as 250mg while others may find they require up to forty times this much—10g or more a day. For when less than truly adequate amounts of ascorbic acid are taken, although symptoms of acute scurvy can be prevented, many people nevertheless develop chronic symptoms of 'subclinical' deficiencies which include lack of mental alertness, bleeding gums, borderline anaemia, irritability, and a strong susceptibility to infections and age-related degeneration. And requirements of the vitamin in an effective programme of supplementation for ageless ageing are likely to be even higher—probably between 10 and 15g a day for most people. Although many ageing experts take much more. Herman Le Compte, for instance, swallows 30g of ascorbic acid daily.

Daily doses of this size and larger have been shown to have quite remarkable effects on human beings. Susceptibilities to colds or flu usually disappear. Injuries, broken bones and bruises heal rapidly. Even cancers and tumours have been regressed, and the lifespans of animals have been significantly prolonged on high daily doses of ascorbic acid. Many researchers, including Stone, claim that such doses will delay wrinkling and other visible signs of ageing as well as prolonging youthful vitality.

Of Apes and Men

Current recommendations for daily intake of vitamin C are about 60mg a day. For an 11 stone man this is proportionally less than 1mg for each kilogram of body weight. When you compare this requirement with the Nutrient Requirement of Laboratory Animals from the Committee on Animal Nutrition it seems very low indeed. Drawing on their recommendation of 55mg per kilogram of body weight for monkeys, one would expect proportionally it to be almost 4g (4000mg) for a man. The average adult gorilla living in the wild (who like us cannot produce his own ascorbic acid) consumes in excess of 4500mg of the substance every day, while animals who are able to synthesize it in the liver tend to produce even higher quantities of it— about 70mg per kilogram of body weight. Under stress of any kind or when they are ill, this production more than triples. Pauling and others have often pointed out that since civilized man is continually under stress, an 11 stone man can need somewhere near 15,000mg of the vitamin a day to maintain a high level of well-being and protection from degeneration. One of the reasons why a high-raw diet of fresh foods can be so useful in slowing down degeneration and even in rejuvenating the body biochemically and physiologically may be because, compared to the average overprocessed and overcooked foods most people eat, it is quite rich in natural vitamin C. But even a high-raw diet cannot supply that much.

Ascorbic-Acid Scares

If you intend to take 10g or more of ascorbic acid a day, is it safe? After all, there has been a lot of negative publicity about vitamin C—particularly from some areas of the medical Establishment who claim not only that it is not effective in preventing or curing the common cold, but even that it can cause a deficiency of vitamin B_{12} and/or kidney stones. Dismissals of ascorbic acid's many health-promoting properties tend to come from professionals who have little or no experience in using it either for prevention or therapy. Most criticism of high-dose usage comes from early studies done to validate Pauling's original findings that the vitamin has antiviral and antibacterial properties. A number of these studies were carried out in which subjects were given supplements of vitamin C in low doses—amounts in the fifties and hundreds of milligrams a day. These studies showed no increase in their subjects' ability to resist infection nor did they give any indication that extra vitamin C helps speed the healing of colds. And their findings received a lot of press coverage and brought forth not a few expressions of disdain from physicians who had never used the vitamin. What the publicity did not make clear is that the amounts of the vitamin which had been tested had been far too low to be effective— sometimes as much as fifty times less than those Pauling, Stone, Ewan Cameron, Robert Cathcart and the other experts were using for the same purpose.

Other worries began in 1974 when two doctors, Victor Herbert and Elizabeth Jacobs, published an experiment suggesting that large doses of vitamin C could destroy vitamin B_{12} in foods and lead to a B_{12} deficiency in the body. This too brought a lot of publicity in its wake. But when the methods these researchers used for analysis were examined, it became obvious that their findings could not be considered reliable. For their experiments had been carried out in the presence of oxygen which is involved in the reaction that destroys B_{12}. This is highly unlikely to occur in a living organism, where the pressures of oxygen in its digestive system are very low indeed.

Finally there has been the worry about the possibility that large doses of ascorbic acid might cause kidney stones. Since some ascorbic acid is converted in the body to oxalic acid, a few professionals have expressed fear that someone who takes both a lot of vitamin C and calcium could produce calcium oxalate urinary stones. But there have been no actual reports of this. Quite the contrary. Many studies have shown that a high intake of vitamin C actually *reduces* the incidence of several types of urinary stones. And, provided you get sufficient magnesium and vitamin B_6 in your diet, even the faint possibility of producing kidney stones is eliminated. Another concern which is commonly voiced about taking large amounts of ascorbic acid regularly is that you will develop a tolerance to it so that it is no longer effective. Seldom has this been reported. Soviet scientists eliminate even this possibility by giving high-dose C supplements for three or four weeks and then stopping them for the same period.

Morbidity Index

When ascorbic acid goes to work in your body to detoxify wastes and protect against oxidation and free-radical damage, much of it is metabolized into dehydroascorbic acid, which is in effect 'oxidized' vitamin C. One of the most useful and interesting ways of using ascorbic acid as a diagnostic and prognostic tool—a way of estimating the biological state of your vitality and resistance to illness and degeneration—is by measuring the ratio of ascorbic acid to dehydroascorbic acid in your blood. Stone calls this ratio the 'morbidity index' (although it could as easily be looked at from the opposite point of view as a 'vitality index'). Normal healthy people have a morbidity index of about 15—that is, 15 parts ascorbic acid to 1 part dehydroascorbic acid. Critically ill people have a morbidity index of about 1·0. When they convalesce after serious illness the morbidity index improves dramatically. This measurement is a diagnostic tool which is enormously helpful in indicating the overall state of the body and in estimating just how much oxidation-stress you have been exposed to. It is now just beginning to be used as a biometer for ageing as well.

How and How Much?

Doses of vitamin C are important, both when you are using it for its health-promoting, age-retarding anti-oxidant purposes and when it is being used to treat illnesses. Because it is a water-soluble vitamin, ascorbic acid is not stored in the tissues. Once your tissues have been saturated, any excess is excreted in the urine. Many of the opponents of high-dose therapy complain that the only benefit this leads to is the rather questionable one of having very expensive urine. But scientists with experience in megascorbic therapy for the prevention of illness and ageing say that this flushing and the elimination of excess is an important part of the benefit that the vitamin can bring the body. It neutralizes toxins, free radicals and activated oxygen molecules and constantly keeps undesirable wastes moving through the body, helping to get rid of them.

Ascorbic acid in quantities greater than the body can use beneficially tends to cause loose bowels. Robert Cathcart, an American physician who is known throughout the world for his therapeutic uses of the vitamin, believes this can offer a good indication of just how much at any particular time—sick or ill—you need. He uses doses of the vitamin ranging from 10g a day up to 200g taken orally to treat serious illness. To determine the proper dose he quite literally 'titrates to bowel tolerance' to determine just what dose is appropriate. It should be just below the point at which this loose-bowel phenomenon occurs, says Cathcart. At least 80 per cent of normal adults, he says, will tolerate 10–15g of ascorbic-acid fine crystals in one half cup of water in four divided doses per twenty-four hour period before this happens.

Vitamin C comes in many water-soluble forms—ascorbic acid, calcium ascorbate, sodium ascorbate, and so forth—both in powder form and in tablet form. Most experts in vitamin C use claim that the best form of the vitamin (and the cheapest) is quite simply the crystalline powder of ascorbic acid itself. This you can stir into fruit juice or spring water and drink three or four times a day. High doses of vitamin C tablets sometimes cause distress to sensitive stomachs. Tablets also contain fillers which, if you are taking megadoses of them over a period of time, you are probably better off without. The advantage of the ascorbate forms of the vitamin is that, unlike ascorbic acid which has a low pH, they are more alkaline. But many people actually come to like the rather acid flavour. The way I like best to take vitamin C is by dissolving three level teaspoons of ascorbic acid powder in a litre of sparkling mineral water which I drink throughout the day to supply a steady supply of about 9g of the vitamin per day. It makes an enormously refreshing and stimulating drink and, at the same time, keeps ascorbate levels in the tissues nicely elevated so you can make good use of its natural protection as an anti-ageing nutrient. There is also one oil-soluble form of vitamin C. Called ascorbyl palmitate, it too is a powerful anti-oxidant and it is nontoxic. In the food industry it is used to prevent cut apples from turning brown and to cure meats. Because it is fat-soluble, it offers far more protection against lipid-peroxidation damage to the cells than the water-soluble forms do. It can be sprinkled on foods or added to salad dressings. It is an excellent complement to water-soluble vitamin C, which is why most longevists take both.

The Amazing Bioflavinoids

In nature vitamin C occurs together with certain pigments of flowers, fruits and vegetables called bioflavinoids. They are a remarkable group of brightly coloured plant-derived substances that were also discovered by Szent-Györgyi and which together with vitamin C make up what is commonly called the 'C complex'. These substances, which are called by various names, include hesperidin, rutin, vitamin P, flavones, flavonals, nobiletin, tangeretin, eriodictyol and so on. They potentiate the effects of ascorbic acid in the body as well as strengthening cell membranes and capillaries. Scientists working with refined techniques which enable various bioflavinoids to be isolated and tested have shown that some help prevent blood platelets from abnormal clotting by exerting anti-adhesive actions on red blood cells. In the plants from which bioflavinoids come they act as primitive defence systems protecting them from disease. They appear to have similar actions on man. Many studies indicate that various bioflavinoids, either on their own or in combination, actively combat infectious bacteria, viruses and fungi. If you are going to follow a mega nutrient approach to retarding ageing it is probably a good idea to include these substances in the list of supplements you intend to take.

SEVENTEEN

Radical Fighters

Anti-oxidant nutrients are helpful in slowing down the rate at which you age not only because they deactivate free radicals and unstable oxygen species in the body. As we've seen, the same nutrients enhance the immune system and improve your resistance to disease—infections, food and chemical allergies or sensitivities and chronic degenerative illnesses. They also offer protection against many of the life-eroding hazards of twentieth-century life in industrialized societies. These include the vast array of environmental threats to which we are subjected—from the pesticides which are sprayed on our fruits and vegetables to the more than 200,000 chemicals to which we are exposed every day of our lives—chemicals which fifty years ago were little present in our environment: water-borne carcinogens formed when the chlorine used to purify our drinking water chemically interacts with industrial effluents; solvents; the halogenated hydrocarbons in air and water; formaldehyde; chlorine gas; heavy metals such as lead and cadmium; asbestos and even radiation. They have become a serious threat to health.

The airborne pollutants are particularly worrying since air is the single thing which we cannot live for more than a few minutes without. The air we breathe contains a long list of nasty-sounding substances which not only erode the marble and granite of buildings but can cause serious harm to lungs and skin and encourage premature ageing on a wide scale. Two of the most destructive oxidant air pollutants are ozone and nitrogen dioxide. The first comes mostly from the burning of petrol in cars, buses and lorries, although gas fires and stoves are another source. The second is created in photochemical smog by reactions involving nitrogen oxides, oxygen and unburnt petrol vapours. Both cause oxidation damage to the lungs by oxidizing the polyunsaturated fatty acids of lung cell membranes. Because they are so useful in protecting from environmentally caused damage, anti-oxidants are on their way to becoming almost necessities in twentieth-century urban life. Where the Hunzas, Vilcabamba Indians and Soviet Georgians were able in their unpolluted environment to live long and healthy lives based entirely on *natural-law* anti-ageing practices, for us this appears virtually impossible. We appear to need the *high-tech* help from extra anti-oxidants for us to manage it. As always they are synergistic—they work best in combination. But three are particularly important in counteracting the destructive effects of environmental pollutants in our air, water and food—vitamin E, selenium and vitamin A.

Tocopherol Power

When vitamin E was isolated from wheatgerm oil in 1936 researchers discovered it was a mixture of several similar substances which are grouped under the name of tocopherols— alpha, beta, gamma, delta, epsilon, and so forth. There are seven of them and all of them have biological activity and anti-oxidant power, but each to a slightly different degree. The tocopherols occur in highest concentration in nature in wheatgerm, cold-pressed vegetable oils, whole raw nuts and soy beans. Most vitamin E capsules contain alpha-tocopherol acetate, the most biologically active isomer of the series, for which 1mg is equal to one international unit or IU. Some, however, are made up of a mixture of tocopherols or their esters since there is evidence that such a mixture increases alpha-tocopherol's activity in a living system. Vitamin E is a potent anti-oxidant and free-radical scavenger, with a particular bent towards looking after the body's lipid-based structures. So far, it's the only anti-oxidant known to prevent lipid peroxidation within the microsomes and mitochondria so it is terribly important in maintaining cell integrity and ensuring a safe and complete use of oxygen by the cells. It has also been used successfully to treat menopause problems such as hot flushes and chronic muscle cramping as well as to prevent and treat some kinds of anaemia and cancer. Large doses of vitamin E have been shown to significantly extend the lifespans of animals.

Early research with vitamin E got it rather a bad reputation because it became associated in people's minds as the 'sex vitamin'. This is because tocopherols exist in high concentration in the anterior pituitary where they oversee the production of male hormones, and because animal experiments showed that they are necessary in the female for normal reproduction to take place. Indeed vitamin E does protect sex hormones and other vital hormones from oxidation, but perhaps its most important role in the body is that it encourages a more efficient use of oxygen by the cells. It plays a vital role in cellular respiration and this is why it is so important in protecting the heart from damage. In addition it causes dilation of the blood vessels so that more blood gets through and it is an effective inhibitor of clots.

Vitamin E also gives your muscles and nerves the ability to function on less oxygen and in this way increases endurance and stamina. It is concentrated in the parts of cells most involved with oxidation and with respiration reactions, such as in the mitochondrial and microsomal membranes. These sites of energy transfer are where nutrients enter to be metabolized and wastes are eliminated. Researchers have found that a vitamin E deficiency dramatically lowers cellular oxygen use at these sites while it increases peroxidation and the formation of free radicals. This is particularly important in muscle tissue where a shortage of the vitamin can result in a 40 per cent decrease in endurance capacity. That is why vitamin E has long been used by top athletes. The vitamin's ability to minimize oxygen starvation on a cellular level appears to play an important role in protecting the arteries and veins from the build-up of cholesterol which has a tendency to collect in areas where oxygen is particularly sparse.

Pollution- and Age-Protector

Experiments with animals have shown that vitamin E even in relatively low doses can protect against the damage which nitrogen oxide and ozone in our air do to lungs and tissues.

American biochemist Roger Williams points out that a vitamin E deficiency is often observed to cause physiological and bio-chemical changes which parallel those of old age. And Russian scientists report that as a supplement for ageing people vitamin E has brought about a disappearance of wrinkles on the face, increased strength and stamina, improved sleep patterns and even turned greying hair back to normal. The tocopherols also offer protection from ageing by enhancing immune responses. This way they also help protect your body from illnesses. When mice infected with pneumonia were given extra doses of vitamin E, over 60 per cent of them were able to resist the disease compared to the control group fed on the ordinary laboratory diet—all of whom caught the illness. But for top immune protection—the kind needed for ageless ageing—it appears that we, like these lab animals, need considerably more of the vitamin than is available in the average diet. One of the world's experts on the vitamin, Robert Tengerdy at Colorado State University says that we appear to require six times more than what is usually thought to be nutritionally adequate.

Vitamin E's anti-oxidant properties are strongly synergistic with other nutrients. For instance this vitamin reduces the amount of vitamin A you need by preventing it from breaking down and forming other substances that can be harmful to your body. Vitamin E has a similar effect on saturated and unsaturated fatty acids. It also protects the B complex vitamins and vitamin C from oxidation in the digestive tract and enhances the anti-oxidant activity of both selenium and the amino acid cysteine (see Chapter 18), both of which are central to any nutritional programme for ageless ageing. The more fat there is in your diet the more vitamin E you will need.

How Much Is Enough?

All the experts on vitamin E insist that, thanks to widespread use of refined flour which eliminates the vitamin from it and to the high-fat diet we eat which quite simply burns it up, few of us get adequate E to maintain good health, let alone be able to make substantial use of its anti-oxidant properties for age-retardation. Most nutritionists suggest that supplements of 400

IU a day are needed to maintain good immune functions although this need increases with the amount of fat and oils you consume. Many longevists take as much as 1600 IU a day or more. Although there are no known side-effects of taking such a high dose of vitamin E, there have been some recent reports in the popular media that on prolonged high doses of the vitamin some people develop exhaustion and fatty livers—that is, on doses as high as 1600–2000 IU a day for months on end. Lab animals have produced abnormalities of the adrenals, thyroid and sex glands on prolonged extremely high doses. People who have high blood pressure, heart damage from rheumatic fever, or an overactive thyroid are advised not to take vitamin E in large doses. In some people when supplements of very high doses of vitamin E are begun suddenly this can temporarily elevate blood pressure. That is why many physicians begin with a smaller dose of the vitamin, say 100 IU a day, and gradually work up to their optimum amount over a period of several weeks. What is the optimal amount for ageless ageing? Again it depends on the person. Most ageing experts recommend building up to between 600 and 1200 IU a day together with the other anti-oxidant nutrients. Vitamin E should always be taken with meals, as it is absorbed best where there is some oil or fat in the digestive system, and it is a good idea to take it along with vitamin A and selenium with which it works closely. Because it has a slightly calming and relaxing effect on the nervous system, many people prefer to take it with their evening meal.

Superlative Selenium

In many ways the most exciting of all the anti-oxidant nutrients is selenium—an essential micro-nutrient found in minute quantities in your body. It can preserve elasticity of the skin by preventing oxidation of polyunsaturated fatty acids which can result in cross-linking of proteins. It also helps protect from cancer and premature ageing, and it works closely with vitamin E. How much selenium you get in your diet depends entirely on how much is found in the soils in which the foods you eat are grown, although seafoods, particularly tuna which has been packed in water not oil, are good sources of the nutrient. In areas of high-selenium soils cancer incidence is significantly lower than in areas of low selenium. For many years nutritionists largely ignored selenium because, like vitamins C and E, in high doses it is toxic: it can inhibit the actions of important enzymes and replace sulphur in biological compounds. These symptoms however have only been reported in areas of exceptionally rich selenium soils of which there are very few.

A powerful anti-oxidant and free-radical scavenger, selenium is part of the glutathione peroxidase molecule which you may remember from Chapter 16 is one of three enzymes that are part of the body's first line of anti-oxidant defences. This protective enzyme is responsible for turning lipid peroxides, which damage cells and collagen, into harmless hydroxy acids. And it cannot function properly in the absence of selenium. This anti-oxidant enzyme is absolutely essential to protect your body from the many forms of environmental pollutants that are linked both to age-degeneration and to the development of cancer. It is also a vital force in protecting you from airborne allergies and environmental sensitivities, and selenium itself appears to be the most important of all the anti-oxidant nutrients for people who are sensitive to the chemical environment. In fact a number of clinical ecologists report that supplements of 400mcg of selenium a day can clear up symptoms in approximately 60 per cent of people suffering from chemical allergies.

The Anticancer Nutrient

Selenium also detoxifies the body of heavy metals such as mercury and appears to be a potent anticancer agent. Researchers have only recently discovered this fact. The discovery has a certain irony about it because in the early days of nutritional research selenium was believed by some scientists to be a cancer-causing element.

Its power *against* certain forms of cancer is of particular relevance to anyone concerned about retarding the ageing process since so many of the changes on a cellular level associated with the development of cancer are paralleled in cellular ageing. It has been demonstrated from several different research approaches. Epidemiological studies have shown that where the dietary intake of selenium is highest the rate of breast cancer is lowest. For instance, in the United States the average daily intake of selenium is 68mcg and the incidence of breast cancer is 22·2 per 100,000. Thanks to their high consumption of fish, people in Japan have an intake of 287mcg and only a 4·0 in 100,000 incidence. In the Philippines where the average daily intake is 189mcg the breast cancer rate is 5·4 per 100,000. Other studies have confirmed these findings and indicate that selenium not only helps protect from cancers of the colon, stomach, lungs, breast, liver and prostate, but from other chronic illnesses as well. These include heart disease, high blood pressure and arteriosclerosis. All of them are less prevalent in areas of high-selenium intake.

Other studies have shown that people with low selenium have an increased risk of skin cancer and still others that selenium supplementation can reduce the incidence of breast tumours in mice from 80 per cent to 18 per cent. In Germany researchers took fifty animals and fed them extra selenium while fifty remained untreated. They were then all irradiated to cause cancer. It developed in thirty-one of the untreated group. Only fourteen of the selenium group succumbed to the disease, however, and the tumours in these animals were less than half the size of tumours in the untreated group. Researchers stated, 'We must infer that selenium must be one of the few chemical elements to which a tumour preventative effect can be attributed . . . the results of our own investigations enhance and amplify present knowledge of this anticarcinogenic action of selenium.'

Heightened Immune Defences

Selenium's role in glutathione-peroxidase activity and its ability to detoxify the body of carcinogens are no doubt important in its ability to protect from cancer and to retard the ageing process. But so too is the direct action it has on the immune system— improving immune functions as no other single nutrient appears able to do. Selenium is a necessary ingredient in raising your body's defences against foreign invasion from bacteria, viruses and toxic chemicals. Supplements of selenium have been shown to increase the numbers of B-cells—the white blood cells which form an important part of immune defence. Animals treated with selenium show that lymphocytes are also increased in the blood when this micro-nutrient is given over a period of time. Meanwhile rabbits injected with selenium show increased numbers of white blood cells, heightened phagocyte* activity and an increased ability to kill bacteria.

Where From and How Much?

Seafood is the best source of selenium. Fruits and vegetables are usually poor sources unless they happen to have been grown in selenium-rich soils. Wholegrains, onions, garlic, cabbage, mushrooms, asparagus, broccoli and soy beans can all be good sources provided they come from adequate soils. People who live on the average Western diet, high in refined and processed foods, are often very selenium poor. Brown rice contains fifteen times as much selenium as its white counterpart. How much is enough is still a matter of great debate in scientific circles. Most nutritionists err on the side of caution and recommend 200mcg per day despite the fact that the Japanese take in much more than twice that in their daily diet and appear to get nothing but benefits from it.

Selenium is a poison in too high doses and selenium supplements are always measured in micrograms (millionths of a gram) instead of milligrams. But you would have to swallow an awful lot of it to develop a reaction. Official reports state that 'Chronic selenium toxicity would be expected in human beings after long-term consumption of 2400 to 3000mcg daily.'

Most longevists take a minimum of 400mcg a day and few go as high as 2000mcg. When you take this micro-nutrient together with vitamin E and vitamin C both its activity and its safety in the body are enhanced. The most easily absorbed form of selenium is a chelated form in which it has been chemically bound to an amino acid for easy uptake in the system. Nutritional supplements of selenium sometimes include the amino acids it works with in the body to form glutathione

* Literally, 'big eater' white blood cells.

peroxidase as well as the other nutrients, such as vitamins A, E and C, with which it is particularly synergistic.

Retinol and the Carotenoids

Vitamin A or retinol is an oil-soluble nutrient named after the retina of the eye which has a special need for it in order to remain healthy. It is also an effective anti-oxidant and free-radical protector from damage with a particular role to play in guarding the lungs from damage caused by the airborne pollutants to which we are exposed. Closely related to vitamin A are the carotenoids (named after carrots in which the most well-known carotenoid—the yellow pigment beta-carotene—is found in abundance). Beta-carotene is sometimes called pro-vitamin A because it is converted to the vitamin itself by your body when you eat foods containing it. Vitamin A helps maintain soft, smooth, young-looking skin, protects the mucous membranes of your mouth, nose, throat and lungs, and reduces your susceptibility to infection. Recent studies show that if you are deficient in vitamin A you increase your risk of lung cancer. There is also a definite relationship between your cells' ability to synthesize new RNA and adequate intake of vitamin A or beta-carotene in your diet. As far back as the 'forties researchers at Columbia University showed that they were able to extend the lifespan of rats between 10 and 20 per cent by supplementing their diets with vitamin A.

Vitamin A, which occurs in good quantity in liver and fish, is one of the oil-soluble nutrients which can build up in the body. In adults more than 85,000 IU of it a day quickly becomes toxic and can be responsible for symptoms of nausea, vomiting, headache and dizziness. This is why vitamin A is never used in mega doses. Most longevists recommend between 20,000 and 35,000 IU a day—no more.

Beta-carotene or pro-vitamin A is different however. It is absorbed from your foods through the intestinal wall. And it is non-toxic. Eat too many carrots and all you are likely to end up with is a slight colouring of the skin that looks like a mild tan. Indeed this colouring property of some of the carotenoids is often taken advantage of by people wanting to tan naturally without the sun. One of the carotenoids, canthaxanthin which occurs naturally in some mushrooms and shrimps, is available in Britain and Canada as a natural tanning supplement which you take for a few weeks before exposing yourself to sunlight (see page 276). How much beta-carotene you absorb depends partly on the kind and quantity of fats that you have also eaten. Some of it is converted into vitamin A in the intestine and then stored in the liver, the rest circulates in the blood. The fact that, unlike retinol itself, beta-carotene does circulate in the blood appears to be important in the kind of anti-oxidant protection against age-degeneration which it offers the cells and tissues of your body—particularly the skin and the lungs. To put it simply it goes easily where it is needed. And the fact that it is non-toxic makes it an important adjunct to vitamin A in the collection of natural anti-oxidants for ageless ageing. Most age-researchers and doctors using anti-oxidant nutrients as age-retarders use 15,000–35,000 IU of retinol together with about 25mg of beta-carotene. This much beta-carotene provides about 40,000 IU of potential vitamin activity.

Natural Support System

All the enzymes involved in free-radical protection from damage demand trace elements or B vitamins as co-enzymes. For instance the trace elements copper, zinc and manganese are essential to the superoxide dismutases, selenium is needed for glutathione peroxidase, and iron is essential for catalase and some forms of peroxidase. That is why a truly adequate intake of these trace nutrients is essential for protection against free-radical-produced diseases and ageing. They should be included in any effective anti-ageing supplement. In fact several of the B complex vitamins, including vitamin B_1, pantothenic acid, B_6, PABA, B_3, choline, inositol, and B_{12}, and some of the minerals such as zinc, either appear to have their own anti-oxidant properties, are immune-stimulants, or play other specific anti-ageing support roles in the body. For instance the vitamin niacin, B_3, is not itself an anti-oxidant but it is used in NADPH—one of your body's major electron-carriers; B_2 is also not an anti-oxidant but it is necessary for the natural anti-oxidant-recycling enzyme glutathione reductase. Lecithin is an anti-oxidant. A phospholipid manufactured by your body, it also acts as an emulsifier and has an affinity for water. It breaks down fat into minute particles so it can be dissolved, and appears to bind with cholesterol and to help prevent the build-up of cholesterol in the arteries.

SOD Against Ageing

Other natural anti-oxidants which have recently received a lot of publicity are the superoxide dismutases or SOD. You may remember that, as enzymes, SOD is part of your body's first line of defence against free radicals and unstable oxygen species. It is found in all the body's cells and its primary function is to protect them from toxic effects of oxygen. SOD levels in mammals appear to be closely correlated with ageing and directly proportional to their lifespans. It is the fifth most prevalent protein in humans. Recently SOD given by injection has been shown to have some remarkable healing and degeneration-reversing effects: it reduces inflammation, alleviates the pain of arthritis, ameliorates or prevents the side-effects of high-dose radiation, and may even prevent the growth of cancer cells. You will find SOD supplements sitting on the shelves of health-food stores. But before you include it amongst your nutrients for ageless ageing you should know that so far there is no conclusive evidence that it can be of use when taken orally. It is a long-chain protein which, even if it avoided being broken down in the digestive system, most biochemists believe could not be expected to cross cell membranes.

Synergy Has the Last Word

The single most important principle on which any sound nutritional programme must be based is synergy. Just as there is never a deficiency of only one vitamin or mineral, there is never any vitamin or mineral action which takes place by itself. It is always the multiple interactions of essential nutrients which constitute the basis of their biological functions. This is never more true than when you are relying on natural anti-oxidants and immune-supporters for ageless ageing. How successful they are in slowing the clock for you depends on their being supplied together with a good balance of all the other nutrients necessary for what you might call 'biochemical housekeeping'— the day-to-day running of things in your body. This means that your way of eating has to be right—not too much, and based on the natural wholesome foods that supply a full range of essential nutrients plus whatever as yet undiscovered factors are part of the structural information necessary for high-level health. Many high-potency-supplement reigmes for slowing down ageing are doomed to failure simply because they forget this principle so that complementary nutrients are not sufficiently available in the system to make proper use of the high-powered anti-agers. Such an approach is not only a waste of money (the anti-oxidant nutrients don't come cheap), it could also seriously unbalance your system.

EIGHTEEN

The Amazing Aminos

If somebody said you could take a pill which would make your body look slimmer, firmer and younger you would probably think they were either a charlatan or quite mad. That is certainly what I thought. That is until I learned about the amazing aminos. And this is only one of the many ways in which they can be used to counteract the effects of ageing. Specific free-form amino acids—that is amino acids which have been chemically separated from the long-chain proteins to which they normally belong—are the most exciting development in nutrition in the past twenty years. Different sorts of free aminos are currently being used to cure food allergies, eliminate drug addictions, alter mood, and improve intelligence. They can be helpful in slowing down the ageing process because they detoxify the body, they act as free-radical scavengers and they stimulate immune functions, as well as performing a myriad of other useful tasks which are subtly connected with protecting the body from degeneration.

Why Amino Acids Matter

Amino acids are the building blocks from which proteins are made. There are twenty-two of them so far identified which commonly occur in proteins. Eight are called *essential* because your body can't manufacture them itself. They therefore have to be taken in through foods you eat. The rest can be made in the body out of other amino acids. For man the essential amino acids are isoleucine, leucine, lysine, methionine, phenylalanine,

PHENYLALANINE
This cannot be metabolized if a person is deficient in vitamin C. Congenital deficiency of phenylalanine hydroxylase causes inadequate formation of tyrosine, and increased serum phenylalanane in babies produces brain damage which results in severe mental retardation. Another result is melanin deficiency, predisposing the individual to skin diseases such as eczema.

GLYCINE
Serves as an inhibitory neurotransmitter as well as helping in the healing of a swollen or infected prostate.

GLUTAMIC ACID
May serve as an excitatory neurotransmitter. It provides gamma-aminobutyric acid.

TRYPTOPHAN
This provides niacin, which prevents pellagra and mental deficiency. Tryptophan is better for depression than for energy. Deficiency causes insomnia.

ISOLEUCINE
Needed in haemoglobin formation (there are very limited amounts in beef).

TYROSINE
Precursor of catecholamines, and of importance in the regulation of emotional behaviour. Important in the eventual synthesis of the hormone thyroxine, thus aiding in prevention of hypothyroidism, cretinism and myxoedema.

CYSTEINE AND METHIONINE
These are natural chelating agents for heavy metals. They help break down calcium plaques. Both aid in producing beautiful skin. Methionine can be substituted for choline, which aids in reducing fat in the liver and protects the kidneys.

HISTIDINE
Precursor of histamine. There are increased concentrations in haemoglobin synthesis.

THREONINE
Prevents the accumulation of fat in the liver.

VALINE
Deficiency results in negative nitrogen balance in the body.

LEUCINE
Leucine is found to be lacking in alcoholics and drug addicts, as are three other amino acids: l-glutamine, alpha-amino-n-butyric acid, and citrulline.

ARGININE
Helps increase sperm count.

LYSINE
Deficiency may cause nausea and anaemia. Dry heating of protein destroys much of its lysine.

ACTIONS OF AMINO ACIDS IN THE HUMAN BODY

threonine, tryptophan and valine. Cysteine and tyrosine are synthesized in the body from methionine and phenylalanine respectively. All these ten amino acids occur in proteins in your cells. Another ten amino acids—alanine, arginine, aspartic acid, asparagine, glutamic acid, glutamine, glycine, histadine, proline and serine—are present in most proteins. Two more, hydroglycerine and hydroproline, are present in collagen. The body has the ability to synthesize these from simple precursors. That is why they are called non-essential. Recently however experts in amino acids have begun to insist that the concept of 'essential' and 'non-essential' amino acids is fallacious and that for high-level well-being and ageless ageing all of the amino acids should be available through the foods you eat. This is because, although your body can itself manufacture the so-called non-essential aminos, some like arginine cannot be manufactured in sufficient quantity to supply the need. Further, these can put strain on enzyme systems and use up supplies of co-enzyme nutrients which are better left free for other duties in the organism.

These twenty-two amino acids can be linked together to form more than 50,000 different proteins. In fact your body is continuously breaking down the proteins you eat into amino-acid complexes and free amino acids, then recombining them to form whatever new proteins it needs to maintain itself. Amino acids supply the raw materials for maintaining the genetic code—DNA—as well as for repairing damaged muscle tissue, for cell division, for making enzymes (together with vitamins as co-factors and minerals as activators), for building new connective tissue and—particularly important—for making hormones which regulate bodily processes and neurotransmitters which are responsible for brain activities.

From Protein to Amino Acid

The common belief amongst doctors and most nutritionists is that deficiencies of amino acids simply don't exist—at least not in the Western world where we all eat plenty of protein. But what this belief ignores is the fact that the proteins we eat have to be broken down into their respective amino acids before our bodies can make use of them. This process of break-down is a complicated one and one which involves the actions of enzymes which are themselves made from amino acids. The proteins you take in through your foods are first attacked by pepsin, an enzyme secreted in the gastric juices. This is followed by other proteolytic enzymes from the pancreas and the mucosa of the small intestine. All of these enzymes are themselves made from amino acids. If your system is deficient in the free amino acids which you need in order to make digestive enzymes, your body will be unable to make proper use of the proteins you eat. So despite the fact that you may be taking in plenty of good-quality protein (indeed in Britain and the United States most of us eat far too much) you could be suffering an amino-acid deficiency which, like a vicious circle, only gets worse as the years pass. It goes something like this: if you have insufficient pancreatic proteolytic enzymes you digest proteins poorly and don't get the amino acids from them that you need. This amino-acid deficiency in turn creates a kind of chain reaction throughout your body. Since proteolytic enzymes are built from amino acids when these are deficient then digestive enzymes become deficient as well. Also if amino acids are deficient then they fail to evoke proteolytic enzyme secretions from the pancreas. So a deficiency of amino acids at one level leads to a further deficiency at another level which leads to a further deficiency at yet another level and so on.

Poor Digestion Leads to Degeneration

This is no hypothetical theory either. Experts say it is a common occurrence as we age. Deficiencies in hydrochloric acid in the stomach, in pepsin and particularly in the pancreatic proteolytic (protein-digesting) enzymes is widespread in people over thirty who have lived on a typical Western diet. They can suffer from digestive degeneration and malabsorption so that they do not break down their food proteins adequately and do not get the amino acids they need to carry out all of the essential biological functions which are dependent on them. Also, when as a result of insufficient enzymes proteins are incompletely broken down, they putrefy in the small intestine, producing by-products which are toxic and can result in food allergies, and mental and emotional disturbances, and which appear to contribute significantly to a number of other problems—from rheumatoid arthritis and gout to poor skin and premature ageing. So important is proper protein digestion in protecting your body from age-degeneration and deterioration that many nutritionally oriented physicians recommend that over the age of thirty-five or forty their patients take supplements of digestive enzymes (usually together with hydrochloric acid) to ensure better protein break-down in the gut. Many also recommend that a balanced free-amino-acid supplement also be taken in any serious programme for ageless ageing. This is for two reasons. First because the person can be sure of getting adequate free aminos for enzyme production and second because some free aminos such as methionine and cysteine are themselves superb free-radical scavengers. They help protect against the cross-linking and peroxidation damage of the ageing process.

Checks on Amino Status

In recent years a few farsighted scientists and physicians have been using 'quantitative urine amino-acid screening' to check on how well their patients break down proteins into their constituent amino acids and to identify areas of deficiency, and sluggish or retarded metabolic pathways as well as probable vitamin and mineral deficiencies (which prevent the formation and activation of enzymes). It is a valuable diagnostic tool. For it indicates exactly how and in what quantities specific combinations of free amino acids, vitamins and minerals can be used as nutritional supplements to correct them. In combination with hair, blood and urine analyses of minerals and vitamins, it is the best way of outlining an effective and highly personalized programme for anyone serious about pursuing an ageless-ageing lifestyle. On such a programme, a patient's mental and physical health often improve dramatically.

One of the areas in which amino-acid therapy appears to offer the greatest help is in the treatment of resistant emotional disturbances and mental illnesses—particularly those such as depression which have been long associated with ageing.

Screenings of hundreds of patients with psychological problems as varied as anxiety, depression and hallucinations show that almost all of them have distorted amino-acid pictures. When the results from each patient's amino-acid assays are used to design a personal programme of amino-acid supplementation for them, many longstanding emotional disorders simply disappear. Another area which currently appears to offer great potential for amino-acid therapy and which is closely related to their use as anti-ageing substances is in the treatment of cancer.

Even without personal amino-acid screening, there are many ways in which an ageless ager can use specific aminos as part of an effective programme for age-retardation. They can be used in combinations of 'complete' amino acids for revitalizing a flagging digestive system and to encourage the healing and rebuilding of muscle tissue, hormones and enzymes in the body. Some, such as phenylalanine, tyrosine, and tryptophan can be used to alter mood, mind and behaviour or to relieve age-related aches and pains (see Chapter 29). Others such as histidine can dramatically improve the quality of many people's sexual responses and enjoyment. Some are superb aids to weight loss and can help turn flaccid muscles into firm youthful contours, and still others such as ornithine and arginine are natural immune-stimulants which reinforce the health and functioning of the immune system and can therefore strengthen your body's resistance to ageing on a broad front. But in relation to ageing probably the most important of all are the sulphur-based amino acids which are themselves powerful anti-oxidant nutrients—useful tools for protecting your system from free-radical damage and cross-linking. These sulphur-based aminos are central to any serious programme for ageless ageing.

Stay Young with Sulphur

Seldom do nutritionists concern themselves with sulphur and yet dietary sulphur is not only an essential mineral and a potent protector against radiation and chemical pollution, it has even been shown to prolong the lifespan of animals. The molecules of most amino acids are made up of carbon, hydrogen, nitrogen and oxygen atoms only. Those which also contain sulphur in their molecules, such as methionine, cysteine and taurine, besides being helpful in building enzymes, hormones and new protein tissue in the body, are also important anti-oxidants, free-radical scavengers, neutralizers of toxic wastes and aids for protein synthesis. Their ability to offer protection from radiation of many different sorts—from x-rays to low-level nuclear radiation—makes them particularly important in the late twentieth century when radiation has become such a widespread threat to high-level health. Much of the damage from radiation comes because of radioactivity's ability to steal electrons from water molecules in the body, turning them into hydroxyl radicals which in turn get together to form peroxides. These peroxides emasculate anti-oxidant enzymes such as catalase by damaging their sulphydryl groups. When sufficient sulphur amino acids are present in the body then sufficient sulphydryl groups are available to be sacrificed by combining with free-radicals and peroxides so that anti-oxidant enzymes remain protected to carry out their jobs. After this occurs the amino acids themselves are simply turned into other harmless substances.

The Methionine Connection

Methionine is a constituent of haemoglobin, tissues and serum and it has an essential part to play in the activity of the spleen, lymph system and pancreas. It is one of the important agents in preventing excessive build-up of fat in the liver and it is often used to eliminate toxic metal loads from the body. Methionine also helps convert a toxic substance, guanidine, to a relatively nontoxic chemical, methyl-guanidine. This is particularly important in countering the kind of fatigue which often accompanies getting older since this toxin is an important cause of chronic fatigue in the body. Methionine, like many of the natural anti-oxidants, works in a synergistic way with other important nutrients for ageless ageing. For instance it helps your body make good use of selenium.

Taurine, another sulphur-based amino, as well as being an anti-oxidant and free-radical deactivator, plays an important role in cellular health by helping to stabilize membrane excitability in the heart, skeletal muscles and the central nervous system, all of which contain taurine in high concentrations. Taurine has been used therapeutically to lower blood pressure in people with essential hypertension and also as an effective treatment for epilepsy. It also helps the passage of minerals such as calcium and magnesium, sodium and potassium through cell walls. Taurine is in very high concentration in human breast milk. Many scientists now believe that it is an important substance in the healthy development of the brain and in the prevention of strokes. Taurine is often not included in anti-oxidant formulas for ageless ageing simply because it can be synthesized in the brain from other amino acids, but many experts in the field of amino-acid biochemistry insist it should be.

Cysteine—the Youth Connection

Cysteine is probably the most important sulphur-based amino acid of all. It has a pleasant garlic-like taste and you can sprinkle it on your foods instead of eating salt. But you have to be sure to keep it in a tight container since it is also an amino which tends to draw water from the atmosphere. In fact cysteine, which many serious longevists include in their list of supplements in good quantity by taking between 500 and 2000mg of L-cysteine hydrochloride a day, is really a stable form of the sulphur-rich amino acid cysteine. One gram of cysteine hydrochloride contains about 180mg of sulphur. Your body can convert one into the other as it needs it. Cysteine occurs in good concentration in the hair and nails and is one of the most useful supplements in improving the health and good looks of both. It is equally important in keeping your skin smooth and young looking and in helping skin recover from damage. Like selenium, cysteine is particularly useful in protecting the body from chemical pollutants. It can also help protect the body from the destructive effects of radiation.

Cysteine is a central component of the body's important anti-oxidant enzyme glutathione peroxidase. It is also able to chelate or tie up metals such as copper, cadmium and mercury and help eliminate them from the body. And it is an important agent to counteract the effects of acetaldehyde and other chemicals which build up in the body as a result of smoking and drinking. When researchers dosed rats with enough acetaldehyde to kill 90 per cent of a control group, an amazing 80 per cent of those treated with cysteine half an hour before testing survived the challenge. Cysteine is particularly bound up with the use of vitimin B_6 in the body. That is why it is important if you take the one that it is complemented with the other. Cysteine is not given as a supplement to diabetics except under medical supervision since it is capable of inactivating insulin. And most ageing experts agree that if you are going to take a very large dose of cysteine as an anti-ageing supplement you should also take three times the dose of ascorbic acid. This, they say, will protect your body from any possibility of its developing kidney or bladder stones from very high doses of this amino acid.

Don't Forget the Eggs and Garlic

Your body contains about 140g of sulphur, almost a gram of which is lost every day and which needs to be replaced through the foods you eat. Foods which are a good source of sulphur amino acids include eggs, cabbage, garlic and onions. Eggs can be particularly important as part of any nutritional programme for ageless ageing. Each egg contains about 65mg of sulphur. Unfortunately over the years, as a result of the notion that eggs contribute to the accumulation of cholesterol, many people have been shortchanging themselves of the support that these sulphur-rich foods can bring. Recent research has shown that this belief is completely unfounded. For although eggs do indeed contain cholesterol they also are a good source of iron, lecithin, zinc and sulphur as well as other trace minerals which are active elements in converting cholesterol into useful steroid hormones and other substances in the body. As twice Nobel laureate Linus Pauling says, 'We must educate people away from the dangerous idea that you can control heart disease by not eating foods such as eggs, butter and milk. This over-simplified idea is totally wrong.' Don't neglect your eggs. Years from now you will be glad you didn't.

Sex and the Aminos

Two amino acids have particularly useful sexual connotations. The first is arginine which is especially important for men because it is such an essential constituent of seminal fluid and can increase sperm count as well as sperm motility. A large proportion of seminal fluid is arginine and in one interesting study, forty-two men who were being treated for infertility experienced a 100 per cent increase in sperm count.

The other amino acid which can play a particularly useful sexual role is histidine. Histidine is a precursor to histamine, the amine found in all organic matter which helps regulate blood pressure and gastric secretion and which is released by certain immune cells during an allergic reaction or when you have a cold. People with allergies often have the suppressor cells in their immune system out of balance. They have too many helper cells and not enough suppressors. Many physicians have found that, because histidine supplementation can rebalance this problem, it can be very helpful in treating allergic symptoms.

Histidine is also essential to the body during growth and you will find increased concentrations of it during haemoglobin synthesis. Experimentally it has been used to change brain waves from the alert beta-dominated wave patterns to the alpha waves characteristic of light meditation. It appears to have a calming effect on the nervous system and some physicians have used histidine supplements to help people stop biting their nails as well as to relieve the serious miseries of arthritis. Histidine together with tryptophan are the only free amino acids included in Professor P. P. Saksonov's famous vitamin-amino acid-adaptogen complex which was given to Russian astronauts as a 'nonspecific pharmacochemical protective' medicine and a specific radiation protector on their journeys into space. In the realm of sexuality histidine has some interesting applications. In fact, American psychologist and expert in amino-acid screening and the applications of amino acids for therapeutic uses Robert Erdmann says of histidine, 'It is the best kept sex secret of the century.' Erdmann and others have used it with enormous success to heighten sexual feeling in people in whom it has been repressed. Among other things it dramatically intensifies the experience of orgasm for many people. It has even been used successfully in the treatment of 'frigidity' and of non-orgasmic women. Used in this way it is generally taken with niacin and vitamin B$_6$ which are necessary to convert histidine to histamine in the body.

Tri-peptide Anti-oxidants and Immune-Supports

Many of the growth-hormone-releaser (GHR) amino acids such as ornithine and arginine have a strengthening effect on the immune system. They have been shown to improve immune response to bacteria, viruses and tumour cells in animal experiments. They have also been used to increase the weight of the thymus gland—the master gland of immunity—and to increase important T-cell production. These immune-supporting functions, coupled with the anti-oxidant capabilities of some amino acids we have already mentioned and the characteristic that many of them have of being able to detoxify the body and of encouraging full functioning of the body's anti-oxidant enzymes and digestive enzymes, make free amino acids potent nutritional tools for ageless ageing.

One particular tri-peptide known as glutathione which is composed of three amino acids—L-cysteine, L-glutamic acid, and glycine—offers particular support to the body's anti-oxidant defence system. You may remember we spoke of the body's first and second lines of defence against free-radical attack and cross-linking. The second line of defence is composed of all of the anti-oxidant nutrients from ascorbic acid to methionine which act as free-radical scavengers in the system. Glutathione plays an important part in our first line of defence. It works something like this. The primary enzyme defending against activated species of molecules is composed of super-oxide dismutase, glutathione peroxidase and catalase. SOD takes care of converting activated oxygen molecules to hydrogen peroxide. But hydrogen peroxide itself is still mildly toxic. It has to be further metabolized either by catalase or by glutathione peroxidase. Glutathione has been used for many years in injectable form to stimulate glutathione peroxidase activity in the body with excellent results. Recently it was discovered that, unlike SOD, whose effect when taken orally is highly controversial, glutathione taken orally as a nutritional supplement appears helpful in guarding against fat peroxidation as well as in detoxifying the body of wastes. It has been used with particular success to clear away debris and harmful bacteria from the lungs in the case of infection or when a person has been exposed to a high level of air pollution. Like all of the free-radical scavengers it works best in combination with others. Selenium is particularly important since it is essential for the formation of glutathione peroxidase in the body.

Make Friends with Aminos

If you want to make use of some of the benefits which have been reported from using free amino acids as part of a programme of ageless ageing, how do you go about it? And what kind of cautions do you need to exercise? Let's look at cautions first. Arginine and ornithine are not usually given to schizophrenics; tryptophan and the GHR aminos (see page 206) are not given to pregnant or lactating women; cysteine is not given to diabetics and is always taken with three times the amount of vitamin C; phenylalanine is given with caution in cases of high blood pressure; histidine is taken with an equal quantity of vitamin C and not by people who already have high histamine levels or by manic depressives; tyrosine is not given to people who are taking the MAO inhibitor anti-depressant drugs; neither is phenylalanine or tryptophan.

Although many people use certain free aminos such as tryptophan for relaxation or L-glutamine as a mental pep-up with no problem whatever, if you are planning to take them over a long period of time it is a good idea to have an amino assay done to clarify your own individual pattern of amino-acid use and to indicate the best nutritional supplement for your specific needs. Unfortunately as yet few physicians offer this service and it can also be quite expensive. Is there an alternative?

Robert Erdmann, who has spent fifteen years researching the clinical and preventative use of free amino acids as nutritional supplements, advises anyone taking them longterm to ensure they have a 'complete' formula in addition to any specific free amino they may be using for a certain effect—say histidine to increase sexual response or cysteine as a means of improving hair condition—as well as a well-balanced formula of vitamin and mineral supplementation. For like all anti-oxidant nutrients it is important to ensure that you get sufficient co-factors for their use—vitamins such as B_6, B_{12} and C, selenium, zinc and so forth—to be able adequately to draw from them all of the support for high-level energy and well-being which they potentially offer. This way one can be absolutely sure of supplying the body with all of the nutrients—amino acids as well as vitamins and minerals—it needs to function at a high level of vitality. This way too you can be sure of not causing any imbalances in the system. An example of a good balanced formula would be one which has been based either on the amino-acid balance naturally found in an egg or in spirulina—a freshwater alga.

Most free amino acids are best taken on an empty stomach at least forty-five minutes before a meal. They are available from health-food stores and by post from suppliers. By far the best way to take any of them is in pure white crystalline form simply by stirring a teaspoon or more of the powder into a glass of mineral water or in simple gelatin capsules, since this means you avoid any of the incipients (i.e. the binding ingredients) which are used to put them into tablet form. Be sure when buying amino acids that you buy absolutely the best and don't be misled by manufacturers who are trying to get on to the amino-acid bandwagon by putting inferior products on the market.

NINETEEN

Slimming Revolution

One of the great worries many people have about beginning to follow an ageless-ageing way of eating centres around their being overweight or their having had to be constantly fighting the battle of the bulge. They are afraid they could never adjust to a high-potency-low-calorie diet because for them the ritual of slimming has always consisted of constant self-abnegation and been a kind of continual battle with guilt and overindulgence. For others it has been a source of constant frustration or impossibility. The amazing free amino acids can help here too. Certain free amino acids, used together with a way of eating which, like high-potency-low-calorie nutrition, particularly stresses fresh raw vegetables and complex carbohydrates, natural grains and pulses, and which is also low in fat and eliminates highly processed and refined foods, can transform the traditional on-again-off-again slimming ritual into a way of life which balances your weight permanently. And it needn't take a gigantic act of will either. That is, provided you make use of the right free amino acids. They can reduce your appetite, encourage the burning of fat in your body, improve your mood and raise your energy levels. No wonder the free aminos are rapidly becoming cornerstones of successful and permanent slimming.

Natural Appetite-Suppressant

The substance now most widely used as a natural appetite-suppressant is the essential amino acid phenylalanine, which appears to have a number of other therapeutic properties as well—from acting as an antidepressant to helping eliminate the chronic pain of arthritis and back injuries. Phenylalanine, which has to be taken on an empty stomach, together with the nutrients and vitamins B_6 and C that are needed for its use, appears to work to reduce hunger in two ways. First it is converted into noradrenaline in the body which is an important brain chemical—an excitatory neurotransmitter which elevates your mood and quite simply makes you feel like eating less. Amphetamines—the prescription drugs used to suppress appetite—also work to release noradrenaline in the brain and to block its reabsorption. Trouble is that with amphetamines you quickly build a tolerance to them so they cease to be effective and you need to take ever-increasing doses to get the effect. Also amphetamines have dangerous side-effects when taken over a period of time. Amongst other things they force your body to produce more noradrenaline than it wants to produce without supplying the raw materials from which it can be made. This can lead to a deficiency of this important neurotransmitter.

Phenylalanine is different and it is safe. It both normalizes brain and nerve levels of noradrenaline, suppresses appetite and makes you feel energetic and positive without the dangerous side-effects or the problem of building tolerance. Phenylalanine appears to be important in another way too. According to recent research, the hypothalamus is the control centre for a chemical called cholecystokinin—CCK—which is made in the brain and in the intestines and is believed to be important in giving you a feeling of hunger or satiety. Too much CCK makes people undereat while too little creates an overeater. Phenylalanine availability has been linked to CCK production through noradrenaline. For high levels of this neurotransmitter in the brain appear to spur the release of CCK which in turn reduces appetite in yet another way.

Phenylalanine comes in various forms. The kind used for appetite control is usually L-phenylalanine or DL-phenylalanine—which is also used for the control of chronic pain (see Chapter 29). It is usually taken with B_6 and vitamin C first thing in the morning in 500mg capsules since they are more readily absorbed than tablets. The one caution about its use is in the case of someone with high blood pressure since this amino acid can heighten blood pressure if used in too high a dose. As with any of the free aminos it is wise to consult a nutritionally aware physician before embarking on a longterm course of them.

The Amino Fat-Burner

L-carnitine is another amino acid currently attracting a lot of attention as a means of encouraging weight loss. Unlike phenylalanine it is not an essential one. It can be made in the liver from two other amino acids, lysine and methionine, in the presence of vitamins C and B_6, niacin and iron. Carnitine is a substance which in the body transfers fatty acids through the membranes of the mitochondria—the cells' minute energy factories—so that they can be burnt and turned into energy. If not enough carnitine is available then fatty acids are not metabolized well. This can lead to a build-up of fat as well as to high blood-fat and triglyceride levels. Supplements of L-carnitine have been shown in animal experiments to improve fat metabolism, reduce blood cholesterol and triglyceride levels and lower blood pressure. Also in experiments in animals L-carnitine is currently attracting interest because of its ability to prolong an animal's lifespan—probably because it enhances the anti-oxidant effects of other nutrients such as vitamins E and C by enabling them to be carried across cell membranes to the mitochondria where the ageing free radicals are generated.

L-carnitine is also widely being used as a supplement for athletes—one to two 250mg capsules a day—because since it enhances the body's ability to burn fat for energy it also increases endurance. It appears helpful for weight loss because of this ability as well and because it protects the body from ketosis—a common problem of many people on weight-reducing diets. Ketosis consists of an accumulation of fat waste products called ketone bodies or ketones which tends to make the blood acidic and leads to the loss of potassium, magnesium and calcium from the body. It can cause kidney damage and even be life-threatening if it goes uncontrolled. Carnitine supplementation can control it. L-carnitine is believed to be the best form of this amino acid for it is the most biologically active and doesn't cause muscle weakness as can the D and the DL forms.

It too is generally given on an empty stomach—usually in doses of between 250mg and 500mg a day.

Muscle Magic with Aminos

Of interest to anyone who has constantly fought the battle of the bulge or who, although not overweight, is concerned about correcting a loss of muscle tone as he or she gets older, is the way in which some free amino acids used as nutritional supplements appear to perform a few hitherto virtually impossible tasks: turning flab into muscle, and improving your emotional state so that while you are losing weight you feel on top of the world. It is a breakthrough in the search for a biochemical means of stimulating weight loss and for making an older softer body look younger and firmer which is nothing less than revolutionary. This use of certain free amino acids to encourage weight loss and to alter the ratio of fat to muscle tissue in the body in favour of more muscle tissue is largely based on the recent discovery that some amino acids such as ornithine, lysine, tryptophan, tyrosine and arginine when taken in their free form and under special circumstances (that is in the presence of vitamins C and B_6 and on an empty stomach) have the ability to trigger the production in the body of what is known as human growth hormone (HGH).

Human growth hormone—also called somatotrophic hormone—is a substance secreted by the anterior lobe of the pituitary gland. It is needed for the maintenance of normal protein synthesis and for growth in young people. Its presence in the body inhibits fat formation, mobilizes fat stores—releasing them into the bloodstream in the form of free fatty acids—and stimulates the immune system to protect the body against illness and premature ageing. Medically HGH has been used to arrest the bone-thinning tendency which old people have, to treat tissue-wasting conditions and to accelerate wound healing. We produce the highest levels of human growth hormone when we are still growing and production falls off sharply when growth is finished and in most people ceases altogether by the time they are fifty. It is high human-growth-hormone production which helps give young people their firm muscular bodies and bestows on them that infuriating ability—so wide-spread amongst teenagers—to eat virtually as much as they want without gaining weight. A decrease in human-growth-hormone production which occurs with age appears to be the major reason why older bodies tend to be less muscular, more flabby and fatter than their youthful counterparts.

Natural Growth-Hormone Triggers

There are a number of conditions which can trigger human-growth-hormone release from the pituitary. One of them is sleep. The release of human growth hormone is part of your body's normal circadian rhythms. It occurs about ninety minutes after you fall asleep at night. If your sleep is disturbed, however, growth-hormone release can be reduced or elimin-ated—an event which, if it occurs regularly over a period of time, can weaken your body's immune system and make you more prone to illness. Another trigger of human growth hormone is exercise. When you exercise regularly and aero-bically—that is so that your heart and lungs get a good workout—you also encourage the release of human growth hormone from the pituitary. This is one reason why people who train regularly are leaner and more muscular than those who are sedentary. It is also one of the reasons that exercise is such an important tool in keeping you young-looking and -feeling. What is particularly encouraging to any would-be slimmer or lean flab-fighter are recent findings that certain amino acids taken in their free forms can be used to stimulate the human-growth-hormone production in the pituitary—each in its own way—and thereby to help people burn fat and build muscle. Together these aminos have become known as Growth Hormone Releasers—GHRs.

GHR Nutrients

Take arginine and ornithine for instance. Both these free amino acids are currently being used to encourage growth-hormone release from the pituitary not only by people watching their weight but also by Olympic athletes intent on improving the strength and size of their muscles. Their ability to trigger the release of human growth hormone in turn stimulates protein production in muscles by increasing the transport of amino acids from which they are made into the cells, causing fat cells to release free fatty acids into the bloodstream and encouraging the liver to increase the rate at which it burns fat. It also strengthens connective tissue, reduces the concentration of urea in the blood and urine and, as a kind of bonus, appears to improve immune functions and may therefore improve the body's resistance to illness and premature ageing.

Arginine occurs in good quantity in the protein of soy beans, chickpeas and sunflower seeds and is particularly important in maintaining your body's nitrogen balance. It is an amino acid which some authorities now classify as 'essential' because normal growth and bodily function appear to demand more of it than can be made in the body itself. In its free form arginine promotes detoxification of ammonia and in men it is used to encourage the production of sperm. Arginine is also proving itself useful in the treatment of liver diseases and in encouraging wound healing after surgery or wounding. Unlike arginine, ornithine is not an amino acid used to make structural proteins or enzymes in the body. But it is an excellent growth-hormone stimulator thanks to its action on the central nervous system. In fact it is twice as effective as arginine. And it has an ability which arginine doesn't have—it can actually be transported to the mitochondria, the cells' energy factories. Many physicians and nutritionists who use GHR stimulants recommend taking ornithine alone instead of both.

Glycine is another amino acid which researchers are now using to stimulate growth-hormone release. In the Department of Endocrinology at Tokyo University researchers have found that an oral dose of 4-8g of glycine brings about a significant increase in serum growth-hormone levels. Glycine is also used in the treatment of progressive muscular distrophy and to build muscle tissue in athletes. Glycine has the added advantage of exerting a calming effect on the mind which can be very helpful to anyone on a low-calorie diet with its tendency to produce nervousness.

Tyrosine—Metabolic Stimulant and Appetite-Suppressor

Other amino acids are currently being used to stimulate weight loss through their biochemical mechanisms as well—say because of their ability to decrease appetite or to be converted in the body into hormones which encourage the mobilization of stored fats for use as energy. Tyrosine is one. Your body uses tyrosine to make several compounds which are important as neurotransmitters—chemicals which carry messages between neurons in the brain and which, among other things, can be powerful determinants of moods, brain functions and emotional drives. Vigorous exercise for periods of between thirty and forty-five minutes a day several times a week has been shown to encourage weight loss not only because of the calories it burns and because it encourages growth-hormone release but also because it stimulates metabolism, increasing the rate at which you burn calories. And the most important biological mechanism by which exercise stimulates metabolism appears to be its ability to raise the levels of a particular neurotransmitter called noradrenaline which both heightens metabolic processes and decreases appetite. By a several-step process L-tyrosine in its free form can be converted into noradrenaline in the body and therefore can also bring about increased energy expenditure and decreased appetite. L-tyrosine is also a precursor of other compounds such as L-dopa which themselves stimulate growth-hormone release when it is converted into them—but by quite different mechanisms than do ornithine, arginine and glycine. So it can help with weight loss and muscle building in a number of different ways. Yet another amino acid, tryptophan, is also helpful. When taken together with vitamin B_3, vitamin C can be converted into another growth-hormone-releasing neurotransmitter called serotonin.

Putting it into Practice

The new knowledge about metabolic stimulation and growth-hormone release is just beginning to filter down from scientific literature into the popular press. Sadly, as yet, few physicians, nutritionists and other health practitioners know how to put it into practice for the benefits of their patients. It can be tricky. There are a few precautions that advocates of amino-acid therapy insist must be carefully observed and there are a few rules, they say, which you need to remember.

One of the first rules is that most of these amino acids which stimulate growth-hormone release and suppress appetite work best in synergy—that is when they are taken in combination and on an empty stomach at least an hour before eating, preferably two. For if free-form amino acids are taken with food then instead of being converted into growth hormone and neuro-transmitters helpful for weight loss and muscle building, they will simply be used (as are the proteins you take in in the form of food) for tissue repair and other tasks. Second, in order to be converted it is necessary that they be accompanied by vitamin C—practitioners recommend somewhere between 1 and 10g a day during amino-acid supplementation—and vitamin B_6—usually between 50 and 150mg a day. They also recommend that anyone taking free amino acids drink at least four pints of liquids each day and that they ensure they are truly getting adequate quantities of other synergistic nutrients which are especially important to growth-hormone conversions, such as manganese and zinc. Then too you need to know that many free amino acids compete with each other to cross the blood-brain barrier, so it is important, for instance, not to take tyrosine (best taken in the morning) with tryptophan (best taken at night), otherwise you risk neutralizing the effect of both.

How much of each amino acid does one take? Practitioners vary in their opinions and, because amino-acid therapy is a relatively young therapeutic tool, there are no hard-and-fast rules. Standard practice, however, is to give somewhere between 6000 and 8000mg of ornithine or arginine (or a mixture of the two) together with 3000-4000mg of glycine, between 500mg and 2g of tyrosine and say 1000-2500mg of vitamin C, plus 100 to 150mg of B_6, a day. These quantities are usually split down the middle into two doses, ensuring that all the tyrosine is taken in the morning an hour or two before breakfast and all the tryptophan at bedtime—both on an empty stomach. One of the most effective ways to use the new GHR nutrients is to take them an hour before aerobic exercise such as swimming, running or cycling.

The Diet

What kind of diet should one follow when taking GHR supplements? The high-potency-low-calorie way of eating is ideal, with the one stipulation that at least for the first week or two you place special emphasis on raw foods, aiming at 75 per cent or more of your foods initially to be eaten raw. This is for several reasons. First, uncooked fresh foods offer the highest complement of essential nutrients—vitamins, minerals, enzymes and fibre—needed to make best use of the GHR supplements. Second, because raw fruits and vegetables tend to make the system alkaline they superbly balance the supplements, many of which are acidic. Finally, a high-raw diet rapidly eliminates many of the cravings for too much food or the wrong kind of food which are the result of longstanding allergy-addictions (the kind of thing which has some people reaching for one biscuit to go with their cup of tea and eating a whole packet).

Another good reason why the high-raw diet is important in making the best use of proteins is the fact that many of the proteins themselves which you will be eating are taken uncooked which makes them of greater value to the body because the amino acids they contain are more available for use.

Words of Caution

For most people the new amino-acid supplements appear to be entirely safe. However they should not be taken by anyone on tranquillizers, MAO inhibitors or antidepressant drugs, nor by diabetics, schizophrenics, pregnant and lactating women, growing adolescents or children. And it is wise for anyone wanting to make use of the GHRs for weight loss or to improve body tone to consult a nutritionally oriented physician who can help them design a formula tailored to their individual needs. For the need for and use of amino acids vary greatly from person to person. GHR nutrients taken over a long period in very high doses—much higher than those mentioned here—have been known to result in enlargement of joints and in a thickening of the skin which returns to normal when they are stopped. Another caution is that you should be very careful when buying amino-acid supplements to buy only the best. For their purity and effectiveness can vary greatly amongst those available from chemists and health-food stores. Read labels carefully. There are a lot of 'pretenders' sold as amino-acid supplements. For instance, protein powders which demand complete digestion are not a source of free amino acids, nor is 'pre-digested protein' nor 'free amino acids in a lactase or protein base' which only have a small percentage of free amino acids and are mostly undigested protein powder. But they are cheap and therefore are more widely sold. Free amino acids reduced from a protein source such as milk are not really very good either since they are not pure and they tend to contain residues which can cause allergic reactions and prevent proper use of the amino acids contained in the formula. The best free-form aminos—the only ones I would take myself for instance—are pure white crystalline substances. They come in a variety of forms—tablets, which give the poorest absorption, and capsules, and as pure crystalline powders, which are unquestionably most easy of all to absorb. By buying the powders themselves and taking some care you can mix your own GHR supplement. Trouble is most of them taste rather like old socks so you need either to stir them into a glass of juice when taking them or put them into gelatin capsules. There are also a few well-formulated growth-hormone-release nutritional supplements on the market.

PART III
The Ageless Body

TWENTY

Move Back through Time

Not only will regular exercise firm your muscles, keep your body young-looking and improve your self-image, it can also rejuvenate your body by altering what are ordinarily considered age-related parameters towards more youthful levels. Research has shown that it can:

- Prevent and reduce overweight
- Improve the heart's output and efficiency
- Make skin look younger and function in a younger way
- Protect the cardiovascular system from otherwise inevitable atherosclerosis
- Improve glucose-tolerance against degenerative changes leading to diabetes
- Lower triglycerides
- Increase the level of high-density lipoproteins (HDL) associated with protecting the heart
- Strengthen bones and prevent their shrinkage
- Increase lean muscle mass
- Improve the oxygen-carrying capacity of the blood
- Lower high blood pressure
- Banish anxicty and depression
- Improve mental functions
- Heighten vitality
- Help you live longer

Exercise and Live Longer

Until recently there was a lot of controversy surrounding the issue of how exercise affects longevity, mostly because a number of well-known research projects, such as the Harvard study of 6300 athletes and the Michigan State Study of 692 athletes, which purport to show that exercise does not increase life-span. The first study showed that Harvard athletes died significantly earlier than their sedentary counterparts while the second recorded no difference in length of life between exercisers and non-exercisers. The trouble is when you examine such research you find some serious mistakes in the way these studies were handled. The researchers defined 'athletes' as men who had been active while in university. They made no attempt to discover if these men had continued with sporting activities or exercise after leaving university. Many athletes stopped training when they ceased playing sports in college and began to lead sedentary lifestyles—they could hardly be called 'regular exercisers'. On the other hand when the data-research projects exploring links between exercise and longevity have been well handled strong evidence emerges that exercise is a powerful tool for age-retardation and life extension—even rejuvenation—for it alters many parameters such as blood-pressure and cholesterol levels, bone mineralization, vitality, and the oxygen-carrying capacity of the blood—all towards more youthful levels.

Calming the Controversy

Exercise can not only make you look and feel younger, it can actually help you live longer. A study by Harvard and Stanford University of nearly 17,000 graduates carried out over five decades showed that regular exercise delays ageing. It is also an important factor in preventing coronary heart disease. Researchers found there was 'a strong inverse relationship between exercise and death from *all* causes, total cardiovascular diseases (including both CHD and stroke) and total respiratory diseases'. They discovered that the adjusted death rate for the most sedentary of the men studied was almost twice that of individuals who regularly burned 2000 calories a week in exercise. But to reap benefit from the life-lengthening effects of exercise it has to be carried out steadily—not in spurts and spells. For even university athletes have a high risk of death if they later become sedentary while sedentary ex-athletes are able to lower their risk if later on they return to regular exercise. Bruce B. Dan, editor of the *Journal of the American Medical Association* which reported the study commented, 'We can now prove that large numbers of Americans are *dying from sitting on their behinds*' [my italics]. Researchers noted, 'If everyone studied had been physically active there would have been a 23 per cent lower incidence of coronary disease.' They also found that how much physical exercise you get can influence your other lifestyle habits for the better. Physical activity reduces your desire to smoke, lowers the chance of your becoming obese, helps control blood pressure and leads both to a better diet and better stress control.

Exercise for Fun and Live Longer

In 1977 Charles Rose and Michel Cohen at the Veteran's Administration Hospital in Boston examined the death records of 500 men by interviewing living relatives about their lifestyle. They discovered that while exercise on the job appeared to have little effect on longevity those men who exercised regularly in their leisure-time lived 7.1 years longer than those who let their exercise decline steadily after their twenties. They also showed that regular exercise carried out throughout life extends lifespan. Meanwhile in Canada Terence Kavanagh and Roy Shepherd examined 128 men and 7 women participants—some top athletes, others simply enthusiastic amateurs, some as old as ninety—who exercised regularly and who were playing in the 1975 World Masters' Golf Championships in Toronto. These exercisers showed significantly fewer signs of ageing than the average person does. For instance where most of us lose height at a rate of about half an inch per decade after the age of 45, they had lost less than half that much. Those between forty and ninety years of age also showed less body fat, had larger muscle mass in their body and better heart and lung function. Their bodies looked younger and stronger, their physiology functioned better and they were able to maintain their bodies even under conditions of 'haphazard' nutrition, thanks to the powerful anti-ageing effects of exercise.

Use It or Lose It

This old adage is never better applied than in the realm of age-prevention. A large part of what generally passes for age-related degeneration in the human body is instead a result of simple *disuse*. In fact, some of the latest research indicates that disuse may be even more important than disease or the passage of time in determining the rate at which you age. Your body was built for movement just as your digestive system was designed to deal with natural foods rich in fibre and structural inform-ation. When—thanks to our sedentary occupations and the hours we spend driving around in cars instead of walking or running from place to place—your body does not get the rhythmic vigorous exercise for which it was designed, it begins in a hundred ways to degenerate. This degeneration is easily measured in terms of loss of calcium and a thinning of the bones, increases in blood pressure and certain blood fats, poor muscle tone and sagging skin. But what has only recently been recognized (indeed even many age-researchers have not tumbled to this fact yet) is that changes in the body due to low levels of physical activity are very close to those commonly attributed to ageing. These changes can come on fast. In only twenty-four hours of inactivity your muscle tissue begins to deteriorate. Let a year go by without exercise and 50 per cent of the health and age-control benefits you may have gained from a lifetime of sports will be lost. For lounge lizards this is the bad news: regular rhythmic exercise is essential to holding back the ravages of time. But there is good news too: it is *never* too late to begin.

Space-Age Research

Much of the awareness of how disuse (often more than the passage of time) is central to the processes of ageing and degeneration has come out of the scientific work involved in putting man into space—in particular plunging him into that novel physiological state known as weightlessness. For weightlessness in physiological terms is a kind of intensified disuse in which the human body does not even have to make the effort to resist the force of gravity. When researchers started to investigate weightlessness they naturally studied the two conditions which most closely approximate it—being in water and being at rest in bed. In either of these states you rapidly lose precious minerals from the bones, making them weaker and more susceptible to breakage, you slow down the elimination of wastes from the tissues, and you get muscle shrinkage and a wasting of the skin and muscles that most people associate with old age.

Your body's single most important function is its use of oxygen. Unlike food or water, you cannot go without oxygen for even a few minutes without suffering damage. And when an organ such as the brain or heart is deprived of oxygen even for a short time it brings about catastrophic results—a stroke or a heart attack for instance. Studying the effects of weightlessness and immobility on the body, researchers such as Walter M. Bortz II at the Stanford University School of Medicine have found that by far the most serious effects of disuse lie in the way it decreases the body's ability to extract oxygen from the atmosphere and to transmit it via the bloodstream to the tissues which use it for energy. They claim that it is not a pill, magic potion or some glamorous and expensive youth treatment which can best reverse the long and rather depressing list of changes that have come to be associated with ageing, but exercise— simply because it dramatically improves your body's ability to extract oxygen.

The measurement of how well you do this is expressed in scientific terms as VO_2 max. Bortz began studying the relationship between age-related changes and inactivity as a result of having his own leg in a cast for six weeks. He noticed when the cast was removed that the 'withered, stiff and painful leg' looked like it belonged on a body which was forty years older than he was. Researching the subject in depth he discovered that by almost every measurement that could be taken, a lack of exercise produced bodily changes which paralleled those associated with ageing. Put yourself into a programme of regular sustained physical activity and you can not only prevent them but even help reverse them when they have already occurred.

VO$_2$ Max—Key to Youth

In most people VO$_2$ max steadily declines after thirty—at a rate of about 1 per cent per year. The decline takes place simply because, unlike our primitive ancestors who remained physically active all through their lives, we lead a largely sedentary existence. As a result we appear to age quite rapidly: our bodies decline in cardiovascular and lung fitness, we lose muscle and bone tissue, our skin wrinkles and thins and we experience a progressive stiffening of the joints. Curiously, these age-related changes occur at just the rate at which your VO$_2$ max declines. But what some of the exciting new studies show is that a decline in VO$_2$ max is not inevitable. When an ageing person of thirty-five, fifty-five or even seventy-five works out regularly he or she can restore their VO$_2$ max levels to that of someone much younger. And as VO$_2$ max increases, energy levels rise, measurements of the state of the cardiovascular system such as heart rate, cholesterol levels and blood lipids, return to more youthful parameters, skin looks younger, high blood pressure decreases, joints regain their flexibility, the loss of minerals from the bones is halted, muscle mass increases and fat is lost. Even intelligence levels improve.

Turn Back the Clock

Physiologist J. L. Hodgson at Pennsylvania State University has carried out studies which show that when an inactive seventy-year-old starts a programme of moderate activity he can expect to improve his oxygen-transporting ability by some fifteen years. If he then goes on to achieve an athlete's level of conditioning, says Hodgson, he could potentially regain forty years of VO$_2$ max and experience many of the physical and physiological effects of rejuvenation in the process. So exceptional is the ability of regular exercise to reverse age changes that, as Bortz has written in the *Journal of the American Medical Association*, 'It seems extremely unlikely that any further drug or physician-oriented technique will approach such a benefit.'

Regular sustained physical activity can go a long way towards preventing age-related changes of all sorts from cardiovascular ones to the look of the skin. It also dramatically increases a person's energy levels. Herbert de Vries, age expert at the Andrus Gerontology Centre at the University of Southern California has shown in a study involving more than 200 people that men and women of sixty or seventy can become as fit and energetic as people thirty years younger. 'Regular exercise quite literally turned back the clock for our volunteers,' says de Vries. When questioned about what they considered the greatest benefit of their regular exercise programmes his subjects most often answered greater energy. The fitter you are the more energy you have. It is the 'body so unused to activity that tires at the slightest effort', he says.

Work Out Your Stresses

De Vries has also explored in depth how exercise might be used to relieve anxiety and depression—two conditions which so-called middle-aged and older people are believed to suffer greatly from. It has long been established that there is a direct correlation via the autonomic nervous system between anxiety and the level of electrical activity in our skeletal muscles. Electromyographic instruments are designed to measure even minute electrical changes in muscles and this in turn indicates the degree of muscular tensions present. De Vries has taken these kind of measurements and correlated the relationship between resting-muscle action potential and the body's oxygen consumption as a whole—something which also reflects both neuromuscular tension and emotional status. He has discovered that even a few minutes of moderate exercise, where you are breathing deeply and your heart is beating well, significantly reduces emotional anxiety. And when you exercise regularly and aerobically by brisk walking, swimming, jogging, cycling and so forth, you dramatically decrease your anxiety levels. The right kind of exercise for the right length of time can bring about a better tranquillizing effect than drugs with none of the side-effects. According to de Vries, to make the most of exercise's tranquillizing effects you need to practise it from five to thirty minutes each session at between 30 and 60 per cent of maximum heart rate.

Defeat Depression

No one is absolutely sure why exercise has such a tranquillizing effect on body and mood. At least in part it probably comes from the decrease in the muscle irritability and the increase in deep muscle heat which it brings about. Partly too it must be a result of how exercise alters brain chemistry. For moderate aerobic exercise has at least two important effects on the brain. First it encourages the production of noradrenaline or norepinephrine—the neurotransmitter which makes you feel 'up'. Athletes tend to have high levels of this hormone in their blood while endogenously depressed people usually show very low levels. Putting a sedentary person into a regular exercise programme quite soon leads to an increase in noradrenaline and therefore to an improvement in mood—making him more optimistic and giving him feelings of having power over his life. Second, exercise greatly increases the body's production of beta-endorphins—natural opiates produced in the pituitary gland and in various structures of the brain which, through their action on the central nervous system, have a calming effect on the whole body as well as uplifting mind and mood. Study after study has shown that when chronically depressed people get into exercise programmes—even as simple as taking long brisk walks a few times a week—their depression lifts.

Rejuvenate Your Skin

Regular physical exercise—the kind you get if you do forty-five minutes of walking, swimming, aerobic workouts, running, rebounding or rowing at least four or five times a week—also makes you *look* younger. It suffuses your skin with blood and increases the ability of your body to carry oxygen and nutrients to the skin's cells and to remove waste products from them. Exercise physiologist James White at the University of California at San Diego carried out an interesting study to discover just how effective exercise can be at retarding and reversing the effects of ageing on skin. He paired older women on a programme of rebounding using mini-trampolines with sedentary women and discovered that the exercisers looked younger, had better skin and colouring and fewer wrinkles than nonexercisers. White was surprised to find that exercise reduces bags under the eyes as well. So, while forty minutes a day of an aerobic activity may not sound as mysterious and romantic as a visit to one of Europe's glamorous rejuvenation centres, in the long run may do you a lot more good. Not to mention the amount of money it can save. You don't have to be an enthusiastic jogger or visit the gym four times a week to reap the benefits of exercise. Activities as gentle as yoga and as pleasant as long brisk walks can do it for you. One of the most important factors in exercising for ageless ageing is the way when it is done with ease and enjoyment it can be a tool for the integration of mind and body. So important is this factor that it merits closer scrutiny.

TWENTY-ONE

Free the Body – Charge the Mind

We live in an age of fitness. Joggers pound the pavements summer and winter, dance studios brim with all sizes and shapes of sweaty women in pink legwarmers, and every month or so a 'new' system of physical exercise appears on the scene. You'd expect to find the world full of strong supple bodies brimming with grace and energy. The reality is somewhat different. The fine muscle tone, buoyant energy and rich mobility of a coordinated, supple and responsive physical body is a rare occurrence in the Western world even amongst those who consider themselves most fit. Instead we are faced with contracted shoulders and sunken chests, distorted thighs and faces which have aged before their time thanks to poor muscle tone and flagging energy. Meanwhile too many of us—fitness freaks and lounge lizards alike—experience our body not as a joy or a finely tuned instrument of expression for our inner being—but rather as a prison incarcerating the Self which cries out for physical expression but is rendered mute by walls of chronic tension, fatigue or postural distortions. Most of us live at only a fraction of our capacity for vitality and we have not the least notion of our body's potential for beauty and for pleasure. For exercise to be of real benefit in ageless ageing, it needs to be an *integrating* activity which draws together mind and body.

The Body as Energy

For just as it's important to recognize that the ageing process as a whole is not only a biochemical phenomenon but is also dependent upon energy changes—structural information that comes to us through our food and our environment, and our mental attitudes and expectations—so a new approach to exercise is needed to make the most of its potential for ageless ageing. Thinkers such as von Bertalanffy and researchers such as Szent-Györgyi and the American orthopaedic specialist and expert in electrobiology Robert Becker are helping to create a new awareness of the physical body and the mind as a single complex. They demonstrate that it is no longer enough to consider the body as a physiological and biochemical phenomenon alone.

Beneath our physiology and biochemistry lies a unifying system of energetics which is subtle and complex as well as enormously potent in its effect on body, mind and overall vitality. Becker has even uncovered a second 'nervous system'—previously unrecognized by science—which he insists controls growth, healing and regeneration of broken bones. This energetic system appears to be influenced by both our environment and by our thoughts. It is currently being used to explain such diverse phenomena as why acupuncture can be used for pain relief and how hypnosis works. So far very little of the new scientific findings about the body as a unified energetic system has filtered down into the awareness of exercise physiologists and teachers. As a result there are still a great many people for whom even a dedicated and dynamic exercise programme followed regularly but mechanically does little good. To an unfortunate few it can even be harmful. To make the most of exercise for ageless ageing, you need not gear yourself up for some superhuman effort. You only need to leave behind the mechanical approach to exercise which tends to treat your body as a machine to be put through its paces—and to get back to basics.

Try Walking for a Start

A number of studies show that for a variety of reasons walking is the best form of natural exercise available for most people—provided it is done regularly, briskly and with true enjoyment. There is another important proviso too: vigorous exercise in any form will serve you best, and you will only avoid strain and injury, if you have worked out enough of your chronic residual tensions to enable you to give your body over to the rhythmic movements it involves (more about that later). Outdoor sports such as tennis, golf, riding and sailing can be fun and helpful although, unlike walking and the other specifically aerobic activities, they do not create a steady demand on your body because of their stop-and-start nature, so it is best to include some aerobic exercise in your lifestyle even if you are an avid games player. If you like more challenging activities than walking, try jogging or running, rowing or swimming, cycling or crosscountry skiing—all excellent aerobic activities. Like regular brisk walking they too get heart and lungs working well and help keep you young-looking and -feeling. They are great if you want to achieve a high level of fitness and—most important of all—if you really like doing them. This sense of enjoyment is a central consideration in whatever exercise programme you choose for ageless ageing. Any physical activity which you carry out with your teeth gritted virtuously thinking that you are, after all, doing your duty though you hate every minute of it, can only be counterproductive. For mind and body are inextricably linked and for you to get all the benefits of exercise you need to make that link a positive one.

Charge the Body—Free the Mind

That's why, for most people, walking is so good. There is something quite extraordinary about the way that walking briskly in low-heeled shoes—particularly if you can walk in the country or in a park amidst trees and flowers—seems to revitalize the body while it sets the mind free for thought. Thoreau used to say, 'The moment my legs begin to move, my thoughts begin to flow.' And Dr George Sheehan, the highly respected cardiologist and sports-medicine expert—himself a passionate marathon runner—wrote recently of walking, 'You will read of this phenomenon again and again in the journals of the great thinkers, writers and artists. They were all great walkers. They found that not only can one train the body while one is using the mind, the mind actually works better when the body is in motion.'

Some interesting scientific studies confirm the notion that walking helps clarify mental processes. At Purdue University, after giving subjects psychological tests to determine their decision-making abilities, researchers put people into a fitness programme in which regular walking was a central feature. They found after six months on the programme they had improved their decision-making skills 60 per cent more than subjects in the control group who did not exercise. George Macaulay Trevelyan, Britain's highly respected historian who had a real passion for long walks used to say, 'I have two doctors, my left leg and my right.' Latest research into the effects of regular brisk walking more than bears out his belief that this kind of moderate exercise can play a central role in keeping the body healthy, young and fit. Besides, walking is the form of exercise least likely to cause injury, it is inexpensive to practise, natural, and efficacious for ageless ageing. It will lift your spirits, help lower if necessary and keep down your weight, tone your muscles and reduce your risk of cardiovascular disease.

Walk Your Way to Wellness

So good is brisk walking as a means of strengthening heart and lungs and improving cardiac resistance that in some studies of different forms of exercise it comes out better than cycling or running. At the University of Wisconsin, for instance, when researchers examined the effects of brisk walking (at a rate of 4 miles an hour or more) on men they found that it pushed some heart rates up to 87 per cent of capacity, which was the same as the cyclists achieved and only 3 per cent lower than the runners. This measure of maximum heart rate is a useful one, whatever kind of exercise you choose to follow. It is determined by subtracting your age from 220 beats a minute. And it will tell you just what kind of workout you are giving yourself.

In an interesting study by David Mymin at the University of Manitoba in Canada and Dan Streja, researchers discovered that the rejuvenating effects of strenuous exercise such as running—including a significant increase in high-density lipoprotein (HDL) and decreases in circulating insulin levels—also take place when people are put on exercise programmes based on walking even at a pace lower than 4 miles an hour. HDL is a lipoprotein in your blood. Generally speaking when it is high the chances you will suffer a heart attack are low. Before the Mymin study it was assumed that only long-distance runners and other active exercisers would have high levels of HDL in their blood. But the study showed that such beneficial changes can take place just from walking. Walking's ability to lower circulating insulin levels is also important for high-level wellness and age retardation. Many people past the age of forty have disturbed insulin levels which can lead to adult-onset diabetes and heart disease. The walkers in Mymin's programme experienced a definite decrease in circulating insulin. Other research confirms the Manitoba findings and shows as well that walking is an excellent way of increasing the amount of oxygen that reaches the cells all over the body. Like any form of rhythmic aerobic exercise it improves lymphatic drainage, stimulates arterial and venous circulation, and promotes the elimination of wastes and morbid materials which can cause free-radical damage and cross-linking on a cellular level. It also brings increased blood supply to all the body's organs. Brisk walking is particularly good for people whose work tends to be mentally or physically passive because it counteracts the tendency of their circulation and their eliminative processes to become sluggish. Max Bircher-Benner always insisted his patients rise early. Then he sent them out into the hills and forests around Zurich for an hour's brisk walk before breakfast. Walking was an important part of his 'order therapy' and still is in every naturopathic clinic in Europe.

Free and Often

To get the most out of walking do it every day. Choose some place you want to walk to, and wearing low-heeled shoes and loose comfortable clothes, set out with your arms swinging free from the shoulders. Breathe deeply and carry your body high. Every few minutes draw in a breath and then after a few seconds, without exhaling, draw in another and after a further interval of a few seconds still another. After the third inhalation vigorously expel all your air. This helps inflate your chest to its full capacity. Most of us don't breathe fully and deeply. We therefore miss out on the full benefits of oxygen for brain and body. After a walk of, say 2 or 3 or 4 miles, if possible, take off your clothes and rub down your skin with a flannel which has been dipped in cold water or take a brief cool shower followed by a brisk rub with a Turkish towel. It will leave you refreshed and renewed with energy to spare in the hours ahead.

And how intense should an aerobic activity—walking or other—be for best results? Most experts insist you should exercise somewhere between 30 and 60 per cent of maximum capacity. This you can figure out by following a few simple steps:

1. Find out what your resting heart rate is by taking your pulse for six seconds and multiplying by ten while you are seated comfortably. You do this by putting two fingers on the artery just inside your wrist. *80*

2. Subtract your age from 220 to determine your maximum heart rate. For instance if you are fifty then your maximum heart rate would be 170. *169*

3. Now find out your heart-rate range by subtracting your resting heart rate from your maximum heart rate. Say for example you are fifty and your maximum heart rate is 170 with a resting rate of 70. Then your heart-rate would be 100.

4. With this information you can now calculate your best exercise level to achieve a good anti-stress, anti-ageing effect. Calculate 40 per cent of your heart rate range (which is 100 in our example) which is 40. Now add this to the resting rate of 70 and you get the figure 110 beats per minute—your target heart rate for exercise.

5. For middle-aged and older people who are not athletes walking moderately or briskly will raise their heart rate to that target rate, which is 40 per cent of ultimate capacity. Younger people and highly trained people will need to run or exercise more vigorously to reach it.

One of the best things about taking a daily walk is that it is such a natural and easy thing to do. You need no special equipment—apart from a good pair of shoes—and because the easy flowing movement of putting one foot in front of another can be so wholehearted it often brings a sense of freedom to the body which so many more mechanical approaches to exercise miss out on.

Exercise and Self-transformation

Not only is such wholeheartedness important if one is to realize the full potential for exercise used as a tool for ageless ageing, the enormous power for self-expression and physical trans-formation which can come through movement only takes place when muscles and exercise are also linked through mind-body awareness. We are not machines, no matter how much flashy books on exercise would have us believe otherwise. When we have treated ourselves as such, either by neglecting to care for our physical needs or by forcing our bodies through exercise routines like automatons, we both create distortions of posture and body shape and dissipate precious adaptive energy instead of renewing it. In fact most of us have quite literally grown up with postural distortions which over the years become so much a part of us they are almost like physical symbols for our personality. When you begin to approach exercise from a more unified perspective it's important to find ways of unlocking some of the residual tensions which underlie these distortions and to set the body free to move naturally so we can make the most of whatever form of exercise we choose to do. A good yoga teacher can help you do this, gradually over a period of time. So can some very simple exercises which I learned from a quite extraordinary movement teacher called Lilla Bek.

Herself a longtime teacher of yoga as well as an acclaimed healer and writer, Lilla Bek's approach to movement is an ancient one—based on the principles of sacred dance where the body is not only put through its physical paces to tighten muscles and firm contours but to balance the body's energies through what in mystic tradition are known as the chakra centres. There are believed to be seven of these, starting at the base of the spine and rising through the solar plexus to finish at the crown of the head. Each chakra is said to be connected with specific endocrine glands and to influence the functions of organs related to it as well as energy in the part of the body it governs. Each is also believed to have specific psychic qualities—

the one in the belly, for instance, is said to be connected with the actions of the will, while the chakra at the throat is a centre for creative energies, particularly artistic ones and for self-expression. The purpose of sacred dance is to revitalize the energetic circuits of the body and mind and to unify the system so that one connects up both with the earth as well as one's own energies and is fed by them. Whether or not the chakra system is ever validated by scientific research, working with exercise and movement in this way can be a superb means of integrating mind and body as well as working out longstanding bodily tensions and postural distortions that make you look and feel older than you are. After a while your body really does become a vehicle for the expression of the inner being. Its movements become naturally graceful and authentic. Over a period of time even the most distorted frame seems to untwist itself as the muscles are freed from chronic postural habits and tensions which deplete energies and undermine natural beauty. But for me the most rewarding thing of all in beginning to work in an energetically aware way with movement is the extraordinary levels of energy it brings. It is as if you create for yourself a link with the earth which supports you at a high level of calm vitality long after the other, more disconnected exercisers have fallen by the wayside.

Postures for Transformation

To begin working energetically rather than mechanically with your body it is necessary to do two things. First you need to identify areas of chronic tension which are distorting body shape and posture, and eliminate them by an active process of letting go. Second you need to begin drawing conscious aware-ness to the ways in which even the smallest movement, whether it takes place while running, dancing, speaking or whatever, affects muscle groups and energy-focus in other areas of the body not directly related to the muscles doing the work. Lilla Bek has worked out some gentle but useful postures which do both.

'Most people,' she says, 'even very active people, have many areas of residual tension which restrict full movement and interfere with the free flow of energy so that they become unnecessarily fatigued. These areas are really the result of how we live and how we use our bodies. Our waking hours are largely spent using only a small amount of space right in front of us—for instance as when we are driving a car or eating, working at a desk or watching television. Every group of muscles in the body has another which works in opposition to it. When we restrict our movement to such a small space we tend to contract the muscles of one group without ever doing any kind of contrastretch to bring its opposing muscles into play. This is how chronically tense muscles lead to body distortions such as dowager's hump, slumped shoulders, excessively curved backs and the rest.'

Undoing the Kinks

The postures Lilla Bek uses to undo longstanding kinks in the body are designed specifically to create a contrastretch for each group of chronically tightened muscles. At the same time, because they are done slowly and deliberately in a deeply relaxed state they make it possible for the person practising them to begin experiencing just how connected up his body is energetically. Take the movements implied in Leonardo's famous spreadeagled man for example. Hold yourself in this position and slowly move your arms from your sides to above your head—palms turned outwards. At each level of movement you will find that a different group of muscles come into action which are quite separate from those of the arms and shoulders involved in the movement. First the lower abdomen is tightened and the energy there is stimulated, then the solar plexus, the chest and the area of the heart chakra come into play. Then the jaw line, the lower face and ears, the roof of the mouth, the eyes, cheeks and forehead each in their turn are activated as you move your arms higher and higher. To someone who has never had any consciousness of the energetic phenomenon of exercise and the unification of body movement such an experience is like a revelation.

Practise a few of the postures which heighten your body awareness and you will find very soon not only that your posture changes as your body becomes more fluid and more supple and a more articulate expression of your being, but when you turn to your aerobics or your yoga or your running or your sacred dance there is a lightness and a freedom which you have never experienced before. Here are five of Lilla Bek's simple postures. Spend two to five minutes on each once a day and you are likely to experience new energy levels as well as a sense of authentic natural grace which no amount of mechanical jogging around the park or sweating it out in pink legwarmers can match.

'The Opening'

This position has a remarkable ability to open out the body, expanding the chest, releasing chronic tension from the neck and shoulders, gradually smoothing out hollow backs, and greatly expanding contracted hip joints.

Here's How

Lying flat on the floor relax and close your eyes. Ask a friend to take a look at the position of your chin. If it is higher than the illustration, place a book under your head to bring it back into alignment. As the natural alignment of your spine improves you will need a thinner and thinner book until you can do without one altogether. Does your back lie flat against the floor or is there a hollow? An arched spine indicates that you normally hold your chin wrongly which stretches the skin of the neck and creates a double-chin look. How far are your shoulders off the floor? Do they differ in this? As chronic tension is released by doing the exercise regularly your shoulders will come closer and closer to the floor, your back will lengthen and your chin will naturally align.

Draw your right foot up while placing your palms downwards on the floor and rest it near your buttocks. Do the same with the other foot placing your heels together, soles flat on the floor. Now, starting with your palms against the sides of your hips, begin to explore space with your arms and notice the parts of your body which your slowly moving your arms outwards and upwards activates. Moving your arms up and out you begin to activate energy first in the pelvic area, then the solar plexus, heart, thymus, forehead and top of the head. When you get to the level where you are lying with your arms in line with your shoulders, let your hands open slightly and you will have reached the level of the throat energies. Explore the feel of each level of the arms in turn by moving them slowly and then leaving them at each level to sink quietly to the floor. If while doing this you gradually open out or close your fingers you will produce many interesting changes in energy at different levels of your body. With your arms extended like this at the sides shoulder blades will separate and then by letting your knees open outwards to the natural pull of gravity you will discover your breathing opens up. Explore this position for two or three minutes before going on to the next.

'Expansion'

This position opens out a collapsed midriff, lengthens the body, energizes the solar plexus and even tightens the muscles of the face.

Here's How

Moving from the first position, now place your feet about 18in apart with soles flat against the floor. Leave your arms at shoulder level and very slowly roll your hips to the right side simultaneously rolling your head to the left. Return to the centre keeping your lower spine in contact with the floor and repeat the movement to the other side. Your knees should gradually fit into the arches of the opposite legs. Don't worry if they don't touch the floor. They will eventually. Most people have a shortened midriff and the solar-plexus chakra which provides the body with dynamic physical energy cannot function properly when this is the case. This position has a remarkable effect on the look of the face when it is practised regularly and can make you look considerably younger. But for this to work you must 'connect up' your face with your body—particularly in the spaces through which the knees move—in your awareness as you carry out the movement. Take a full breath before you begin and exhale as your hips roll to the side then inhale again slowly as they return to centre, exhale in starting position and repeat to the other side.

'The Rainbow'

This is a position of natural grace. It brings a superb stretch to the waistline, lengthens the whole body, flattens and firms the abdomen, and integrates body energies.

Here's How

Lying flat on your back take a full breath, exhale and roll to the left side, bringing your arms together in the same direction. Now bring your right knee across and exhale. Keep your knee down by holding it with your left hand to make sure it will not go back up. Now very gently try to take your right hand up and around your body. If it does not come in contact easily with the floor above your head then the energies from your heart and throat areas are not freed for use. Have a friend calculate in this position how much your arm is off the floor. If it is more than 6in then problems of distortion will be exaggerated in your body and it will take a bit of time to correct. If it is exaggerated it is a good idea not to exercise vigorously until the exaggeration disappears.

'Bow to the Earth'

Not only is this position profoundly relaxing—an excellent way to relieve stress after the end of a long day—it is also wonderful for alleviating lower-back problems and period aches and it encourages energy to rise up the spine flooding the whole body with new vitality and clearing a fuzzy mind.

Here's How

From a kneeling position, bend your body forward, pushing your hands out in front, and stretch forward like a cat. On the in-breath, bring your hands to lie at the sides of your feet and lower your buttocks. If you have difficulty in doing this be gentle but persevere since chronic contraction here can lead to lower-back problems later. On the out-breath, bring the top of your head down in front of your knees. Rest a moment and then bring your hands forwards and place them one palm on top of the other. Rest your forehead on top. Close your eyes and relax

THE OPENING

BOW TO
THE EARTH

THE RAINBOW

EXPANSION

THE
LENGTHENER

FLOOR

Postures to heighten your
body awareness and
eliminate unwanted
muscular tension which can
distort body shape and
structure as you age (see
descriptions in text).

for two minutes or more. The detensing effects of this position work slowly. It can be held for longer than most. It too is excellent for the solar plexus but it is also good for releasing energy that has been blocked at the base of the spine.

'The Lengthener'

This position and the gentle movement which accompanies it activate the base of the spine, improve blood flow to the brain, take pressure off of tired legs, alleviate lower-back tensions, improve circulation in the pelvis and are a superb antidote to stress.

Here's How
Lying flat on your back relax as fully as you can. Now start to raise one leg slowly up as high as you can go. Be aware as your leg moves through the arc that with each 6 or 8in it passes through different parts of your body become energized, starting with the base chakra and moving up through the belly, heart and throat when it reaches a right angle. If you can go beyond this upright position you can also activate head energies. Now with your hand on one knee, don't pull by force but hold your knee with your hands and see how far you can bring it into your body. On the in-breath raise your forehead to the knee. Breathe out as you bring them together, relax and lie back. Repeat with the other leg, going through the whole sequence for two or three minutes. If you are unable to bring your knee all the way to your body do persist with the exercise. It will help protect you from lower-back troubles later. You will get a splendid feeling of lengthening over your whole body after working through this position.

Combine these simple 'untwisters' with a habit of regular aerobic activity—walking, swimming, rebounding on a mini-trampoline, cycling, running, jogging or rowing—and you will not only strengthen your lifestyle for ageless ageing significantly you will also find a new sense of integration takes place. And your energy levels will soar.

TWENTY-TWO

Water Works

One of the most potent of nature's tools for the ageless-ageing body is water. That is why hydrotherapy forms an important part of treatment at most of the world's clinics and spas which are dedicated to using *natural-law* methods of age-retardation and rejuvenation. Yet it has been little used in Britain and the United States. Would you consider pouring a stream of cold water over your face to banish fatigue or prevent your skin from wrinkling and sagging? Would you apply a hot compress of hay flowers to get rid of an aching back or knee, or tennis elbow? Walk in ice-cold water up to your knees every morning to increase your vitality and ward off premature ageing? Or even have jets of cold water directed against your back and legs to help you lose weight. Extraordinary as these things may sound, they are natural methods of treatment with over 100 years of clinical validation behind them. In fact they are part of one of the most elaborate, effective and well-researched methods of healing, health enhancement and age-retardation in the world: Kneipp therapy.

An Officially Supported Treatment

Virtually unknown in English-speaking countries, Kneipp therapy is practised in some seventy spas and 6000 hospitals in Europe. There treatments are supervised by physicians who have been highly trained in the various methods it involves, the most important of which is a complex set of water applications which have profound regenerative and protective effects on the body. Far from being some kind of far-out alternative therapy used only by nature freaks and old women, Kneipp hydrotherapy is supported by government health-insurance schemes in Europe and subsidized by the state both as a preventative and a prophylactic treatment against ageing as well as a means of curing and rehabilitating the seriously ill. The anti-ageing prophylactic use of Kneipp's water treatments is steadily gaining ground simply because it has proved to be less costly to prevent the degenerative conditions of ageing than to cure them. Now Kneipp therapy is used in its various applications—from affusions, where water in a steady stream is poured over specific parts of your body, to hot and cold compresses—as a treatment for a wide variety of these conditions from arthritis, abscesses and heart disease to asthma, diabetes and allergic eczema. Kneipp methods using water in all its many forms can greatly increase your vitality, enhance athletic prowess, help you handle stress better, banish insomnia and counteract a myriad of negative effects usually connected with the ageing process.

The Kneipp system is a means of improving health and raising vitality without resorting to drugs, drastic methods or great expense. As such, in Europe it has become increasingly valued in a world of soaring medical costs and increasing iatrogenic (doctor-caused) diseases. As far back as 1900 Kneipp's water therapy was already being practised all over Europe. Since then his methods have been researched, applied, refined and adapted to contemporary needs by a large number of medical scientists—most of them German—who form the basis of the Kneipp movement world-wide. There are prizes of thousands of German marks given each year to scientists now investigating how the simple application of water can have such a profound effect on the health of the human body.

A Bid to Save His Life

Sebastian Kneipp, after whom European hydrotherapy is named, was born in Bavaria in 1821, the poor son of a humble weaver with an ambition to become a priest. In youth he experienced brutally hard work coupled with extreme poverty.

While studying for the priesthood he contracted tuberculosis: his physicians pronounced him incurable and advised him, in effect, to prepare for death. But Kneipp was unwilling to accept their judgement. He came across an old book written by a German physician on the curative powers of water. He began to experiment on himself by applying water in various ways. This, coupled with a growing awareness of the body's own ability to heal itself in accordance with certain laws of nature, brought him back to full health. This was much to the consternation of some physicians who did not believe (as most still don't) that water applications could have potent healing power, and much to the delight of many of his fellow students who themselves were cured of various minor and serious illnesses by his suggestions. He then went on to develop hydrotherapy into the remarkable therapeutic and preventative system which bears his name.

In 1855 he was sent to the tiny Bavarian village of Worishofen to supervise a Dominican nunnery. Many of his friends insisted that the church had only sent him there to get him away from his fascination with water-healing, in the belief that it was inter-fering with his clerical life. There he acted as father-confessor to the nuns, revived the village's stagnant economy and advised farmers about how to improve their agriculture. But his fascination with health and healing prevailed—when later he was made parson of the village, despite the fact that his days were filled with ecclesiastical duties, he found his time in-creasingly taken up by a growing number of ailing people who had heard of his 'miracle cures', and either did not have enough money to pay for medical care or had been given up as 'hopeless' by their physicians. Kneipp treated them with his water tech-niques and he taught them to treat themselves, gradually developing a complete system for prevention, cure and re-habilitation based on the theory that a human being is a unity of body and soul and that whenever this unity is threatened, or whenever the harmony of nature is disturbed, illness ensues.

Total Therapy

His methods—which include water applications, herbal treatments (many passed on to him by local peasants), nutritional therapy using fresh natural foods simply prepared, movement therapy and the development of a positive attitude to life— formed a course of treatment designed to restore physical and mental unity of the human being with a particular emphasis on the use of the forces of nature (sun, water, food, movement etc). His therapy was intuitive, empirical and directed towards the specific needs of the individual patient.

Kneipp collected his own herbs, taught people how to use them and how to be moderate in the way they lived. He rapidly developed a reputation unequalled amongst nineteenth-century healers—physicians or no. He treated emperors and popes, the peasants and the clergy, all of whom flocked to Worishofen for his care and advice. Kneipp was farsighted enough to insist that his methods be put into the hands of doctors to be further developed and improved. He taught many physicians and be- queathed his herbal formulas to a pharmacist with whom he had worked for several years before he died. The pharmacist began to manufacture them late in the nineteenth century. The same company, Kneipp-Werke, still does. And Worishofen, the village where Kneipp settled, became Bad Worishofen—the largest spa centre in Europe and a centre completely devoted to Kneipp treatment. The town, which now has been carefully developed by the German government, boasts 7000 beds in its many hotels, sanatoria and clinics where people can go to take a 'Kneippkur' and to walk the miles of beautiful pathways through the woods.

100 Ways with Water

What makes Kneipp hydrotherapy unique as a part of a lifestyle for ageless ageing is its exceptional versatility. It uses water in more than a hundred ways of widely varying intensity. They begin with such gentle stimuli as a compress or an ankle- or foot-bath—measures which involve almost no strain on the body—and range on to highly strenuous treatments such as the 'Blitzguss', where a powerful stream of cold water is directed at specific areas of the body to stimulate immunity, strengthen vitality and encourage the complete elimination of harmful waste products from the system. Depending on the general condition of the person, and the kind of ailment being treated, the water can be hot or cold: some treatments involve the use of steam.

Warm water is generally used in Kneipp baths, to which herbal extracts such as melissa, rosemary and pine (either alone or in combination) have been added. Some baths involve the immersion of the whole body, others only a portion. Many Kneipp treatments are based on the use of compresses—to quell fever, to detoxify the body, to bring relaxation to a stressed person. These are applied to various parts of the body for measured lengths of time. Kneipp also developed all kinds of other local applications from treading cold water—Bad Wörishofen is full of beautiful pools in the woods and in the hotels for people to walk in—to walking through dewy grass, on wet cobblestones and even in snow. These treatments, at least one of which is meant to be part of your daily routine, all aim at enhancing immunity and increasing vitality. The system is highly complex and versatile, so physicians prescribing it can carefully gear the treatment to the state of the circulation and the reactive powers—Selye would have called them adaptive abilities—of each individual patient. Each patient is advised to carry out a controlled, gradually intensifying training programme.

Water as a Source of Information for Health

The way each treatment, from the most sophisticated to the simplest form of water treading, is to be carried out for good results is carefully regulated by a number of absolute principles. For hydrotherapy is not something 'innocuous'. These seemingly simple water techniques can be detrimental if used wrongly. There is a real science to it all. It is the temperature of the water when applied to the surface of the body in specific ways which brings about beneficial results. It causes a stimulation to the skin which is transferred by way of the nerves and blood vessels to the organs. The greater the difference between the temperature of the water applied and the body itself, the stronger an effect its application will have.

In terms of information theory applied to biology, specific applications of water could be said to bring to an organism what Brekhman and others call 'absolute', 'connected' or 'structural' information which acts beneficially to bring the body the kind of stimulation it needs to thrive. Augustin de la Pena, author of *The Psychobiology of Cancer: Automatization and Boredom in Health and Disease* describes the kind of beneficial total-body reaction that such stimulation can bring when he says:

> Presentation of a novel or unexpected stimulus produces a generalized orienting reaction. This orienting response is accompanied by an increase in the level of CNS [central nervous system] activation relative to the pre-novel stimulus baseline. The purpose of the physiological changes, in general terms, is to make the individual more sensitive to incoming sensory stimuli so that he is better equipped to discern what is happening and to mobilize the body for whatever action may be necessary.

Water applied to your body, like spring-cleaning 'cures', exercise, and a number of the other *natural-law* tools of ageless ageing, can 'stress' your system in very positive ways—ways which make you stronger and more resistant to illness and which can increase overall vitality and improve biological functioning as well as even providing a healthy mental stimulation which takes one away from the habitualized ways of thinking and being which result in boredom and degeneration of a living organism.

Do-It-Yourself Kneipp

Not every Kneipp treatment has to be administered by a professional in a clinic or a spa. One of Kneipp's most important principles was that hydrotherapy should be simple enough that any otherwise healthy person should be able to benefit from it—both as a prophylactic treatment against ageing as well as to improve the condition of his skin, to eliminate stress and to treat minor ailments from a headache to a cold—without professional help. Simple at-home water treatments can fortify your body against sickness in general, improve circulation and calm frayed nerves. If you decide to make use of water applications as part of a programme for ageless ageing, you need to know a few principles, for good results depend on each application being carried out in the correct way. Whatever water application you make these are Kneipp's general rules to follow:

- Apply cold water only to a warm body, never to a chilled one. It's best to warm up with exercise or be wrapped up snugly in bed just before you begin. If your body doesn't get warm quickly afterwards, then it is best to use alternate warm and cold applications instead of cold ones only, until your system becomes stronger and more resilient.

- Your body should always regain its warmth within fifteen or twenty minutes after a water application. It is a good idea to move about afterwards or rest in a warm bed.

- After any form of warm Kneipp bath, either a full bath or a half bath, (if not followed by a cold affusion) you should rest for half an hour to get the full benefit of the treatment.

- Wait until at least an hour after a meal to carry out any water application.

- Don't dry your skin with a Turkish towel after a water application as this can lessen its benefits. Instead pat dry the wet parts of your body with your hands then cover yourself quickly with warm clothing in natural fibres which are porous.

- For women, during a menstrual period, only make use of applications on the upper part of your body.

Here are a few of the simplest and most useful Kneipp treatments which have good applications for ageless ageing.

Face Affusions for Perfect Skin

An affusion is literally a pouring of running water over a particular area of the body. The fact is, affusion stimulates blood supply to the skin and restores lost tautness and freshness to sagging or faded skin. It is a popular natural treatment in Europe amongst men and women who want to retain their youthful good looks. It helps prevent premature ageing of the skin, eliminates feelings of fatigue and can even cure a migraine.

Here's How

Make sure your body is in a well-warmed state to begin with. Then, using a hose with an opening of about ½ inch (it can be a bathroom hand shower with the head removed) turn on the cold water so that a sheet of water is delivered to the skin when the hose is held 2-4in from it. (There should be no great pressure of water.) When an affusion is done right the water flows smoothly and evenly and there is no 'splashback'. Now, resting your neck on a towel and bending over a sink or the bath, begin by circling your face with the water from just below the temple. Then go back and forth from one side of the face to the other. Now guide the stream several times from up to down starting at the left side and working towards the right. End by circling the whole face again. The entire process is done with cold water and should take only a couple of minutes. Now pat your face gently to remove excess water and then let it dry completely in the air.

To Boost Vitality and Strengthen the Immune Functions

There are several techniques designed to increase vitality and bring protection against illness and age-degeneration. Which you choose depends on your current state of stamina and health. They range from the body wash, which is gentle enough for almost anyone, to the cold Blitzguss which top athletes and other very fit people favour.

The Body Wash

This is quite different from the usual cleansing wash you carry out in the bath or shower using a flannel. It involves the uniform spreading of water over your skin with a rough linen cloth. Afterwards you should not dry yourself. Instead get into a warm bed for a few minutes. It helps relax the body while bracing and strengthening it, and activates natural warmth to eliminate and to prevent the build-up of toxic substances in the blood and tissues which can cause the cellular damage and cross-linking that come with ageing.

Here's How

Having dipped the linen cloth into cold water, begin on the back of the right hand and sweep upwards over the shoulder then down again on the inside to the thumb. Now turn the cloth over and wash the inside of the hand and arm to the armpit and finally the back of the palm. Now dip the cloth in water again quickly and carry out the same movements on the other arm. Then quickly dipping the cloth in water again, with half a dozen vertical movements wash over the chest, abdomen and the fronts of legs. Another dip and do the back (or have a friend help here since it is easier). Finish the body wash by quickly rubbing the soles of the feet. The whole procedure, which must be carried out in a warm room, needs to be very quick (only thirty to forty seconds); then take off excess water from your body's surface, dress warmly and move about, or pop into a warm bed for a few minutes. (It can be a superb way of refreshing yourself after a long day before going out for the evening.)

Water Treading

This takes a couple of minutes. In Bad Worishofen there are beautiful pools in the clinics and hotels and even the woods where you can take off your shoes and socks and walk barefoot in water every morning—summer and winter—even when there is snow on the ground. If you are lucky enough to live near the sea or by a brook both are ideal. But you can get the same results at home using a bath filled with cold water.

Here's How

Dressed warmly, but with your legs and feet naked from the knee down, step into the water and 'walk on the spot', lifting first one foot and then another up out of the water. The sharp reaction will be either a pleasant warm feeling flooding the feet or a sharp cold ache, followed by warmth. Begin by treading water for only thirty seconds or so, then work up to a couple of minutes as your system gets stronger and more resilient. Immediately afterwards put on dry warm socks and shoes and move about. (This is also an excellent treatment for insomniacs—done just before going to bed.)

Blitzguss

A real Blitzguss has to be done by a professional in a special shower using a powerful water-force. But you can get many of its beneficial effects in the shower, particularly if you happen to have a hand-held shower which you can direct on to different parts of your body.

Here's How

Take a warm shower until your skin is really glowing with the warmth. Turn off the hot water and use only cold—directing it over your face, down your arms and legs, over your trunk and abdomen and down your back. The whole process should take no more than thirty seconds. Get out of the shower, pat off the excess water and dress warmly. This will leave your skin glowing with warmth thanks to the reaction against the cold water. Practised every day or so, it will also strengthen your immune system not only against age-degeneration but also against colds, flu and other illnesses. And it will greatly increase your vitality. This is a favourite of top athletes in Germany. It is also my favourite of all the prophylactic treatments with water—and I am a long way from being a top athlete. But I had to work up to it in the beginning by starting with the body wash and with water treading (which I still do when I feel tired but unable to sleep). You shouldn't use the Blitzguss until you are already quite strong.

De-stressors for Better Sleep

The next two techniques are particularly good if you feel stressed or you tend to wrestle with insomnia at the end of the day.

Wet Socks

A favourite of Kneipp himself, this is an easy way to apply a foot compress. It is quite extraordinarily relaxing.

Here's How
Wet a pair of cotton socks in cold water and wring them out so that they are no longer dripping. Put them on and then cover them with a pair of dry woollen socks, then pop into bed. Leave the socks on for at least half an hour although it doesn't matter if they stay on all night should you fall asleep.

Cold Sitz Baths

These last only ten to thirty seconds, according to how quickly and how well you react. They are carried out with the upper part of your body well clothed—always in a warm room. This is also an excellent way of boosting immunity and protecting against minor illnesses—particularly throat and chest conditions—eliminating flatulence, constipation and stress.

Here's How
Fill the bath with enough cold water to reach to your waist. Climb into the bath and stay there for a few seconds, then get out, gently pat the excess water from your skin and immediately climb into a warm bed.

Hot Compress for Digestive Upsets

This is enormously helpful when you have eaten a meal the size or content of which you regret. It rapidly restores normal digestive processes to a stomach overloaded with rich or too much food. It can be a godsend after holiday revelry.

Here's How
Take a linen or pure cotton cloth large enough to be folded twice and still cover your abdomen from waist to upper thighs. Dip it folded into hot water and wring it out well, then lay it over your

abdomen. Now place a hot-water bottle filled with very hot water over that and cover the whole abdomen with a warm blanket which is wrapped all around your body. (An electric heating pad won't work.) Now relax for half an hour or more.

Once you begin to experience some of the extraordinary benefits from these simple treatments you may find you want to explore some of the other natural therapies which are also carriers of vital information for health and ageless ageing. They include air baths, saunas and Turkish baths, herbal treatments using the adaptogens and dry skin-brushing. Not only can each one of them leave you feeling vibrantly well and looking good, together with good nutrition, exercise and relaxation they are some of the means by which your body/mind/spirit can in Schrödinger's words 'drink order' from the environment—just the quality and kind of information needed to keep you well, youthful and vital long after those around you have succumbed to the ravages of time.

TWENTY-THREE

Shed the Skin of Age

Men are more fortunate than women when it comes to ageing skin. Wrinkles on the male skin give 'character' lines. For most women wrinkles strike horror into their hearts. No single aspect of ageing seems to worry people as much as the look of their skin. Nobody likes to see their face look old. To slow down the rate at which wrinkles appear, you need to treat your skin not as a superficial covering to your body but as the living, breathing organism it is, and you need to provide optimal conditions for its health and functioning on a cellular level. This involves both internal and external care. It means making sure you are well supplied internally with free-radical scavengers and anti-oxidant nutrients, detoxifying your body periodically, protecting yourself from ultraviolet-light damage and from water loss, and using specific substances on the surface of the skin either to guard against age-related damage or to encourage cellular repair when it occurs. The time to begin is long before those worrying lines start to show. But if that time has already passed, don't despair. It is never too late to get significant improvement in the smoothness of your skin's surface and its overall appearance, provided you are willing to work for it.

The Mystery of the Wrinkle

For generations dermatologists and cosmetic scientists have been trying to find out why skin wrinkles. They have chemically analysed old skin and compared it to young. They have examined the differences in cell structure between young and old skin and in the ground substance which helps give skin its cushiony feel and smooth contours. They have even taken skin samples from wrinkled areas of a body and compared it with skin taken from smooth areas of the same body. What they have discovered is that there are no fundamental differences between skin taken from wrinkled and from unwrinkled areas. A wrinkle is simply a crease in the skin where the collagen beneath it has been imprinted by continual muscle actions such as smiling or squinting. Wrinkling is but one phenomenon within the whole matrix of complex changes associated with age-degeneration. To prevent it we must prevent them. The more we can protect from them systemically—by treating and caring for the whole organism—the more slowly they will occur.

The rate at which skin ageing takes place depends on your genetic inheritance and your exposure to ultraviolet light, as well as your diet and general state of health. It involves the kind of alterations to the mesenchyme as well as to the cells' genetic material and to cell walls which we've been looking at in previous chapters. These changes tend to lower cell metabolism and to interfere with proper cellular use of nutrients. They also tend to slow down the elimination of wastes.

Atrophy of the sebaceous glands, resulting in lower secretions of sebum, also takes place with age. This makes your skin's surface dry. A decrease in the volume of circulating blood and a loss of subcutaneous fat which gives youthful skin its smooth cushiony look are also part of the process which results in wrinkling. So is a slowing down of cell reproduction at the base of the epidermis, and a decrease in the water content of the dermis. Most of these age-related changes appear to occur thanks to free-radical and peroxidation damage and to cross-linking of collagen in the body. One of the major factors in bringing these things about in your facial skin is being exposed to ultraviolet light day in day out throughout your entire life.

UV light in its many wavelengths acts on skin in a number of ways—all of which can make it look and feel older. It dis-organizes and hardens the collagen fibres and it damages the skin's elastic fibres, destroying its 'stretchability'. Both of these effects encourage the formation of wrinkles and sagging. Free-radical damage and cross-linking also disrupt the natural balance of your skin's mucopolysaccharides which form the gel-like medium in which the cells live which helps your skin retain water. Finally, they damage the cell membranes and even the ability of a cell to reproduce accurately so that, gradually, as cells divide they come in time to be quite different in structure and functioning to the young cells from which they are descended.

Protecting DNA and RNA

As in every other cell of your body, within the nucleus of every skin cell lies the genetic material which makes it possible for that cell to reproduce by dividing—ideally making perfect replicas of the original cell. What ensure this continuity, what make sure that each cell is therefore able to carry out perfectly and efficiently its functions without the skin tissue, are the minute 'blueprints' clustered by hundreds of thousands in every chromosome. These blueprints come in the form of a long spiral molecule which looks like a twisted ladder—deoxyribonucleic acid—DNA. And although there is nothing very special about the components of this molecule, its superb architecture makes it unique among chemicals. Without DNA no life would exist on earth. DNA is simply made up of phosphates and sugars (which form the spirals of the twisted ladder) and bases, which are the nitrogen-containing adenine, thymine, guanine and cytosine. The 'rungs' of the spiral ladder are made out of any combination of two of these bases. The ingenious way in which the DNA molecule is structured in these two intertwined spirals connected by thousands of these rungs enables it to 'spell out' an incredibly complex coded message. Even more important, DNA has an ability which is totally unique in biology: it can reproduce itself.

Your skin's health and good looks depend heavily on this unique skill. It makes it possible for cells to replicate themselves perfectly, thanks to the carefully coded message. That is, it should. But, as we have seen, DNA can become damaged by free radicals and highly reactive oxygen molecules that are present in the body as a result of exposure to chemicals in the atmosphere, cigarettes, alcohol, caffeine from coffee, drugs and metabolic wastes. When such damage takes place, the cell can usually repair itself and continue to reproduce itself (that is unless the damage is so great that it dies) but its genetic coding will no longer be perfect. And unless the damage to the genetic material can be repaired, future generations of cells which come from it will be flawed. An accumulation of such errors in the genetic message can lead to a decline in cellular functioning and promote skin ageing. Of course the human body, like all biological systems, is programmed for success and for survival. So there are trigger mechanisms which come into play when damage to the DNA occurs. One of the most important is a process called 'excision repair' or 'dark repair'. It stimulates the production of specific enzymes which 'excise' or cut out the damage. Then a new section is made to replace the damaged one which has been removed, so that the DNA strand is restored to normal; the offspring cells which are produced by this one will remain perfect.

The only problem is that when skin is exposed to UV light and to other sources of oxy-stress and free-radical damage, as it is day in day out year after year, the DNA can accrue more errors than the normal repair mechanisms can handle before the cells reproduce themselves. Also as you get older the natural repair mechanisms appear to work less efficiently. Together these degenerative changes result in a significant lowering of vitality in the skin and in the build-up of wastes in the tissues. The lower the vitality and the higher the levels of wastes, the more cellular degeneration takes place and the more rapidly your skin is inclined to show signs of ageing.

Cosmetics and Nutrients to the Aid

In the past couple of years a number of products have appeared which contain active ingredients designed to accelerate the skin's natural repair process by at least 40 per cent, thereby increasing the number of repaired cells for reproduction by somewhere between 40 and 50 per cent. Such a complex used daily should help slow down the signs of skin ageing. Even more potent help however can come from providing your system with an *optimal* supply of the nutrients known to promote DNA repair. They include ascorbic acid, biotin, choline, chromium, the amino acid cysteine, folic acid, manganese, methionine, molybdenum, nucleic acids, orotic acid, pantothenic acid, pyridoxine, thiamine, vitamin E and zinc.

Surreptitious Cosmetics

Cosmetic counters are also full of products—from night creams, eye creams and neck creams to ampoules and masks for both men and women—which contain special ingredients claiming to help prevent and counteract wrinkling and other age-related changes in other ways. The 'anti-wrinkle' substances used in such products usually work in one of two ways. Either they aim to increase the skin's water content—something which in itself has been shown measurably (although only temporarily) to decrease the depth of facial lines by 'plumping' up the epidermis—or, more important, they attempt—often surreptitiously— to stimulate skin tissue biologically. A good example of such biological stimulation (and an approach which a number of cosmetic manufacturers take in formulating their products) is the use of specific factors known to increase cell reproduction at the base of the epidermis. Another is to heighten circulation in the dermis thereby bringing increased blood-flow and nutrients to the skin's cells, or to improve the cells' use of oxygen and thereby stimulate skin metabolism.

The reason I say that such stimulation is often 'surreptitious' is because by law cosmetic products are only allowed to treat the epidermis—the skin's outer layer. Anything which is absorbed into the dermis and which has a biological effect on skin's deeper layers is supposed to be classified as a drug. However many of the most effective anti-ageing ingredients in skin-treatment products—such things as placenta extracts, specific amino acids, vitamins and plant extracts—undoubtedly improve the look and feel of skin and help work against age-related changes, not only because of the way they act on the epidermis but because they are in fact absorbed much deeper, where they bring about a stimulation to skin tissue which can improve cell metabolism, strengthen cell walls and even encourage the natural repair process to genetic material, thus helping to slow down the ageing process at a cellular level. Most of the best cosmetics have more than 'cosmetic'—that is superficial—actions. One of the ironies of maintaining such strict controls on cosmetic advertising is that cosmetic ads tend to sound all alike since manufacturers of genuinely active products can say little more about them than those who produce jars full of empty promises. The old idea that cosmetics are only superficial, because they sit on the surface of the skin, is an evasive half-truth. Many biologically active ingredients are drawn deeply into the skin where they act for good or ill. You can make effective use of this fact without spending a fortune on expensive creams and ampoules as well. More about that later.

The Vital Positive Response

In order for any of these biologically active substances to be of use, your skin's potential for good cellular function has to be good. For a fairly high level of potential vitality is necessary for skin to benefit from whatever treatment-product stimulation is being offered it. This is something that the high-potency-low-calorie diet helps provide. The adaptogens can help too (see Chapter 27). So can many specific nutrients with special actions on skin. But without a high degree of potential energy in your skin's cells themselves, using any treatment product, no matter how well formulated, is rather like beating a dead horse. The single most important action to take to improve the responsiveness of your skin to whatever treatment products you are going to use on it is simply to detoxify it by detoxifying your whole body (see Chapter 15). Most skin needs detoxification badly, for people living the sedentary life common to Western man and eating the average Western fare—a diet high in fat, protein and refined carbohydrates, not to mention too much food and alcohol—cannot help but store up waste products in their system. (This is also a major cause of cellulite in women and hair loss in men.) Once there they tend to build up, and impede microcirculation so that the supply of nutrients carried to the cells via the blood is decreased and the elimination of cellular wastes is also slowed down. This results in a kind of tissue sludge which dulls the responses of the skin's cells not to mention those of the cells in the rest of the body so that no matter how good the biological stimulation you are offering it you will get little positive response and therefore little improvement in its health and beauty.

Going on a seasonal 'cure'—a detoxifying diet for from ten days to two weeks—or a well-monitored juice fast, or a regime which is ultra-high in fresh raw vegetables and fruits, can help with elimination and stimulate skin's responsiveness. Even on its own this will lessen the depth of wrinkles and leave your skin looking smoother, softer, better moisturized and firmer within a fortnight. A dynamic exercise programme followed regularly over a few months can do the same thing. So can many of the European treatments for overall body 'rejuvenation'—such as cell therapy or organ-specific RNA treatment. They can also work wonders for some skins because of the way they can improve microcirculation and cell metabolism all over the body.

The Water Margin

Youthful skin holds an amazing 14 pints of water on which its good looks largely depend. Most of its water is found in the deeper layers—the dermis and hypodermis—where, bound within the cells and in the interstitial network, the water forms a semi-fluid gel with mucopolysaccharides and polysaccharides which together with healthy collagen give your skin its healthy and youthful look and feel. So long as the water balance of your body is good, the water content of these deeper layers will be right too. If, however, you take diuretics, you will lose too much water and in time your skin can become flaccid and desiccated-looking. If you eat too many refined carbohydrates—which no ageless-ager would ever dream of doing—or if you suffer from hormone imbalances such as an excess of oestrogen, the opposite can happen. Your skin can grow puffy with too much fluid.

The outer layers of your skin are different. A mere 8 per cent of the skin's water is found in the epidermis—the superficial horny layer of cells on the outside of the body which cosmetics set out to treat. Yet the softness and the smoothness depend greatly on it. Unlike the deeper layers, the moisture level here is strongly influenced by outside factors such as temperature and relative humidity as well as by chemicals you come in contact with—from airborne pollutants to cosmetics. In the modern world, full of artificially heated and cooled buildings and chemical assaults of various kinds, every type of skin is fighting a battle against water loss.

Your skin is always giving up moisture into the air. We lose up to 3½ pints of water a day through the skin. When this water loss is excessive, the skin tends to become fragile and cracked. If the cracks are deep, as in those on hands which have been repeatedly exposed to harsh detergents, then chapping develops. When they are more superficial, the skin flakes. Sometimes these flakes are large enough to be seen with the naked eye. Sometimes they simply give skin a dull, flat look.

Protection From Water Loss

The epidermis itself does its best to control water loss in two ways. First, in the most superficial layer of the epidermis, the horny scales of the cells separate, leaving spaces which are then filled in with the skin's own natural protective emulsion made up from sebum, water and salts. This has an acid pH and thus helps retain some of the available water on the skin's surface. It creates a film which holds water in, rather as petroleum jelly might, although not as successfully. One of the ways that moisturizers work is by creating such a film artificially on the skin's surface.

Naturally oily skin has an advantage in that its sebum is richer in lipids which give better natural protection against water loss. The second way the epidermis works to retain its moisture is internal. The cells of the skin themselves act as a selective filter, regulating both the passage of substances through the skin from outside and also the loss of water from within. They contain hygroscopic (moisture-attracting) substances carefully protected by membranes which are rich in lipids. Another cosmetic approach to moisturization has been to supply the skin with some of these natural moisturizing factors—such as urea, lactates, sugars, electrolytes and other humectants such as sodium pyrrolidone carboxylate (Na-PCA) which appears to be the most hygroscopic of all.

There are a number of good moisturizers on the market

which incorporate both approaches to moisturization in their products. And there is a third approach too. It uses oils that are particularly rich in essential fatty acids such as gamma-linolenic acid which occurs in evening primrose oil. A few moisturizers now offer all three but they are generally very expensive. Sometimes I use them—particularly when travelling. More often I prefer home treatments both to encourage moisture retention and to retard skin ageing with anti-oxidants applied as you would expensive ampoules on the surface of your skin. Let's look at do-it-yourself moisturization first.

Moisture-Gatherer

Some of the best (and most expensive) moisturizers, face creams and treatment ampoules rely heavily for their effectiveness on a particular ingredient—a concentrated solution of Na-PCA. This ingredient is perhaps the skin's most important natural moisturizing factor. So powerfully hygroscopic is Na-PCA that it quite literally pulls water from the air to moisturize the skin. It is found in human skin and is synthesized in the body from glutamic acid, a 'nonessential' amino acid. As we age both the ability of the skin to retain moisture and the concentration of Na-PCA decline. Until recently, unless you happened to be a chemist yourself, you could only take advantage of Na-PCA's ability to improve moisturization of skin and therefore both its texture and look, by buying products which were very expensive. Now however it is available on its own in a spray bottle. You can spray it all over the body after a bath, on the face before make-up and even on hair which has become dried out. It is non-oily and an excellent and inexpensive way of moisturizing skin and it is available in chemists and health-food stores and by post from manufacturers.

Nail, Hair and Skin Help

Essential fatty acids—the most recently discovered tools for improving skin quality and moisturization—(see Chapter 12) are useful both taken internally through foods or supplements and spread directly on the skin either from their capsules or in products which contain them. They can dramatically improve the texture, functioning and look of your skin. Rapidly absorbed through its surface, they reinforce the hydrolipidic film and the intercellular cement, strengthen cell walls so you get better cellular exchange of nutrients and elimination of wastes, and increase your skin's moisture-holding capacity. There are now skin-care products on the market which are beginning to make use of various forms of EFAs. And what has come to light recently, as a result of experiments with various EFAs used to treat such conditions as premenstrual tension and in the prevention of heart disease, is the fact that used as nutritional supplements for many people they offer a number of highly desirable 'side-effects'. For instance many people using these supplements have found that broken and brittle nails become strong and grow long and healthy, while hair texture and quality also improve. I use both Na-PCA and evening primrose oil daily, spraying my skin with the former after cleansing it or after a bath and then, as soon as it has dried, applying the contents of a capsule of evening primrose oil, which I have pierced with a pin, to my skin and massaging it in—morning and evening. Evening primrose oil also forms part of a formula which I devised for myself as an anti-oxidant skin cocktail for ageless ageing (see page 261). So far I have found no cosmetic to equal its effects.

Vitamins for External Use

The notion that you can use vitamins to advantage on the surface of your skin is often dismissed by the uninformed who insist that these relatively large molecules cannot be absorbed into the body through the skin and that they have no therapeutic effect. In fact just the opposite is true. Since just after the last world war scientists have known that the fat-soluble vitamins—A and E and essential fatty acids—were rapidly and easily absorbed through the skin's surface. They found that this was the only way in which they could treat many of the vitamin deficiencies of the concentration-camp victims because their digestive systems had degenerated so greatly that they could not get adequate nutrients through their foods. The effect of topical applications is anything but superficial. It can affect the body systemically. At the Unilever Research Laboratory in Sharnbrook, Bedford, scientists reported that daily skin applications of sunflower-seed oil rapidly correct essential-fatty-acid deficiencies which have been brought about by massive small intestine reactions. Recently much work has been done with the water-soluble vitamins and some of the minerals as well—using them in topical applications with remarkable results. The advantage of using vitamins and nutrients this way is that they can reach the area you are trying to treat—in this case the skin—without being used up or converted into some other metabolite in the body. So even relatively small doses of them applied topically can be helpful.

Topical C for Collagen

Vitamin C, zinc and the bioflavinoids are essential for the production of new collagen in the body. The condition of your skin is to a great degree dependent on how efficiently you can use them to manufacture it. Vitamin C is therefore an important factor in wound healing. Anthony N. Silvetti who is director of the Wound Healing Intensive Care Unit at West Lake Community Hospital in Melrose Park, Illinois, has found that, used in a wound-healing nutrient solution, Vitamin C can successfully heal even chronic bedsores—lesions which in some cases are thirty years old. Vitamin C stimulates the skin's fibroblast cells to produce new collagen. Another American physician, Lawrence Schachner, director of paediatric dermatology at the University of Miami School of Medicine, uses zinc applied topically in a similar way to heal skin rashes and eruptions. Meanwhile doctors at Hadasah University in Jerusalem have discovered that topical zinc almost halves the healing time of herpes simplex sores and Swedish studies have shown that the continued use of zinc after sores have been healed helps prevent their re-occurrence.

Vitamin E has a long history of being used topically. Because of its anti-oxidant properties, applied to the surface of the skin it can help protect cells from the damage caused by exposure to

UV light or chemotherapy. It can also reduce inflammation and heat on sunburnt skin and, thanks to its potentizing effect on Vitamin A, it can make this vitamin more available for healing and good skin-cell functioning. But there are some more interesting things which have recently been discovered about vitamin E. Peter T. Pugliese of the Xienta Institute for Skin Research in Bernville, Pennsylvania, has found that this nutrient also helps restore damaged capillaries that are leaking excessively into surrounding tissue—something which is common with age and in people who have been living on a typical Western diet. Japanese researchers as well have found that vitamin E topically applied constricts capillaries and reduces the kind of excessive permeability which also comes with inflammation. Vitamin A has also been used with good results on the surface of the skin. One form of it—retinoic acid, which is strictly a prescription item—even accelerates cell turnover, which is something that slows considerably as the skin grows older. Albert Kligman, professor of dermatology at the University of Pennsylvania Medical School, has found that it enhances wound healing, increases blood flow to the skin and stimulates fibroblasts to produce new collagen. His wife, Lorraine Kligman, who is also a dermatologist, has even found that it eliminates fine wrinkles and makes deep wrinkles on older skin seem less noticeable.

Skin Cocktail for Ageless Ageing

But most important of all perhaps, when it comes to making use of nutrients applied to the skin for ageless ageing, is the fact that vitamin E, as well as zinc, vitamins C and A and gamma-linolenic acid from evening primrose oil, have anti-oxidant properties. They can mop up free-radicals and highly reactive oxygen species before they have a chance to damage cell materials and cause cross-linking of collagen to occur. And when you apply them neat to clean skin instead of only relying on nutritional supplements taken orally, you get them right where you need them to do their work—you don't have to worry about what has been metabolized into other forms which don't have such a powerful effect on skin.

Having spent several years in search of a simple, relatively inexpensive yet highly effective external anti-ageing treatment, I finally found one which I think works beautifully. It is no glamorous cosmetic product however. Indeed it leaves your skin smelling more like a kitchen or a chemist's shop than a beauty salon. (That is why I sometimes add just half a drop—*absolutely no more*—of pure essential oil of sandalwood to my mixture.) But it is truly a powerhouse for protecting skin, built from the latest research into free-radical biochemistry and anti-oxidant therapies. You can use it once or twice a week as a mask or you can use a course of it for, say, a fortnight at a time several times a year. It is also an excellent formula to use when you are exercising since this increases your skin's absorptive properties. I often use it daily to make sure I have constant protection against free-radical damage, peroxidation and cross-linking of my skin. If I am working at home I simply put it on and leave it there. If I am out and wearing make-up I leave it on for twenty minutes then tissue off any excess before applying make-up or a night cream. It is as good for oily skin as it is for dry skin but if your skin is oily you will probably always want to tissue it off after twenty minutes or half an hour. You must always be careful not to get it into your eyes (I would not use it on my eyelids or just underneath the eyes for instance) and you should be warned that someone with very sensitive skin might react to one of the vitamins used. This is unusual but there is no way of absolutely ensuring that you won't be one of the unfortunate few for whom it is simply too strong a stimulus. If you know you have sensitive skin it would be wise to test it on the inside of your wrist for a day or two before trying it on your face. I call it Anti-Ox.

Anti-Ox—the Recipe

You'll need:

Ascorbyl palmitate (the oil-soluble form of vitamin C) in 'powder' form
100 IU capsule vitamin E
7500 IU capsule vitamin A
500mg capsule evening primrose oil
½ drop pure essential oil of sandalwood (optional)

Pierce the end of each of the capsules. Pour about half a teaspoon of ascorbyl palmitate into the palm of one hand. Squeeze the contents of each of the capsules into the powder and then, using your fingers, mix it all together until you get a fine oily paste. (The longer you mix the finer it becomes.) This is enough to spread lightly all over your face and neck, massaging it gently in. In the beginning you will probably find your skin seems quite literally to drink it all up. It is almost as though it is hungry for the nutrients being offered. Later on the take-up becomes less dramatic. This may indicate that there is no reason to use it twice every day. But I still prefer to do so. I always wipe the excess on my hands. Almost from the first day I noticed that my skin was smoother and my circulation had improved. Now, after having used it for some time, I think I will never want to be without it—that is until I find something which is even better. My skin texture, colour and translucency are now better than they have been for years.

TWENTY-FOUR

To Tan or Not to Tan

Everybody knows that sun damages your skin. UV radiation is the single most powerful accelerator of skin ageing to which you are likely to be exposed. Radiation triggers free-radical and oxidation damage. It also causes collagen to break down so that skin wrinkles, weakens elastin so that it sags, and brings about unsightly pigmentation blotches which are sure signs of getting old. Trouble is, many people love a tan. Until recently you had only two choices—tan and age or stay pale and preserve your skin. Now that is changing, thanks to new advances in cosmetic chemistry and new formulations which make use of them, as well as special natural substances which can help you fake a tan while actually providing you with some protection against the sun's ageing effects when you are exposed to it. And while no one in his right mind should toast himself in the sun, with a little bit of careful manoeuvring and a clear understanding of what is involved in the tanning process you should be able to have your cake and eat it too.

Solar Radiation and the Skin Challenge

You hear a lot about UVA, UVB and the kind of filters in sun preparations designed to protect from them. In fact 'UVA' and 'UVB' are only rather arbitrary designations for wavelengths of radiation. Until relatively recently manufacturers of suntanning preparations concerned themselves mostly with using filters which block out all or part of the shorter-wavelength UVB radiation which is most responsible for sunburning. They paid little attention to the longer UVA waves which are more implicated in the tanning process. The thinking was that if you cut out the burning rays and let the tanning ones through then you would be getting the best from a sun-protection product. It is on this theory that most of the new so-called 'safe' sunbeds—those which cut out all or most of the UVB rays while letting the UVA rays through—have been sold as well. What they didn't know (or what they chose to ignore for commercial reasons) was the fact that it is also the longer UVA rays which may be most implicated in premature ageing, simply because they penetrate the skin more deeply than does UVB radiation. Short of tying people to sunbeds in laboratories for ten years, there is really no way to absolutely validate this, but leading dermatologists such as Albert Kligman at the University of Pennsylvania have referred to these sunbeds as 'automatic ageing machines'. Both UVA and UVB rays in excess are detrimental and both need to be reckoned with. For they react with the constituents of both epidermis and dermis, causing changes in the skin's vital systems which rapidly accelerate skin ageing.

The Harmful Changes

First exposure to UV radiation releases chemical messengers in the skin which produce vasodilation. Your skin rapidly becomes reddened and puffy as plasma proteins pass through cell walls and cause the accumulation of water in tissues. Such exposure also reduces the population of the cells which form your skin's true protective shield, making it more vulnerable to damage on a molecular level. And it is at the molecular level that UV radiation does its most fundamental damage by acting on four kinds of macromolecules—DNA, RNA, the protein of connective tissue and the lysosome membranes. It causes breakages in the molecular chain of the DNA—the cell's genetic material—due to free-radical reactions, and in the RNA—the chemical messenger for the transfer of genetic information in the birth of new cells—so that a breakdown in protein synthesis and cell mutation occur. It alters the structure of the collagen and the elastin, which are responsible for skin firmness and elasticity. It damages the membranes of some important parts within the skin's cells, called lysosomes, which you may remember contain enzymes, so that even more damage is done to the cells. The biochemical consequences of such UV-induced responses are many, including a decrease in your skin's ability to hold moisture in its outer layer, a decrease in elasticity and an increase in the number and depth of wrinkles. And skin ageing as a result of UV exposure is both cumulative and irreversible.

The Natural Protectors

You have two. The urocanic acid contained in sweat has a weak filtering action on UV light reaching the skin's surface. But, far more important, is the natural process of tanning itself—provided it is *carefully controlled*. The new approach to suntanning reflected in some excellent new formulations does just that. They not only provide *both* UVA and UVB protection, they also do a lot of other, sometimes highly sophisticated, things either to accelerate the tanning process or to provide skin with specific help in resisting and repairing UV damage at a deeper level, or both. In fact we are seeing a real breakthrough in skin protection and suntanning. To understand how the new ranges work their wonders, you need to know a little about how the process of tanning itself occurs.

Exposure to UV light brings about two quite separate effects—the immediate pigment-darkening you get after even a few minutes in the sun and real tanning which is called melanogenesis. The first effect is only the result of a photo-oxidation and changes in colour of the melanins or tanning pigments already synthesized in the skin. But real tanning takes place only when new melanins are synthesized. It involves two kinds of cells. Melanocytes at the skin's reproductive layer produce the melanin pigments which are based on an amino acid, tyrosine. Under the action of an enzyme called tyrosinase, tyrosine is converted into pigment in specialized organelles within these melanocytes. Then the second kind of cells, the keratinocytes, come into play. For while the melanocytes are stationary cells, they only manufacture the tanning pigment, it is the job of the keratinocytes to carry these pigments to the skin's surface where they form a coloured screen. Provided no degenerative damage is done in the process, this gives your skin a natural protection from further UV damage as well as creating a beautiful tan.

Most of the highly sophisticated new suntanning products are aimed at optimizing this natural protective process while guarding against damage within the skin. They incorporate highly selective UVA and UVB filters which transmit only a controlled amount of UV radiation—just enough to stimulate the formation of melanin. Many are also formulated to increase melanin synthesis in the melanocytes. This they can do not by using the psoralenes as has been done in the past (since it is by no means certain that these substances are toxicologically harmless), but by providing skin with a melanocyte-stimulating substance to accelerate the activity of tyrosinase as well as other factors such as beta-carotene, glycoproteins and glycopeptides which can also influence the activities of melanocytes. Many of the new products are also formulated to influence the formation of keratinocytes which carry the pigments to the skin's surface so that they have a good capacity for renewal, perfect integrity, perfect elasticity and so that your skin is in the best possible state of hydration, elasticity, smoothness and firmness. Some of these new ranges also incorporate anti-wrinkle and hydrating agents and both can be shown by objective laboratory measurements to leave skin in better condition (firmer, smoother, more moist, less lines) *after* tanning with them than *before*. But just in case you think these new advances in sun-protection make it possible to throw caution to the wind, think again. The sun's rays are still powerful forces for ageing. Go easy with them.

Safe Alternative with a Bonus

Tanning, then, is nature's way of putting limits on the amount of damage the sun can do your skin. There are other ways of providing such protection as well—for instance by ensuring you get optimum quantities of the anti-oxidant nutrients needed. Some nutrients such as PABA, one of the B complex vitamins, are particularly helpful. It can be used either as a nutritional supplement or spread on the skin. In fact it is the main ingredient in many sun-protected products. But the protectors which fascinate me most are the carotenoids—colorants which occur naturally in our foods such as carotene, which turns carrots orange and which, as a precursor to vitamin A, has potent free-radical-scavenging abilities. One carotenoid—canthaxanthin—which is a red pigment found in certain edible mushrooms and shellfish, can be taken as a nutritional supplement to 'artificially' turn the skin a lovely bronze colour. It is the colorant which turns flamingos' feathers pink, and is one of the natural food additives permitted in the UK.

For artificial tanning canthaxanthin is usually taken two or three times a day and over a period of a fortnight to three weeks you gradually develop colour in your skin. And it appears to be safe—overdoses are said to cause nothing more serious than stomach upset. What colour your skin becomes depends on your genetic inheritance and your ability to produce melanin naturally when you are exposed to sunlight. So Mediterranean skins and even Scandinavian skins will tend to bronze nicely while the peaches-and-cream skin types will unfortunately gain far less colour. But what is particularly nice about the carotenoids is that the ones which have been tested show an ability to protect skin from UV damage. Thanks to their anti-oxidant abilities they also appear to have anti-cancer properties.

Five years ago the idea that you could tan to protect your skin from ageing rather than tan to age it would have been unthinkable. Now it is on its way to becoming a reality. It is a pleasing prospect. But it will still be a long time before you'll be able to bask on the summer beach with impunity.

TWENTY-FIVE

Cellular Therapy

The most controversial of all the natural treatments for re-vitalizing the body is cellular therapy—the injection of fresh animal embryo cells into living organisms. It is a treatment which is outlawed in Britain and the United States, where it has been the focus of orthodox medical hostility for more than thirty years. Meanwhile in Germany, Switzerland and Austria (and now in Mexico and further afield) some 8000 physicians and surgeons have been regularly using it not only to treat chronic skin diseases and those connected with ageing and degeneration such as arteriosclerosis and arthritis but also as a technique for improving the Down's syndrome condition in children, a treatment for resistant obesity, and as a way of eliminating sexual dysfunctions. There is also a rapidly growing medical literature on the subject—some 800 papers in foreign scientific journals and more than 50,000 medical reports on its therapeutic effectiveness. In 1982 it was estimated that more than 2 million patients in the world had so far received cellular therapy—a technique made famous by the charismatic and highly con-troversial Swiss surgeon Paul Niehans at his Clinique La Prairie.

During his lifetime Niehans' patient records were filled with the names of the rich and famous. According to close medical colleague Wolfram Kuhnau and others, Niehans numbered amongst his clients no less than Churchill, De Gaulle, Eisen-hower, and Adenauer as well as both the Duke and Duchess of Windsor, Picasso, Noel Coward and Somerset Maugham. But what first brought cellular therapy to the attention of the world at large was his treatment of Pope Pius XII. Summoned to the

Vatican to inject fresh cells into the ailing pope, Niehans drew popular attention especially when Pius went on to live for another four years and insisted that the Swiss doctor had saved his life. Since then cellular therapy has largely been a source of confusion to most of us. There has been so little reliable information about it in English and it seems to be practised in so many guises at different centres throughout the world. Add to that the fact that amidst the thousands of conscientious doctors and surgeons using it there have been a few money-mad charlatans more intent on increasing the size of their bank balances than on benefiting humanity and it is little wonder the aura surrounding the technique has become murky, muddled and morally questionable.

It is time some of the confusion was cleared up. For cellular therapy offers a potential for revitalization and for healing of the human body which needs urgently to be examined. And far from becoming some kind of dated medical curiosity, it too has developed as a technique. It is currently being used in Germany, Switzerland and Mexico in conjunction with nutritional techniques for health and lifestyle changes which together create a methodology of treatment that goes far beyond what can be achieved by cellular therapy alone.

A Total Approach to Healing

One of the leaders in the use of cell therapy as part of an historic approach to total health is Swiss physician and octogenarian Franklin Bircher. Bircher worked closely with Niehans in the early days. He is the second son of the famous Swiss doctor Max Bircher-Benner. Also one of the world's experts in micro-circulation, Bircher has been combining fresh-cell treatments with dietary principles for two generations. Like many of the physicians using cellular therapy in a total programme of physical revitalization, his successes have been legion. Ironically perhaps, Franklin Bircher came to use cellular therapy because of his failures. Amongst the many patients treated with diet and lifestyle changes, there were a few who just didn't seem to get better. The food, exercise and psychological therapies didn't seem enough for them. They needed some kind of boost to raise

them out of the biological inertia into which they had sunk—
perhaps some kind of immune-support or the rebalancing of
their hormonal system at a deep level. He was not sure what. He
was even less certain where it could be found.

A vigorous campaigner for public health and a laboratory
researcher as well as a physician, Bircher is a man with an
insatiable desire to discover what could be put to practical use.
He met Niehans, worked with him and found that in this simple
technique of injecting fresh cells from carefully selected foetal
glands and organs, the majority of these resistant cases got
better. This he was able to measure in three ways: by the
disappearance of symptoms, by clinical and laboratory checks
on blood lipids, blood pressure, hormone balance and other
standard medical parameters, and finally by a technique for
which he later became famous all over Europe: microscopic
examination of the microcirculation of a patient before and after
treatment with fresh cells and diet.

His technique is, I believe, unique in the world. It involves
the examination of the patient's underlip through a microscope,
which is done by stretching the lip over the field of the microscope and illuminating it from beneath. This way Bircher and
his colleagues have been able to evaluate blood flow through the
tiny capillaries while it is taking place. Then by photographing
these microscopic blood vessels he is able later to examine the
exact size and configuration of capillaries. Many of these microscopic photographs have been blown up to immense size. Some
are remarkably beautiful. In the past forty years he has discovered that the shape and condition of the walls of the
capillaries give a strong indication not only of the patient's
overall state of health but even of the particular ailments from
which he is suffering. He has also found that for many people
changes in diet alone, towards a way of eating which is low in fat
and protein and rich in fresh vegetables and fruits and whole
grains, are enough over a period of a few months to quite
literally rejuvenate the body—to normalize these tiny capillaries
and restore proper blood flow to the tissues. The condition of
your microcirculation is of central importance both in maintaining a state of high-level health and in protecting your body
from ageing.

Microcirculation and Health

The capillaries—very thin blood vessels which radiate throughout the body—together make up the microcirculation. If the capillaries in your body were attached to each other end to end they would measure 60,000 miles in length—more than twice around the world. Their state largely determines the condition of your body as a whole because they are arbitrators of both nutrition and elimination. It is through these capillaries that nutrients and oxygen are carried via the bloodstream to the cells, organs, glands and tissues of the body. The capillaries have tiny 'pores' in them which let plasma but not red blood cells seep through and pass into the body fluid. This is how nutrients are delivered and wastes eliminated from the cells. But capillaries can become twisted, distended and highly porous as a result of poor diet or age-degeneration. When they do, blood proteins seep through and deposit themselves between the tissues and the capillary walls to interfere with proper exchange of nutrients and the elimination of wastes—gradually starving cells, tissues and organs of what they need to function properly. Such changes in microcirculation not only lower overall vitality since none of the body's parts are receiving the oxygen and nutrients they need to function, they also predispose you to degenerative illnesses and to rapid ageing both of the skin and of the body as a whole. Restore normal microcirculation and you can, in a very real way, offer the body rejuvenation at a cellular level. For most people simply changing to a diet high in fresh raw foods and eliminating all highly processed and refined foods will do this gradually over a period of several weeks. For a few such a diet is not enough and that is where cell therapy appears very helpful.

The Protocol

Cellular therapy consists of intramuscular injections given in the buttocks of preparations taken from endocrine glands and other tissues of animal embryos—usually calves or lambs. These injections are prepared from tissue excised from a freshly killed embryo which is homogenized and placed in isotonic salt solution to prevent it from autolysis. They are made as quickly as possible so as to preserve the living properties of the cells and they are taken from embryos to minimize the chance of any allergic reaction and to keep the patient's immune system from rejecting foreign material. This entails having to have a laboratory where the animal can be slaughtered and dissected in conjunction with a sanatorium where the treatment is given.

Because of the difficulty of doing this, a number of alternatives to fresh cells have been developed—lyophilization, for instance, where cells are suddenly frozen at a low temperature with dehydration under vacuum, and extracting only RNA and DNA from the cell preparations (both of which are designed to preserve the actions of the cells)—which enable them to be given in a doctor's office or at home instead of a special clinic. There is little question that these alternatives are nowhere near as good as fresh cells extracted from an embryo and injected almost immediately. Both methods greatly reduce biological activity. And though they may prove economically therapeutic and easy to use for practitioners employing them, they are not treatments of choice.

Ordinary freezing is another method. Cells are preserved in liquid nitrogen so they can be sent around the world without being harmed to the doctor using them who gives them immediately on defrosting. This method is a close second-best to fresh cells, and far more convenient than giving fresh cells on removal from the animal.

The Diagnosis

Exactly which tissues and glands are given depends on careful patient workups on the part of the physician prescribing cellular therapy. To determine this he will put the patient through a complete physical, take a lengthy case history, and examine a number of medical parameters the most important of which is the patient's hormonal status. He will then order cells from each of the glands or organs which he believes need treatment. These can include the pituitary, the adrenals, the ovaries, the thymus, the thyroid, the liver and so forth. Each preparation is given in a separate injection and a patient may receive anywhere from four to twelve injections at once. Daunting as this sounds, in the hands of a competent physician they are actually completely painless. The patient is then forced to stay in bed for a period of from two to six days during which time his diet is carefully controlled and the fresh-cell preparations begin to work.

Cell therapy is currently being used, apparently with considerable success, not only to revitalize the system as a whole and to slow down the rate at which you are ageing but also to treat diseases ranging from chronic skin disorders—such as psoriasis, eczema and allergies—and arteriosclerosis to multiple sclerosis, muscular dystrophy, cancer, congenital defects of all kinds, mental and physical retardation, Down's syndrome, narcolepsy, obesity, pancreatitis, chronic systemic metabolic dysfunctions, liver cirrhosis, many sexual dysfunctions, chronic nephrosis and all kinds of auto-immune disorders. How does it work? The fact no one has a clear answer to this question is one of the major reasons that cell therapy has met with such violent hostility from the British and the American medical community. Thanks to burgeoning continental European research into the mechanisms by which it affects the body however, there are some important hints.

The Mysteries of Fresh Cells

Niehans described the actions of cellular therapy as:

> . . . a method of treating the whole organism on a biological basis, capable of revitalizing the human organism with its trillions of cells by bringing to it those embryonic or young cells which it needs. Cells from all organs are at our disposal; the doctor's art is to choose the right cells. Selective cellular therapy offers new life to the ailing or diseased organism.

This claim which doctors using cellular therapy continue to make for these fresh embryo cells—that when they are injected into the body the cells migrate towards their related organs, glands and tissues—is one that most 'nonbelievers' find hard to swallow. Once there they are said to transfer their essential biological characteristics to their human counterparts. Such a notion has not been acceptable to many members of the scientific community because such 'cell migration' is thought to be a physiological impossibility. Yet radioactive tagging of fresh cell material has shown that, just as the cellular therapists have claimed, this cellular material (or at the very least something from it) does indeed find its way to target glands and tissues. This work was done mostly by Professor A. Kment, chairman of the physiology department at the University of Vienna Veterinary College of Medicine and Professors F. Schmid and H. Lettre at the University of Heidelberg. Thanks to their research, it is now believed that this occurs due to the actions of the immune system's scavenger cells which may link with the fresh cells, dissolve them into their constituent elements—nucleoproteins, enzymes and so forth—and then migrate to the specific receptor sites. Working with animals Kment has found that the injections of fresh cells improve learning and perception, elasticity and resilience to damage in the skin, cardiovascular system and connective tissue. They also enhance cellular respiration and improve intra-extra cellular exchanges of nutrients and the elimination of wastes.

Quality Not Quantity

Doctors with many years of experience using cell therapy such as Franklin Bircher in Zurich and Wolfram Kuhnau in Mexico agree that in using cell injections on patients it appears to be the quality rather than the quantity of cell material given which brings results. Each cell in a living organism appears to have an innate ability for self-organization. In some way, that is as yet not completely understood, the information contained within each kind of cell reacts in such a way that cells become identifiable as tissues. Because there are no essential differences between the functional capacities and enzymic functioning of human and animal cells, it would seem that the well-organized constituents of these animal cells may help provide biological information needed to restore harmonious functioning to the human cells which they are being used to treat.

The transfer of this fresh cellular information to the body's ailing cells has been found to take place within the first forty-eight hours after injections are given. During this time patients are made to rest and are given no drugs of any kind. Neither are they usually allowed any proteolytic (protein-dissolving) enzymes in their diet such as those which occur in pineapple and papaya. Like Bircher and Kuhnau, many physicians insist on giving vitamin supplements as well—particularly the anti-oxidant nutrients such as vitamins C and E, and others which help protect the newly injected cells from free-radical and peroxidation damage to cells. Some even recommend injections of anti-oxidant enzymes such as superoxide dismutase, catalase or dimethyl sulphoxide (DMSO).

Despite the many conditions which appear to respond favourably to cellular therapy, practitioners insist that there are some for which it should not be used. For instance it is not given to patients suffering active inflammatory diseases (which appear to dissipate the beneficial effects of the fresh cells), nor to patients who have recently suffered a heart attack or a cerebral haemorrhage, nor to patients with chronic kidney disease or known allergies to certain drugs and vaccines, nor to patients with a high risk of thrombosis. It also appears to be ineffective where metal toxicity—a high level of lead or cadmium or aluminium for instance—is present in the body. They must be removed by chelation before cellular therapy can be effective.

Hormonal Actions

The basic intention of cellular therapy is to normalize bodily functions and to restore biological harmony to a living organism. This appears to take place in no small part thanks to the effects that injected embryo cells have on the body's hormonal functions—restoring a harmony to endocrine functions which is virtually impossible to achieve by giving specific hormone concentrations. Just how long this takes to happen depends greatly on the individual patient (another factor which irks members of the British and American scientific community who prefer results cut and dried). In tests of hormone metabolites in the urine before and over a twenty-four hour period just after cellular injections physicians report normal readings are restored, at least temporarily, almost immediately. But the generalized benefits to body and mind can take several weeks or even months to show themselves. Most patients experience an immediate lift (some describe it as a kind of relaxed euphoria) for the first couple of days. Then there often follows a period of mild weakness or fatigue which in turn is followed (between six weeks and six months later—it is a highly individual thing) by a dramatic improvement in how they look and feel.

Cell therapy is something which is often given as a prophylactic treatment every few years to boost the body's own resistance to ageing and degeneration. Although as Franklin Bircher will tell you, most of his patients who make dietary and lifestyle changes at the time of cell therapy and then who continue to follow more health-enhancing ways of living, never need more treatment. Injections are never repeated before six months or a year after the original treatment has been given except in the case of treating mongolism, where they are often given every five or six months until the child reaches the age of about ten when the therapy is usually no longer necessary, and in the case of cancer where cellular injections are sometimes repeated as often as every week to once a month.

What the Future Holds

Ask any experienced cell therapist why there is such long-standing and often hostile resistance in Britain and America to this much used continental European technique for healing and rejuvenation and they usually cite two things. First ignorance. Because most of the laboratory research into cellular therapy and most clinical reports of its effectiveness have been published in foreign languages, English-speaking doctors have little access to it. Second, in a medical community which leans heavily for its treatment approaches on drug-based therapies, cellular therapy has little place. It is a simple natural technique which, like the orthomolecular approaches to treatment, offers no financial opportunities for development to multinational drug companies. Then, of course, there are many, such as vegetarians, who object to using animal tissues on humanitarian grounds. I have great sympathy with their pleas and am completely against the unnecessary slaughter of animals. Yet, so potent a tool for human healing can this technique be that I cannot but feel that sometimes its use is justified.

Happily, at least one of those factors—ignorance—appears to be being gradually replaced by knowledge that is coming from pure research at least. Not long ago the prestigious *New England Journal of Medicine* carried (to my knowledge for the first time in any English-language medical publication) a report of how seventeen children had been treated for a resistant immune-suppressive condition known as histiocytosis-X by being given daily intramuscular injections of thymus extract from five-day-old calves. Ten of them, the report shows, experienced complete remission from the condition.

Hopefully this is a first step. For in a world in which degenerative diseases—for which we have no effective treatments in our repertoire of drug therapies—have reached epidemic proportions we cannot afford to ignore the clinical experience of physicians like Franklin Bircher and others like him and the methods they use for restoring harmony and balance to the person as a whole. Cellular therapy certainly has a place among them.

TWENTY-SIX

Hormone Magic and Nucleic Wonders

As far back as the papyrus of Eber, physicians have prescribed raw glandular substances for healing and rejuvenation. Homer tells how Achilles took bone marrow from lions for strength. In 1400 BC the Indian doctor Susrata counselled eating sex glands from tigers to cure impotence. In the past hundred years numerous reports have appeared in scientific journals about the successful use of raw glands such as thyroid, pancreas, pituitary and so forth in the treatment of disease and age-related degeneration. In fact it was the discovery that these raw glands from animals or extracts derived from them could dramatically improve glandular insufficiencies in human beings that led pharmaceutical companies at the beginning of the century to make these preparations available for common medical use and which lent power to the newly developing science of endocrinology. In recent years, however, orthodox medicine has tended to discard the use of whole glands and glandular extracts in favour of specific hormones such as insulin, pancreatin and thyroxine, which have either been isolated from them or chemically made.

Out of this work has come the development of the contraceptive pill, the use of insulin in drug therapy for diabetes and a number of other important treatment modalities using powerful chemicals which have potent actions. The problem is they can also have powerful side-effects. For the entire endocrine system is a delicately balanced interwoven complex of chemical messengers—the hormones—which are interdependent. Giving excessive amounts of one of them on its own can *seriously* imbalance the whole system, leading to harmful side-effects.

Isolated hormones such as testosterone—the male sex hormone—oestrogen, insulin and so forth are not as safe as the whole raw glands from which they have been derived, which is why they are only available on prescription and why they need to be handled very carefully by specialists. Whole-gland extracts are different.

Natural Chemical Messengers

Glands, or more specifically endocrine glands, secrete hormones. They release these chemical messengers directly into the bloodstream. The hormone messengers are then carried through the circulation to specific points in the body where they excite action. It is largely because of the minute quantities of hormones and polypeptides which glands secrete—usually measured in micrograms per millilitre of blood serum—that the body's organs and systems can communicate with each other. In the body there are complex biochemical cycles involving hormones from one gland which trigger actions in organs and other glands, and there are also superbly controlled feedback loops for slowing or stopping the functions of an organ or another gland when a particular task is finished. Ten glands are known to have endocrine functions, including the pineal, the hypothalamus and the pituitary in the brain, the thyroid and the parathyroid in the neck, the thymus in the chest, the adrenals, kidney and pancreas in the abdomen and the gonads or sex glands in the pelvis.

As the body ages, many essential hormones are in increasingly short supply, while at the same time imbalances between various hormones and the glands that secrete them tend to develop. According to experts in cell therapy, one of the reasons why, when properly administered, it can be so useful in restoring vitality to an organism and improving immunity is because the majority of cells used are taken from endocrine glands. And, provided these are well chosen according to a patient's need, they appear able to rebalance the endocrine system and are able to a remarkable degree to restore depleted hormone levels near to normal.

While not as potent in its actions as injected cells, oral

glandular therapy—the clinical evidence for which was established as long ago as sixty to eighty years—appears to have considerable therapeutic value as an anti-ageing tool. That is provided of course that the glandulars are carefully processed. The major controversy now is not so much *whether* they work but *how* they work.

Oral Glandular Therapy

For many years after the endocrinologists began to isolate individual hormones and use them for treatment the idea of giving the extract of a whole raw gland orally instead was dismissed on the belief that, because the biologically active hormones and enzymes in these glands were proteins and polypeptides, taken orally these would only be broken down into their constituent amino acids and peptides in the stomach and therefore could exert no specific action on the body's own endocrine glands or hormonal secretions. Recent investigation has shown however that even very large molecules such as enzymes can penetrate the gut. It has been suggested by researchers such as W. A. Hemmings that about half of the food proteins which pass through the stomach into the small intestine are not broken down into amino acids and small peptides in the gut but pass as intact molecules into the circulatory system. There is also biochemical evidence that a significant percentage of the food proteins which have left the bloodstream and entered the tissues—possibly more than 20 per cent—retain their original characteristics as complex animal proteins. Clinically too, there is evidence that substances in properly prepared glandular tissues—factors such as enzymes, hormones, polypeptides, essential fatty acids and even prostaglandins—have clinically significant effects which may account for the therapeutic value of oral glandular therapy.

There are a number of glands which are available for oral use. They can be purchased from health-food stores and by post from manufacturers of nutritional supplements. Because proper endocrine balance and the restoration of good hormone levels are so important to ageless ageing, these natural substances are commonly used by physicians employing non-drug methods for age-retardation—usually after a careful consideration of the endocrine status of the individual patient. The most commonly used gland is the thymus because this gland, which is often called 'the master gland of immunity', governs immune functions which in turn play such a central role in how rapidly the body ages. It is usually given in amounts of between 200 and 800mg of thymus tissue a day in two doses.

Other common glands used orally in anti-ageing treatment include the pituitary, the pancreas, the thyroid, the adrenals and the male and female sex glands. Most longevists agree that raw glandulars can also be useful taken as a complex which includes not only the glands themselves but other bodily tissues particularly susceptible to age-degeneration: liver, stomach, heart, brain, kidney, spleen, pancreas, duodenum, thyroid, thymus, adrenal, parotid, parathyroid, pineal, adrenal and pituitary. This can be taken together with an ovarian and uterus glandular extract for women and a prostate and orchic (taken from the testicles) glandular concentrate for men. Raw glandulars are usually taken for a period of about six weeks at a time three or four times a year and they are best utilized when the body has good supplies of the nutrients needed to make use of them—vitamins C, A, E, folic acid, B_6, zinc, B_{12}, manganese, B_1 and B_2.

The Key Lies in Processing

Health-food stores abound in glandular products many of which are of very poor quality either because they have been heat-processed, which destroys much of the biological activity of the raw substance, or because they have been extracted from animals which are not healthy or which have been treated with growth hormones such as di-ethyl stilbestrol (DES) to make them fatten quickly for market. Avoid them. Poorly processed glandular material cannot be effective if the biologically active materials it contains have been eliminated or destroyed. These materials tend to be stable at temperatures below freezing but they can be destroyed by heat. There are three ways of process-ing raw glandulars which are widely used: the azeotropic method of co-distillation, salt precipitation and freeze-drying.

While the azeotropic method produces a final product which is quite high in enzyme activity, it removes the fat-based substances present. And, since many of the active fat-soluble hormones are present either in the fat surrounding the gland or in the interstitial fat these are removed in the process. So are essential fatty acids and prostaglandins. The salt precipitation method involves maceration—steeping the fresh frozen glands in liquid—after which salt and water are added and then the mixture is centrifuged to separate the fat. But even after the processing is finished the salt remains.

The best way of processing glandular extracts is by freeze-drying them. This process, in which they are treated under vacuum, avoids removing the fat within the glands and produces a product which is stable over long periods when exposed to air. You end up with a product which has at least five times the raw coagulable protein and enzymes of glandular tissue prepared by other methods. It is also very important to make sure that the glandular materials themselves come not from animals which have been raised on feed lots but from livestock which has been grazed. Glandulars from New Zealand are particularly good since there are strict regulations there prohibiting the use of insecticides or synthetic hormones and their livestock is range-grazed. When choosing a supplement for oral glandular therapy it is also important to look for one which is prepared in such a way that each tablet is protected from stomach acid so that as much of the biologically active glandular substances as possible reach the small intestine where they can be absorbed by the lymph system.

Nucleic Acids for Prolonged Youth?

You may remember from Chapter 23 that one of the major problem areas in ageing on a cellular level is the missynthesis of proteins and especially the nucleic acids which carry the cell's genetic information—DNA and RNA. When this occurs, amongst other things cell vitality is lowered and, unless the damage is repaired, a cell can no longer reproduce itself accurately. Nucleic acids—DNA and RNA—have continually to be synthesized in the cells and there has long been a controversy about whether supplying these substances dietetically or in the form of supplements, together with the various vitamins, minerals and amino acids needed to manufacture them, can promote the repair of damaged genetic material and boost the synthesis of healthy protein. There is some evidence that taking between 1200 and 2000mg of nucleic acids five days a week for a two-month period at a time can do this.

This theory has mostly been propagated by a Swiss-trained American physician, Benjamin Frank, who has written several books on the subject of nucleic-acid supplementation and who has for more than twenty-five years been using nucleic acids either as dietary supplements or encouraging people to eat foods which are high in them, such as sardines, very often. Frank claims that the body is not always able to synthesize enough DNA and RNA. This results in a breakdown of genetic encoding that eventually leads to degeneration. He asserts that by providing supplementary nutrients, 'Exogenous RNA, especially when combined with metabolically associated B vitamins, minerals, amino acids and sugars, will enter the cell and aid in normal regeneration of the decayed metabolic organization of the cell and in so doing will bring about normal enzyme synthesis and activation.'

Frank believes that supplementing your diet with nucleic acids increases the production of ATP—the cell's basic energy currency—and that this in turn stimulates cell repair and normal functioning. ATP itself can be synthesized from nucleic acids. If one can increase the production of ATP, claims Frank, then your cells are able to use oxygen more efficiently and therefore oxidation damage to them will be reduced. He claims that several weeks on such a regime brings improvements in health, including an increase in stamina and vitality. Facial lines become softened and begin to disappear while the skin becomes moist and glowing as a result of improved cell functions and increased production of one of the skin's most important moisture-retaining factors—hyaluronic acid. The Frank diet stresses foods which are particularly high in nucleic acids such as brewer's yeasts (the richest source), sardines, pinto beans, lentils and so forth. Nucleic acids are also available as supplements from health-food stores.

The Nays

The most common objection to Frank's techniques is twofold. First, dissenters claim that nucleic acids are not needed in the diet because the body can make them out of proteins and carbohydrates. Frank is quick to counter this argument by pointing out that nucleic acids are actually taken in when we eat many foods and that we have both digestive enzymes which are able to break nucleic acids down into nucleotides as well as biochemical pathways for resynthesizing nucleic acids from these nucleotides in the cells. So, he claims, it would appear that nature intended for us to get at least some of them in our diet. The second common objection to nucleic-acid therapy lies in the fear that they might increase the level of uric acid in the blood and encourage gout. But, provided vitamin B_5 and thiamine are present in sufficient quantities this should not happen. Vitamins C, A and E as well as the essential fatty acids also help detoxify the body of excess uric acid.

Unfortunately nobody so far has done much to try and validate Frank's work, so there is little more than his clinical records to go by in evaluating the treatment. However there has been quite a lot of research into how exogenous nucleic acids affect animals. For instance as long ago as 1928 Australian scientists experimented by feeding 25mg a day of yeast-derived nucleic acids to mice from weaning to death. They recorded a 16 per cent increase in lifespan. If this were to be translated into human terms you would have to eat a lot of yeast—about 70g (2½oz). Another researcher, T. S. Gardner, later fed 2.5mg again of yeast-derived nucleic acids to mice, starting when they were 600 days old—well on the way to old age. He found they lived 9 per cent longer than the control group and also that they kept their vigour and had significantly less tendency to senile changes than their counterparts.

Organ-Specific RNA

In Europe, particularly in Germany, there is a well-established tradition of using RNA and DNA derived specifically from glands and organs for rejuvenation and restoring hormonal balance. The best-known mixture is called Regenerensen or RN-13. It is made up of organ-specific RNA from testes, ovaries, placenta, hypothalamus, adrenals, liver, pituitary, thalamus, spleen, blood vessels, brain and kidneys plus some yeast-derived RNA. It is meant to encourage proper protein synthesis in all the corresponding glands, organs and tissues of the body. (This treatment is an offshoot of the original cellular therapy.) Organ-specific RNA is usually given by injection but it is also available in tablet form. Anyone taking either organ-specific RNA or dietary supplements of yeast RNA orally is usually advised to take the tablets five out of seven days a week, to ensure he gets all of the vitamin and mineral factors which are particularly important in the synthesis of new nucleic acids and to drink plenty of water while following the treatment. I personally have never tried either, while I have several times used oral glandulars with good results. People whom I know who have, however, claim to have found them very helpful. Most of them insist that Frank is right—dietary supplements of RNA do improve the look and feel of the skin dramatically.

TWENTY-SEVEN

Nature's Anti-Agers

Amidst the growing awareness of what high-tech biochemistry boasts—in the form of the anti-oxidant nutrients—against degeneration and what expensive treatments such as cell therapy can do to improve your appearance, to slow down the rate at which you are ageing and to revitalize your system, we often give little thought to what simple natural substances have to offer. Take herbs and roots and animal tonics for instance—some with a history going back several thousand years. Amongst them all, the most exciting, the finest and most effective belong to a group called 'the adaptogens'. The adaptogens, which include a number of very different natural substances—from Panax ginseng and eleutherococcus (sometimes called 'Siberian ginseng') to an exotic-sounding preparation made from the horn of a deer—have been widely investigated in recent years, by Soviet scientists, and in centuries past, mostly by the Orientals.

Most of the adaptogens belong to long traditions of folk medicines and most have been held in high esteem for thousands of years in the pharmacopoeia of the world's medicine. What is so special about these natural products and why they are grouped together under the name is that they are all substances which, in carefully conducted laboratory and clinical studies, have been shown to enhance an organism's 'non-specific resistance' to ageing, illness and fatigue. In practical terms they enhance your body's ability to adapt itself to all forms of stress—from the stress of fatigue, of illness, of exertion and of ageing to emotional hardship—while at the same time helping to normalize biochemical activities. Taken as 'medicines for well people' they can be remarkably helpful in keeping your body young and full of vitality. So remarkable are the positive effects that adaptogens have been shown to have on a living organism that it is a constant source of wonder to me that they have not been more widely investigated and used in Europe and in America. Meanwhile Soviet and Oriental scientists have spent the last forty years working with certain natural products which, when taken in a form unadulterated by heat or heavy processing, have a remarkable ability to improve health. They appear to be high in structural information.

Structural Information for High-Level Health

As Soviet scientists I. I. Brekhman and others have shown, not only are the chemicals and nutrients which can be extracted from natural plant or animal substances in the laboratory—vitamins, minerals, protein, organic acids, oils, etc—important for health, so is the complexity of the way they and other as yet unidentified factors are synergistically combined. In Brekhman's terms certain natural products (many of the folk remedies) are rich in 'structural information'—a high-quality health-supporting energy which cannot be measured in chemical terms alone. He is particularly interested in certain natural pharmacological substances such as ginseng which appear to supply a high degree of structural information to an organism and thereby support a high level of health and energy. There is something quite special in the way the constituents of such natural products seem to work together and have a natural affinity for the body. They have been shown to increase physical stamina and endurance, stimulate protein repair on a cellular level, protect from radiation damage, increase antibody production, detoxify your body and improve your stamina and vitality. In a way the adaptogens could be considered the 'elixirs of life' in the late twentieth century. They are perfect natural tools for ageless ageing.

Stress without Distress

It was Soviet scientists who first developed the notion of an adaptogen, from the work of Hans Selye, Director of the Institute of Experimental Medicine and Surgery at the University of Montreal, whose work on stress has become universally accepted. His 'general adaptation syndrome', the GAS, you may remember from Chapter 6, describes the way in which when your body is stressed by whatever agent—from cold to fatigue to emotional upset to overwork to chemicals in your air or foods—its homeostasis, that is its natural balance, is threatened. Immediately it draws upon its resources to resist the threat and to maintain well-being. And indeed, provided you are young and strong and well it can go on resisting any damage from stress for a long time. But, alas, eventually it enters the final stage of the GAS in which exhaustion takes over. Then your body's weakest system starts to break down and chronic illness, fatigue and (if the stress is great enough) even death can follow. What in effect has happened is that your body's adaptive energy—its ability to cope— has finally become exhausted.

Selye pointed out that the ageing process itself can be viewed as the GAS on a wider scale. He emphasized that the capacity to adapt virtually disappears in old age and that this loss, equivalent to a loss of vitality, is characteristic of senescence. Selye was always fascinated by the notion that it might be possible to discover or to develop 'medicines for well people' which could enhance the body's own adaptation mechanisms—substances which could prolong your body's ability to resist age-degeneration and exhaustion. They would be different from usual medicines in that, unlike drugs, they would not be aimed at a specific effect such as lowering blood pressure or eliminating pain. Nor would they be intended for the treatment of illness. Instead they would belong to a new category of medicines for health for they would improve the body's *nonspecific resistance* to illness, ageing and fatigue.

That's where the adaptogens come in—substances which can increase your general capacity to overcome external stresses through adaptation. Their use has an important part to play in protecting skin from ageing, in maintaining a high level of health and vitality and even in enhancing mental abilities. Russian researcher I. I. Brekhman, at the Far-East Scientific Centre of the Academy of Science, Vladivostok, has done more than any other single scientist to explore adaptogens and to test their effects on both animals and humans. In fact it was Brekhman's teacher, the Russian expert in pharmacology N. V. Lazarev who first coined the word in order to describe these substances with the remarkable ability of strengthening and rebalancing the whole system. One of the first natural substances which Brekhman and his co-workers investigated and which they found had this ability was Panax ginseng—the root that was first used for medicinal purposes more than 4000 years ago 'to restore the five internal organs, tranquillize the spirit, calm agitation of the mind, allay excitement, and ward off harmful influences . . . The continual use of ginseng makes for long life with light weight of the body.' It is probably the most well known and highly respected natural medicine in the world.

Useless in Perfect Harmony

Traditionally ginseng has been prescribed only in states of imbalance. It is used to treat toxicity in the body, sluggishness, anaemia, weakness and fatigue. But like most of the nutritional and natural tools for health, in a perfectly healthy and balanced person it is supposed to have no effect whatever. Because, as your body ages, its ability to withstand stress and to maintain homeostasis declines, ginseng has become a prime anti-ageing remedy. For generations in the West the value of ginseng has largely been dismissed as an old wives' tale. In part this is because the very notion of a medicine for health finds no place in the thinking behind Western orthodox medicine. But in part too it is probably because some of the few studies which have been carried out to test claims made for it have been done on inferior crops or on ginseng which had been heat-treated and heat-treating destroys many of the beneficial effects of most of the adaptogens.

A number of well conducted studies—both on animals and humans—carried out by Brekhman and others in the Soviet Union and by European researchers in Switzerland, Sweden and Germany and Britain show quite conclusively that ginseng has extraordinary adaptogenic properties. It improves the body's ability to use oxygen—important in staving off ageing as well as increasing mental and physical stamina and in enhancing athletic performance, all of which it has been shown to do. It helps lower blood pressure that is too high, but doesn't affect normal readings. It offers protection against radiation-caused damage—also important in slowing down the rate at which your body ages. It increases your resistance to illness and against harmful effects of chemicals in the environment. It heightens mental faculties and is a natural stimulant to the central nervous system—improving reflexes, longterm and shortterm memory, and making learning easier. But unlike coffee and most other stimulants, it does not produce a sudden rise in body activity followed by an unpleasant dip in energy, or depression. Nor is there any danger of becoming dependent on it. Like all of the adaptogens, ginseng has a gradual build-up effect on the body when you take regular doses of it over about three weeks.

Staving off Exhaustion

If, like me, you like to work long hours but still be reasonably fresh and responsive afterwards, you can use ginseng as a means of staving off exhaustion, while improving mental and physical functioning and maintaining a sense of mental and physical balance. At the Maudsley Hospital in London, Stephen Fulder gave ginseng to nurses involved in stressful and exhausting shifts and an identical placebo to others. He found that although performance in pyschological as well as physical tests, and overall mood, vitality and competence, were undermined by the stressful conditions in which they worked, ginseng improved many of these parameters in those who took it. In the Soviet Union ginseng was given to fifty soldiers on a 3km race while to another fifty a placebo was given. Those who had taken the ginseng finished an average of 53 seconds sooner than the rest. At the University of Minnesota researchers tested the exam-taking abilities of students giving some ginseng and some a placebo. The exam results from the ginseng group were significantly higher than the placebo-takers. In repeated animal trials Brekhman and others have found that ginseng acts as a stimulant without causing insomnia and that not only does it help stave off fatigue and strengthen the organism's ability to cope with stressors of all sorts, the beneficial effects of taking ginseng appear to multiply and build up over the period in which it is taken. Also, ginseng's benefits last long after you stop taking it. As Brekhman says:

> After a series of experiments on men it was established that daily doses of ginseng preparations during 15–45 days increase physical endurance and mental capacity for work. The increase was noted not only during the treatment itself, but also for a period of time (a month to a month and a half) after the treatment had been over. The increase in work capacity was attended by a number of favourable somatic effects and a general improvement of health and spirits (appetite, sleep, absence of moodiness, etc).

Siberian Ginseng

Another adaptogen which has now been widely investigated, particularly in the Soviet Union, is eleutherococcus or Siberian ginseng. Unlike ginseng, eleutherococcus has not been used for generations for health. Indeed its therapeutic properties have only been discovered in the past fifty years. Siberian ginseng is a prickly plant known as 'devil's shrub' with leaves similar to ginseng and beautiful yellow and purple flowers. It is the plant's hot and spicy roots which are used medicinally. Like ginseng it has an ability to strengthen the body's ability to resist illness, degeneration and fatigue while never upsetting your body's natural physiological functions. It is a mild stimulant. Take it now and this stimulant action will last between six and eight hours. Its tonic effects are accumulative—they come gradually over a few weeks. They include increased stamina, better sleep patterns, better memory, clearer thinking and improved athletic performance. Eleutherococcus has particular relevance to any anti-ageing programme because it is a natural protector against the kind of free-radical oxidation which leads to cross-linking of proteins and, among other things, skin sagging and wrinkling. It also appears to have potent anti-cancer properties. Brekhman and many Russian researchers believe that eleutherococcus is a better adaptogen than ginseng. It has been shown both to increase the work capacity of people in factories and also to reduce the incidence of absence from work because of illness.

And it is considered by Russian physicians to be a treatment of choice for both high and low blood pressure thanks to its ability to harmonize bodily functions. It is also used widely to treat anaemia and to treat atherosclerosis in the Soviet Union. Like ginseng and all of the adaptogens it is best taken regularly over a period of several weeks. It can however be taken year round without any loss in beneficial effects.

Stringent Demands for Adaptogens

Ginseng and eleutherococcus are the two adaptogens most widely available in Britain and America (not, alas, always in active forms however—you have to be careful what you buy). But there are others too: pantocrine (an extract of deer horn); Schizandra chinensis (the red berries of a Chinese plant which are widely used as a tonic); and more—most with long Latin names—which are still under rigorous investigation. Each has its unique properties but they have a great deal in common both in the way they act on the body and in their safety even when used regularly over long periods of time. In fact Russian scientists are very careful about the requirements that need to be fulfilled if a natural medicine is to qualify as an adaptogen. In Brekhman's own words:

1. The substance, whether herbal or animal in origin, must be absolutely safe to the body. It must also have a wide range of therapeutic and protective properties while only bringing about minimal alteration to bodily functions.
2. Its action must be nonspecific. That is it must increase resistance to a wide variety of harmful chemical and biological influences.
3. It must have a normalizing action regardless of the direction of pathological changes it may meet with in the person's body. In other words in a person with blood pressure which is too high it should help lower it while it should have just the opposite effect on an organism in which blood pressure is too low.

When you think just how remarkable these requirements are you begin to realize why the Chinese have traditionally believed many of the adaptogens to be worth their weight in gold. It is also easy to understand why the Western mind has such difficulty grasping the idea of an adaptogen at all. After all, we are used to a totally different approach: mostly this is because of our strong emphasis on symptomatic medicine.

Our science has investigated a number of pharmacological preparations designed to do specific things, such as improve circulation or increase oxygen uptake by cells during surgical operations. However most of these drugs, such as the derivatives of phenothiazine and ganglio-blocking agents, bring about side-effects which make them inappropriate for any healthy person to use as part of a programme for increasing vitality, promoting high-level health and encouraging ageless-ageing. We take substances such as the phenylalkylamines, like amphetamines and their analogues, as a means of suppressing an overactive appetite, or we drink coffee with its caffeine or other purine derivatives to pep us up, and we can turn to the bromides and sedatives such as the herb valerian to calm us down, but we find it hard to conceive of something that could do both or either depending upon our specific mental and physical state when we take it. As a result little investigation of possible new adaptogenic substances is going on here. Good candidates would be bee products such as pollen, propolis and royal jelly and even honey itself.

Bee Power

'Use thou honey,' commanded Solomon, 'for it is good.' Just as ginseng has a long history of being used to increase vitality and protect from ageing, so folklore is filled with advice about the medicinal use of honey and other bee products such as pollen, propolis and royal jelly, which have been employed throughout history to increase stamina, heal sickness, beautify skin and retard ageing. A natural antiseptic with a proven ability to kill bacteria, honey and all its 'by-products'—pollen, propolis and royal jelly—have antibiotic properties. And although honey has been scientifically analysed for the last fifty years, there appear to be a number of its constituents which remain unidentified. Scientists who have attempted to break it down into its parts and then to put it together again have failed. Although honey is made up of 75 per cent natural sugars and 17 per cent water it is also a good source of many of the B group of vitamins, vitamin C, carotene and organic acids, and of many important minerals including potassium, magnesium, iron, sodium, calcium, sulphur, phosphorus and lime. This sweet golden substance has a reputation for prolonging life. While researching longevity another famed Russian scientist—biologist and experimental botanist Dr Nicolai Tsitsin—discovered that of the 200 people in Russia whom he surveyed claiming to be over 100, a large number were beekeepers. All of them claimed their principal food was honey.

Natural unprocessed honey has been shown to increase calcium retention and to raise haemoglobin count—it is traditionally used to treat anaemia. It also appears to speed the healing process in a great many conditions from arthritis and poor circulation to liver and kidney disorders, poor skin and insomnia. Some researchers even believe that, thanks to its high aspartic-acid content—an amino acid important in the proper functioning of sex glands—it has rejuvenating properties. But just in case you're tempted to rush to your local supermarket and buy the first jar of golden stuff you come across you should know that it is not the honey itself which appears to be the most potent source of health-promoting qualities but the pollen-rich waste matter which lies at the bottom of honey containers. Tsitsin found that beekeepers tended to sell the 'good' honey and to eat the 'dirty residue' themselves. The dirty residue—which is a constituent of natural unfiltered and unprocessed honey and appears to have such exceptional properties for health—is too often filtered off from commercial honeys. Most have also been heated, which further limits the structural information they carry and therefore depletes their health-promoting value. Honey, by the way, keeps indefinitely thanks to its anti-microbial properties so you need never worry about it spoiling.

Royal Bee Power

Even more interesting than honey are the other bee-based products—propolis, royal jelly and pollen. Propolis is a sticky resin made out of the substance bees gather from the leaves and bark of trees. It is secreted via their pharmageal glands. They use it as a binding material when making hives. It has strong antibiotic properties and is much used in Sweden and Denmark to combat minor infections. Royal jelly is a white jelly-like substance produced by glands in the heads of very young worker bees. It contains almost every life-supporting element known. The queen bee, who lays over 2000 eggs a day, lives on the stuff and it appears to have remarkable benefits for beauty both when it is taken internally and when it is used in beauty products. Royal jelly contains virtually all the life-supporting elements plus an unidentified 3 per cent which scientists have been unable to break down. In the south of France royal jelly is a common sight for sale by the roadside. People take a 'cure' of it for a month or so twice a year. It is also said to be beneficial for anyone suffering from stress or exhaustion or for people recovering from an illness. Bulgaria is often called 'the country of royal jelly' because beekeeping and all its products have formed an important part of the economy since feudal times. The Bulgarians have also done a great deal of research to establish the health benefits from royal jelly, pollen, honey and propolis. They have found for instance that royal jelly has an ability to protect against radiation, that it increases fecundity in animals, that it improves the body's use of oxygen, lowers blood pressure, speeds regeneration of damaged tissue, lowers cholesterol and, like the official adaptogens, increases tolerance to stress. It even stimulates and encourages better functioning of the immune system.

Priceless Pollen

Pollen is the male germ seed of flowering plants. A fine powder that plants need to make seeds, it is gathered by bees in the process of collecting nectar for honey and harvested by pollen-collectors as the bees fly back into the hive. Not only does it contain all the water-soluble vitamins including the elusive B_{12}, it is a good source of carotene, and vitamins E and K, and it offers a rich supply of minerals, trace elements and enzymes as well as hormonal substances beneficial to human beings. As such it is probably the perfect 'skin food'. Pollen is a rich natural source of rutin as well—one of the bioflavinoids which, together with vitamin C and zinc, is particularly important in the formation of collagen (the structural protein which gives skin its contours and much of its strength). A thrice daily dose of raw pollen can do wonders for ailing skin—whether the problem is acne, excessive dryness or hypersensitivity. It can also improve the look and feel of normal healthy skin. But pollen's health-promoting properties don't stop there. It has been a favourite of Olympic athletes since ancient times and still is. Those who use it claim it increases strength and endurance, improves performance and helps prevent minor infections.

A Cure for Allergies?

One of pollen's more curious attributes—particularly important in springtime—is its ability to render many hayfever sufferers free of symptoms, provided oral doses of the stuff are taken regularly for several weeks before the season begins—another example of one of those folk remedies which is supported by the experience of a number of physicians who still use it successfully every year. One more interesting attribute of pollen of interest to anyone concerned about preventing premature ageing is its ability to protect the body from some of the damaging effects of radiation. It has been tested on irradiated animals and given to cancer patients subjected to radiation doses with excellent results. Finally, and most important, pollen taken in this way, like many of the natural substances which are high in structural information, seems to possess an ability to restore balance to a body. It is said to be particularly helpful in weight regulation—whether the person taking it is underweight or too fat.

The Proof of the Pudding

Using any adaptogen as a tool for increasing vitality, protecting health and resisting ageing is simple. It is taken every day, usually on an empty stomach, and an average longterm restorative dose is usually 1–2g a day in the case of ginseng and Siberian ginseng. Benefits tend to accrue over the time one is taking it and the best results come from taking it regularly over a period of a month to six weeks at least. Often people take it twice a year as a 'cure'. What is not so simple is making sure that the product you are taking has been properly grown, harvested and processed in order to preserve its biological activity. For instance there are dozens of ginseng preparations on the market which are virtually empty of ginsenosides—the active ingredients in ginseng. And if eleutherococcus has been heated too much in its processing its effectiveness is either reduced or completely destroyed.

Panax ginseng comes from Korea or China and the best quality are the big red roots which are six years old. Second are the white roots and third are the red grown in Japan, so look for country of origin when buying them and also for the Korean 'Office of Monopoly' seal on the pack. The whole roots are the best, with root pieces and extracts following in that order. Ginseng tablets and powders often contain 'fillers' and are much less potent, and the instant ginseng teas contain almost no active ingredients at all. American ginseng—Panax quinquefolium—is usually less effective than Panax ginseng unless you can get large old roots, and they are hard to come by.

The best form of Eleutherococcus senticosus (Siberian ginseng) comes in extract direct from the Soviet Union. It has been carefully low-heat processed to preserve its biological activity. This form of extract is used in some of the German Siberian ginseng preparations. Most experts in adaptogens insist that Panax ginseng is primarily a man's preparation, although it can be useful for women past menopause, and that eleutherococcus is excellent for both men and women. People with very high blood pressure are usually given eleutherococcus instead of ginseng. It is best to steer clear of coffee while on a course of ginseng or you may have trouble sleeping, and to follow a light diet without too much meat.

Bee products—all of them—are also best taken unheated in small quantities daily. In the case of pollen and propolis, which usually come in tablets, the recommended dose is usually two to three tablets a day on an empty stomach. Royal jelly is best bought raw, kept refrigerated and taken in amounts of between

250 and 500mg a day under the tongue where it is absorbed by the mucosa in the mouth and bypasses the digestive system. It can also be bought in less biologically active forms as capsules and suspended in tonic solutions.

TWENTY-EIGHT

Think Young

Almost everybody has heard of death curses. Psychological literature is laced with accounts of how Aboriginal witch doctors have quite literally brought about the death of the young and healthy by cursing them. No sooner do these people learn of the fate which has been cast for them than they begin inexplicably to sicken and eventually to die. It appears that through complex biological processes, their simple belief in the curse brings about destruction of their organism.

Modern-Day Death Curses

In civilized society we tend to look upon such phenomena as anthropological curiosities—products of primitive superstition which simply don't touch us in our more enlightened age. What we are not aware of however is that many of us in the civilized world are also under our own brand of 'death curses'. They may be subtler than those issued by witch doctors but they can be every bit as potent in bringing about the physical and mental decline which we have come to associate with ageing. Common (and usually unconscious) notions such as 'retirement', 'middle-age', 'It's all down hill after forty', and 'At your age you must start taking things more easily', are widely held. They can exert a powerful effect on the process of ageing by creating destructive self-fulfilling expectations about age decline. Instead of facing the future full of confidence and excitement about what lies ahead, optimism is replaced by anxiety as we are warned to 'Be careful', or 'Don't take chances on a new career at your age.'

The list of commonly proffered 'sensible' advice is a long one. Such well-meaning suggestions often lead people to make changes in their lifestyle which encourage physical decline—for instance decreasing the amount of exercise they get, altering their eating habits away from fibre-rich natural foods towards 'softer' foods, and even decreasing the amount of social and intellectual stimulation they have been used to. Even worse, this kind of advice can undermine your self-image and destroy self-confidence, which in turn interferes with the proper functioning of the immune system which plays such a central role in protecting your body from ageing. An essential ingredient in ageless ageing is a strong awareness of just how powerfully your emotions, state of mind, and your unconscious assumptions can influence both your susceptibility to illness and the rate at which you age. Once that awareness has penetrated your consciousness then you can begin to make use of some simple and pleasant mind-bending techniques you can put to use in aid of ageless ageing.

Mind-Body Connections

The notion that your state of mind can influence your health and the rate at which you age was once something which had to be taken on faith. Now it is not only being scientifically proven, it is even being put into effective practical use thanks to a rapidly developing scientific discipline with a tongue-twisting name: psychoneuroimmunology (PNI). PNI has discovered that your body's immune system, that bulwark of defence, is undeniably affected by your unconscious assumptions, your emotional states and your behavioural patterns. They can lead either to an increased resistance to ageing or to an increased susceptibility to degeneration and illness. In simple terms the happier you are, the better you feel about yourself and the more positive are your expectations about the future, the more likely you are to age slowly and gracefully and the less likely you are to fall prey to degeneration and illness of whatever sort—from a common cold to a life-threatening disease.

No area of ageless ageing is more fun to explore than this one. I always think of its positive side as 'Zorba the Greek' consciousness. It can make possible the most amazing physical and mental feats by quite ordinary people living quite ordinary lives. Take the man who is able to work eighteen hours a day, drink whisky by the tumblerful, dance on tables until the early hours of the morning and still live to be 110 thanks to the sheer joy of his experience of life. I have seen it too amongst saints and holymen who carry out their day-to-day activities, from writing letters to peeling potatoes, in a state of bliss—samadhi. Take a look at their superbly unlined faces. They could as easily be thirty as seventy. Psychoneuroimmunologists are working to find out why.

So new is the PNI discipline (the name was only coined in 1981) that the average physician is unlikely even to have heard of it. But so profound and wide-reaching are the consequences of its findings that they quite literally threaten to revolutionize medical theory about the origins and development of degeneration. Research into psychoneuroimmunology is already describing the pathways through which mind and body are inextricably bound together. These pathways include neurological connections linking glands and organs with the brain, the anti-oxidant system and the blood, thanks to hormonal secretions triggered by thought patterns and emotions and—most important of all—via the immune system. PNI researchers have discovered for instance that several kinds of lymphocytes involved in your body's immune response carry receptors which recognize hormones found in the brain that alter mind and mood. They have also found that some of these neurotransmitters or peptide hormones stimulate T-cells to produce more lymphokines such as interferon while others have the opposite effect. In fact listening to leading PNI researchers talk about mind-body connections makes you realize there is probably no state of mind which is not faithfully reflected by a state of the immune system.

Beyond Psychosomatic Consciousness

Western medicine has long acknowledged that emotional states such as anxiety and depression can make a limited number of illnesses worse. These include asthma, diabetes, peptic ulcer, ulcerative colitis, migraine and cardiovascular problems. But until the advent of PNI it has paid little attention to examining the nature of their psychological components nor has it explored ways and means of improving these conditions by altering a patient's mental state or behavioural patterns. Meanwhile it has almost completely ignored possible psychological components in the vast majority of other illnesses—from lung disease and cancer to rheumatism and allergic reactions—treating them instead as pure physiological occurrences little affected by whether the patient experiencing them felt good or bad in himself.

This is mostly because Western medicine, bound by the Cartesian notion of a split between mind and matter, has failed to consider the people it treats as psychobiological units—total beings whose feelings, thoughts, expectations and perceptions are intimately bound to their physiology and biochemistry. Happily this is now changing in no small part thanks to a few visionary scientists who began asking some penetrating questions. Why for instance do some people who smoke forty cigarettes a day for twenty years end up with lung cancer while others following exactly the same pattern don't? The first, most obvious answer is that the former have an hereditary disposition to the disease. True, genetics are important, but these scientists found that they were by no means the whole answer. A large and very important piece of the puzzle was still missing. So they began to look at psychological factors.

Let Go and Live Longer

In a pioneering study carried out over twenty years ago, Scottish researcher Dr David Kissen examined more than 1000 Glaswegian industrial workers suffering from respiratory complaints. Before diagnosing them he gave each man a psychological test designed to delineate personality patterns. He came up with some quite fascinating and highly significant results. He discovered that those who were later found to have cancer showed a striking inability to express their emotions. Intrigued by Kissen's study and other similar investigations which suggested that emotional repression was an important component in the development of cancer, two doctors, R. L. Horne and R. S. Picard, at the Washington University School of Medicine in the United States, decided to carry out an in-depth study of the psychosocial risk factors in lung cancer as measured on a psychological scale developed from the findings of previous studies including Kissen's. They confirmed that emotional repression was indeed the central component of a complex personality pattern which led to the development of the disease. In fact, so important were the relationships between psychological states and the development of lung cancer which they uncovered that the two researchers found they could predict with an amazing 73 per cent accuracy which men had cancer and which men had simple lung disease, from psychological testing alone. They discovered that cancer sufferers, because of their emotional repression, tended to find great difficulty coping with life's challenges and sorrows. After losing an important relationship such as a job or a wife the cancer victims often suffered profound depression for from six to eighteen months before the discovery of the illness. These findings have been confirmed by others.

Mind and Biochemistry

Similar studies linking other psychological factors to other diseases, including infections, arthritis, allergies and premature ageing, have also recently appeared. One of the best known is that done by Meyer Friedman and Ray Rosemann which demonstrated that what they called 'type A behaviour'—a behaviour pattern characterized by a fierce and unrelenting struggle to do ever more things in less time against harsh competition—appears to cause a number of bodily changes predisposing one to coronary heart disease. They include alterations in blood-fat and blood-sugar levels, changes in circulation and increased levels of the hormone noradrenaline. And each disease is beginning to appear to have its own collection of psychological characteristics.

Studies have now established that psychological factors are primary determinants in a host of illnesses while in others psychological factors appear to interact with biological ones determining whether disease tendencies, initiated either by heredity or your environment or both, will in fact turn into degeneration or whether your body will be able to fight them off. But how does it all work? Through what physiological mechanisms do emotional repression in the case of cancer, a frustrated power drive in the case of high blood pressure, and all the various other psychological and behavioural traits linked with their illnesses help create their respective illness and age decline? Perhaps even more important, once one can find these physiological mechanisms how can we make use of them first to prevent ageing and even perhaps to reverse some of its processes once they have occurred? The key to both questions appears once again to lie in the immune system.

Rat Magic

You'll remember that the immune system exists to defend your body against antigens—foreign invaders such as bacteria, viruses and chemical toxins. It is also a watchdog against the development of cancer cells and premature ageing both of which can be induced by chemical damage, radiation, viruses and other bodily changes. It does this by being able to recognize 'self'— that which belongs naturally to the body—from 'non-self'— that which is foreign to it. If your immune system is under-active you will find yourself highly susceptible to infection and to cancer. If it is working too hard you will be prone to allergies. If it is simply misfunctioning and unable to differentiate 'self' from 'non-self' you can end up with one of the auto-immune diseases such as multiple sclerosis or arthritis. Until quite recently scientists assumed that the immune system was an independent physiological entity—something beyond the influence of psychological influences. Then Dr Robert Ader, professor of psychiatry and psychology at the University of Rochester School of Medicine (who himself coined the word 'psychoneuroimmunology') carried out some mysterious experiments with animals. He gave rats saccharin-flavoured water and at the same time injected them with a drug known to cause digestive disturbances and to suppress immune function. The rats rapidly developed an aversion to the flavoured water as he expected them to. But what was surprising was that a number of the rats also died when later they were offered the flavoured water even without the drug. Why? Perhaps, Ader reasoned, it was a brain-triggered response. Perhaps the rats died because they had been conditioned, rather as Pavlov's dog was conditioned to salivate at the sound of a bell, so that their immune system reacted to the flavoured water as it would have done to the immuno-suppressive drug, thus dramatically reducing their susceptibility to disease.

To check out this theory Ader then conditioned another group of rats, challenging their immune system with a common antigen after first conditioning them with water flavoured with saccharin and the drug. They were divided into three groups. The first received another injection of the drug and as researchers predicted their antibody production was suppressed. The second group, which was neither treated further with the drug nor given the flavoured water, had normal antibody responses. But the third group who got only the flavoured water without the drug showed a marked decrease in immune reaction—their antibody response to the challenge was significantly less than normal. They had learnt to react to the flavoured water in the same way that they did to a chemical that suppressed the immune system. Ader concluded, 'The fact that learning could alter antibody response in this manner demonstrates a clear, direct link between the brain and the immune system.' His conclusion has since been firmly supported by a host of scientific studies showing how anxiety, depression and discouragement interfere with good immune functions and create susceptibility to illness and ageing.

Mysteries of Mind and Immunity

You may recall that the immune system has two major branches, each with its own particular kind of defence cells or lymphocytes. It also includes other less important factors such as large scavenger-type cells called macrophages which gobble up antigenic material. The first branch confers on your body what is known as *cell-mediated* immunity and is responsible for about half of your body's resources for defence. It is centred around

T-cell leucocytes—warrior cells produced in the thymus which battle the thousands of potentially lethal organisms, cancer-inducing ultraviolet radiation from the sun and toxic chemicals from our highly industrialized environment. T-cells also produce a group of hormone-like substances such as interferon. They are called *lymphokines* and are considered the immune system's natural drugs. Some are poisonous to foreign tissue, others trigger white blood cells to keep an immune reaction going. The second branch of the immune system offers *humoral-mediated* immunity. It relies on what are known as B-cell lymphocytes, which produce antibodies specific to whatever invaders the body is being challenged by. B-cells are carried in the blood. They can combine with antigens in the body and neutralize them or they can coat them, making it simple for white blood cells to destroy them.

The actions of both T and B cells are mediated through the thymus gland—often called the master gland of immunity. As we have seen the rate at which you age appears to be very much influenced by the function of the thymus gland and the state of the immune system which it governs. It has also been well established that immune functions can be disrupted or depressed by such things as malnutrition, free radicals, infection and certain drugs. Recent research shows too that lymphocytes from people suffering from all kinds of stress and from grief, say after the death of a close relative, have a markedly decreased ability to rise to the occasion when challenged by antigens threatening the health of the body. What psychoneuro-immunologists are now trying to explore in experiments with animals and in studies of people are the pathways between brain and body through which this occurs—to delineate the means by which mind affects immunity both as a result of direct input from the brain and the indirect influence of hormones associated with specific emotional states and personality patterns.

Stress and Immunity

One of the questions currently being most seriously investigated by PNI researchers is how biological changes associated with stress diminish immune response and increase susceptibility to illness. Stress of any kind triggers the 'fight or flight response'—

a matrix of hormonal reactions designed to prepare the body for action. Adrenaline is released, for instance, and corticosteroid hormones from the adrenal glands. They in turn trigger other hormonal reactions. PNI researchers have now found that within fifteen minutes of its hitting the bloodstream even a small dose of adrenaline challenges the immune system and triggers the release of lymphocytes. It also inhibits the function of mature white blood cells needed to ward off invasion. Other studies have shown that the corticosteroids can also seriously depress immune functions and increase your susceptibility to disease. They inhibit the functions of both lymphocytes and macrophages and they undermine the ability of lymphocytes to reproduce themselves in the body. In fact if stress is prolonged enough and the levels of corticosteroids become high enough in the body they even cause a withering away of lymphoid tissue altogether.

Stress has been shown to increase susceptibility to cancer in mice and to exacerbate the condition once it is present. And cancers appear to grow fastest and to result in earliest deaths in animals with no way of coping with stress. The same appears to be true of people. At St Luke's Medical Center in Chicago, Dr Richard Shekelle headed a research project which examined death certificates of more than 2000 men who had been tested psychologically for depression and other emotional states seventeen years before. He found that the death rate of men who had been very depressed at the time of testing was twice that of the rest.

One of the most widely held theories about cancer states that each of us develops small malignancies all the time in our body but that these are rapidly destroyed in a healthy person thanks to the actions of his immune system. If however you have strong feelings of helplessness or depression this can result in elevated corticosteroid levels and other changes which impede your immune system from doing its proper job and rejecting the cancer cells before they can take hold.

PNI Alters Paradigms

The mind-body links which PNI research is uncovering are

beginning to have far-reaching consequences—consequences which ultimately will go far beyond helping people avoid life-threatening diseases and slow the ageing process. There is a strong resonance to be found between PNI and much of the new physics which is busily exploring the view that the observer is essential to the creation of the universe just as the universe is creator of the observer. As Nobel laureate Roger Sperry has said, 'Current concepts of the mind-brain relation involve a direct break with the long-established materialist and behaviourist doctrine that has dominated neuroscience for many decades. Instead of renouncing or ignoring consciousness the new interpretation gives full recognition to the primacy of inner conscious awareness as a causal reality.'

It is a causal reality that you can begin using to your advantage right now. For just as prolonged unmitigated stress, depression and anxiety can suppress immune functions, a positive frame of mind and a sense that you can cope with whatever comes your way offers potent protection against illness and age-degeneration.

At Beth Israel Hospital, another researcher, Dr Stephen Locke, has used psychological tests to evaluate students' abilities to cope with the shocks and challenges of their lives. He has found that the 'poor copers'—those who tend to succumb to anxiety, depression and a sense of helplessness when life difficulties arise—show suppressed immune functions, while the 'good copers'—people who feel they can deal effectively with whatever comes their way—had normal immune functions even when faced with major life changes. Meanwhile in a well-controlled study of women suffering from breast cancer who underwent mastectomy, British researcher Dr Steven Greer discovered that women who react to their diagnosis with a denial that they are ill or with a determination to conquer the illness are far more likely five years later to be free of the disease than those who stoically accepted the diagnosis or who felt hopeless or helpless.

Making Immunity Work for You

What can you do, starting right now, in the way of using your mind as a tool for ageless ageing? You can begin by exploring the benefits of mind/body techniques which can help alter your mental attitudes and emotional states from negative to positive and therefore encourage good immune functions and hence slow down the rate at which you age. There are many. Dr Herbert Benson of Harvard Medical School developed the simple meditative technique, called the relaxation response, which consists of sitting with your eyes closed for fifteen or twenty minutes morning and night and repeating a single word—say 'one' or 'peace'—over and over again silently. Practised regularly it will not only counter the immune-suppressing tendencies of stress but even bring about major psychological shifts in belief systems that can gradually change a self-defeating 'poor coper' into an optimistic 'good coper'.

You can also explore just how many negative expectations you have connected with ageing. Then you can quite simply and methodically go about changing them. For instance, how many of the following notions would you agree with? They have been adapted from a quiz designed by well-known gerontologist Erdman Palmore from Duke University Medical Center in the United States and they appeared in the scientific journal *The Gerontologist* not long ago. Take the quiz and then check your answers at the end. It is a good way of helping you become aware of how many false ideas you have about ageing. (In each case tick 'T' for 'true' or 'F' for 'false'.)

Quiz: How Much Do You Know About Ageing?

T F 1. The majority of old people (past age sixty-five) are senile (ie defective memory, disoriented or demented).

T F 2. All five senses tend to decline with age.

T F 3. Most old people have no interest in sex.

T F 4. Lung capacity tends to decline in old age.

T F 5. The majority of old people feel miserable most of the time.

T F 6. The majority of old people are seldom irritated or angry.

T F 7. At least one-tenth of the aged are living in long-stay institutions (ie nursing homes, mental hospitals, homes for the aged etc).

T F 8. Aged drivers have fewer accidents per person than drivers under age sixty-five.
T F 9. Most older workers cannot work as effectively as younger workers.
T F 10. About 80 per cent of the aged are healthy enough to carry out their normal activities.
T F 11. Most old people are set in their ways and are unable to change.
T F 12. The majority of old people are working or would like to have some kind of work to do (including housework and volunteer work).
T F 13. It is almost impossible for most old people to learn new things.
T F 14. The reaction time of most old people tends to be slower than reaction time of younger people.
T F 15. In general, most old people are pretty much alike.
T F 16. The majority of old people are seldom bored.
T F 17. The majority of old people are socially isolated and lonely.
T F 18. Older workers have fewer accidents than younger workers.
T F 19. Older people tend to become more religious as they age.
T F 20. Most medical practitioners tend to give low priority to the aged.

The answers to this quiz are that the even-numbered questions are true and the odd numbered ones are false.

Contrary to popular opinion only 2 or 3 per cent of old people are institutionalized because of psychiatric disorders. Neither do the vast majority of old people have memory defects. Most people over sixty-five continue to be interested in sex, and sexual relations continue well into the eighties between healthy men and women. Studies made of morale and happiness amongst the elderly show no difference between their enjoyment of life and that of younger people.

People over sixty-five have fewer accidents per person driving than do younger drivers. They also have fewer accidents at work. The majority of old people are not set in their ways although it does take them longer to learn something new than the young. Studies show that few old people suffer from boredom. Neither are they socially isolated or lonely. More than 10 per cent of old people work and two-thirds of those who don't would like to. Finally old people are seldom irritated or angry. This has been determined by three separate studies.

Visualize Age Anew

Becoming aware of false assumptions about ageing is a good first step. The next is to create a new vision of what it means to have time passing. Make use of creative visualization techniques where in a state of relaxation you allow your mind to play on positive images of yourself five, ten, thirty years from now. There are some excellent books available on the subject which you can use as a guide. But really the technique is very easy. It is only a matter of letting yourself indulge in positive daydreaming. Or practise a meditation or deep-relaxation technique a couple of times a day and finish off by repeating silently to yourself Coué's formula for personal growth and healing, 'Every day in every way I am getting better and better.' It is exquisitely simple yet enormously powerful when practised daily in a deeply relaxed state so that it is your imagination rather than your will which is brought into play.

Affirm Youth and Well-being

Another simple technique which has real power for altering unconscious expectations and creating new realities is that of writing out 'affirmations'—seven times seventy—for a week or two. This can be something as simple as 'I am well and will continue to be so as the years pass' or 'I let go of past confusion and day by day make my life anew.' The mere act of writing out such words over and over for several days helps break through old thought patterns and negativity that may be hampering you from realizing your full psychobiological potentials. You might be surprised at how quickly they penetrate your consciousness and bring about positive shifts in expectations and in your reality. For they can generate positive mental states and emotions and make them your common everyday experience of reality. And, just as PNI researchers have been discovering, it is the simple positive experiences and emotions like love, hope, faith, laughter, playfulness and creativity which can not only make life worth living, they can actually keep us alive, youthful and well. As effective as massive doses of anti-oxidant nutrients, fresh-cell therapy and all the other biological methods of age-retardation available to you? Very probably. Besides they'll cost you absolutely nothing but a smile.

TWENTY-NINE

The Ageless Brain

Of major concern to age-researchers is the brain. Many believe that alterations in the brain are central to age-related changes elsewhere in the body. Others focus on the way in which the behaviour can alter when people get older so that they show signs of confusion or memory loss or some curtailments in mental facility. Such impairments can be responsible for the irritability, depression, restlessness and even withdrawal which some older people experience, as well as for alterations in sleep patterns—the wake-often-and-sleep-little syndrome associated with ageing. Just what does happen in your brain as you get older? What relationship do these happenings have to the state of your body as a whole? And—most important—can some or all of the age-related brain changes and mood alterations which accompany them be halted or reversed?

Loss of Brain Cells

At about age twenty your brain weighs about 1400g if you are a man and about 1300g if you are a woman. Although this can vary considerably from person to person, brain weight tends to decline in your sixties. Mostly this is because of a loss of protein and fats and to a lesser degree because it also loses water. Accompanying this loss in weight which amounts to about 3g between the ages of thirty-five and seventy-five, a loss in volume takes place. Both may be due to the fact that most people lose about 100,000 cells—cells which are never replaced—from their brain each and every day from their mid-thirties onwards.

IDEAS OF THE BRAIN: OLD AND NEW

The complex association of nerve cells called the brain has puzzled and intrigued scientists for centuries. It is now known to govern nearly every phase of life; sensory and muscle centres have been pinpointed, and the processes responsible for speech, hearing, vision and so on have been located (*above left*). But today's scientists are not as bold as sixteenth-century savant Georg Reisch, who distinguished between such functions as 'imagination' and 'fantasy' (*above right*). However, while we know that his ideas were wrong, our own understanding of the brain is still far from complete.

This may sound like a great deal, and the loss of certain cells can be important to brain and body function, but since within this 3lb or so of grey material are woven tens of billions of nerve cells and since so much of our brain's resources remain untapped throughout our whole life anyway, it is likely to be far less important to brain function than it might seem. As the brain gets older its ridges and convoluted patterns grow deeper and more well defined. There are other brain-changes which appear to be of more concern. For instance, in the brains of most older people a substance called lipofuscin or 'age pigment' builds up as they get older. This pigment, which many gerontologists believe is a kind of build-up of waste products in the cells, also accumulates in other tissues of the body too, such as the heart and the skeleton, causing a kind of cellular constipation which is important because it interferes with normal cell functions and leads to further age-related changes in the body.

Finally, since the hypothalamus, which is buried within the brain tissue, and the pituitary are involved in the control of so many bodily functions, a few researchers have postulated that changes in these two glands which occur in time may trigger the release of some kind of 'age hormone' which acts as a biological clock causing age-related damage throughout the body. But so far this is only speculation.

What is interesting about the brain in relation to ageing is the fact that much of what used to be considered inevitable mental and emotional changes connected with ageing such as senility, depression, and an inability to learn rapidly, now appear to be much less time-dependent than they have always seemed. Only some 10 per cent of the population have the slightest tendency towards senility and many of the moods and mental restrictions which naively used to be considered an inevitable consequence of ageing are nothing of the sort. Instead they usually stem from two causes, both of which can be relatively easily dealt with: either they are part of the expectations people have about getting older and therefore become self-fulfilling prophecies or they are a direct result of a decline in certain brain hormones called neurotransmitters—a state which with relative ease can be altered by nutritional means.

Oxygen-Induced Brain Damage

Senility is also unquestionably a result of excessive oxy-stress and free-radical damage to tissues, and the anti-oxidant nutrients which form an important part of any effective programme for ageless ageing will help protect the brain from damage. As Bruce Ames, chairman of the biochemistry department of the University of California and an expert on ageing and cancer says, 'The brain uses 20 per cent of the oxygen consumed by man and contains an appreciable amount of unsaturated fat. Lipid peroxidation (with consequent age pigment) is known to occur readily in the brain, and possible consequences could be senile dementia or other brain abnormalities.' Abram Hoffer, the Canadian expert in orthomolecular treatment of mental disorders, believes as Ames does that anti-oxidant nutrients are important in protecting against age-related brain degeneration. But then so are certain specific nutrients which are not generally classified as anti-oxidants such as niacin (vitamin B_3), and vitamin B_1.

Deficiencies Cause 'Age' Symptoms

Although your brain accounts for less than 2 per cent of your total body weight an amazing 25 per cent of the body's total metabolic activity takes place there. That may be why it is so sensitive to even the slightest nutritional deficiency. And as people get older, unless they follow a lifestyle for ageless ageing or have an extraordinary genetic inheritance which is looking after them, nutritional deficiencies become common. One of the very first places they show up is in the brain.

James Goodwin of the University of New Mexico School of Medicine is a leading geriatrician with a particular interest in brain chemistry and its relation to ageing. He points out a long string of so-called psychiatric symptoms associated with ageing which are in reality signs of subclinical deficiencies of essential nutrients which have not been well enough supplied or well enough absorbed in the diets of older people. For instance even mild vitamin B_{12} deficiencies can result in a wide range of psychiatric symptoms from indifference and irritability to hallucinations and obvious psychotic behaviour. A vitamin B_1 deficiency can result in the person simply being unable to learn anything new. Lack of folic acid can result in symptoms of senility or dementia and so forth. These symptoms are certainly not a sign of normal ageing as most of us have been led to believe. Neither need they be permanent. But, as a number of recent studies in Britain and America show, such nutritional deficiencies are widespread and they tend to get worse the older people get.

In an interesting study carried out by British researcher J. C. Brocklehurst, eighty residents of an old people's home were selected and half of them were put on to a multiple-vitamin formula with the other half taking a placebo. Neither patients nor staff knew which was which. Reasoning that the vitamin group would perhaps improve in subtle ways in their behaviour, six months later researchers asked the staff to guess which old people had been getting the vitamin supplement and which the placebo—thus making them rely on their overall impression of behaviour and not on any specific test. The attending doctor guessed all of those who had been receiving vitamins because the improvement in their behaviour and mental acuity had been so dramatic.

New Life for Ageing Brains

Many symptoms of neuropsychiatric disorders result from imbalances in the functioning of the brain's neurotransmitters and/or from a deficiency in the specific nutrients needed to manufacture them for the brain. A nerve cell or neuron has a very special structure in order to enable it to carry information quickly from one part of the body to another. It has long projections called axons which reach out from the cell body to make contact with another nerve cell, creating a kind of relay system of circuitry in the brain. But they never directly contact each other because there is a tiny gap called a synapse between each neuron and its neighbour. The way that messages get passed on from one to the next is that the neuron's axon releases a chemical messenger—a neurotransmitter—which diffuses across the gap and stimulates a receptor site causing a minute electrical current on the next neuron which in turn passes the message on to the next and so on in a process so rapid and so efficient that it occurs in virtually no time at all.

It is thanks to the actions of these neurotransmitters that motor messages get carried, that thoughts link up and that emotions can be felt. Some are excitatory in character—they rapidly trigger another electrical discharge. Others are inhibitory, in which case they suppress the spontaneous electrical firing of the nerve cells they come in contact with. Science has now identified some forty neurotransmitters but there could be hundreds as yet undiscovered. They are made in the body out of nutrients from the foods you eat and there is very good evidence that many of the most important neurotransmitters are diet-dependent—the levels of them in your brain are directly related to how many of the specific nutrients such as amino acids, vitamins and minerals needed for their manufacture are supplied through your diet.

There is much evidence that there is absolutely no reason for brain power to decline with age. Neither should you expect that feelings of depression or apathy or even longstanding fatigue are a 'normal' sign that you are getting older. They are nothing of the kind. They are rather a sign that something needs to be done to improve things and there are so many possibilities.

Brainfood—Phosphatidyl Choline plus Lecithin

One of the most important of the precursor nutrients with power to alter mental tendencies usually associated with getting older is phosphatidyl choline. Studies show that taken as a dietary supplement, granular lecithin enriched with extra phosphatidyl choline can enhance learning, improve memory, stimulate lagging brain functions in older people and even help regulate the dramatic mood-swings of manic depressives. Healthy brain function, on which clear thinking and feeling rely, is dependent on the action of many neurotransmitters. And perhaps the most important of all of these is acetylcholine. When there is too little of it available the ability to reason, remember and control muscles all over the body goes awry. Insufficient acetycholine is also associated with a number of illnesses as well as with the

CEREBRAL CORTEX (histidine)

HISTIDINE is the precursor for histamine, a potent vasodilator. As histamine is highly localized in the nerve endings, it probably acts as a neurotransmitter. It is a chemical stored in many cells throughout the body, being released in allergic reactions and causing many of the symptoms of such reactions. It is highly concentrated in the hypothalamus and is released during orgasm.

GLUTAMIC ACID may serve as an excitatory neurotransmitter, although its precise functions in the brain are difficult to determine. Nevertheless, its concentrations in the brain are higher than those of any other amino acid. Derived from it by decarboxylation is *gamma-aminobutyric acid* (GABA), one of the best known amino-acid neurotransmitters, which slows the firing rates of neurons.

TRYPTOPHAN is the precursor for serotonin, which regulates sleep and wakefulness: decreased serotonin causes insomnia. Tryptophan is also important in that from it can be derived small quantities of niacin, a vitamin which must otherwise be ingested in food.

TYROSINE is the precursor of the catecholamines, and is of great importance in regulating emotional behaviour.

HYPOTHALAMUS (glutamic acid, gamma-aminobutyric acid, tryptophan, tyrosine, histidine)

CEREBELLUM

BRAIN STEM
(glycine) A major inhibitory neurotransmitter, of importance especially in the spinal cord and brain stem. It helps regulate blood sugar.

LIMBIC SYSTEM

PITUITARY GLAND

ACTIONS OF AMINO ACIDS IN THE HUMAN BRAIN

The amino acids play a vital role in the functioning of the brain, not only because they help maintain ionic balance in the cell but also because they give rise to amines that are physiologically active; moreover, they take part in the biosynthetic changes that maintain the structure of the cell. As precursors, the amino acids yield neurotransmitters.

development of senility. It can result in a number of symptoms in otherwise healthy people as well—from foggy thinking to nervousness, anxiety, hyperactivity in children, slowed reflexes and sluggishness.

Your body manufactures acetylcholine from the vitamin choline, one of the few nutrients which can be transferred directly from blood to brain. The amount of acetylcholine produced is entirely dependent upon how much phosphatidyl choline is available for its production. Researchers at Massachusetts Institute of Technology showed that if students were given 3g of choline a day their learning abilities and memories improved. But taking choline on its own as a nutritional supplement has its disadvantages, one of the main ones being it tends to give your breath and skin a fishy smell. Not so when it is taken in the form of lecithin of which it is a major constituent. In fact granular lecithin itself, which is an emulsifier, appears to enhance the actions of the phosphatidyl choline it contains. It has recently been used successfully as a part of treatment for manic depression and vascular diseases. There are now available some excellent formulas of phosphatidyl choline—the best come in the form of enriched lecithin granules which you can sprinkle on to cereals, soups or salads or mix in fruit juice. They provide as much choline as twelve high-potency lecithin capsules and are quite pleasant-tasting. The other use for such a product is in helping to lower cholesterol levels in people whose blood fats tend to be high.

Precocious Precursors

Some of the free amino acids (see Chapter 18) are themselves either neurotransmitters or precursors to neurotransmitters. When taken as nutritional supplements they can be very useful as mind-stimulants, mood-enhancers, natural relaxers and even pain-killers. Probably the most important of all the natural mood-elevators is DL-phenylalanine. It is a highly effective natural antidepressant and is also useful in the control of chronic aches and pains such as those of stiff joints or of arthritis. It is also very safe, non-toxic both in shortterm and longterm therapy; unlike coffee and pep-up pills it does not bring about excessive arousal; toxic overdose of DL-phenylalanine is virtually impossible; and finally it does not have adverse side-effects.

Statistics show that depression tends to increase with age and also to be higher in women than in men (although the suicide rate is higher in men). Its symptoms can be as diverse as changes in sleeping or eating patterns, early morning waking or prevailing sleepiness or insomnia. The body seems low in energy and the person often feels a lack of direction or meaning in life. Doctors have had remarkable results using DL-phenylalanine as an antidote to depression, particularly what is known as endogenous depression (depression which is longstanding and very difficult to treat) and involutional depression—the sort that is associated particularly with ageing. In fact this amino acid has been found to be 89 100 per cent effective in the treatment of such depression and without the dangerous side-effects associated with antidepression drugs such as the MAO inhibitors. To my knowledge there is no other substance, natural or otherwise, which can claim similar results. How does it work?

The Perfect Antidepressant?

DL-phenylalanine appears to have three quite separate antidepressant effects on the brain. First it increases the levels of endorphins in the brain by inhibiting enzymes which break down endorphin hormones. These are the body's natural opiates which give runners their euphoric high, eliminate pain from the experience of natural childbirth, and appear to be an important biochemical reason for the bliss that comes in certain states of meditation. Second, DL-phenylalanine increases the production of phenylethylamine or PEA—a neurotransmitter-type natural brain-stimulant. Finally, DL-phenylalanine can also be converted in the brain into the neurotransmitter noradrenaline which is a natural stimulant and mood-elevator. (Athletes tend to produce a lot of it and depressed people to have very low levels. DL-phenylalanine can change all that.) Many antidepressant drugs aim to increase the levels of noradrenaline in the central nervous system as well. But this they do in very different ways than DL-phenylalanine—ways which produce in many people serious side-effects, from nausea and drowsiness to anorexia—and these drugs also prevent reabsorption of the neurotransmitters into nerve terminals. What this eventually does is deplete the cells' stores of neurotransmitter material and therefore interfere with good brain function. Not only does DL-phenylalanine not have these negative effects, it can even help restore brain levels to normal. But this is by no means its only use either. Many women find it helpful in relieving the symptoms of premenstrual tension. One study using it reports that over 80 per cent of women using it for this purpose gained 'good to complete relief'. It also appears to be an effective natural pain killer—particularly useful for chronic pain such as that from arthritis.

The Nuts and Bolts of Use

DL-phenylalanine is available in white crystal-powder form or made into tablets—usually of 375mg each. Most physicians and nutritionists using it suggest that to start with you take three tablets of this size each day—each one just after a meal. The dosage needs to be divided up, they claim, in order to get the full anti-depressant effect. Once this occurs then they often reduce the dose to one tablet per day. Some people don't even need to continue taking it at all to maintain benefits of mood improvement because, like a lot of the natural substances used in orthomolecular health (and unlike drugs) they help restore normal functioning to tissues so they are no longer needed. DL-phenylalanine is most effective taken with the vitamins which encourage its conversion to brain chemicals. They are vitamins B_1, B_2, B_6 and C. How long does it take to get results? Many people notice them within a few days but if the depression is longstanding it is usually four to six weeks before it lifts. There are three important cautions: DL-phenylalanine should not be taken by pregnant or lactating women nor by people who suffer with phenylketonuria (an inborn error which can result in a mentally retarded condition that occurs when the body cannot convert phenylalanine into tyrosine naturally). It should be used with caution in the case of anyone with high blood pressure as well. Something that I find DL-phenylalanine particularly good for is in helping people who feel discouraged about themselves and their life to experience the new hope and enthusiasm and energy necessary to make lifestyle changes, such as improving their diet or getting more exercise, which will eventually lead them towards a permanently heightened experience of wellness and vitality.

The Tryptophan Connection

Another free amino which has been used to treat depression is tryptophan. Tryptophan, which is also an excellent natural tranquillizer and sleep-inducer, and which for many psychologically 'normal' people appears to enhance their sense of mental and emotional well-being, is a precursor of serotonin. Serotonin is a neurotransmitter which is involved in many metabolic processes. Studies show that when serotonin levels are low in animals they tend to be aggressive, to overreact to stimuli and even show signs of abnormal sexual behaviour. Many authorities believe that because tryptophan is the least abundant amino acid in most foods, many people don't get enough of this substance to experience the natural stress-relief, sleep improvement and relief from anxiety and depression which it can offer.

W. M. Ringsdorf and E. Cheraskin, authors of *Psychodietetics*, believe that the standard recommended daily requirement of 500mg of tryptophan for adults every day is not enough for many people. In an experiment where sixty-six normal people increased their daily intake of tryptophan to 1001-1331mg a day they report 'a remarkable decrease in the number of psychological complaints'. A number of studies have demonstrated how effective tryptophan supplementation can be in dealing with insomnia when you take 1g of the amino acid twenty minutes before going to bed. Tryptophan is something I like to use to help combat jet lag. It is an excellent supplement to take when you arrive in a city and it is bedtime there but you are not in the mood for sleep. I use another amino acid—tyrosine—in the opposite condition, that is when I arrive in a city and I feel like sleeping but I have to work. I find they can make a remarkable difference in how you cope with crossing time zones.

Using Tryptophan

Reaping the many benefits of tryptophan used as a nutritional supplement requires a little skill. It is not just a question of eating tryptophan-rich foods. For tryptophan is one of the amino acids which needs special treatment to get it through the blood-brain barrier for conversion to serotonin. For one thing, it is best taken together with vitamins B_6, B_1, B_2 and niacin which enhance its benefits. For another it needs to be taken with a little carbohydrate, which heightens brain pick-up of the amino acid—say a small piece of wholegrain bread or a glass of fruit juice; and it must not be taken with protein foods. Protein foods discourage brain take-up and encourage the tryptophan to be diverted to other tasks in the body such as the formation of enzymes and the rebuilding of protein tissue.

Natural Tranquillizers

All of the brain's natural opiates—substances such as enkephalin and the endorphins which uplift mood while they calm a restless mind and leave you feeling exceptionally well—are made from amino acids. And one of the most useful things you can do with the free amino acids is to apply them as natural tranquillizers. There are four which can be particularly helpful because either directly or as precursors they form the inhibitory neurotransmitters. These brain hormones will calm an overactive mind and create a mental state akin to that which comes from deep relaxation or meditation. They are L-tryptophan, L-glycine, L-taurine and L-histidine. A mixture of these four aminos has been used clinically to alleviate anxiety and depression, calm anger, banish phobias, halt obsessive-compulsive behaviour, and treat high blood pressure. It can also be simply an excellent way to switch off when you are under stress, without the help of alcohol or drugs.

A Look at L-Glutamine

L-glutamine is the amide form of glutamic acid, a 'non-essential' amino acid which has generally been considered nutritionally unimportant but which acts as a high-energy brain fuel and can have some remarkable effects on the body, such as detoxifying it of ammonia which is poisonous to living cells. It has also been shown to improve intelligence, speed the healing of ulcers, help control alcoholism, schizophrenia and the craving for sweets. And it is one of the best banishers of fatigue you will find anywhere.

Because glutamic acid itself does not pass easily through the blood-brain barrier but the amide L-glutamine does, and once there it is transformed into glutamic acid for use as fuel, it is in this L-glutamine form that it is usually taken. American biochemist Roger Williams first discovered that L-glutamine helps protect the body against the poisonous effects of alcohol and that for many people it even banishes the craving for it altogether. He and others have used it in doses of 1-4g daily for this purpose. L-glutamine's ability to help many people who have a craving for sweets probably works through the same mechanism as it does in helping to eliminate addiction to alcohol—via the hypothalamus. Abram Hoffer has used L-glutamine against senility, schizophrenia and mental retardation with good success, and H. L. Newbold, author of *Mega-Nutrients for Your Nerves* uses it regularly to treat fatigue. As a brain fuel to increase intelligence or for eliminating cravings it is usually taken in 500mg capsules twice a day for the first week, and then 500mg three times a day working up to two 2000mg a day in split doses the third week until you find the level which seems to work best for you.

Make Brain Aminos Work Hard

It is a good idea to take ascorbic acid—from 1 to 10g a day—and vitamin B_6 when taking any amino-acid product because these two vitamins work synergistically with the aminos. It is also wise to ensure you drink plenty of water—3-4 pints a day—when using amino acids regularly. You also need to make sure you have a good supply of all the known nutrients—vitamins, minerals, essential fatty acids and so forth to work with them. There is no such thing as a single pill which will do everything or solve a particular problem. The body is a complex organism whose functioning depends on a good balance of essential nutrients and the right kind of structural information not only to function in optimum health but also to make the best use of these quite remarkable natural products in any programme for ageless ageing. Get to know them one by one. Choose those which are right for your needs. Chances are they will become for you what they have become for me—good friends I can call on whenever I or any member of my family need them for special boosts or problem-solving. They should not be taken by diabetics except under the guidance of a nutritionally trained physician since some of them can influence insulin levels. And because each of us is a biochemical individual there are no set quantities of each which are right for everyone. They take a little experimenting.

THIRTY

Ageless Ageing for Life

In this world of sophisticated biochemistry, psychoneuro-immunology, complex treatments for face and skin and body, and mind-bending nutrients, how do you gather together what you need in order to begin creating a lifestyle for yourself which will help you live long and well and look your best year after year? Probably the best way to start is to consider what you need most help with and begin there. For instance, you may already be eating well and sparsely and it may be only a matter of cutting out the negative things in your diet such as coffee or sugar and increasing the number of fresh foods on your table to bring you in line with the high-potency low-calorie nutrition which appears ideal for ageless ageing. But, perhaps you have sadly neglected the state of your muscles and the conditioning of your body through exercise. And perhaps you have a tendency to become easily stressed by overwork or worry. Then you might start by promising yourself a brisk walk for at least half an hour four days a week and keeping that promise. And you might consider exploring what some of the natural anti-anxiety antidotes—one or two of the free amino acids—could offer you. Someone else, a marathon runner for example, might be superbly fit and have lots of energy, yet be suffering (as so many athletes do) from haggard-looking skin and a diet which is not supplying all of the essential nutrients in optimum quantities. (And strenuous physical exercise can dramatically increase body demand for many of them.) In this case a substantial programme of nutritional supplements stressing the anti-oxidant nutrients could be a good idea. So might making use of the Anti-Ox formula for skin once or twice a day (see page 270).

Each of us is an individual with particular needs, interests and weaknesses. And the best way for anyone to make ageless ageing a part of their life is to start with one or two techniques which are specifically applicable to their needs and then build from there—slowly. Leaping into some elaborate programme in which you try to do everything all at once is doomed to failure. For valuable and lasting change almost always has to come slowly and gradually. Then the things you take up for your benefit are not just curious fads to be tried and dropped. They become integrated parts of your life—solid, stable ways of living which can both bring you closer to the ordered harmony of *natural-law* age-retardation as well as reaping the benefits from *high-tech* science.

Slow and Not So Steady Change

For many of us, change also comes in starts and stops. More than fifteen years ago I first came upon a physician using a high-raw diet and was fascinated by how such a simple tool could be so transformative. But I am a compulsive experimenter and a great doubter and I have to test something out twenty times before I will believe it. I began to experiment with more fresh foods in my own diet and found that they did indeed improve the way I looked and felt. But then, because of social convention or basic cynicism, I would return to the usual stodge I had been eating before. It took several years of doubt and experiment (as well as a dawning awareness that at some level I then had a real commitment to *worseness* rather than *wellness*) for me to gradually come to a point where a high-raw way of eating has become my normal lifestyle.

Probably I am slower than most to learn. Several years ago I read in a scientific journal about experiments designed to test animal intelligence. In the 'discussion' part of the paper researchers stated that basic intelligence is directly proportionate to the number of times an animal has to experience a stimulus— say an electric shock every time it touches a switch or a reward of grain whenever it goes through a trap door—before it learns whether the stimulus is of positive or negative value. Only then does the beneficial response become integrated into an animal's behaviour. I remember thinking at the time that I definitely belonged with the lowest level of rats since I tend to have to beat my head against a brick wall a hundred times before I finally twig to the fact it hurts. Yet, like a lot of creatures which are slow to learn, once I do, I actually *know* not just in my head the way I would know a fact but on a deeper and more permanent level—the way once you learn to ride a bicycle it becomes almost an unconscious response and you *know* it forever.

It is that kind of knowing which is valuable in creating an ageless-ageing lifestyle for yourself. And, unless you are one of the very fortunate few who are able to quickly grasp new ideas and techniques and to integrate them into your way of life easily and sensibly, it is going to take time. It also takes experiment to separate out what works best for you from what doesn't work at all. And it may take the help of a doctor or health practitioner who is well versed in nutrition.

The Orthomolecular Approach to Ageless Ageing

The orthomolecular approach to health is based on an extremely simple nuts-and-bolts hypothesis: we are made of vitamins, minerals, amino acids, fatty acids and so forth, working together according to a living molecular logic. Because we are alive, that life provides the consciousness to utilize these nuts and bolts. It is these nuts and bolts which—when insufficient—create pathology and degeneration. This simple concept is fundamental to nutritional supplementation for ageless ageing. It is also, I believe, a concept which will eventually change the course of medicine and science.

If you want to use the anti-oxidant nutrients as part of an orthomolecular approach to ageless ageing it is a good idea to consult with a nutritionally oriented doctor or health practitioner who can help you work out a supplemental programme personally tailored to your individual needs. Each of us is biochemically highly individual so that where one person may need only moderate quantities of a specific nutrient such as vitamin B_6 or zinc yet high levels of vitamin C, another may need quite exceptional amounts of zinc and B_6 yet have only a moderate need for ascorbic acid. There are a number of useful diagnostic tools which in conjunction with an examination of the foods you eat and your lifestyle as a whole can be helpful in establishing this.

In Chapter 18 we looked at Quantitative Amino Acid Screening. This technique, in which the level of specific amino acids is determined from a urine sample, can tell an experienced nutritional practitioner a great deal about how your metabolic pathways are working and where extra nutritional support in terms of vitamins, minerals, essential fatty acids or amino acids can be helpful to improve them. Hair analysis of minerals can also be useful, as can urinalysis of blood levels of both vitamins and minerals. All of these tools work best when used together since one offers a check against the others. Hair analysis on its own can never give a complete picture. So far there are few physicians in this country using these techniques but an awareness of what they offer in helping a person create a nutritional programme for high level wellness and longevity is rapidly growing within the medical profession.

It can also be helpful to look at what a typical selection of supplemental nutrients designed for ageless ageing looks like. For although age-researchers can disagree about specifics, the general principles of age-retardation through supplementation are becoming well established. One thing which is absolutely vital to remember is the rule of synergy. It is no good taking large doses of a few vitamins with anti-oxidant properties unless you also provide your body with adequate supplies of *all* the other nutrients you need in smaller quantities, to create an orthomolecular environment which enables it to use them.

Sample Programme of Supplementation for Ageless Ageing

Name of nutrient	Optimum daily allowance[a]	Ageless-ageing dose range	How it is taken
THE VITAMINS (and related nutrients)			
Vitamin A	10,000–35,000 IU	15,000–35,000 IU	in one dose with a meal

Name of nutrient	Optimum daily allowance[a]	Ageless-ageing dose range	How it is taken
Beta-Carotene	unknown	15–45mg	same
Vitamin C (ascorbic acid) as fine powder	250–2000mg	5–20g	divided doses in liquids between meals
Vitamin C (ascorbyl palmitate)	none	1–3g	in one dose with a meal
Bioflavinoids	unknown	500–2000mg	divided doses with a meal
Vitamin E	50–400 IU	800–1600 IU	same 400
Vitamin D	200–400 IU	200–400 IU	same
Vitamin B_1 (thiamine)	5–10mg	100–1000mg	same
Vitamin B_2 (riboflavin)	6–15mg	100–300mg	same
Vitamin B_3 (niacin)	25–100mg	250–3000mg	same
Vitamin B_5 (pantothenic acid)	10–50mg	250–3000mg	same
Vitamin B_6 (pyridoxine)	10–20mg	50–150mg	same
Vitamin B_{12}	10–100mcg	100–1000mcg	same[b]
Vitamin B_{15} (pangamic acid)	unknown	150–250mg	same
Folic Acid	2000–4000mcg	800–5000mcg	same
PABA	unknown	250–750mg	same
Biotin	unknown	150–750mcg	same
Choline	unknown	500–3000mg	same
Inositol	unknown	500–3000mg	same

Name of nutrient	Optimum daily allowance[a]	Ageless-ageing dose range	How it is taken
THE MINERALS			
Calcium	800–1500mg	1000–2000mg	divided doses with acid fruit or juice
Magnesium	400–700mg	500–1000mg	same
Iron	10–30mg	5–10mg	same
Zinc	15–35mg	10–25mg	same
Manganese	2.5–5mg	10–25mg	same
Molybdenum	250–1000mcg	250–1000mcg	same
Chromium[c]	10–20mcg	50–200mcg	same
Selenium	100–200mcg	250–800mcg	same
Kelp	none	250mg–1000mg	same

The great variation in dosage of B vitamins takes into account the amount of stress present. The higher the stress levels, the greater the demand.

AMINO ACIDS AND OTHER ACCESSORY NUTRIENTS

L-Methionine	unknown	500–1500mg	on empty stomach ½ hour before a meal or at bedtime
L-Cysteine	unknown	500–1500mg	same
L-Glutathione	unknown	500–1500mg	same
Ginseng	none	1000–3000mg	same
Eleuthero-coccus	none	1000–3000mg	same
Royal Jelly	none	250–500mg	same
Evening Primrose Oil	none	1500–3000mg	divided doses with meals

Name of nutrient	Optimum daily allowance[a]	Ageless-ageing dose range	How it is taken
Nucleic Acids	none	X1200–2000mg	with meals
Lecithin	none	3–15g	same
Raw Glandulars	none	200–1000mg	same

Notes:

a. Figures taken from *Nutrition Desk Reference Manual* by Robert Garrison Jr and Elizabeth Somer, New Canaan, Connecticut: Keats Publishing, 1985.

b. With sorbitol on empty stomach for 30 days then stop for 2 months.

c. GTF form if possible.

Guidelines for Ageless Ageing

Although nutritional supplementation is a highly individual affair, not every aspect of an ageless-ageing lifestyle is so personal. There are a few simple 'don'ts' which anybody can benefit from adhering to. And while science has not yet provided us with the knowledge which will enable us to live to 200 they should go a long way towards helping us reach 120:

Don't smoke.

Don't drink more than a couple of glasses of wine a day.

Don't let yourself become a victim of negative expectations about ageing.

Don't take drugs unnecessarily.

Don't overeat.

Don't eat sugar and other refined carbohydrates or highly processed foods.

Don't push yourself beyond your limits.

Don't put off a change of lifestyle—such as giving up smoking or getting more exercise—which you know will improve your health. Do it now.

There are also some equally important 'do's' for longevity and ageless ageing:

Do increase the number of fresh (as many as possible eaten raw) vegetable and wholegrain foods—particularly organically grown—in your diet.

Do exercise to between 30 and 60 per cent of your maximum capacity for at least thirty minutes three to five times a week.

Do investigate what nutritional supplements including the anti-oxidant nutrients can do for you under the guidance of a nutritionally oriented doctor or health practitioner.

Do learn to listen to the messages of your own body so that you sleep when you are tired, eat only when you are hungry and follow what your conscience tells you is right. What works for someone else may not be right for you.

Do make a friend of stress by taking enough relaxation when you need it, by talking problems out with other people when they arise instead of swallowing them and by seeking out what your own intrinsic goals are and then following them.

Do go easy in incorporating any of the new approaches to ageless ageing from this book into your own life and don't try to take on more than you can handle at any one time. It's important to be circumspect and to move towards newer methods of life extension with caution, wisdom and sensitivity to your own responses.

Do begin to view ageing as a positive process which can lead you to even better health, greater stamina and more creativity and happiness. These expectations help create your future.

Do allow yourself to experience joy in your work and when you are at play. It is the natural birthright of every human being and can do more to improve your health and longevity than any other single thing.

Do seek out new challenges which keep your mind alert and stimulate your interest in life and in other people.

Do, as Hans Selye counsels, 'Reach for the highest aim yet never put up resistance in vain.'

Postscript

Thanks to our growing understanding of the natural laws of health and advanced research into high-tech biochemistry, what was once little more than a pipe dream—the notion that the length of human life can be extended—is becoming a reality. Gerontologists have now challenged the maximum life-spans of many species of animals. Man is next. Already physicians are using anti-oxidant nutrients, electromagnetic techniques and other anti-ageing tools to prevent physical degeneration and to restore health and balance to ailing bodies. Meanwhile psychiatrists and psychologists trained in bio-chemistry and in the orthomolecular treatment of the brain are not only beginning to cure mental and emotional problems associated with age, they are even using the tools of their trade to expand consciousness. It becomes important to ask the question, 'With what consequences?'

Boon or Burden?

The first worry about life extension for most people is usually, 'What will we do with these old people we are creating?' 'Won't they be yet a further burden to society?' Naturally they want to know about the effect that longevity will have on housing, medical costs and the rest. Such questions are valid. But it is also important to penetrate the point of view from which they come—the assumptions and paradigms which underlie them.

Our society has imprinted its members with negative concepts about being old. In the book for which he won a Pulitzer Prize, *Why Survive? Being Old in America*, Dr Robert Butler outlined the enormous practical problems of dealing with the aged: housing, pensions, personal security, need for meaningful occupations and the rest, and the horrific conditions in which many old people in modern Western society live. He also pointed out that we hold many unconscious assumptions about the aged which continue to create these conditions. They are always with us and they greatly distort our view of ageing, old people and their place in society. These assumptions include a belief that the aged are inflexible, senile, unproductive people waiting for the inevitable arrival of the grim reaper. Basically not interesting, of little value, they are people worthy of being assigned to a forclosed existence. Alex Comfort refers to these common views of age and the elderly as 'agism' which he defines as 'the notion that people cease to be people, to be the same people or become people of a distinct and inferior kind, by virtue of having lived a specified number of years'. The assumptions of 'agism' lie behind many of the most often asked questions about the social and political consequences of ageless ageing. They make such questions impossible to answer adequately from our current perspective and with our current views of reality. They also force us to ignore a number of important realities.

We forget for instance that chronological age at its very best is only a limited indication of biological and functional age. Even our present old people are capable of far more than society allows them to express or contribute—indeed more than they themselves allow. We also forget that every major disease is age-dependent and all of the major causes of death and disability are secondary to the progressive degeneration of ageing. Little wonder, for until now, after the age of 30 we have been witnessing a steady and inexorable increase in the probability of morbidity and mortality from one disease or another. But people living by the principles of ageless ageing will be different. Highly resistant to the ravages of degeneration which manifest themselves in our major destructive chronic diseases such as cancer, coronary heart disease, arthritis and the rest, they will be *less* rather than *more* of a burden to the state in terms of medical, social and psychiatric care. Application of these life-lengthening and life-enhancing principles to health on a wide scale should lead to an increase in the ratio of productive to non-productive men and women with prolonged life spans. This has been the conclusion of Yale's Professor Larry Kotlikoff, one of the few academics to look seriously at the issue. Kotlikoff initiated an inquiry into the economic effects of increased life-span. He also concluded that this increase in the ratio of productive to non-productive people would result in an increased *per capita* output whether or not the working period increased year for year with life expectancy.

With the increased longevity and the improved resistance to degeneration which are the natural outcome of applying the findings of age-researchers to our everyday lives, the population of our old people will also change. So will our attitudes to them. No longer a burden, like the Vilcabamba Indians or the Abkhazians of the Soviet Caucasus, they will become not 'old people' but 'long lived people'. Such a simple shift in attitude could revolutionize us as human beings not only in terms of politics and economics but by shifting us towards a more value-oriented society. At that point the question of 'What will we do with all these old people?' begins to take on quite a different meaning. For the challenge now becomes not how we house, feed, and care for a growing sector of the non-productive population but rather how we can best channel and use the energy and wisdom of the older members of our society.

A Time For Reaping

At the moment we have about a quarter of a century allotted to us in which to grow to adulthood. The next forty years are generally directed towards accomplishment in the outside world, realizing the goals of adulthood, procreation and raising a family. Then we tend to slide headlong downhill until we die. The character Vitek in Karel Capek's celebrated play *The Makropoulos Secret* describes the plight of modern man:

> . . . he hasn't had time for gladness, and he hasn't had time to think, and he hasn't had time for anything except a desire for bread. He hasn't done anything. No, not even himself . . . What else is immortality of the soul but a protest against the shortness of life? A human being is something more than a turtle or a raven; a man needs more time to life. Sixty years— it is not right. It's weakness, it's innocence, and it's animal-like.

Within the confines of our three score and ten years and under the pressures of contemporary social values, modern man and modern woman have become quite extraordinarily obsessed with accomplishment. Since for most of us the time for worldly accomplishment is limited to this middle period we push ourselves forward, often at health-breaking and heart-breaking speed. To many of us the concern with fulfilling ourselves in our career, paying the rent, buying the baby a new pair of shoes, during what are supposed to be the best years of our lives, forces us to postpone the pleasures of a time to dream, a time to think and a time to play—in the very highest sense of the word. If we are to find a means of coping with the problems of our society—problems of poor statesmanship, overpopulation, Third World famine, pollution and economic inequities—we desperately need this time to dream. We need this time to recreate our own world and to take our destiny responsibly into our own hands, aside from the demands of adult life.

Connectedness—A Priority

Nobel laureate novelist Hermann Hesse wrote about such a time-expanded world in his *Glass Bead Game*. There, time's limits become the rules of the game of life and each human being is freed to order his existential choices. Such a time-expanded world could help us draw together our learning and re-synthesize our knowledge. It might enable the coming together of disciplines such as mathematics, physics, philosophy, biology, medicine, psychology, anthropology, art, literature, politics, theology and law—in fact the whole gamut of human concerns and disciplines—into a kind of connectedness which is urgently needed in the excessively fragmented post-industrial society which has become our home. Healthy longevity—ageless ageing—would make available to us the steadily maturing wisdom of our old people—people whose experience and awareness have not become distorted by ill-functioning minds and rapidly waning energies. Such wisdom is, I believe, exactly what we need to help guide our species into its further evolution. Moreover, such time expansion takes hold of our personal sense of the present and in a very real way draws it into the future. For when we are able to project ourselves into the future, that future becomes not an abstract consideration but of active concern to all of us. The future of the earth is *our* future. We become responsible for it and we will live to see it as caretakers instead of as irresponsible tenants of a rented property. Ageless ageing will help us become its owners and like all owners we are far more likely to look after our property.

In George Bernard Shaw's preface to *Back to Methuselah*—the play in which his character Dr Conrad Barnabas promotes an extended lifespan of 300 years—he writes: 'Men do not live long enough; they are, for the purposes of high civilization, mere children when they die.' He then goes on to consider some of the creative possibilities of our being able to lengthen life:

> This possibility came to me when history and experience had convinced me that the social problems raised by millionfold national populations are far beyond the political capacity attainable in three score and ten years of life by slowgrowing mankind. On all hands as I write the cry is that our statesmen are too old, and that Leagues of Youth must be formed everywhere to save civilization from them. But despairing ancient pioneers tell me that the statesmen are not old enough for their jobs . . . We have no sages old enough and wise enough to make a synthesis of these reactions, and to develop the magnetic awe-inspiring force which must replace the policeman's baton as the instrument of authority.

Creators of Destiny

For me this magnetic awe-inspiring force of which he speaks is nothing less than man's potential to become the creator of his destiny on earth. The situation in which we live with all the global dangers to which we are exposed—from the possibility of mass nuclear extinction to world economic collapse—are not accidents of nature. They have been created by us. And no act of God can suddenly remove their potential destructiveness from our future. Only we ourselves have the possibility of doing that. If we are to succeed, we will need to call forth every resource which we have—intelligence, wisdom, strength, courage, patience, wit, compassion—and work with them. Ageless ageing can help us do that.

Life extension, the freedom from mental and physical degeneration, is no curious artifact of twentieth-century science. Who cares if, at the age of 85, we are all capable of running a marathon or if we look 30 years younger? Such things matter little on their own. But the high-level health, mental clarity and wellbeing which are rewards of ageless ageing are of urgent concern to our future as residents of the earth. They form the foundation on which we as human beings can build if we are to make use of our full potential for creativity. In the full use of such creativity lies the future of ourselves, our children and our planet. Again in the words of Capek's Vitek:

> Let's give everyone a three-hundred-year life. It will be the biggest event since the creation of man; it will be the liberating and creating anew of man! God, what man will be able to do in three hundred years! To be a child and pupil for fifty years; fifty years to understand the world and its ways and to see everything there is; and a hundred years to work in; and then a hundred years, when we have understood everything, to live in wisdom, to teach, and to give example. How valuable human life would be if it lasted for three hundred years! There would be no fear, no selfishness. Everything would be wise and dignified. Give people life! Give them full human life!

An idealistic plea in the midst of the profound disillusionment with man that is so much a part of late twentieth-century life? A dream? Perhaps. Yet our dreams become the myths by which we live. And right now we urgently need new myths to give our life direction—dreams which, having been tempered by the wisdom of age and experience, are large enough and rich enough to take us forward. Such dreams have power. They also have a remarkable way of becoming reality:

> All men dream; but not equally. Those who dream by night in the dusty recesses of their minds wake in the day to find it was vanity: but the dreamers of the day are dangerous men, for they may act their dream with open eyes, to make it possible.

T. E. Lawrence

Useful Names and Addresses

Suppliers of Vitamins, Minerals and Amino Acids

Nature's Best, P.O. Box 1, Tunbridge Wells, Kent TN2 3EQ
Tel: 0892 34143.
Suppliers by post of high-quality vitamins and minerals including many forms
of Vitamin C in capsules and powders. They have the most comprehensive
range of high-quality amino acids in Britain. Nature's Best also do Na-PCA
spray for skin, a canthaxanthin supplement for artificial tanning called Natur-
Bronze and the best anti-ageing formulation I have come across on either side
of the Atlantic. Called New Leaf Anti-Oxidant Capsules, it is a unique formula
along the lines of the Ageless Ageing vitamin and mineral supplements (see page
338) which can be taken either in small quantities by using 3 to 6 capsules a day
or as a mega supplement by taking much more. It needs to be used with extra
quantities of Vitamin C.

G. R. Lane, Sissons Road, Gloucester.
Manufacturers of high-quality nutritional supplements which are available in
health food stores, Lanes do an excellent granular lecithin and the best
phosphatidyl choline enriched lecithin. It is called Hipolec and comes in
convenient little sachets for sprinkling on cereals or other foods. Lanes also do
good-quality herbal products and other vitamins.

Britannia Health Products, 7–11 High Street, Reigate, Surrey.
Producers of Effamol evening primrose oil which is available in chemists and
health food stores in capsules.

Nature's Own, Cheltenham, GI50 1HX.
This company produces a small range of excellent nutritional supplements
carefully formulated to ensure their uptake in the body.

Natural Flow, Burwash Common, East Sussex, Tel: 0435 882482.
Natural Flow import top-quality American vitamins and minerals, RNA and
glandulars. They can be ordered by post and are also available in health food
stores. They also do a very good natural bristle brush for skin brushing.

Cantassium, Larkhall Laboratories, 225 Putney Bridge Road, London SW15,
Tel: 01-870 0971.
A large range of nutritional supplements of good quality are available from
Cantassium either by post or in health food stores.

Suppliers of Herbs and Adaptogen Products

Salus-Haus, Fern Reach, Delph Lane, Daresbury, Warrington, Cheshire, Tel: 0925 74236.
Importers of excellent German herbal tonics and remedies. They do a top-quality eleutherococcus (Siberian Ginseng) tonic as well as a Ginseng tonic both of which have been carefully manufactured at low heat to preserve the adaptogenic properties of the natural plants.

Ortis, 7A Church Street, Esher, Surrey, Tel: 78 66468.
Probably the best source of Royal Jelly in Britain. They import the fresh royal jelly as well as other forms of the substances. The fresh form must be kept under constant refrigeration.

Cell Therapy

Cempami Bircher, Centre for Molecular Pathology and Microcirculation, Theaterstrasse 2, 8001 Zurich, Switzerland, 01-691133.
The centre of Franklin Bircher's work in cell therapy and microcirculation in Zurich where he has treated patients from all over the world for many years.

Dr Wolfram W. Kuhnau, 190 E Calle Primero, San Ysidro, CA 92073, USA.
Kuhnau heads the clinic in Mexico offering cell therapy there and is one of the world's most well informed doctors on the subject.

Body Realignment

Lilla Bek, PO Box 151, Wallington, Surrey, SM6 9PL. Tel: 01-647 4146
For information about sacred dance and movement for realigning the body.

Pilates Technique, Alan Herdman, 17 Homer Row, London W1. Tel: 01-723 9953.
An excellent method of body realignment which can transform posture and muscle shape in a few weeks. It uses special equipment in a gym.

Alexander Institute, Dr Wilfred Barlow, 3 Albert Court, Kensington Gore, London SW7, Tel: 01-589 3834.
The Alexander technique is the finest method I have ever come across for altering consciousness, expanding creativity and improving health simply by changing the way you move and use your body.

References

Chapter 1

Compendium of Health Statistics, 4th ed, London: Office of Health Economics, 1981.

Mortality Statistics, 1979, Office of Population Censuses and Surveys, series DH1, No 8, Table 22.

Special Report on Aging, 1979, NIH, Pub No 79–1907, 1979.

Bjorksten, J. 'Approaches and prospects for the control of age-dependent deterioration', *Annals of the New York Academy of Sciences*, 7 June 1971, 184:95–102.

Coronary Heart Disease: The Scope for Prevention, London: Office of Health Economics, 1982.

Gruenberg, E. M. 'The Failures of Success', *Millbank Memorial Fund Quarterly*, winter 1977, 55(1):3–24.

Harris, A. *Handicapped and Impaired in Great Britain*, London: HMSO, 1971.

Leaf, A. 'Every Day Is a Gift when You Are Over 100', *National Geographic*, 1973, 143(1):93–119.

Leaf, A. *Youth in Old Age*, New York: McGraw-Hill, 1975.

Medvedev, Z. A. 'Caucasus & Altay Longevity: A Biological or Social Problem?', *The Gerontologist*, 1974, 14:381.

The Surgeon General, *Healthy People: The Surgeon General's Report of Health Promotion and Disease Prevention*, DHEW, Pub Nos 79-55071 and 79-55071A, Washington DC, 1979.

Thoms, W. J. *The Longevity of Man: Its Facts and Fictions*, London: J. Murray, 1873.

Walford, Roy. *Maximum Life Span*, New York: W. W. Norton & Co, 1983.

Chapter 2

Brown-Séquard, Charles E. *Société Biologique*, Vol II, Paris: 1851.

Codellas, P. S. 'Rejuvenation and Satricons of Yesterday', *Ann. of Med. Hist.*, Vol IV, 1934.

Comfort, A. *The Biology of Senescence*, London: Routledge & Kegan Paul, 1956.

Comfort, A. et al. *The Process of Aging*, New York: Signet/NAL, 1964.

Hayflick, L. *Scientific American*, March 1968: 218.

Hayflick, L. 'Cell Biology of Aging', *Federal Proceedings*, 1979, 38(5):1851–1856.

Hayflick, L. and Moorhead, P.S. *Expl. Cell. Res.*, 1961, 25:585.

Lambert, Gilbert. *Conquest of Age*, London: Souvenir Press, 1960.

Niehans, Paul. *Introduction to Cell Therapy*, New York: Pageant Books Inc, 1960.

Niehans, Paul. *Die Endokreinen Drusen des Gehirns, Epiphyse und Hypophyse*, Berne: Hans Halen, n.d.

Rosenfeld, A. *Pro-Longevity*, New York: Avon, 1977.

Trimmer, Eric J. *Rejuvenation*, London: Robert Hale, 1967.

Chapter 3

Bender, A. D. et al. *Expl. Gerontol.*, 1970, 5: 97.

Bjorksten, J. 'Cross Linking: Key to Ageing?', *Chemical and Engineering News*, 9 May 1955, 33:1957.

Bjorksten, J. *Longevity: A Quest*, Madison, Wisconsin: Bjorksten Research Foundation, 1981.

Bjorksten, J. 'Biochemistry of Aging', in *Clinical Biochemistry: Contemporary Theories and Techniques*, Vol 2, ed H. Spiegel, New York: Academic Press, 1982.

Bjorksten, J. *Dialogue on Death*, Bjorksten Research Foundation, Houston, Texas, n.d.

Cranton, E. M. and Frackelton, J. P. 'Free Radical Pathology in Age-Associated Diseases: Treatment with EDTA Chelation, Nutrition and Antioxidants', *Journal of Holistic Medicine*, spring/summer 1984, 6(1).

Frank, B. S. and Miele, P. *Dr Frank's No-Aging Diet*, New York: Dell, 1976.

Haugaard, Niels. 'Cellular Mechanisms of Oxygen Toxicity', *Physiological Reviews*, April 1968, 47(2).

Kent, Saul. *The Life Extension Revolution*, New York: Quill, 1983.

Kugler, Hans. *Slowing Down the Aging Process*, New York: Pyramid, 1974.

Levine, Stephen and Reinhardt, Jeffrey. 'Biochemical-Pathology Initiated by Free Radicals, Oxidant Chemicals and Therapeutic Drugs in the Etiology of Chemical Hypersensitivity Disease', *Journal of Orthomolecular Psychiatry*, Third quarter 1983, 12(3).

Levine, Stephen. *Antioxidant Biochemical Adaptation: Doorways to New Science and Medicine*, Publication preview copy from author, 1984.

Mann, John A. *Secrets of Life Extension*, San Francisco: Harbor Publishing, 1980.

Passwater, Richard. *Supernutrition*, New York: Pocket Books, 1976.

Pelletier, Kenneth. *Longevity: Fulfilling Our Biological Potential*, New York: Delacorte Press/Lawrence, 1981.

Rosenfeld, Albert. *Pro-Longevity*, New York: Avon, 1977.

Tappel, A. L. 'Will Antioxidant nutrients slow aging processes?' *Geriatrics*, October 1968.

Williams, R. J. 'Medical Research Leading to the Acceptance of the Orthomolecular Approach', *Journal of Orthomolecular Psychiatry*, 4(2):99.

Chapter 4

Bjorksten, J. 'Cross Linking: Key to Ageing?' *Chemical and Engineering News*, 9 May 1955, 33:1957.

Bjorksten, J. *Longevity: A Quest*, Madison, Wisconsin: Bjorksten Research Foundation, 1981.

Bjorksten, J. *Dialogue on Death*, Bjorksten Research Foundation, Houston, Texas, n.d.

Demopolos, H. B. 'The Basis of Free Radical Pathology', *Federation Proceedings*, 32:1859–1861 symposium issue.

Goodhart, Robert S. and Shils, Maurice. *Modern Nutrition in Health and Disease*, Philadelphia: Lea & Febiger, 1978.

Guyton, Arthur C. *Textbook of Medical Physiology*, Philadelphia: W. B. Saunders, 1976.

Levine, Stephen. 'Oxidants, Anti-oxidants and Chemical Hypersensitivities', Parts I and II, *International Journal of Biosocial Research*, 4:51–54 and 4:102–105.

Levine, Stephen, and Kidd, Parris M. *Antioxidant Biochemical Adaption: Doorway to the New Science and Medicine*, San Francisco: Biocurrents Research, 1984.

Rosenfeld, Albert. *Pro-Longevity*, New York: Avon, 1977.

Chapter 5

Amkraut, A. and Solomon, G. F. 'From the symbolic stimulus to the pathophysiologic response: Immune mechanisms', *Int. J. of Psychiatry in Medicine*, 1975, 5(4):541–63.

Anderson, R. et al. *Am. J. Clin. Nut.* 1980, 33:71.

Barton, G. M. G. and Roath, O. S. *International Journal of Vitamins and Nutritional Research*, 1976, 46:271.

Bjorksten, J. in *Theoretical Aspects of Ageing*, ed M. Rockstein et al, 43–59, New York: Academic Press, 1974.

Brook, M. et al. *Am. J. Clinical Nutrition*, 1968, 21:1254.

Chandra, R. K. *Nutrition Immunity and Infection*, New York: Plenum Press, 1977.

Hayflick, Leonard. 'On the Facts of Life', *Executive Health*, June 1978, XIV, 9.

Herbert, V. and Das, K. C. in *Vitamins and Hormones*, Vol 34, eds P. L. Minson et al, New York: Academic Press, 1976.

Holland, J. J. *Scientific American*, Feb 1974:32.

Hume, R. and Weyers, E. *Scott. Med. J.*, 1973, 18:3.

Lewin, S. *Vitamin C: Its Molecular Biology and Medical Potential*, London: Academic Press, 1976.

Milne, J. S. et al. *Br. Med. Journal*, 1971, 4:383.

Pisciotta, A. V. et al. *Nature*, 1967, 215:193.

Scrimshaw, Nevin S. 'Synergistic and Antagonistic Interactions of Nutrition and Infection', *Federation Proceedings*, Nov-Dec 1966, 25:1679–1681.

Siegel, B. V. and Morton, J. I. *Experientia*, 1977, 33:393.

Stein, M. et al. 'Influence of brain and behavior on the immune system', *Science*, 6 Feb 1976, 191:435–440.

Walford, Roy. *The Immunologic Theory of Ageing*, Baltimore: Williams and Wilkins, 1969.

Walford, Roy. *Am. J. Clin. Path.*, 1980, 74:247.

Walford, Roy. *Maximum Life Span*, New York: W. W. Norton, 1983.

Wilson, C. W. M. and Loh, H. S. *Lancet*, 1973, 1:1058.

Yonomoto, R. H. *Int. J. Vitam. Nutr. Res.* 1979, Suppl 19.

Chapter 6

'It's Not the Amount of Stress You Have, It's How You Respond to It', *Executive Health*, February 1983, XIX(5).

Khorol, I. S. 'Einstein and Selye', *Rejuvenation*, July 1978, VI(3):54ff.

Selye, Hans. *The Story of the Adaptation Syndrome*, Montreal: Acta Inc Medical Publishers, 1952.

Selye, Hans. *In Vivo: The Case for Supramolecular Biology*, New York: Liveright, 1967.

Selye, Hans. *Stress Without Distress*, London: Hodder & Stoughton, 1974.

Selye, Hans. *The Stress of Life*, New York: McGraw-Hill, 1975.

Selye, Hans. *Stress in Health and Disease*, Reading, Mass: Butterworths Inc, 1976.

Chapter 7

Bray, H. G. and White, K. *Kinetics and Thermodynamics in Biochemistry*, London: J. & A. Churchill, 1957.

Brekhman, I. I. *Man and Biologically Active Substances*, Oxford: Pergamon Press, 1980.

de la Pena, A. M. *The Psychobiology of Cancer*, New York: Praeger Publishers CBS Educational and Professional Publishing, 1983.

Komarov, L. V. 'Life as a Notion and Gerontology', *Rejuvenation*, June 1984, XII(1–2).

Pardee, A. B. and Ingraham, L. L. 'Free Energy and Entropy in Metabolism', in *Metabolic Pathways*, Vol 1, ed D. M. Greenberg.

Polanyi, M. 'Life Transcending Chemistry and Physics', *Chemistry and Engineering*, 21 Aug 1967.

Schrödinger, Erwin. *What Is Life? and Mind and Matter*, Cambridge: University Press, 1980.

Szent-Györgyi, A. *Bioenergetics*, New York: Academic Press, 1957.

Szent-Györgyi, A. *Introduction to a Submolecular Biology*, New York: Academic Press, 1960.

Szent-Györgyi, A. *Bioelectronics*, New York: Academic Press, 1968.

Szent-Györgyi, A. *The Living State*, New York, Academic Press, 1972.

von Bertalanffy, L. 'General Systems Theory: A Critical Review', *General Systems Yearbook*. Society of General Systems Research, 1962, 7:1.

von Bertalanffy, L. 'The Mind-Body Problem: A New View', *Psychosomatic Medicine*, 1964, XXVI(1).

von Bertalanffy, L. *Robots, Men and Minds*, New York: George Braziller, 1967.

von Bertalanffy, L. *Problems of Life: An Evaluation of Modern Biological Thought*, New York: Harper Torchbook, 1980.

Chapter 8

Becker, R. O. *Electromagnetism and Life*, Albany, NY: State University of New York Press, n.d.

Becker, R. O. 'Electromagnetic Forces and Life Processes', *Technological Review*, Dec 1972.

Becker, R. O. 'The Basic Biological Data Transmission and Control System Influenced by Electrical Forces', *Annals of the New York Academy of Sciences*, 11 Oct 1974, 238:236–241.

Becker, R. O. 'An Application of Direct Current Neural Systems to Psychic Phenomena', in *Psychoenergetic Systems*, 1977, 2:35.

Becker, R. O. 'Electromagnetic Fields and Life', *Psychoenergetic Systems*, 1979, 3:119–128.

Becker, R. O. 'Electrical Control Systems and Regenerative Growth', *Journal of Bioelectricity*, 1982, 1(2):239–264.

Becker, R. O. 'Electromagnetic Controls over Biological Growth Processes', *Journal of Bioelectricity*, 1984, 3(1 and 2):105–118.

Becker, R. O. *The Body Electric: Electromagnetism and the Foundation of Life*, New York: William Morrow & Co, 1985.

Burr, Harold Saxton. *Blueprint for Immortality*, London: Neville Spearman, 1952.

Chimoskey, J. E. et al. 'Time Varying Magnetic Fields: Effects on DNA Synthesis', *Science*, 24 Feb 1984, 223:818ff.

Crile, George. *The Bipolar Theory of Living Processes*, New York: Macmillan, 1926.

Crile, George. *The Phenomenon of Life*, New York: W. W. Norton, 1936.

Galvani, Luigi. *Commentary on the Effects of Electricity on Muscular Motion: A Translation of Luigi Galvani's De Virbis Electricitatis in Motu Musculari Commentarius*, Cambridge, Mass: E. Licht, 1953.

Goodman, Reba et al. 'Pulsing Electromagnetic Fields Induce Cellular Transcription', *Science*, 17 June 1983, 220:1283ff.

Kenton, L. and S. *Raw Energy*, London: Century, 1984.

Komarov, L. V. 'On the possible use of permanent magnetic fields for the artificial prolongation of the specific lifespan', in *Rejuvenation*, 1975, 3(4).

Lakhovsky, G. *L'Origine de la Vie*, Texas: University Press, 1947.

Lawden, D. F. 'Separability of Psycho-physical systems', *Psychoenergetics*, 1981, 4(1):1–10.

Lawden, D. F. 'A Berkeleian Model for Psychic Phenomena', *Psychoenergetics*, 1983, 5(3):185–198.

Szent-Györgyi, A. *Introduction to a Submolecular Biology*, New York: Academic Press, 1960.

Chapter 9

Bjorksten, J. 'The Theoretical Base of the First Law of Le Compte', *Rejuvenation*, May 1975, III(4).

Bjorksten, J. 'Pathways to Longevity', *Rejuvenation*, June 1978, VI(2).

Bjorksten, J. *Longevity: A Quest*, Madison, Wisconsin: Bjorksten Research Foundation, 1981.

Bjorksten, J. 'Biochemistry of Aging', in *Clinical Biochemistry*, New York: Academic Press, 1982.

Colgan, Michael. *Your Personal Vitamin Profile*, New York: Quill, 1982; London: Blond & Briggs, 1983.

Le Compte, Herman. 'Le Compte's Law', *Zeitschrift für Altersforschung*, 1965, Band 18, Heft 2.

Le Compte, Herman (with Northcote Parkinson). *The Law of Longer Life*, Troy, Alabama: Troy State University Press, 1980.

Le Compte, Herman. Personal communication with the author.

Nutrition Search. *Nutrition Almanac*, New York: McGraw-Hill, 1979.

Pfeiffer, C. *Mental and Elemental Nutrients*, New Canaan, Connecticut: Keats Publishing, 1975.

Pfeiffer, C. and Banks, J. *Total Nutrition*, New York: Simon and Schuster, 1980.

Szent-Györgyi, A. 'On a Substance that Can Make Us Sick if We Do Not Eat It', *Executive Health*, June 1977, XIII(9).

Williams, Roger J. and Kalita, D. *A Physician's Handbook on Orthomolecular Medicine*, New Canaan, Connecticut: Keats Publishing Inc, 1977.

Chapter 10

Gatsko, G. G. et al. 'Combined Effect of Periodic Feeding and Using the Vitamin B Complex upon Biological Age, and Some Metabolic Indices of the White Rat', *Rejuvenation*, January 1982, X(1).

McCay, Clive. 'Clinical Aspects of Ageing and the Effect of Diet upon Ageing', in *Cowdry's Problems of Ageing*, 3rd ed, New York: Williams & Williams Co, 1952.

Ross, M. H. et al. 'Length of Life and Caloric Intake', *Am. J. of Clin. Nut.*, Aug 1972, 25:834–838.

Ross, M. H. et al. 'Food Preference and Length of Life', *Science*, 10 Oct 1975, 190:165–167.

Ross, M. H. et al. 'Dietary practices and growth responses as predictors of longevity', *Nature*, 12 August 1976, 262(5569):553–584.

Ross, M. H. et al. 'Dietary Behavior and Longevity', *Nutrition Reviews*, Oct 1977, 35(10).

Ross, M. H. et al. 'Dietary Practices of Early Life and Spontaneous Tumours of the Rat', *Nutrition and Cancer*, 1982.

Schlenker, E. D. *Am. J. of Clin. Nut.*, Oct 1973.

Walford, Roy. *Maximum Life Span*, New York: W. W. Norton, 1983.

Walford, Roy. 'On Retarding Ageing by Nutrition', *Executive Health*, Sept 1983, XIX(12).

Young, Vernon. 'Diet as a Modulator of Ageing and Longevity', *Federation Proceedings*, 6 May 1979, 38(6).

Chapter 11

Ames, Bruce. 'Dietary Carcinogens and Anticarcinogens', *Science*, September 1983, 221:1256ff.

Bircher, Franklin. 'The Relationship Between Clinical Symptoms and Disturbances in Microcirculation', 9th European Conference on Microcirculation, Antwerp, 1976. *Bibl. anat.* 16:249–252, Basel: Karger, 1977.

Bircher, Ralph. 'A Turning Point in Nutritional Science', Milwaukee, Wisconsin: Lee Foundation for Nutritional Research, reprint, n.d.

Bircher-Benner, Max. 'The Healing Community', unpublished translation by Hilda Marlin.

Bircher-Benner, Max. 'The Prevention of Incurable Disease', unpublished translation by Hilda Marlin.

Bircher-Benner, Max. 'The Meaning of Therapeutic Order', unpublished translation by Hilda Marlin.

Brekhman, I. I. *Man and Biologically Active Substances: The Effect of Drugs, Diet and Pollution on Health*, Oxford: Pergamon Press, 1980.

Brekhman, I. I. and Kublanov, M. G. 'The Concept of Structural Information in Pharmacology and Nutrition', Vladivostok: 1983.

Eppinger, H. et al. 'Transmineralisation und vegetarische Kost', *Ergebnisse der Inneren Medizin und Kinderheilkunde*, 1936, 51.

Eppinger, H. et al. 'Uber Rohkostbehandlung', *Wiener Klinische Wochenshrift*, 1 July 1936.

Eppinger, H. et al. *Die Permeabilitätspathologie als Lehre vom Krankheitsbeginn*, Vienna: 1949.

Goodhart, Robert S. and Shils, Maurice. *Modern Nutrition in Health and Disease*, 6th ed, Philadelphia: Lea & Febiger, 1980.

Hall, R. H. 'Is Nutrition a Stagnating Science?', *New Scientist*, 2 January 1975:7ff.

Heddle, J. A. (ed). *Mutagenicity: New Horizons in Genetic Toxicology*, New York: Academic Press, 1982.

Kenton, L. and S. *Raw Energy*, London: Century, 1984.

Kenyon, Julian. 'Food Sensitivity—A Search for Underlying Causes: A Case Study of Twelve Patients', photocopy from the author.

Liechti von Brasch, Dagmar. 'Seventy Years of Experience in the Bircher-Benner Therapy of Order', unpublished translation by Hilda Marlin.

Stich, H. F. et al. *Mutat. Res.*, 1981, 90, 201 and 1983, 116, 333.

Sugimura, T. and Sato, S. *Cancer Research supplement*, 1983, 43, 2415s.

Szent-Györgyi, A. *Introduction to a Submolecular Biology*, New York: Academic Press, 1960.

Chapter 12

Bircher, Ralph. 'The Question of Protein', typed paper from author.

Challem, Jack Joseph and Lewin, Renate. 'Keeping the Mind Young', Feldmore Newsletter No 44.

Colgan, Michael. *Your Personal Vitamin Profile*. New York: Quill, 1982; London: Blond & Briggs, 1983.

Eastwood, M. A. and Mitchell, W. D. 'The Place of Fibre in the Diet', *Brit. J. of Hosp. Med.*, Jan 1974:123.

Ershoff, B. H. 'Antitoxic Effects of Plant Fiber', *Am. J. of Clin. Nut.*, 27:1395–1398.

Horrobin, David. *Clinical Uses of Essential Fatty Acids*, London: Eden Press, 1982.

Issel, Josef. 'Nutritional Protection against Cancer', *Tjidskrift fur Halsa*, Stockholm, 1975, 1–3.

Karstrom, Henning. *Ratt Kost*, Gavle: Skandinavska Bokforlaget, 1982.

Katenkamp and Stiller. *Histochemistry of Amyloid*, Jena: VEB Gustav Fischer Verlag, 1975.

Katenkamp and Stiller. 'Das Amyloid', *Hippokrates*, 41(1):5–23.

Kelsay, J. 'A Review of Research on Effects of Fibre Intake on Man', *Am. J. of Clin. Nut.*, Jan 1978, 31:142–159.

Kruiswijk, H., Oomen, H. A. and Hipsley, E. H. *Voeding*, 1969, 30/5:225–230.

McCully, Kilmer S. *Am. J. of Pathology*, 1970, 59:181–193 and 61:1–8.

McCully, Kilmer S. *Am. J. of Clin. Nut.*, May 1975, 28.

Spiller, Gene. 'Interaction of Dietary Fiber with Other Dietary Components: A Possible Factor in Certain Cancer Etiologies', *Am. J. of Clin. Nut.*, Oct 1978:231–232.

Winick, M. 'Slow the problems of Aging and Quash its Problems—With Diet', *Modern Medicine*, 15 February 1978:68–74.

Chapter 13
Kenton, L. & S. *Raw Energy*, London: Century, 1984.

Kenton, L. & S. *Raw Energy Recipes*, London: Century, 1985.

Kunz-Bircher, Ruth. *Eat Your Way To Health: The Bircher-Benner Approach to Nutrition*, London: Allen & Unwin, 1984.

Polunin, Miriam. *The New Cookbook*, London, Macdonald, 1985.

Chapter 14
Ash, J. E. 'The Blood in Inanition', *Arch. Inter. Med.*, July 1914, 14:8–32.

Buchinger, Otto. *About Fasting*, Wellingborough, England: Thorsons, 1961.

Buchinger, Otto. *Uber Moderne Heilfasten Kuren*, Beitigheim: Turm-Verlag, 1970.

Carlson, A. J. 'Hunger, appetite and gastric juice secretion in man during prolonged fasting', *Am. J. Physiol.*, 1918, 45:120–46.

Child, C. M. *Senescence and Rejuvenescence*, Chicago: University Press, 1915.

Cott, Alan. *Fasting As a Way of Life*, New York: Bantam Books, 1977.

Cott, Alan. *Fasting: The Ultimate Diet*, New York: Bantam Books, 1981.

De Vries, Arnold. *Therapeutic Fasting*, Los Angeles: Chandler Book Co, 1963.

Hazzard, L. B. *Fasting for the Cure of Disease*, Physical Culture Pub Co, 1910.

Hills, Christopher. *Rejuvenating the Body*, Boulder Creek, CA: University of the Trees Press, 1979.

Kent, Susannah. 'Fasting', *The Vegetarian*, Nov 1974.

Maleskey, Gale. 'The Truth about Fasting', *Prevention Magazine*, Oct 1984.

Morgulis, S. *Fasting and Undernutrition*, New York: E. P. Dutton & Co.

Morgulis, S. 'Contributions to the physiology of regeneration', *J. Exp. Zool.*, 1909, 7:595–642.

Shelton, H. *The Science and Fine Art of Fasting*, Chicago: Natural Hygiene Press, 1978.

Sinclair, U. P. *The Fasting Cure*, M. Kennerly, 1913.

Szekely, Edmond Bordeaux. *The Essene Science of Fasting and the Art of Sobriety*, Cartago, Costa Rica: International Biogenic Society, 1978.

Chapter 15
Airola, P. O. *Health Secrets from Europe*, New York: Arco, 1972.

Airola, P. O. *How to Get Well*, Phoenix: Health Plus Publishers, 1974.

Dalas, Nergis. *Yoga for Rejuvenation*, Wellingborough, Northants: Thorsons, 1984.

Dhillon, Sukhraj. *Health, Happiness and Longevity*, Tokyo: Japan Publications, 1983.

Guyton, A. C. 'Interstitial fluid pressure-volume relationships and their regulation' in Wolstenholms, G. E. W. and Knight, J. (eds) *Ciba Foundation Symposium on Circulatory and Respiratory Mass Transport*, London: J. & A. Churchill, 1969.

Guyton, A. C. *Basic Human Physiology: Normal Function Mechanisms of Disease*, Philadelphia: W. B. Saunders Co, 1971.

Kluger, M. J. 'On Fever: Does it really harm or help?', *Executive Health*, March 1984, XX(6).

Knowles, William. *Knowles Breathing Course*, privately published, 1960.

Lederman, E. K. *Good Health through Natural Therapy*, London: Pan, 1978.

Lindlahr, Henry. *Natural Therapeutics*, Vol 2, Saffron Walden, Essex: C. W. Daniel, 1981.

Powell, Eric. *The Natural Home Physician*, Saffron Walden, Essex: Health Science Press, 1962.

Turner, R. N. *Naturopathic Medicine*, Wellingborough: Thorsons, 1984.

Wareland, Are. *In the Caldron of Disease*, London: A. G. Berry, 1934.

West, Samuel C. *Trapped Protein: The Major Cause of Pain, Loss of Energy and Degenerative Disease*, Mesa, Arizona: The New Way of Life Health Foundation.

West, Samuel C. *Excess Protein*, Mesa, Arizona: The New Way of Life Health Foundation, Jan 1978.

Yoffrey, J. M. and Courtice, F. C. *Lymphatics, Lymph, and Lymphoid Tissue*, Baltimore: Williams & Wilkins, 1967.

Chapter 16

Bjorksten, J. 'A Theoretical Base for Multivitamin Therapy', *Rejuvenation*, Oct 1976, 4(4).

Cameron, Ewan and Pauling, Linus. *Cancer and Vitamin C*, New York: Warner Books, 1981.

Cathcart, R. 'The method for determining proper doses of Vitamin C for the treatment of disease by titrating to bowel tolerance', *Journal of Orthomolecular Psychiatry*, 10(2):125ff.

Committee on Animal Nutrition, *Nutrient Requirements for Laboratory Animals*, Publication No 990: National Academy of Science.

Cranton, E. M. and Frackelton, J. P. 'Free Radical Pathology in Age-Associated Diseases: Treatment with EDTA Chelation, Nutrition and Anti-oxidants', *Journal of Holistic Medicine*, spring/summer 1984, 6(1).

Crary, E. et al. 'Potential Clinical Applications for High-Dose Nutritional Anti-Oxidants', *Medical Hypothesis*, 1984, 13:77.

Davis, A. *Let's Eat Right to Stay Fit*, New York: Signet Books, 1970.

Demopolus, H. B. et al. 'Theoretical Basis for Free Radical Damage and Review of Experimental Data' in *Neural Trauma*, New York: Raven Press, 1979.

Gilbert, D. L. *Oxygen and Living Process*, Springer-Verlag, 1981.

Halliwell, B., and Gutteridge, J. *Lancet*, 23 June, 1984, p 1396.

Pauling, L. 'For the Best of Health: How Much Vitamin C Do You Need?', *Executive Health*, Dec 1975, 12(3).

Pauling, L. *Vitamin C and the Common Cold*, New York: Berkley Books, 1982.

Roos, D. et al. 'Oxygen Free Radicals and Tissue Damage', Ciba Symposium, 65, Amsterdam: Excerpta Medica—New Series.

Stone, Irwin. *The Healing Factor: Vitamin C Against Disease*, New York: Grosset & Dunlap, 1972.

Chapter 17

Bjorksten, J. *Longevity: A Quest*, Madison Wisconson: Bjorksten Research Foundation, 1981.

Goodhart, Robert S. and Shils, Maurice E. *Modern Nutrition in Health and Disease*, Philadelphia: Lea & Febiger, 1980.

Hoffer, Abram and Walker, Morton. *Orthomolecular Nutrition*, New Canaan, CT: Keats, 1978.

Kent, Saul. *The Life Extension Revolution*, New York: Quill, 1983.

Kirschmann, John D. ed. *Nutrition Almanac*, New York: McGraw Hill, 1985.

Kraus, V. K. and Mahan, L. K. *Food, Nutrition and Diet Therapy*, London: W. B. Saunders Co., 1979.

Kugler, Hans. *Slowing Down the Aging Process*, New York: Pyramid, 1974.

Levine, Stephen A. and Kidd, Parris M. *Antioxidant Adaptation: Its Role in Free Radical Pathology*, San Leandro, CA: Biocurrents Division, Allergy Research Group, 1985.

Newbold, H. L. *Mega-Nutrients*, New York: Peter H. Wyden, 1975.

Rosenfield, Albert. *Pro-Longevity*, New York: Acon, 1977.

Stryer, Lubert. *Biochemistry*, San Francisco: W. H. Freeman and Company, 1975.

Tappel, A. 'Will Antioxidant nutrients slow aging processes?', *Geriatrics*, October 1968.

Williams, Roger. *Physicians' Handbook of Nutritional Science*, Springfield, Illinois: Charles C. Thomas, 1975.

Williams, Roger. *Biochemical Individuality*, London: University of Texas Press, 1979.

Chapter 18

Journal of Clinical Nutrition, 1953, 1:232.

Orthomolecular Psychiatry, Vol 4, 1975, 4:297ff.

Science, 1973, 179:588–591.

'Growth Hormone Releasers', Newsletter 53, Feldmore Health Publications, Tunbridge Wells. Has excellent list of references on free amino acids used for GHR.

Brown, P. E. *Nature* 1967, 213:363.

Cutting, W. C. *Handbook of Pharmacology*, New York: Appleton-Century-Crofts, 5th ed, 1972.

Erdmann, Robert. Private communications with the author.

Freidman, H. et al. *Nature*, 1965, 205:1050ff.

Goodhart, R. S. and Shils, M. E. *Modern Nutrition in Health and Disease*, sixth ed, Philadelphia: Lea & Febiger, 1980.

Guyton, A. C. *Textbook of Medical Physiology*, Philadelphia: W. B. Saunders, 1976.

Hoffer A. and Osmond, H. *How to Live with Schizophrenia*, New Hyde Park, NY: University Books, 1966.
Meiss, D. et al. 'Amino Acid Analysis: An Important Nutritional and Clinical Evaluation Tool', *Nutritional Perspectives*, 1983, 6(2):19–24.
Pearson, D. and Shaw, S. *Life Extension* and *The Life Extension Revolution*, New York, Warner Books, 1984.
Pfeiffer, C. *Mental and Elemental Nutrients*, New Canaan, Connecticut: Keats Publishing, 1975.
Philpott, William H. and Kalita, Dwight K. *Victory over Diabetes*, New Canaan, Connecticut: Keats Publishing, n.d.
Pryor, W. A. *Scientific American*, Aug 1970: 70ff.
Schauss, A. *Diet, Crime and Delinquency*, Berkeley: Parker House, 1981.
Sprince, H. et al. *Federal Proceedings*, 1974, 33:233.
Svacha, A. J. et al. *Federal Proceedings*, 1974, 33:690.
Williams, R. et al (ed). *A Physician's Handbook on Orthomolecular Medicine*, New Canaan, Connecticut: Keats Publishing, 1979.
Williams, R. *Nutrition Against Disease*, New York: Bantam Books, 1981.

Chapter 19

'Growth Hormone Releasers', Newsletter 53, Feldmore Health Publications, Tunbridge Wells. Has excellent list of references on free amino acids used for GHR.
Bjorksten, J. *Longevity: A Quest*, Madison, Wisconsin: Bjorksten Research Foundation, 1981.
Goodhart, Robert S. and Shils, Maurice. *Modern Nutrition in Health and Disease*, Philadelphia: Lea & Febiger, 1978.
Guyton, A. C. *Textbook of Medical Physiology*, Philadelphia: W. B. Saunders, 1976.
Kent, Saul. *The Life Extension Revolution*, New York: Quill, 1983.
Kugler, Hans. *Slowing Down the Aging Process*, New York: Pyramid, 1974.
Mann, John A. *Secrets of Life Extension*, San Francisco: Harbor Publishing, 1980.
Passwater, Richard. *Supernutrition*, New York: Pocket Books, 1976.
Pearson, D. and Shaw, S. *Life Extension* and *The Life Extension Revolution*, New York: Warner Books, 1984.
Pfeiffer, C. *Mental and Elemental Nutrients*, New Canaan, Connecticut: Keats Publishing, 1975.
Rosenfeld, Albert. *Pro-Longevity*, New York: Avon, 1977.
Stryer, Lubert. *Biochemistry*, San Francisco: W. H. Freeman, 1975.

Chapter 20

British Journal of Dermatology, Aug 1978.
Journal of the American Medical Association, 16 Nov 1979 and 27 July 1984 (252(4): 491).
Psychosomatic Medicine, Oct 1983.
'On Walking: Nature's True—and Painless—Elixir', *Executive Health*, June 1984, XX(9).

Bortz, Walter M. 'Effect of Exercise on Aging—Effect of Aging on Exercise', *Journal of the American Geriatric Society*, Feb 1980, XXVIII(2):49ff.

Bortz, W. 'On Disease, Aging, and Disuse', *Executive Health*, Dec 1983, XX(3).

Colgan, M. *Your Personal Vitamin Profile*, New York: Quill, 1982; London: Blond & Briggs, 1983.

de Vries, H. 'On Exercise for Relieving Anxiety and Tension', *Executive Health*, Sept 1982, XVIII(12).

Finch, C. E. and Hayflick, L. *Handbook of the Biology of Aging*, New York: Van Nostrand, 1977.

Moorehouse, L. *The Physiology of Exercise*, 7th ed, St Louis: Mosby, 1976.

Polednak, A. P. *The Longevity of Athletes*, Springfield, Ill: C. C. Thomas, 1979.

Sidney, K. H. et al. *Am. J. Clin. Nut.*, 1977, 30.

Wood, P. D. and Haskell, W. L. *Lipids*, 1979, 14.

Chapter 21

'On Walking: Nature's True—and Painless—Elixir', *Executive Health*, June 1984, XX(9).

Belozerova, L. M. 'Aging and Motor Activity', *Rejuvenation*, April 1982.

Bortz, Walter. 'On Disease, Aging and Disuse', *Executive Health*, Dec 1983.

de Vries, Herbert. 'On Exercise for Relieving Anxiety and Tension', *Executive Health*, Sept 1982, XVIII(12).

Kenton, L. 'Secret Sources', *Harpers & Queen*, Feb 1985.

Leonard, George. *The Ultimate Athlete*, New York: Avon Books, 1974.

Sperryn, Peter. *Sport and Medicine*, London: Butterworths, 1983.

Spino, Mike. *Beyond Jogging*, Milbrae, California: Celestial Arts, 1976.

Sprague, Ken. *The Athlete's Body*, Los Angeles: Tarcher, 1981.

Syer, John, and Connolly, Christopher. *Sporting Body, Sporting Mind*, London: Cambridge University Press, 1984.

Chapter 22

Angele, K. H. *Your Daily Health Care with Kneipp*, Bad Worishofen: Kneipp-Verlag, 1980.

Bruggemann, W. *Kneipp Vademecum Pro Medico*, Würzburg: Sebastian Kneipp Publications, 1982.

de la Pena, A. *The Psychobiology of Cancer*, New York: Praeger Publishers CBS Educational and Professional Publishing, 1983.

Kneipp, Sebastian, *My Water Cure*, Northants: Thorsons, 1979.

Lederman, E. K. *Good Health Through Natural Therapy*, London: Pan, 1976.

Leibold, Gerhard. *Practical Hydrotherapy*, Wellingborough, Northants: Thorsons, 1980.

Lindlahr, Henry. *Natural Therapeutics*, Vol 2, Saffron Walden, Essex: C. W. Daniel, 1983.

Vogel, A. *Swiss Nature Doctor*, Teufen, Switzerland: Edition A. Vogel, 1980.

Chapter 23

Acta Dermato-Venereologica, 1980, 60 and 1975, 55, suppl 74; *British Journal of Cancer*, 1983, 48; *British Journal of Dermatology*, 1981, 104; *Lancet*, 6/4/74.

Bjorksten, J. *Longevity: A Quest*, Madison, Wisconsin: Bjorksten Research Foundation, 1981.

Frank, B. S. and Miele, P. *Dr Frank's No-Aging Diet*, New York: Dell, 1976.

Goodhart, Robert S. and Shils, Maurice. *Modern Nutrition in Health and Disease*, Philadelphia: Lea & Febiger, 1978.

Guyton, Arthur C. *Textbook of Medical Physiology*, Philadelphia: W. B. Saunders, 1976.

Kent, Saul. *The Life Extension Revolution*, New York: Quill, 1983.

Kugler, Hans. *Slowing Down the Aging Process*, New York: Pyramid, 1974.

Maleskey, Gale. 'Vitamins for External Use Also', *Prevention*, July 1984.

Mann, John A. *Secrets of Life Extension*, San Francisco: Harbor 1980.

Passwater, Richard. *Supernutrition*, New York: Pocket Books, 1976.

Pelletier, Kenneth. *Longevity: Fulfilling Our Biological Potential*, New York: Delacorte Press/Lawrence, 1981.

Rosenfeld, Albert. *Pro-Longevity*, New York: Avon, 1977.

Stryer, Lubert. *Biochemistry*, San Francisco: W. H. Freeman, 1975.

Chapter 24

Blum, H. F. *Carcinogenisis by Ultraviolet Light*, Princeton NJ: Princeton University Press, 1959.

Johnson, B. E. et al. 'Response of Human Skin to Ultraviolet Light' in *Photophysiology*, Vol. IV (Ed. A. C. Giese), London: Academic Press, 1968.

Magnus, I. A. *Dermatological Photobiology*, Oxford: Blackwell, 1976.

Urbach, F. ed. *The Biological Effects of Ultraviolet Radiation With Emphasis on the Skin*, Oxford: Pergamon Press, 1969.

Chapter 25

Bircher, F. 'Thérapie cellulaire des troubles circulatoires terminaux', report of the Third French Congress of Cellular Therapy, Paris: Edition du Centre Méd. D'Etudes, ed de Rech., 1959, 65–67.

Bircher, F. Private communications and conversations.

Kment, A. Third International Cell Therapy Congress, Paris, 1961.

Kment, A. 'The objective demonstration of the revitalization effect after cell implantations', in *Cell Research and Cellular Therapy*, ed Schmid, F. et al, Thoune, Switzerland: Ott, 1967.

Kuhnau, W. *My Three Decades with Live Cell Therapy*, Tijuana, Mexico: Kuhnau, 1983.

Lumière, Cornel. *The Fountain of Youth: Not a Legend*, Geneva: Editions Mont-Blanc, 1971.

Niehans, Paul. *Einführung in die Zellular Therapie*, Huber, 1957.

Osband, M. et al. 'Demonstration of abnormal immunity, T-cell histamine H-2 receptor deficiency, and successful treatment with thymic extract', *New England Journal of Medicine*, Jan 1981, CCIV: 146.

Schmid, F. 'Down's Syndrome: Treatment and Management, *Cytobiol. Rev.* 1978, 2:25–32.

Chapter 26

American Journal of Anatomy, 1913, 15:431; *Berl. Klin. Wochenschr.* 1887,

5(371); *British Medical Journal*, 1920, 2:807; *Comp. Ther.* 1978, 2:49; *Endocrinology*, May-June 1934; *Journal of the American Medical Association*, March 1922, and 1924 (83:1380); *Journal of Chiropractic Economics*, 1983, 26(2); *Med. Record*, 3 March 1917; *Medico-Chir. Trans.*, 1878, 81:57; *Rev. Med.* 1886, 6(297); *South. Med. J.* 1979, 72(5):593; *World J. Surg.* 1977, 1:605ff.

'Antigen Absorption in the Gut', Lancaster: MTP, 1978.

Birch, T. W. et al. *Nature*, 1936, 138:27.

Bland, Jeffrey. *Glandular-Based Food Supplements: Helping to Separate Fact From Fiction*, Bellevue-Redmont Medical Laboratories, 1980.

Callahan, E. J. et al. *Med. Rec.*, 1936, 149, 167.

Frank, B. S. *A New Approach to Degenerative Disease and Aging*, New York: Patria Press, 1964.

Frank, B. S. *Nucleic Acid Therapy in Aging and Degenerative Disease*, Lisbon, Portugal: Fiquima, 3rd ed, 1975.

Frank, B. S. and Miele, P. *Dr Frank's No-Aging Diet*, New York: Dell, 1976.

Gardner, T. S. *J. Gerontol.*, 1946, 1:445.

Goodhart, Robert S. and Shils, Maurice. *Modern Nutrition in Health and Disease*, Philadelphia: Lea & Febiger, 1978.

Guyton, Arthur C. *Textbook of Medical Physiology*, Philadelphia: W. B. Saunders, 1976.

Hemmings, W. A. ed. *Antigen Absorption by the Gut*, Baltimore: University Park Press, 1978.

Hemmings, W. A. ed. *Protein Transmission Through Living Membranes*, Oxford: Elsevier/North Holland Biomedical Press, 1979.

Kugler, H. J. *Slowing Down the Aging Process*, New York: Pyramid, 1973.

Kugler, H. J. *American Laboratory*, Nov 1976, 8:24.

Ralli, E. P. *Recent Advances in Nutritional Research*, New York: National Vitamin Foundation, 1952.

Robertson, T. B. *Australian Journal of Expl. Biol. Med. Sci.*, 1928, 5:47.

Stryer, Lubert. *Biochemistry*, San Francisco: W. H. Freeman, 1975.

Vorhaus, M. G. *Acta. Rheumatol.*, 1938, 10, 8.

Chapter 27

'Experimental rationale and trial of the therapeutic use of bee-raising products in cardio-vascular disease', *Kardiologiia*, May 1983, 23(5).

Brekhman, I. I. *Man and Biologically Active Substances*, Oxford: Pergamon Press, 1980.

Brekhman, I. I. 'New Substances of Plant Origin which Increase Nonspecific Resistance', *Annual Review of Pharmacology*, 1969, 9.

Brekhman, I. I. 'Pharmacological Investigations of Glycosides from Ginseng and Eleutherococcus', *Lloydia*, March 1969, 32(1).

Brekhman, I. I. 'Ginseng, Eleutherococcus and Another Adaptogen', speech given at Chelsea College, 1979.

Curtze, A. 'Eleutherococcus senticosus Maxim: Officinal plant of adaptogenic effect', *Der Deutsche Apotheker*, 1977, 29, 8.

Forgo, I. et al. 'The effect of different ginsenoside concentrations on physical work capacity', *Notabene Medici*, 1982, 12(9):721–727.

Fulder, Stephen. *An End to Aging?* Northants: Thorsons, 1983.

Hacker, B. and Medon, P. 'Cytotoxic Effects of Eleutherococcus senticosus', *Journal of Pharmaceutical Sciences*, Feb 1984, 73(2).

Medon, P. J. and Ferguson, P. W. et al. 'Effects of Eleutherococcus senticosus Extracts on Hexobarbital Metabolism in Vivo and in Vitro', *Journal of Ethnopharmacology*, 1984, 10:235–241.

Peichev, P. et al. 'Results of the Complex Use of Certain Apiary Products—Honey, Royal Jelly and Pollen from Bees—In Elderly Persons', *Folia Medica* (Bulgaria) 1966, 8(6).

Petkov, V. 'Effect of Ginseng on the Brain Biogenic Monoamines and 3', 5'–AMP System', *Arzneimittel-Forschung/Drug Research*, 1978, 28(3):388–393.

Sandberg, Finn. 'The Ginseng Root: A New Examination of an Old Drug', *Oesterreichische Apotheker-Zeitung*, 1971, 25(12):205–209.

Sandberg, Finn. 'Vitality and Senility: The effect of the ginsenosides on performance', *Svensk Farmaceutisk Tidskrift*, 1980, 84(13):499–502.

Selye, Hans. *Stress Without Distress*, London: Hodder & Stoughton, 1974.

Selye, Hans. *The Stress of Life*, New York: McGraw-Hill, 1976.

Wilson, R. B. 'Royal Jelly: The Medical Aspects', *American Bee Journal*, 97(9 and 10):356–359 and 396–399.

Chapter 28

Brain Mind Bulletin, 10 Dec 1984, 10(2).

'Hope That Sustainer of Man', *Executive Health*, December 1983, II, XX(3).

Benson, Herbert. *Beyond the Relaxation Response*, NY: Times Books, 1984.

Cousins, Norman. 'How Doctors Cause Disease', *Medical Self Care*, 1983.

Frank J. D. 'Psychotherapy of bodily disease', *Psychotherapy and Psychosomatics*, 1975, 26:192–202.

Frank, J. D. 'The Faith That Heals', *Johns Hopkins Medical Journal*, 1975, 137:127–131.

Frank, J. D. 'The medical power of faith', *Human Nature*, Aug 1978: 40–49.

Hammer, Signe. 'The Mind as Healer', *Science Digest*, April 1984.

Maddox, John. 'Psychoimmunology Before Its Time', *Nature*, 31 May 1984.

Mason, L. John. *Guide to Stress Reduction*, Culver, Calif.: Peace Press, 1980.

Morton, Marion. 'Attitudes and Responsibilities to the Elderly and of the Elderly', *Rejuvenation*, June 1984, XII(1–2).

Pelletier, Kenneth. *Mind as Healer—Mind as Slayer*, New York: Delta, 1977.

Pelletier, Kenneth. 'A Long and Happy Life', *Medical Self Care*, winter 1983.

Simonton, Carl O. *Getting Well Again*, Los Angeles: Tarcher, 1978.

Chapter 29

'Clinical Symptoms Developed During Histidine Deprivation', *Nutritional Review*, 1975, V(33):201.

Ames, Bruce. 'Dietary Carcinogens and Anticarcinogens', *Science*, 23 September 1983.

Aprison, M. et al. 'Glycine, Its Metabolic and Possible Transmitter Role in Nervous Tissue', in *Handbook of Neurochemistry*, Vol 3: 391, New York: Plenum Press, 1969.

Bartus, R. T. et al. 'Age-Related Changes in Passive-Avoidance Retention: Modulations with Dietary Choline', *Science*, 1980, 209:301.

Bland, J. (ed). *Medical Applications of Clinical Nutrition*, New Canaan, Connecticut: Keats Publishing, 1983.

Cheraskin, E. and Ringsdorf, W. M. *Psychodietetics*, NY: Bantam, 1976.

Clark, Michael. 'Obsessive-Compulsive Behavior Linked to Low Serotonin Levels', *Medical Tribune*, 21 June 1978: 19.

Goodwin, J. S. et al. 'Association between nutritional status and cognitive function in a healthy elderly population', *Journal of the American Medical Association*, 3 June 1983.

Goodwin, J. S. 'On Nutrition and Memory', *Exec. Health*, Oct 1984, XXI(1).

Growdon, J. H. and Wurtman, R. J. 'Dietary Influences on the Synthesis of Neurotransmitters in the Brain', *Nutrition Reviews*, 1979, 37:129.

Jackson, I. V. et al. 'Treatment of Tardive Dyskinesia with Lecithin', *Am. J. Psychiatry*, 11/79, 136:11.

Kalita, D. and Philpott, W. H. *Brain Allergies*, New Canaan, Connecticut: Keats Publishing, 1980.

Mesulam, M. and Weintraus, S. 'Cholinergic Therapy for Dementia', presented at the International Study Group on Memory Disorders, Zurich, 1979.

Nutrition Search Ltd. *Nutrition Almanac*, NY: McGraw-Hill, rev. ed, 1979.

Pfeiffer, Carl. *Mental and Elemental Nutrients*, New Canaan, Connecticut: Keats Publishing, 1975.

Williams, R. *Physician's Handbook of Nutritional Science*, Springfield, Illinois: Charles C. Thomas, 1978.

Chapter 30 and Postscript

Butler, R. N. *Why Survive? Being Old in America*, NY: Harper & Row, 1975.

Baines, J. *Aging and World Order*, The Whole Earth Papers, no. 13, East Orange NJ: Global Education Associates, 1979.

Capek, Karel. *The Makropoulos Secret*, Boston: Int. Pocket Library, 1925.

Comfort, Alex, *A Good Age*, New York: Simon and Schuster, 1976.

Erikson, E. H. 'Identity and the Life Cycle', *Psychological Issues*, 1:18, 1959.

Fontana, A. *The Last Frontier: The Social Meaning of Growing Old*, Beverley Hills CA: Sage Publications, 1977.

Hesse, Hermann. *The Glass Bead Game*, London: Penguin, 1972.

Kotlikoff, L. J. 'Some Economic Implications of Life Span Extention' in *Aging, Biology and Behaviours*, ed J. March et al., NY: Academic Press, 1982.

Lawrence, T. E. *Seven Pillars of Wisdom*, Brodie, 1963.

Rendricks, J. and Hendricks, C. D. *Ageing in Mass Society: Myth and Realities*, 2nd ed, New York: Winthrop Publishing, 1981.

Shaw, George Bernard, *Back to Methuselah* in *Complete Plays with Prefaces*, Vol II, New York: Dodd, Mead, 1963.

Index

Organic compounds with prefixes are listed under their root-names; e.g., 'DL-phenylalanine' is listed under 'phenylalanine'. Page numbers in *italics* refer to illustrations.

thickening of 218; wasting of 225; other
references 193, 200, 221, 291, 301, 302; *see
also* wrinkles
skin-brushing 161, 162–4, 256
sleep 81, 187, 213, 299
slimming diets 105; *see also* weight loss
smoking 5, 6, 39, 48, 161, 174, 176, 204, 223,
259, 310, 341
SOD *see* superoxide dismutase
sodium 118, 203, 302; ascorbate 182; dioxide
116; nitrite 35; pyrrolidone carboxylate (Na-
PCA) 264, 265, 266
sodium–potassium balance 144
soils 110, 114, 188–9, 191
somatotrophic hormone *see* growth hormone
sperm 205, 214
Sperry, Roger 316
spleen 45, 202, 289, 293
spring-clean dieting, spring-cleaning *vii*, 159–
70, 250
slimming 186, 187, 299, 301
starches 130; modified 113
stasis 130, 131
Steinach, Eugen 15, 16
steroid hormones 29, 204; corticosteroid 315
stimulants 298, 299
stimulation 336–7
stomach 199, 289; cancer 190
Stone, Irwin 175–81 *passim*
Streja, Dan 233–4
stress 52–62, 176–7, 314–16; adaptogens and
294, 295–6, 303; exercise and 223;
hydrotherapy and 246, 249, 254, 255;
individual responses to 61; nature of 52, 55;
and protein-consumption 126; Selye's theory
of 53; other references 19, 40, 41, 48, 50, 84,
317, 335
strokes 93, 203, 222, 225
sugars 130, 259, 264, 335, 341; in blood 59, 108,
131, 132, 150, 311; cooking and 116–17;
white 106; *see also* glucose
Sugimura, T. 116
sulphates 92
sulphur 93, 189, 201–204, 302; dioxide 39
sulphydryl groups 202
Sumner, James Batcheller 90
sunflower-seed oil 267
superoxide dismutase (SOD) 38, 44, 193, 194,
206–207, 283
supplements 336–41, 342; amino-acid 114, 200,
201, 207–12 *passim*, 216–18, 333–4, 340; anti-
oxidant 30, 84, 93–4, 112, 113–14, 178–83,
187–8, 189, 337, 342; L-carnitine 211–12;
cysteine 203, 204, 340; digestive-enzymes
200; essential-fatty-acid 135; 136; nucleic-
acid 291–3, 341; phenylalanine 210–11; DL-
phenylalanine 330; phosphatidyl-choline
326; selenium 189, 190, 191; vitamin A 192,
193, 338; vitamin C *see* vitamin C; vitamin E
187–8, 283, 339; tryptophan 331, 332; other
references 6, 37, 96, 102, 104, 107, 132, 200;
see also dosages; minerals; vitamins
suppressor cells 205
sweat 273
Sydenham, Thomas 167
synapses 325
synergy 94, 107, 172–3, 185, 187, 192, 194–5,
202, 215, 338

syphilis 146
Szent-Györgyi, Albert 65–6, 73–4, 78, 79, 91,
122–3, 174, 186, 231

tangeretin 183
tanning 193, 271–5; artificial 275
tannins 142, 143
taurine 202–203; L-taurine 332
T-cells 45–9 *passim*, 134, 206, 309, 314
tea 143, 144, 157, 161; herbal 143–4, 157, 161
Tengerdy, Robert 187
testicles 14, 15, 289, 293
testosterone 95, 287
thalamus 293
thiamine *see* vitamin B$_1$
Thoreau, Henry 232
threonine 197, 198
thrombosis 283
thymine 259
thymosin 45, 47, 48, 95
thymus 44–50 *passim*, 206, 280, 287, 289, 314;
extract 285
thyroid 188, 280, 286, 287, 289
thyroid hormone 95, 96
thyroxine 286
tissue 202; connective 198, 214, 272; *see also*
muscle tissue; vascular tissue
tissue rejection 16, 45, 47, 280
tissue repair 94
tocopherol: alpha-tocopherol acetate 185; *see*
vitamin E
tooth decay 94
toxaemia 119, 126
trace elements 92–6 *passim*, 100, 193–4, 303; *see
also* minerals
tranquillizers: drugs 217; exercise 228; natural
331, 332
trans-fatty acids 135
transplants 9, 15, 47
Trevelyan, G.M. 233
triglycerides 108, 211, 221
tri-peptides 206–207
trophic factors 68–9, 113
Tropp, Kaspar 118, 119
tryptophan 197, 198, 201, 205, 207, 212, 215,
216, 327, 331–2; L-tryptophan 332;
supplements 331, 332
Tsitsin, Nicolai 302
tumours 178–9, 206; *see also* cancer
type-A behaviour 311
tyrosinase 273, 274
tyrosine 197, 198, 201, 207, 212, 215, 216, 273,
327, 330, 331; L-tyrosine 215

ulcerative colitis 47
ulcers 59, 309, 333
ultraviolet light 39, 45, 63, 257, 258, 260, 268,
271–5, 314; UVA 271–2, 273, 274; UVB 271–
2, 273, 274
unified theories: ageing 63, 71; disease 30;
medicine 53–4
urea 214, 264
uric acid 292
urine: acetone in 149; analyses 200, 338;
calcium in 95; urea in 214; vitamin C in 182
urocanic acid 273